Crisis, Challenge and Change:
Party and Class in Canada Revisited

Carleton Library Series
Number 148

crisis, challenge and change

Party and Class in Canada Revisited   Janine Brodie   Jane Jenson

Carleton University Press
Ottawa, Canada
1991

Reprinted 1991

ISBN 0-88629-074-0 paperback

Printed and bound in Canada

Canadian Cataloguing in Publication Data

Brodie, M. Janine, 1952-
  Crisis, challenge and change

Includes bibliographical references.
ISBN 0-88629-074-0

1. Political parties – Canada – History. 2. Social classes
– Canada – History. 3. Canada – Politics and government –
1867-   . 4. Canada. Parliament – Elections – History. I.
Jenson, Jane, 1946-. II. Title.

JL195.B76 1988   324.271   C88-090237-X

Distributed by: Oxford University Press Canada,
                70 Wynford Drive,
                Don Mills, Ontario,
                Canada   M3C 1J9
                (416) 441-2941

Cover design: Chris Jackson

Acknowledgements

Carleton University Press gratefully acknowledges the support
extended to its publishing programme by the Canada Council and the
Ontario Arts Council.

To Jean and Glenn Brodie
and F. D. Crowley

Contents

Acknowledgements ix

1. *Party and Class in Canada: An Introduction 1*

2. *1867-1905—The Emergence of a Two-party System 20*

3. *1905-1917—Exporting the Party System Westward 53*

4. *1917-1921—Two Parties in Crisis 87*

5. *The 1920s—The Pursuit of "Normal Politics" 119*

6. *The 1930s—The Depression Election 156*

7. *1936-1945—The Contest for Labour 187*

8. *1945-1965—Social Democracy for an Affluent Society 217*

9. *The Lull Before the Storm: 1965-1974 262*

10. *Into the 1980s: The Politics of Uncertainty 293*

Appendices 330

Index 338

Acknowledgements for the Revised Edition

This book is a revised version of *Crisis, Challenge and Change: Party and Class in Canada*, originally published in 1980. It is not a second edition, in the usual sense of the word, because only some of the chapters have been revised. Chapters One, Nine and Ten are new to this revision, while the rest remain as they were in the 1980 book.

Support for the revisions came from the Center for International Affairs, Harvard University and from the Department of Political Science, York University.

Revising a book first written almost a decade ago has meant responding to the comments—both positive and negative—of several generations of undergraduate and graduate students. As we read their exams and course papers and saw what they read in our book, the direction for revisions took shape. Therefore, our first debt is to our students at Carleton, Queen's and York Universities. We also thank Daiva Stasiulis, who had the original idea of doing this revision, and Neil Bradford and Lise Gotell for their many helpful suggestions on the new chapters. Finally, our greatest thanks go to Greg Albo for his generosity of time and ideas, in the form of his always trenchant comments.

Chapter 1

Party and Class in Canada: An Introduction

Since the beginning of the twentieth century, politics in Canada has appeared as an exception to a more general rule. In other advanced industrial societies party politics often could be described as the "democratic translation of the class struggle." Workers seeking redress from the inequities of capitalism formed their own political parties—whether social democratic or communist—to gain access to and influence over the political process in order to implement a project of societal reform and transformation. Yet in Canada federal elections seldom took this familiar form. Class differences were never a strong line of cleavage among the three parties and the parties which claimed to be representative of workers seldom gained strong support from that constituency. Since many studies of party politics have equated class-based voting and "class politics," Canadian electoral politics seems to be a case of "non-class politics." Moreover, because class politics in the traditional sense of clashing political parties is invisible, many people have argued that class differences do not exist or are irrelevant in federal politics. Instead, parties supposedly aggregate preferences on other, more immediate, issues.

In at least two fundamental respects, this book takes issue with such interpretations of the connection between class and party in Canada. First, the book assumes that in any society characterized by capitalist social relations, politics will represent, in one way or another, the basic pattern of such social relations. Thus, "class politics" exists, even when class-based voting is not present; class politics simply takes another form. Second, the conception of political parties used here does not see them as simple aggregators of individual voters' preferences. Instead, it assumes that, while each party system has developed in the context of particular social structures which constrain partisan activities, the parties themselves partially direct and shape the politics in each system through their strategic actions. Political parties in liberal democracies play a crucial role because they help to define the form and substance of electoral politics. They identify which among a broad range of social differences and tensions will be raised and debated in elections, and they nurture and sustain the criteria by which an electorate divides against itself in a more or less stable system of partisan alignments. Parties, of course, are not alone in this process; other institutions play important roles. Nevertheless, political parties, as the organizers of elections, have the greatest influence on the "definition of politics."

It is in this process of defining the political that class interests are either advanced and protected or suppressed and rejected in elections. The conflictual social relations of capitalism may at times organize electoral contests, but whether they do or not depends in large part on the actions of all political parties as they compete from one election to the next. The dynamic of the situation is one in which workers' parties struggle to introduce the assumptions of class politics into the definition and practice of elections while bourgeois parties use their own strategic resources to limit partisan politics to less threatening social differences. To the extent that non-class definition of politics are the basis of political discourse, elections will not be recognized as events of class conflict. Only if the activity of the challenger succeeds would we expect to observe the pattern of class-voting made familiar in the experience of other advanced industrial societies.

Throughout this history of the Canadian federal party system we show how the two major parties have hindered subordinate classes— workers and at times farmers—from organizing their own political parties. In this way, they also have defused threats to the power of capital which might have followed from the activities of a strong social democratic party. The major parties have done this by mobilizing their considerable resources and prestige, employing the coercive powers of the state, and repeatedly relying on two themes which constituted an alternative definition of politics to that which left-wing parties have tried to introduce into political discourse. The first theme is the social diversity of Canada resulting from the existence of two separate cultures within a single state and from distinct regional variations in economic and political orientations. The second theme then stresses the need for consensus amid diversity. This consensual view argues the irrelevancy and illogic of class conflict in a country rich in resources and opportunities. These themes have penetrated deep into the country's political consciousness, reinforced as they have been in election after election. These themes, as we shall see, have served as substitutes for class-based definitions of politics and as such their continued use and popular resonance have become a formidable obstacle to the success of new parties.

This book also argues for historical analysis as the best way to understand the party system and forms of party politics. While at any one moment the hegemonic definition of politics is important in shaping the pattern of partisan relations, this system of relations and its definition is not given once and for all time. With the emergence of political actors representing new social forces, the definition of politics may alter. Such changes often subject bourgeois parties to intense pressure to adapt, as well as providing an opportunity for a left-wing party to emerge. The reactions to novel circumstances, while the result of real strategic choices by political parties, nevertheless also reflect the limits set by previous rounds of electoral competition. In other words, history simultaneously makes possible and limits the changes which elections can bring. It is the interaction between such limits and possibilities which provides the story of electoral contests.

Our emphasis on parties as shapers of political discourse and as limited but not completely constrained by history has one important implication. If electoral politics does not exhibit class-based voting, for reasons of party strategy and history, we *can not* conclude that elections are, as institutions, devoid of class content or of importance to class relations. The electoral organization of class relations also occurs if bourgeois parties can successfully maintain an ideological and organizational dominance which defines politics in non-class terms. It is precisely non-class definitions of politics which help to disorganize the subordinate classes and which place some limits on their demands on capital or for changes in the social relations of capitalist society.

This book argues, then, that the key to understanding Canada's federal party system is an historical examination of both the bourgeois parties' response to the tensions between capital and the subordinate classes and the failure of parties of the subordinate classes to challenge successfully the definition of politics generated by that response. Since 1867 workers and farmers have organized, or attempted to organize, an alternative definition of politics into elections. At some points their efforts did constitute a threat to the bourgeois parties. Yet, up until now the subordinate classes have not sustained the challenge, nor have they generated an electorally successful left-wing party at the federal level. In the following chapters we trace how a definition of politics stressing both bicultural and regional diversity and the need for consensus emerged and continued from election to election and how the existence of such a definition has diverted demands of subordinate classes into forms which obscured the class bases of the political project of Confederation.

Parties and Class in Canada: A Brokerage System

Canada provides a somewhat perplexing case study of the partisan organization of class relations in liberal democracies. The country has had an advanced capitalist economy since the turn of the century and high levels of industrialization since the First World War. Nevertheless, partisan politics is not organized around the class cleavage between workers and owners which is familiar in countries with similar levels of economic development. There is only minimal evidence of this particular type of partisan organization in the federal party system.[1] In addition, the programmes and policies of the Liberal and Conservative parties reveal few real and consistent differences in the class interests they claim to protect or advance.[2] The New Democratic Party, like its left-wing predecessors, resembles other social democratic parties in terms of its membership, financial base, and formal links to the trade-union movement. Yet, it enjoys nowhere near a majority of the support of its claimed constituency—working people. Study after study has documented that the electorate does not divide its support for political parties according to the occupational structure of capitalist economies or even according to the position voters think they hold in a subjective status ranking. In election after election, the bourgeois parties gain more votes from workers than Canada's self-styled social democratic party, the NDP.[3]

Such patterns of non-class voting have been explained by students of Canadian politics who describe the party system as a "brokerage" one.[4] By this term they mean that essentially similar parties appeal to the many interests which exist in Canadian society.[5] They depict the parties as undifferentiated by principled stands or ideologies, being more like Tweedledum and Tweedledee. The party system is a competition between the "Ins" and the "Outs", as teams of office-seekers present platforms and discuss issues in ways designed to maximize their support across the electorate. Any electoral coalition may house many different interests and these coalitions often change in response to parties' calculations about the electorate's preferences. As a result, there is no reason to expect parties' platforms to be consistent across time, although differences among parties may exist at any single point in time. Because brokerage parties are constantly on the lookout for new supporters there is, moreover, no basis for the systematic exclusion of any group sufficiently influential to articulate its interests. While parties may construct class-based appeals from time to time, such a focus is never an exclusive one. Numbers, not principle, are the currency of electoral politics. Elections are "fought on the plains of consensus rather than from the heights of competing principles."[6]

At least two interpretations of Canadian partisan politics designate the federal parties as brokers. The first, an organizational explanation, assumes that the sole goal of political parties is electoral success. Employing a "market analogy," the model depicts parties competing for votes just as firms compete for customers. The second is more sociological, emphasizing the social divisions in Canadian society and the role of elites who must broker divergent interests in order to maintain social harmony. This interpretation can be labelled the "complex cleavage" explanation.[7]

The "market analogy," as its name suggests, assumes political parties are like department stores whose success depends upon sensitivity to customer (i.e., voter) demand for new products (i.e., policy positions).[8] Party platforms, like mail order catalogues, change from season to season. Politics lacks any structured or systematic relationship to society or the economy. Party politics can be a pure partisan calculation of short-term costs and benefits, although the electoral process does place some constraints on the seller. Parties adhere to the principle of minimum differentiation of the product, warily peddling the same set of ideas and policies which have worked for them in the past. They are disposed to be afraid of new ideas, for fear of making costly mistakes which may lose support they already have, without making compensating gains.[9]

In other words, the negative effects of differentiated products account for the similarity and generality of Canadian parties' positions.

This argument is based on traditional assumptions about the behaviour of firms under conditions of perfect competition, where there are so many competitors (parties) that they all necessarily respond to demand and no single firm can impose a product on customers. Therefore, transferred to the political realm, the claim is that "consumer sovereignty" exists and party platforms reflect voter demand. If, however, the situation actually resembles oligopolistic competition, the analogy begins to look much less benign. Under conditions of oligopoly, firms shape the demand structure and thereby, the assumption of autonomous demand is lifted and replaced by a more subtle analysis of the manner in which customer preferences are moulded by a more active seller.[10]

Continuing with the analogy that political parties resemble oligopolistic firms in imperfect markets, we see how *this* interpretation of the brokerage nature of the Canadian party system could lead to the notion that parties both forge political preferences and restrict the range of choices available to the electorate. Political parties carry a legacy from earlier party competition which creates strategic, ideological, and organizational constraints, just as the product life-cycle limits oligopolistic firms. Parties are not meccano sets, constructed anew at each election. Their supporters identify with the product and any process of adjustment may cause disruption.[11] In many cases, then, we would expect parties to find it easier to "re-educate" the customers to like the product they are already producing rather than to adapt in any dramatic way to changes in consumer preferences.

This first version of a brokerage argument is quite consistent with the notion that political parties construct an ongoing definition of politics, which shapes the meaning of politics for the electorate. Nevertheless, this market analogy can neither explain the development of the definition of politics in the first place nor reveal why one version takes hold and others are still-born. Therefore, it does not solve the puzzle of why party politics in Canada has diverged from the Western European experience. Solutions to that riddle must be located somehow in the history of Canadian society.

No doubt it is the failure to theorize any link to social cleavages and ongoing institutional constraints which accounts for the market analogy's lack of popularity. In general, studies of Canadian politics have converged on two major topics: the prospects for social stability in a religiously, linguistically and regionally divided society and the repercussions of the institutional arrangements of federalism in all political domains. People have tried to understand how parties are influenced or constrained in their behaviours by social and economic relations and/or the institutional context within which they operate. Since the market analogy does not address such matters, sociological arguments which attempt to account for the character of the party system by an examination of Canadian society have generated greater enthusiasm.

Proponents of these approaches both portray several deep social divisions which have culminated in a pattern of "complex cleavages" and assume that the major function of political parties in advanced industrial societies is to assure societal integration.[12] Since deep, divisive and persistent religious, linguistic, and regional cleavages divide Canadian society, the country's parties must harmonize competing interests and, in so doing, perform the heroic task of promoting social stability in a divided polity.[13]

Advocates of the complex cleavage thesis disagree, however, about the best way for parties to perform this integration function. For some, aggregation should occur across a wide variety of interests. By spanning several social cleavages, parties prevent any single one from dominating and dividing the society. Where multiple cleavages exist, parties try to cut across them all and bring together a variety of people under a common umbrella. Yet other analysts see the politicization of multiple cleavages as itself destabilizing and call for societal integration around a single one— that of class. These latter are the proponents of what they call "creative politics," and they argue that the pattern of multiple cleavages preserved in the Canadian party system reinforces rather than reduces social fragmentation.[14] They look to European history where the appearance of class-based politics seems to have solved the very integration crises that analysts fear.[15] Accordingly, they conclude that a party system "creatively" divided along class lines can move politics beyond the very conflicts which threaten national survival, as francophones and anglophones, easterners and westerners, Catholics and Protestants all unite around a common sense of class identity and support for class-based parties.

Behind this debate about the ideal configuration of electoral cleavages, we can discern the structural fault in the complex cleavage thesis. Canadian society *is* complex in its social divisions. Nevertheless, if Canadian politics remains segmented by cleavages of religion, language and region, it can not simply be because there are many more cleavages in Canada than elsewhere. Different religions, languages and pronounced regional differences in economic development also exist in many European countries, yet these real social differences no longer dominate politics. Usually they do remain visible in electoral politics but they are either accompanied by or, more usually, subordinated to class-based politics.[16] Therefore, if party politics in Canada remains trapped by a multiplicity of cleavages, it is not that Canadian society is more complex than others but simply that the party system remains divided by many cleavages. This pattern still cries out for explanation.

For such an explanation we can not turn to "society," as so many political sociologists have. Nor can we have much faith that a voluntaristic enthusiasm for creative politics will force the system to change; such voluntarism has never been sufficient to form classes into active and politically-conscious entities. We must, instead, cultivate our curiosity about the way that societal differences are translated into politically mobilized differences. We must ask what the party system contributes to the deepening of regional and cultural political differences within classes rather than helping to alleviate them and what pushes such non-class cleavages to the forefront of political discourse. To answer this question we will examine the history of the party system and the ways in which the definition of politics developed over time. In doing so, we will move away from the functionalist version of the complex cleavage thesis, which describes parties as compelled by their place in the social system to perform the function of societal integration, as well as away from the advocacy of creative politics as a panacea for a divided polity.

Partisan Politics in Liberal Democracies: An Organizational Analysis

In considering the Canadian party system it is important to remember that discussions of the party system as a brokerage one are popular because they do rather effectively *describe* how parties behave in federal elections. The Liberals, Progressive Conservatives and, to a lesser degree, the NDP do have similar platforms which change from election to election. The Liberals and Tories often do abandon promises once the exigencies of office demand something else and they do not emphasize ideological differences because they appeal to many, often the same, interests— whether they be linguistic, regional or economic—in their perennial search to construct a winning coalition. Although parties may sometimes develop quite coherent and even principled positions, these constructions are fragile and easily reversed when conditions change.[17]

Nevertheless, even if parties are part of an on-going brokerage system, we must still ask what reproduces this partisan formation. It is this question which none of the approaches described here has succeeded in answering. Despite their descriptive accuracy, they can not adequately explain *why* the party system has taken a brokerage form or *why* parties follow a brokerage strategy. In order to do this we must explore theoretically and historically the links between social relations and politics in capitalist societies.

From the outset, it is important to reject any notion that there is a necessary and easy link between the form of social relations in any country and its politics. Too often both political sociologists and some Marxists assumed that the stage of development of a particular society determined partisan politics. They argued that industrialization was followed by the emergence of class-based parties in which the line of demarcation ran between those who, according to the laws of the economy, control the production process and those who, according to the laws of liberal democracy, can gain some political control over production and distribution of profit. A corollary of this argument was that politics in advanced capitalist societies would focus primarily on questions of control over production, distribution and consumption. It is, obviously, this particular organization of partisan relations which is missing in Canada. Yet, such a deterministic analysis is far too simplistic. The apparent absence of class-based voting can not be taken, as it sometimes has been, as evidence that *class politics* does not exist and that elections and partisan politics do not organize class relations in a particular way. An initial assumption about the importance of the social relations of production in capitalist societies does not lead inevitably to a deduction that workers will be organized into one party and the bourgeoisie into another. A class-based electoral cleavage has been observed in many countries, but it is not inevitable.

A less deterministic examination of the last hundred years of industrial capitalism leads to the following perspective: while capitalism has proceeded in all countries in similar—although not always exactly the same—directions towards centralization, the growth of large monopolistic corporations and an increase in state intervention in the economy, the political expression of class conflict has varied in important ways. The politics of capitalism can and has taken quite different forms. Such diversity suggests that it is necessary to entertain the possibility that political parties—as organizations which pursue strategic goals—have a crucial effect on whether class conflict is mobilized in party politics. If the political formation of classes is not an automatic consequence of social conditions, we must ask what role parties themselves play in shaping class identities. At the same time, however, it is also obvious that elections do not occur in a vacuum, lacking historical legacies. The conditions which parties face are never completely transient and unstructured. They reflect previous decisions and actions, embedded in the practices and discourses with which all such actors confront their worlds.

In the following chapters we argue that the Liberal and Conservative parties have, as a result of their strategies over more than a century, managed to dominate the field of electoral activity. The partisan and electoral expression of class conflict has been repeatedly avoided, reinterpreted, or simply repressed. "Third parties" have been plagued by organizational difficulties in the face of this dominance and they have played a minor role in federal elections. Nevertheless, this hegemony exists only under stress, because the potential for periodic outbreaks of class-based partisan protest, whether in the form of new parties or mass migrations between parties, is always present. The bourgeois parties' strategies have successfully retarded but never eliminated the growth of class-based parties and, therefore, class-based voting.

Democracy, Class and Party

The experiences of political parties are closely linked to the unfolding relationship between capitalism and the liberal democratic form of government. Many liberal democracies passed through two distinct phases: They were first liberal, and democratic institutions followed much later.[18] In Britain, for example, merchants and industrial capitalists seeking freedom from the remnants of out-dated economic and political constraints of feudalism were the major social forces behind liberalism's innovations such as free choice in the marketplace, individual mobility in the labour market, and responsible government.[19] While political "factions" appeared at this time of social transformation, they were small and fragile coalitions of powerful men whose political position depended on a very restricted franchise. Mass democracy came much later. Universal suffrage, regular elections, and guarantees of freedom of speech and association were secured only after protracted and sometimes bitter confrontations between the politically powerful, whose social base was in the capitalist class, and the growing working class of industrial capitalism.

One of the legacies of this period of liberal politics is a particular understanding of elections and politics, deeply embedded in the ideology of bourgeois parties. The fundamental ideological principle of capitalism, according to liberals, is the notion that the relations of production are relations between individuals who deal with each other as buyers and sellers of labour. This notion was transferred to the realm of political discourse, where it emerged as the idea that society is composed of individuals and democratic politics provide those individuals with the opportunity to express their preferences. Casting a ballot is, then, simply the act of an individual who is proferring a vote to a political party in exchange for a probable policy outcome. Within this meaning system, free and equal voters trade their votes in the same way that consumers demand goods and services or workers exchange their labour for wages.

Of course, within such a liberal world view, in order for relations of exchange to develop, there must be an intermediary which can link the expression of individual preferences to the state, from which policy outcomes emanate. Mass political parties came into being as the suffrage expanded. At first many people had feared an expanded franchise because they assumed that workers—nearly a majority in many industrializing countries—would use their political rights to eliminate the glaring inequities of late nineteenth century societies and perhaps even to dismantle the capitalist system.[20] To many people's surprise, these consequences did not materialize but there were other important changes in the ways that party politics functioned under the conditions of mass democracy. As the size of the electorate mushroomed, cadre parties which had previously only co-ordinated the business of the legislature expanded their organizations and their outreach activities. The specifics of party appeals varied from one country to another but they all urged the new voters, in casting their individual ballots, to support the parties' vision of the "national interest."

But bourgeois parties were not the only mass parties which became active in these years. In the last quarter of the nineteenth century and the first decades of the twentieth, a number of new parties emerged in most industrialized countries. The new socialist, social democratic, and communist parties claimed to speak for workers and their allies and they challenged the legitimacy of the capitalist system and the political power of capital.[21] The appearance of these class-based parties had a profound impact on the prevailing meaning systems of politics. Left parties rejected the bourgeois parties' proclamations that they were different from each other, accusing all bourgeois parties of representing the same class interest. The left-wing parties asserted that politics was fundamentally a conflict between class interests and only they could act for workers. Once these left parties advanced a class-based definition of politics, the bourgeois parties had to defend their own view of partisan relations.[22] Time and again bourgeois parties retorted that class-based understandings of politics were inappropriate and even dangerous and that politics was best understood as the search for consensus around the "national interest."[23] Despite repeated efforts to fend off the challenge of the new parties, the bourgeois parties of most of Western Europe could not prevent electoral politics from being recast along class lines, and the terrain was frozen into its familiar shape.[24]

Left-wing parties have been quite explicit about the fact that they provide—as an integral part of their partisan activity—definitions of politics. They have understood the importance of piercing the interpretative veil of the bourgeois parties' claim that a healthy capitalism inevitably and automatically benefits everyone. They have advanced practical visions of how politics can change distribution and production relations. In doing so, the parties attempt to convince the electorate to adhere to their political ideology as well as to support their candidates. In these activities, they challenge liberalism's notions that voting is simply an individual act of choice. Rather, voting is an act in ongoing class relations.

Left-wing parties are not the only ones which promote particular meanings about politics, however. All parties do. Through their everyday actions and pronouncements, all parties in liberal democracies integrate individuals into an ongoing system of partisan relations. In this process of integration, parties provide voters with a *definition of politics*. In other words, political parties help to *shape the interpretation of which aspects of social relations should be considered political, how politics should be conducted, what the boundaries of political discussion most properly may be and which kinds of conflicts can be resolved through the political process*. From the vast array of tensions, differences, and inequalities characteristic of any society, parties treat only some as alternatives in the electoral process and thereby influence how the electorate will divide against itself. This activity of parties is profoundly important because before electoral cleavages come into being, a definition of what is political must exist. Whether an issue is considered to be a religious, economic, private or political question is set by this definition. Matters which do not achieve the status of worthy of partisan debate will remain invisible and absent from the political realm.

This understanding of the importance of definitions of politics leads back to a consideration of the relationship between class and party in liberal democracies. Social classes are a product of the social relations of production, which include not only factors like technology, organization of work and structures of authority, but also processes by which meaning is constructed. Any set of workplace or living conditions acquire meaning as they are interpreted in specific social settings. The particular features of the interpretations can never be predicted in advance, however, because they are the product of concrete actions undertaken by actors in specific national settings.

We can say, in general, however, that it is wrong to assume that subordinate classes will spontaneously recognize the political implications of their location in capitalist relations of production and vote according to their class position, regardless of whether a political party exists which defines their class position to be indeed political. Class-based voting must be preceded by the development of a class-based organization which challenges hegemonic definitions of politics that interpret social and political relations in non-class terms. People occupying similar positions in the production process must become aware that they are members of a class, and the nurturing of this awareness demands, as a prerequisite, ideological and organizational activity.[25] In other words, *classes must be formed*, and only with such class formation will they be active and self-conscious social actors, since class is defined by people as they make their own history.[26] Political struggles about class legitimate a class-based world view and permit individuals to see themselves (that is, to identify) as part of a class with a political project for fundamental social change.

Social conditions, such as the existence of different language groups, the labour process, or the gender division of labour, can set parameters around the range of organizations possible in any society, but they will never determine which groups will mobilize in elections. If the existence and characteristics of class conflict are exposed by the activities of a well-developed trade-union movement or an influential party of the left, then there should be evidence, at the level of voting, of class-based politics. Without these prior conditions, class differences are submerged, distorted, and rarely visible in voting behaviour.

Elections are always events of conflict and competition, but the substance of electoral politics is not automatically given. For example, electoral politics can be understood as the aggregation of individual preferences, the expression of religious sectarianism, one place to redress gender inequalities, or a mechanism for expressing and resolving class conflict.[27] Since the late nineteenth century, left parties have used this latter definition and in so doing have offered the electorate an alternative basis for electoral alignment which threatens the very basis of support of one or more of the bourgeois parties. The perception of class relations as conflictual and the recognition of the unequal structure of capitalist social relations depends, in large part, on how successfully socialist parties organize the electorate behind their meaning systems.

Any analysis of class and party must account for the nature of the hegemonic definition of politics and its organizational manifestation, as well as the way that it vanquished its competitors. Organizations which challenge this definition face no easy task. They must overcome the weight of an ongoing meaning system and successfully substitute their own. This is often difficult.[28] The implication of this theoretical discussion is that accounting for the observed lack of class-based voting in Canada is less a matter of accounting for, independent of the configuration of parties, the absence of a class cleavage and much more a matter of first explaining the absence of an electorally successful workers' party. It implies moving from an analysis of the patterns of social relations to a consideration of the behaviour of organizations as strategic actors. The investigation of democracy, class and party in Canada demands, then, an historical exploration of the barriers impeding as well as the potential space for organizations and parties offering competing definitions of politics.

The Mobilization of New Definitions of Politics

Throughout this introductory chapter we have emphasized that the political organization of class relations results in large part from the strategic actions of parties. Such a perspective suggests a research agenda which assesses both the strengths of and the constraints mitigating against the success of a class-based party at any point in time.

The first constraint to note is that any new party enters an already existing party system. It must operate according to the rules and institutional constraints already in place and within an ideological and organizational configuration not of its own making. A definition of politics—more or less hegemonic—already exists and patterns of support and allegiance are established. Parties of the subordinate classes must constantly struggle not only to gain concrete programmatic concessions but also to impose their understanding of capitalist social relations.[29] Therefore, a party hoping to mobilize a subordinate class and its allies must struggle simultaneously to create itself as an organization and to popularize its definition of politics. It must undertake class formation, expanding the class consciousness of its supporters, as a basic element of its activity. The hegemony of an existing definition of politics is, then, a fundamental obstacle to the success of a new party representing the subordinate classes.

To the extent that an existing definition of politics is all-encompassing, widely-accepted and unchallenged by other organizations, the space for a new party is severely restricted. A class party generally begins its life within a discursive context which describes electoral politics in non-class terms. As a result, most of the tensions and inequalities arising between classes are considered by many people not to be political questions at all. They see them as the problems of individuals, to be resolved by private action or perhaps by collective action in the workplace but not in elections. Thus, any new party immediately faces the task of translating the predominant view of the political world into broader terms of class relations.

Under normal circumstances such a translation is a very difficult undertaking. There are periods in a country's history, however, when voters are more likely to question and even reject the hegemonic definition of politics. During periods of crisis, when the major parties no longer appear to work for the national interest, when the system clearly does not produce "benefits for all," and when disputes over power are to the fore, usual partisan ties may come undone and a new definition of politics might take hold. Such a crisis in the social fabric—a war or depression, for example—might lead to a breakdown in the prevailing system of partisan alignments. When the voters' usual partisan ties are broken, the prevailing definition of politics is exposed and vulnerable to criticism. The instability in the party system creates possibilities for parties to challenge the hegemonic definition and even to change it.

Whether voters detached from the dominant system of partisan alignments will go to a new party with a class-based definition of politics depends both on party strategy and on the activities of other actors which have some influence over the voters. Indeed, social organizations only peripherally attached to the party system may either reinforce the hegemonic definition of politics, direct voters detached from this definition towards one party or another, or even help to create the space for class parties in the electorate in the first place. Other organizations of the subordinate classes—farm groups, trade unions, reform movements— play an important role here. In the past, trade unions have been particularly important in the creation and support of left-wing parties because they often were the first bodies which began to organize workers as a class and to provide an alternative interpretation of capitalism. In many European countries it was the union movement which pushed forward the establishment of a "political arm" of labour.

The analysis and strategy of occupational groups, co-operatives and unions, therefore, are crucial variables in the study of the ongoing relationship between class and party. If these bodies adopt a critical view of capitalist relations of production, the space for a progressive and class-based definition of politics is greater. If, however, organized labour accepts a definition which interprets capitalist social relations as a private matter or resolvable in the workplace, the socialist party faces a strategic dilemma. It must either contradict the labour unions or accept the same stance and try to insert itself into the electoral arena on that basis. Either strategy harbours dangers. If the party contradicts the unions, it sets itself up as a competitor for the support of workers, a competition which divides the labour movement against itself. It is difficult to win in this way, especially if the unions are well-established. Yet if the left party offers no class-based reading of politics, it forfeits its chance to mobilize around an alternative definition of politics. It risks becoming indistinguishable from its competitors, the bourgeois parties.

This sketch of the strategic dilemma facing a left-wing party demonstrates that one of the crucial factors for the explanation of a party's success or failure is the dynamic relationship within the labour movement as a whole. The level of mobilization of workers by unions, the ideological stance of the unions, and their partisan activities are all important factors advancing or constraining new left-wing parties. The same holds true for the interplay between agricultural organizations and farmers' parties.

Finally, the experience of a new party will depend upon whether it can defeat the historically-given opposition which usually has great resources. The existing bourgeois parties can mount a number of different strategies to combat the threat of a new party. There is no general theory of these strategies but only a tendency to seek self-preservation. These strategies are not always successful, of course, and new parties do seize political space and even displace older competitors.

The Alliance Strategies of Socialist Parties

Despite the neat analytic division of capitalist society into the bourgeoisie and the working class, any social formation contains groups and classes which do not easily fit into either of these two categories. Remnants of the major classes of earlier modes of production exist. For example, there are independent commodity producers (farmers, artisans) who are producers but are neither capitalists employing labour nor workers selling labour for a wage. In addition, the development of advanced capitalism has generated new occupations, new places in the production process which do not have exactly the same relation to capital as industrial workers. New technology demands technicians and deployers of scientific knowledge who do more than or something other than tend the machinery of a factory. New white collar and service workers, performing several kinds of functions, have become more visible components of both the private- and public-sector labour forces. The implication of these changes for the strategy of left parties is not obvious. These new groups might be seen as potential members of the working class, because they do sell their labour for a wage. But they also might be seen as members of other classes, for example the petite bourgeoisie, or they might even be considered to constitute a new middle class on their own.[30]

Whatever the characterization of these classes and groups, any social formation is complicated by the existence of such variety and the left party must develop a strategy which takes them into account. Members of the traditional working class rarely comprise an electoral majority by themselves. This has always been the case in Canada where workers employed in manufacturing have been outnumbered by farmers and people employed in other sectors of the economy. Yet, if parties accept the rules of the parliamentary game, they accept the requirement of attempting to win elections by garnering at least a plurality of votes themselves or entering into alliance with other parties. This necessity has several effects on the strategies that they develop. Yet, while alliances are generally a requirement of the structure of elections in liberal democracies, the particular strategy, the potential selection of allies, and the basis of the appeal is a matter of choice. And, the choice made will profoundly affect the direction of policy appeal, the programmatic efforts, and the ideological colour of the party. Building alliances thus involves decisions made by parties, but within structured political and ideological contexts as well as economic conditions which produced the potential allies in the first place. In other words, the alternatives are limited by past decisions and current conditions.

Some alliances are more likely than others. They are easier to build and maintain when workers share similar conditions with other groups. Socialist parties have frequently allied with farmers and other fractions of the petite bourgeoisie because they all have somewhat similar experiences with capitalism. Rising prices set by monopolistic corporations, the effects of urbanization, of loss of personal autonomy, and the costs of being "underprivileged" are, among others, some of the bases for wide appeal. But not all the voters to whom the appeal goes have precisely the same needs as workers nor do they experience capitalism in exactly the same way. Therefore, parties of workers must take these differences into account when they develop electoral programmes. The existence of such differences and the need for alliance creates hard choices for socialist parties. They must decide which appeal to make, the form it will take, the common experiences to emphasize, and the differences to downplay. They must do this without risking the loss of the votes of workers and without de-mobilizing the basis of their support by obscuring the unique position of the party vis à vis the workers, which makes a class identity possible in the first place.[31] The remaining chapters of this book recount the ways that workers' parties in Canada have constructed alliances and difficulties they have encountered in identifying and maintaining a viable alliance strategy.

Conclusion

Federal elections in Canada provide an example of the failure of a left-wing party to challenge successfully the predominant view of partisan relations and to mobilize fully the working class. A focus on two dimensions of partisan politics—the mobilization of workers and the alliance strategy of left-wing parties—provides the *raison d'être* for the chapters which follow. Each of them examines the repeated attempts by left-wing parties to develop a definition of politics and search out alliances within the changing context of economic development and the responses of the bourgeois parties. Canadian history can be read as a series of moments when a crisis in partisan relations arose and a challenger attempted to remake the definition of politics and mobilize workers behind a new political project. Thus far the bourgeois parties have succeeded in fending off the challenge and they continue to organize politics around other themes than class. But this past experience can promise nothing about the future. In fact, these very past strategies and past victories of the two major parties may now constitute severe limits on the range of possible reactions to future mobilization efforts of progressive political parties.

NOTES

[1]The expectation of class-based cleavages in elections is found in many works. For two classic statements of the theme, see S.M. Lipset, *Political Man* (New York: Anchor, 1963) and R. Alford, *Party and Society* (Chicago: Rand McNally, 1963). For discussions of the importance of class as an explanatory variable in Canada see, *inter alia*, H. Clarke, J. Jenson, L. LeDuc and J. Pammett, *Political Choice in Canada* (Toronto: McGraw-Hill Ryerson, 1978), Chapter 4; R. Lambert, J. Curtis, S. Brown and B. Kay, "In Search of Left/Right Beliefs in the Canadian Electorate," *Canadian Journal of Political Science*, vol. 19, 1986; M. Stevenson, "Ideology and Unstable Party Identification in Canada: Limited Rationality in a Brokerage Party System," *Canadian Journal of Political Science*, vol. 20, 1987.

[2]R. Ogmundson, "On the Measurement of Party Class Positions: The Case of Canadian Federal Political Parties," *Canadian Review of Sociology and Anthropology*, vol. 12, no. 4, 1975 provides a review of the literature on this question as well as an empirical classification of the parties. This similarity is reflected in the financing patterns of the Liberals and Conservatives, both of which rely on business sources for most of their private funding. See K.Z. Paltiel, "The Control of Campaign Finance in Canada: A Summary and Overview," in H. Thorburn, ed., *Party Politics in Canada*, 5th ed. (Toronto: Prentice-Hall, 1985).

[3]Clarke, *et al., op. cit.*, p. 110; Lambert, *et al., op. cit.*

[4]It is important to recognize that a distinction is made here between the shifting positions of electoral politics—the public appeals and proposed programmes of the parties—and the actions of governments. The consistency and continuity to governmental programmes often are not reflected in the content of electoral politics. This is due first to the distinction between party and state and the fact that the Canadian state is influenced by much more than the political parties. A second reason is that much of the actual content of electoral politics focuses on matters other than policy. For example, leaders and leadership, style and image form much of the everyday discussion during elections.

[5]H. Clarke, J. Jenson, L. LeDuc and J. Pammett, *Absent Mandate: The Politics of Discontent in Canada* (Toronto: Gage, 1984), pp. 10-16 describes the characteristics of a brokerage party system. For an overview of several approaches to explaining brokerage politics see Thorburn, *op. cit.*, Chapter 3.

[6]R. Gibbins, *Conflict and Unity* (Toronto: Methuen, 1985), p. 56.

[7]The term is from Thorburn, *op. cit.*, p. 27.

[8]For works employing this analogy see J. Mallory, *The Structure of Canadian Government* (Toronto: Macmillan, 1971) and P. Brimelow, *The Patriot Game: National Dreams and Political Realities* (Toronto: Key Porter, 1986). See Stevenson, *op. cit.*, for a further consideration of this model in studies of electoral politics.

[9]Mallory, *op. cit.*, p. 201-02.

[10]C.B. Macpherson, *The Life and Times of Liberal Democracy* (London: Oxford, 1977), 89ff.

[11]For a discussion of this process and its effects for voters' identification with parties, see J. Jenson, "Party Strategy and Party Identification: Some Patterns of Partisan Allegiance," *Canadian Journal of Political Science*, vol. 9, no. 1, 1976 and M. Stevenson, *op. cit.*, pp. 816-821.

[12]Such approaches have a strong functionalist tinge to them because of their overriding concern with analysing the conditions of social stability. For the intellectual lineages of such approaches see W. Buxton, *Talcott Parsons and the Capitalist Nation State* (Toronto: University of Toronto, 1985), Chapters 9-10 and J. LaPalombara and M. Weiner, eds., *Political Parties and Political Development* (Princeton: Princeton University Press, 1966), p. v.

[13]For a classic statement of this position see F.C. Engelmann and M.A. Schwartz, *Political Parties and the Canadian Social Structure* (Toronto: Prentice-Hall, 1967), chapters 1-3. See also J. Meisel, *Cleavages, Parties and Values in Canada*, Sage Papers in Contemporary Sociology, vol. 1 (London: Sage, 1974).

[14]The best-known of these theorists are, of course, J. Porter, *The Vertical Mosaic* (Toronto: University of Toronto, 1965), Chapter 12 and G. Horowitz, "Towards the Democratic Class Struggle" in T. Lloyd and J. McLeod, eds., *Agenda 1970: Proposals for a Creative Politics* (Toronto: University of Toronto, 1968).

[15]The argument was that the arrival of left-wing parties permitted the transcendence of religious and regional conflicts which had been so controversial during nation-building. The intellectual similarity is worth noting to the classic argument by S.M. Lipset and S. Rokkan, *Party Systems and Voter Alignments* (New York: The Free Press, 1967), Chapter 1.

[16]We ought never forget that Great Britain, often cited as the polity where, for most of the twentieth century, class-based politics provided the organizing principle, is in fact composed of three different nations, with different languages and cultures, as well as sharp divergences in regional economic patterns.

[17]The principled positions which Doern attributed in 1983 to the Liberals and described as the most coherent in years had disappeared by 1984 when the party acquired a new leader. See G.B. Doern, *How Ottawa Spends: The Liberals, the Opposition and Federal Priorities* (Toronto: Lorimer, 1983); also M. Prince, *How Ottawa Spends, 1986-87: Tracking the Tories* (Toronto: Methuen, 1986).

[18]G. Therborn, "The Rule of Capital and the Rise of Democracy," *New Left Review*, vol. 103, 1977.

[19]C.B. Macpherson, *The Life and Times of Liberal Democracy* , Chapter 2.

[20]C. Offe, *Contradictions of the Welfare State* (London: Hutchison, 1984), p. 179.

[21]These parties were usually founded outside the legislature, sometimes as an outgrowth of trade-union organization. Their leadership had few ties to the dominant class nor did it gain financial support from it. Rather, these parties were tightly organized with a dues-paying membership and they often had formal links to trade unions, which saw the new parties as one means of achieving the political victories upon which the success of the unions' workplace struggles in part depended.

[22]A. Przeworski, *Capitalism and Social Democracy* (Cambridge: Cambridge University Press, 1985), Chapter 2.

[23]For a good discussion of this process in Britain see R. Miliband, *Parliamentary Socialism: A Study in the Politics of Labour* (London: Merlin, 1961).

[24]Lipset and Rokkan, *op. cit.*, pp. 50-54.

[25]A. Przeworski, "Proletariat into Class: The Process of Class Formation From K. Kautsky's "The Class Struggle" to Recent Controversies," *Politics and Society*, vol. 7, 1977.

[26]This sentence is obviously an adaptation of E.P. Thompson's famous definition of class. See *The Making of the English Working Class* (New York: Vintage, 1966), p. 11.

[27]For a discussion of recent controversies over the definition of politics, and the fragmenting effects this debate has had on left-wing parties, see G. Ross and J. Jenson, "Postwar Class Struggle and the Crisis of Left Politics" in R. Miliband, *et al., The Socialist Register 1985-86* (London: Merlin, 1986).

[28]For example, if politics is defined as conflict among ethnic groups, it is more difficult to unite for partisan action members of the same class who have different ethnic backgrounds.

[29]Of course it is not only class parties which must struggle to impose a new definition of politics. Any group wanting to alter the definition of politics must fight this two-front war. For a discussion of the process with regard to the women's movement and its actions see J. Jenson, "Struggling For Identity: The Women's Movement and the State in Western Europe," *West European Politics*, vol. 8, no. 4, 1985.

[30]Ross and Jenson, *op. cit.*, discuss the political importance of such groups. G. Ross, "Marxism and the New Middle Classes: French Critiques," *Theory and Society*, vol. 5, 1978 considers the theoretical debates over meaning.

[31]Przeworski, "Proletariat. . ." *op. cit.*

Chapter 2

1867–1905—The Emergence of a Two-party System

Introduction

The history of the Canadian party system displays crucial divergences in the timing of political developments in several regions. More specifically, the eastern half of the country had a relatively stable system of partisan relationships before the western party system itself took shape. These divergences arise from the time of acquisition of provincial status, patterns of settlement in the new provinces and the effect of different franchise regulations. More fundamentally, however, they stem from the way in which the developing Canadian economy was fitted into the pattern of commercial and industrial relations in North America and in the international economy. Different explanations of this situation were developed by the organizations which drew the population into political activity. Each of these complex and interacting factors must be considered before it is possible to describe the growth of the two-party system until 1905.

By the turn of the century, the eastern provinces had developed a system of partisan alignments in which politics was termed to be about national development, and the electoral debate was increasingly occupied with the relations of the two founding cultures. The familiar division of support of language and religious groups between the parties had been established. By then, the Liberals were predominant among Francophone voters while the Conservative support was increasingly confined to areas with large English-speaking populations, especially those with large Protestant representation. This pattern developed after a series of partisan struggles and false starts, but it was firmly established before Saskatchewan and Alberta entered Confederation and before much of the population of the western provinces had arrived.

The hegemony of the bourgeoisie, as a class, was not subject to threat in the federal elections of this period. Its values, with regard to national development and the experiment of Confederation, remained predominant and were shared by both major parties. Confederation itself was an expression of these values. It was a strategy to realize the immense possibilities of a new country stretching from sea to sea. The potential for material abundance was great but the costs of this, particularly for some regions and the subordinate classes, were not organized as conflict between parties. The western areas, which bore high costs for the new strategy, were still too weak to gain more than minor redress from the representative institutions set up in 1867. It was in this context of ideological consensus that expansion in the western areas was first conceived and carried out.

The potential grievances were neither recognized nor accommodated in the existing party system. By 1905, the eastern party system had grown from a loose and flexible grouping of parliamentarians to one which was organized by large and fairly cohesive political parties with mass electorates ranged behind them. In the process, many of the familiar characteristics of the party system emerged. The party system was characterized by a single primary cleavage, that of culture. Elections were organized around issues relating to this cleavage, though other matters were discussed in each election campaign of the period. It was the parties' appeal to the cultural loyalties of the voters, however, which constituted the basic distinction between the Liberal and Conservative parties.

This party system did not debate the class interests inherent in the strategy of economic and national development. How did it happen that, after Confederation, the hegemony, both political and ideological, of the bourgeoisie was consolidated and assured without challenge? How did it happen that any effective political opposition that was expressed came dressed as regional dissent rather than as the class grievances of western farmers or industrial workers? Answers to these questions are found within the pattern of Canadian economic development, the resulting class formation and the expression of political conflict within the party system. Canadian elections were conducted in a particular context, and it is only by understanding this context that it is possible to understand the nature of party development.

The Establishment of the Canadian Political Economy

The policy and actions of the political parties in post-Confederation Canada were influenced by efforts to establish a viable and integrated national economy according to the initial goals of the political union. With the policy decisions taken by the new federal state, industrialization began in earnest. With this industrialization came the development of a new type of labour force and the beginnings of the modern trade union movement. The population increased dramatically with the influx of huge numbers of immigrants, who took up land and began wheat farming in the West. The continued expansion of these two groups, industrial workers and western farmers, would become of fundamental importance for partisan politics in later decades. In the meantime, by 1905, a structure of partisan relations was in place which differed from what had existed for the elections of the early years of Confederation and which minimized the partisan expression of conflict between capital and the newly emerging industrial working class. Political discussion and dissent focussed on a series of other issues and emphasized that the "national interest" would be best served by a "National Policy" of economic development.

This is not the place to retrace changes in the international economic order which led to the decision to establish a more unified and expanded country in British North America. In brief outline, the position of colonial advantage which Canadian colonies enjoyed in their trade with the United Kingdom was steadily reduced by the abandonment of the mercantile system, which had given preferential treatment to the colonies by incorporating some measure of free trade. The aggressive economic development of the United States also threatened the continuation and geographic expansion of the British colonies.[1]

Throughout its history, both as colonies and as a nation, the basis of Canadian economic development has been the export of staple products. These agricultural and other primary products find their market outside the country and do not require elaborate processing before export.[2] This form of economic development leads to a particular type of class formation based upon the activities of specific economic interests. In a country with a staple-based economy, merchant capital is often the dominant fraction of the bourgeoisie because such economies, first and foremost, depend upon trade and commercial activities. Thus, the success of merchant capital is necessary to ensure the success of the economic system as a whole. The export of staples leads to capital accumulation, earns foreign exchange and provides the foundation upon which other sectors can develop.[3] This development, however, is profoundly influenced by the predominance of a particular staple. For example, some staples are labour-intensive and, therefore, encourage population growth, while others do not. Some require the creation of large-scale infrastructure projects before the staple can be exploited, and this infrastructure can often only be put into place with public intervention of some kind.[4] Therefore, the size and location of the labour force, the market for consumer and capital goods, the type of ownership of the means of production and the nature of the demands for state activity are all matters which reflect the characteristics of the currently dominant staple industry.

In the 1850s and 1860s, the Canadian colonies were in a difficult position because, if they were to expand and develop, further exploitation of the agricultural staple had to be assured.[5] In addition, trade in other products had to be expanded. In the face of competition from American trading routes and lost advantages in the free-trading United Kingdom, one path of expansion was westward, beyond the physical barrier of the Canadian Shield. This strategy, however, demanded more railways over new routes, displacement of the Hudson's Bay Company from control of the lands west of Ontario, a force to establish Canadian sovereignty over those lands, and a population to farm the Prairies. These were the goals of the Fathers of Confederation when they met to discuss the union of the divided and increasingly weakened colonies of British North America.[6]

The demand for union arose out of the colonies' changing relationship with both the United Kingdom and the United States. The strategy of confederation involved a decision to create a transcontinental "Canadian" economy which would be less vulnerable to British trading policy and which could exist independently of the industrializing giant to the south. The idea of an east-west economy parallelling that of the United States was in sharp contrast with the popular hope of previous decades that the economy would benefit from closer economic ties with the United States either through reciprocity or annexation.[7] These hopes were abandoned when it became painfully clear that the Americans were no longer interested in establishing special economic arrangements with the British colonies. Therefore, an east-west orientation to trade and economic activity was sought to replace an inaccessible north-south one.[8]

The realization of this new economic unit required alterations in the existing political arrangements. It implied the immediate necessity of constitutionally linking the Maritime colonies with the two central ones so as to remove barriers of trade between them. It also meant that these four colonies would have to extend their jurisdiction to the North-West.

Nation-building also required railroad links, first, eastward (the Intercolonial from Quebec to Nova Scotia) and then westward (to British Columbia). These extensions promised to strengthen shipping and trading in the St. Lawrence region. Without these new transportation links, Canadian products would move south to New York and Boston or to the Chicago-centred network. In essence, Confederation was to create a larger domestic market, which would allow some independence from the international economy and provide for development within Canada alone.[9] Such a market required the removal of tariffs between the colonies, the extension of the market across the country and an increased population. Therefore, the justification for Confederation in 1867 was an expanded, more self-contained economy which would continue to depend on international trade, but under slightly less variable conditions.[10]

The strongest supporters of the new constitutional arrangements were those people who benefited from a Canada which was a resource-rich, resource-extracting and trading nation. The federal state, with more resources than the small and separate colonies, would be better able to implement the strategy of the architects of Confederation.[11] What was needed was a state which could acquire the western lands from the Hudson's Bay Company; provide for a transcontinental railway network to link all parts of the former colonies and the new areas as far as British Columbia; and recruit immigrants who would work the new farm lands and buy Canadian goods.

It is important to note at this point what Confederation was not. It was not designed to create the conditions for an industrial nation or a nation independent from the ties of the imperial network.[12] Rather, it was to pursue a limited set of goals to offset some new developments in the international economic order. In addition, the new political system was to smooth over, rather than solve, the differences of language, religion and culture which had plagued relations between the colonies. These issues, it was hoped, could be relegated to the provincial level of government, leaving the federal state free to pursue the developmental strategies envisaged by the Fathers of Confederation. Thus, above all else, the federation provided a framework for a larger market, an instrument to organize trade potential and a means to develop access to an expanded hinterland.

These goals provided the basis for the arrangements of Confederation, and they help to account for the kind of partisan politics that developed. The state was to be an active participant in nation-building, through the implementation of the provisions of the National Policy, a policy which acquired its name only in the 1870s but which existed much earlier in outline form.[13] The class involved in the establishment of this state was the bourgeoisie, specifically that fraction of the bourgeoisie involved in mercantile activities. These men pursued vigorously, in both their private corporate activities and their dealings with the federal government, a strategy of nation-building and railroad-building that would facilitate the continuation and further exploitation of an export-oriented, resource-extracting, staple-based economy. In the early years of Confederation, the political home of this fraction was the Conservative Party of Sir John A. Macdonald.[14]

Opposition to this strategy came from a hodgepodge of positions. There were those, particularly in rural Ontario, who felt that the abandonment of the continental policy and reciprocity with the United States was premature. And there were the Maritimers, especially the Halifax merchants, who saw the emphasis on central development as a threat to the position that they enjoyed during the period of British mercantilism. There was also ideological opposition from free-trading liberals.[15] Finally, there was fear of assimilation among the Francophone minority.[16] All of these positions, however, did not fuse into a successful and cohesive alliance against the movers of Confederation. They remained divided in their opposition to the Conservative leadership, sometimes loosely coalesced, sometimes not.[17] It was only in the 1890s that the Liberal Party managed to create a national party that could successfully challenge the electoral dominance of the "nation-builders", the Conservatives. However, it did this, not by contesting the idea of the national dream, but rather by embracing it.

The bright prospects of the new nation were not immediately realized. The Canadian nation was welcomed into a world which was quickly slipping into a major economic depression. The crisis of the 1870s created numerous problems for an economy founded on international trade. As prices for products fell and markets retracted, Canada began to lose population to the industries of the United States at a disturbing rate. An addition to the original formula was needed, and the proposal which came forward was industrialization through the medium of tariff protection.[18] The full-blown National Policy (NP), to be written henceforth with capital letters, was unveiled.[19]

The fundamental goal of the Conservatives, the party of Sir John A. Macdonald and the others who had designed Confederation in the first place, was to make the thing work. The promised economic expansion had to be realized. With the depression of the 1870s, there was a need for action and into the breach stepped the Conservatives, armed with protection for Canadian industry. The increased tariffs, prescribed by the NP, would provide a protective wall behind which industry located in Canada could grow and prosper, free from the terrific competition of American-produced goods and other imports. This National Policy, just as the national policy of the pre- and immediately post-Confederation years, was designed to protect Canada from the effects of an unstable international economic order. A tariff on imported manufactured goods provided the federal government with a source of income to finance its activities. But more importantly, it gave Canadian goods a competitive advantage over imported goods, particularly those from the United States, which, without the tariff, would have been less costly than Canadian goods on the domestic market. Thus, the tariff ensured that the needs of the western region as well as those of the original colonies would be supplied by Canadian manufacturers. At the same time, it sponsored the growth of industry in Canada and thereby slowed the outward flow of population which had jeopardized the original goal of a bigger domestic market and the need for a population sufficiently large to open up the western prairie. Finally, it ensured that eastern Canadian goods would fill the boxcars of the new railroads. In all these ways, the tariff reinforced the original goals of Confederation. It was a policy that offered protection and markets to the central Canadian bourgeoisie.

The bourgeoisie was united in its support for the National Policy. There was no longer competition between mercantile and manufacturing interests over state activity, and there was little ground for partisan competition between these fractions. They sought the creation of a western market of wheat farmers strung along the railway lines behind a tariff wall.[20] Even elements of the Maritime bourgeoisie could be pleased with the tariff because it provided a potential escape from its dependence on the declining West Indian and British trade. Maritimers could move into industrial capitalism and share in the westward-moving national economy.

Wheat was the linchpin commodity in this development strategy. The marketing of wheat was profitable to merchants and to railroad investors. Wheat earned foreign exchange, keeping the balance of payments in proper order, and employed the new immigrants who swelled the population of the West. In turn, these immigrants provided an expanded market for the new tariff-induced industries growing up in the central provinces.[21] The transportation network was in equilibrium because the trains could carry immigrants and manufactured goods west and bring back wheat to the East.

And so the circle went.[22] It seemed to constitute a perfect balance, with each of the three elements of the National Policy–tariffs, immigration and the railways–necessary for the others. The perfection, however, was more apparent than real because the economy was still very dependent on international conditions, in particular the level of demand and price for wheat.[23] The fruition of the policy in the 1890s was produced by an expanding export market for primary goods. Without this market, the dangers of an export-oriented economy which relied on imports of capital for industrialization would become apparent. Vulnerability and instability were inherent in the formula.

This development strategy also led to a change in the balance of domestic forces. Regional disparities, resulting from metropolitan dominance and hinterland dependency, were structured into the Canadian economy as a necessary effect of the NP. Resulting industrialization, especially after 1900, created a large body of industrial workers.[24] Both these effects would come into play in the later rounds of political conflict and would constitute the basis of future crises and challenges to policies of the bourgeoisie. The solution to the economic crisis of the 1870s, the National Policy, created the grounds for subsequent challenges to those who had put the decision into place. However, the expression of these challenges would, of necessity, occur within a system of political arrangements and practices also established in that period. But this is the future. It is the changes in the class structure and the possibilities and limits of their political expression prior to 1905 which concern us here.

Despite an international depression of major proportions, the last three decades of the nineteenth century were,

> . . . a period of substantial growth, increasing localization of industry and increasing specialization of the production of firms. Part of this growth may be attributed to the influence of staple industries . . . while a further significant portion may be attributed to the intensive development of secondary manufacturing within the region of Central Canada.[25]

Much of the growth in manufacturing occurred in the period from 1870 to 1890, with an average rate of growth above any other post-Confederation period.[26] In addition, growth was greater in secondary manufacturing than in the more simple primary manufacturing, stimulated both by staple exports and the National Policy of transportation and tariffs. Larger cities came into being and grew rapidly as locations for new industries and as distribution centres.

As a result of these changes in the economy, new groups and classes were created, and the potential for their political organization increased. One of these groups was obviously that of urban workers employed in secondary manufacturing. There was a steady increase in this category throughout the period, as Table 2:1 shows. These workers were concentrated in the two central provinces, Quebec and Ontario, where most of the industrial development fostered by the National Policy occurred. A second group was the western farmers, immigrants to the new provinces who found themselves inserted into an economic structure dependent upon the continued expansion of wheat for export. It was their production which provided the motor for economic development. The economy would function as long as they remained in their proper location as producers of the staple and consumers of the goods and services of the East. Yet neither group organized a strong opposition to confront the bourgeois parties over their conception of the "national interest" during this period. Why the politics of class remained constrained in the early post-Confederation party system is the subject of the next section.

The Contest for Workers in the East

This expansion of two categories of voters–workers and western farmers–raised an obvious possibility of an electoral alliance between the two groups most likely to desire a change in the distribution of the benefits of the strategy of economic development. The alliance, however, was difficult and not realized immediately, for reasons which will become clear as subsequent chapters unfold. The first reasons were demographic and legal. There was not much settlement in the West until after the initial period of party growth and the congealment in the East of a system of partisan alignments. It was after 1896 that the wheat economy of the Prairies really took form. The western farmers were weak politically for much of this period simply because there were so few of them. A similar argument about size applies to the eastern workers, at least until well into this period. There were just not enough to effectively mount independent party actions. In addition, franchise restrictions and the working of the electoral law weakened the potential influence of these groups. These factors will be described in the next section of this chapter. Newly brought into both a capitalist labour market and a democratic electoral system, workers were introduced to party politics of a very particular sort. The newly enfranchised in Canada learned that, unlike the situation in many western European nations, partisan politics was about the conflict between ethnic and religious groups rather than between classes. As one federal election followed another, the Liberals and Conservatives became increasingly embroiled in religious and ethnic controversies. Thus, even though the franchise gradually allowed more Canadian workers to vote, the politics of culture limited the political options available to them. The absence of an organized opposition allowed ethnicity and religion to dominate the federal partisan debate. It is the absence of an organized opposition to this definition of politics which must be explained.

In many respects the failure of the working class to organize a political opposition can be traced to the experiences of the early labour movement itself. The characteristics of the Canadian trade unions and the decisions they took prior to 1905 set the stage. The effects were felt for many years to come.

The history of the Canadian union movement bears some recounting because, as in the United States but not in Europe, instead of linking workers to political organizations expressing labour interests, the movement frequently denied the value or even the acceptability of such links. By the end of this period, the Canadian labour movement was firmly established on a path which minimized the opportunity for direct political activity by way of party formation. The union movement's tendency not to engage in direct political action was challenged at later points in time. Other forms of political activity by workers and their organizations did develop. However, the choices made in this period became the tradition of the Canadian labour movement, and they could only be displaced by opposition, sometimes violent opposition, to that tradition and the already strong workers' organizations which embodied it.

In its early years, the labour movement did begin to undertake actions which might have resulted eventually in the successful organization of a party of workers in the federal party system. However, attempts to introduce the language of class conflict into partisan politics, by means of a socialist or a workers' party, were always undertaken at great odds. At first, workers were in a minority position in a system of production which was based on the export of virtually unprocessed primary products. Yet, even as the Canadian economy developed new staples and more modern forms of manufacturing, much of the movement maintained a political strategy explicitly opposed to separate partisan action by workers. It was this decision, more than any other, which undercut the possibility of support from organized labour for a party of the working class. A potential ally of a party directed toward and motivated by the interests, needs and position of workers in a capitalist economy was lost.

Any party appealing to workers, as workers, had to face entrenched opposition not only from the bourgeoisie and the state, but also from the bodies which organized workers in the workplace.

Few Canadian workers were organized in 1867. There were some trade unions as early as the 1820s in Upper Canada, and, by the 1830s, the printers and the boot and shoemakers, in particular, had created unions in the major urban centres.[27] Thereafter, the growing manufacturing sector gradually spawned associations, and by 1900 labour was organized in a way which mirrored national economic development. The movement was concentrated in the centre of the country, and fledgling organizations were small and isolated from one another. Moreover, it was only after legal restrictions on labour organizations were removed in 1872 that membership could begin to increase and the organization and structures of the Canadian labour movement could be formalized.

Early trade union activity differed from trends within the movement in the twentieth century in several ways. Specifically, unions did exhibit a desire for political action, as well as an organization which permitted independent partisan intervention by workers and their associations in the federal party system. Nevertheless, the possibility that they might organize a class cleavage into elections in opposition to the dominant system of partisan alignments was circumscribed almost from the beginning. The prevailing religious and ethnic definitions of what constituted politics were skilfully utilized by the bourgeois parties to capture the allegiances of the newly enfranchised workers. This process was in turn reinforced and stimulated by the influential religious and social organizations of the period. Finally, in 1902, the potential for a socialist or labour party opposition in the party system virtually evaporated when American craft unionism, complete with its political ideals and practices, firmly entrenched itself in the Canadian union movement.

The particular institutions and class practices that maintained bourgeois dominance in the organization of the party system were different in English- and French-speaking Canada. However, the outcome was essentially the same. The party loyalties of the mushrooming labour sector were shaped without challenge to the class biases in the party system. In consequence, struggles between the worker and the capitalist, or their representatives, were confined to economic negotiations conducted by trade unions and, thus, were isolated from partisan political debate.

Examining the situation of English Canada first, we see that organized labour did undertake, before the turn of the century, some partisan activity based on class analyses and positions. First, trade unions developed structures and forms of organization which favoured and facilitated their own electoral and other political activity. Skilled and unskilled, service, craft and industrial workers alike began to co-operate on local and regional bases as early as 1871. The Noble Order of the Knights of Labor, active in Canada from the 1870s, grouped together all types of workers into local bodies.[28] Differences in skills and in industry were ignored in favour of comprehensive organization of a locality. This strategy was particularly appropriate in Canada, given the very real structural constraints on organized labour throughout the period. Industrial activity was minimal and unevenly distributed both within and across the provinces. No single category of worker dominated the labour force, although the combined manufacturing, construction and service sectors comprised approximately one-half of the labour force as early as the 1880s (Table 2:1). Therefore, the tendency to organize all types of workers into local and district trade assemblies provided a viable and

Table 2:1
PERCENTAGE DISTRIBUTION OF PERSONS WORKING BY SELECTED INDUSTRY IN CANADA, SELECTED YEARS (1871–1931)
(horizontal per cent)

	Agriculture	Other Primary Industry	Manufacturing and Construction	Tertiary Industry (Public Utilities and other service industries)
1871	50.0	—	13.1	17.0
1881	48.0	3.2	29.4	19.4
1891	45.8	3.7	26.3	24.2
1901	40.2	4.1	27.9	27.8
1911	34.3	5.2	27.1	33.4
1921	32.8	3.8	26.5	36.9
1931	28.8	3.8	16.5	50.9

Source: O. J. Firestone, Canada's Economic Development, Series VII (London: Bowes and Bowes, 1958), p. 185.

stronger centre at a time when splits along craft lines or even industry differences would have been enfeebling.

A second form of local association was a council grouping representatives of unions active in a particular city and, later, a province or the nation. The first of these was the Toronto Trades Assembly, founded in 1871, which brought together fifteen unions from that city. These councils, designed to provide a mechanism to further common goals of labour, soon expanded. In 1873, the Toronto Trades Assembly convened unions from other cities to establish a national central organization, the Canadian Labour Union (CLU), which, despite its name, was confined to Ontario. However, similar organizations were set up in Quebec, Manitoba and British Columbia by the 1880s. The CLU was followed by several other national centres, culminating in the founding of the Trades and Labour Congress of Canada (TLC) in 1892.[29]

The utility of both these forms of local organization was quickly evident. The potential for such assemblies to improve local conditions and influence the state was realized almost immediately. In the Toronto Printers' Strike of 1872, a united labour front (acting in support of the striking printers) induced the federal Conservative government to remove legal restrictions on trade union activity. Such restrictions had been frequently used in the past to ban or weaken, or otherwise interfere with, collective bodies. Their removal was a major step forward.

Moving on from successes such as this, labour organizations began to propose a formal labour opposition in the party system. The Trades and Labour Congress called for independent political action by workers on no less than eight occasions in the period between 1883 and 1899. This included the proposal for a labour party to represent the interests of the workers in the parliamentary system. Several independent labour candidates were elected in cities and towns around the country. However, most spectacular was the political activity of trade unions in British Columbia and their co-operation with the socialists. Political activism characterized the BC labour movement almost from its conception. Trade unionists had contested political office as early as 1882 and had participated in the formation of various socialist and reformist parties which sprang in and out of existence during the period. Although at times fractious, this co-operation proved politically advantageous. In the 1903 provincial election, for example, the Socialist Party of British Columbia gained no less than 11% of the popular vote.[30]

Another factor which favoured the political organization of workers, as workers, before the turn of the century was the national autonomy of the Canadian labour movement. In the early years, Canadian unions were independent bodies, free from ties to unions located outside of the country, particularly those in the United States. While the tendency to establish loose associations with British and American unions existed, national trade unions were predominant throughout the period. In addition, and in contrast to the situation later, the international bonds which did exist were not restrictive. By and large, affiliation with an international union did not imply ideological or strategic control of Canadian trade union activity from outside. Rather, prior to 1902, it was generally recognized by both Canadian and American unionists that cross-national differences in the conditions of work and the structure of government necessitated a large measure of local autonomy, particularly in relation to political strategy and action. Thus, before 1902, Canadian union locals and federations were free to engage in whatever activity they thought necessary to realize their particular and local needs. They could be active participants in partisan politics without the fear of expulsion from the international union with which they were affiliated. And, as has been shown above, unionists in Canada did seize the possibilities to organize separate labour partisan activity.

Generally speaking, then, the early labour movement in English Canada, while small and often isolated, was characterized by several tendencies which encouraged the partisan mobilization of the working class as a class. They were, if not totally autonomous, at least free to pursue their own political strategies; they recognized the need for an organized partisan labour opposition; and their structures provided the requisite strength to support such political action, particularly in urban centres. This was to change drastically and soon. The changes which weakened all three of these tendencies arose as a result of competition between labour organizations and strategies. The situation was resolved by the adoption in Canada of a solution first developed in the United States. There is no need here to go into a description of the evolution of this position across the border. It will be sufficient to show how it was accepted in the Canadian affiliates of the American international unions.

A new approach to labour's political activity was adopted, leaving organized labour with an unrealized potential for electoral politics in English Canada. It magnified the influence of currents within the movement which wished to confine trade unions to non-partisan struggles and advocated that trade unions use their political power by bargaining for concessions from one or the other of the bourgeois parties. While there would be frequent demands that the TLC take political action and even some initiatives, the emphasis on non-partisanship and anti-labour party activity remained predominant. The division of power within capitalism was accepted by the labour movement, and its role became that of getting a better deal for workers, without substituting a new set of class relations for those in existence.[31]

The decision of the Trades and Labour Congress not to organize its own political party for direct political action resulted from the struggle for ascendancy between craft-based and industry-wide labour organizations in the United States. The contest between the American Federation of Labor and the Noble Order of the Knights of Labor was decided in the US in the 1880s. It was a struggle for dominance over the increasingly large and potentially politically powerful American labour force. It was a contest between competing organizations, between competing ways of organizing workers, and it was a struggle of ideology. In essence, the resolution of the struggle set the American labour movement on the path of craft-based unions, organized by the AFL, with an ideology of class collaboration, based on acceptance of the class relations and political expressions of American capitalism. The struggle spilled over into Canada, where both the AFL and the Knights of Labor had affiliated unions.

The actual conflict between industrial and craft unionism in the United States initially had little impact in Canada. However, after the ascendancy of the AFL had been firmly established south of the border, elements within the TLC saw that certain advantages could be gained from joining forces with the international craft union centre. Some hoped that affiliation would provide the TLC with the funds it desperately needed to organize Canadian craft workers and thereby enable it to dominate the trade union movement in Canada as the AFL did in the United States. For others, affiliation promised an international union card which was increasingly a prerequisite for employment in the United States. Moreover, it was hoped that this card would help Canadian craftsmen looking for seasonal work avoid American alien labour legislation. But there were also many dissenters who argued that Canadian workers would be best served by a wholly autonomous and national trade union centre. Thus, the question of affiliation with the AFL was put to the floor of the Trades and Labour Congress convention held in Berlin, Ontario in 1902.[32] The result of the vote was to divide the movement for decades. Commonly referred to as the "Berlin Victory," the Congress amended its constitution to exclude from its membership national and international unions that did not accept the jurisdiction of the AFL.

This decision had several consequences for labour's direct participation in partisan politics. First, the practice of gathering together all types of workers in a particular locale was abandoned in favour of organization of unions by craft. This was, of course, the organizing principle of the AFL, and it was this strategy which had precipitated its struggle with the Knights of Labor. The craft unions claimed sole jurisdiction over skilled workers, which implied that these workers could no longer be organized, even concurrently, on the basis of common geography. The ties between workers were henceforth to be those of craft rather than locale. As a result, Canadian labour lost some of its strong local assemblies, organized by the Knights of Labor. Second, being tied so closely to the AFL, the TLC fell subject to the political philosophy of the president of that body, Samuel Gompers. In effect, "Gomperism" was transferred to the Canadian political system from the United States where it was gaining ascendancy. This view of labour's place in industrial capitalism emphasized that labour should not (and thus, unions could not) form a labour party or even sponsor labour candidates. Instead, they should "shop" between the existing parties, in this case both bourgeois parties, to find the one which would give the best deal to labour. Third, this decision to accept the AFL's jurisdiction and its interpretation of the proper mode of organization (by craft) meant that any move to group workers into unions based on the industry which employed them (miners, for example) was nipped in the bud.[33] This question of mode of organization would surface again and again, causing conflict, distress and political machinations until the 1940s. Thus, the final and somewhat ironic effect of the 1902 decision, designed to create continental unity, actually brought deep cleavages to the union movement in Canada. This division weakened any initiatives for party formation. The terms of the 1902 decision required the expulsion of a large number of national and industrial unions which were either unable or unwilling to accept the jurisdiction of the AFL. They had to be expelled from the central, the TLC, which had housed them to that point. As the following chapter indicates, the resulting strains within the labour movement corresponded to the regional strains built into the post-Confederation development strategy. From the beginning, the 1902 "victory" brought with it a good deal of disorganization, resentment and weakening of the Canadian labour movement.

The experience of labour in Quebec during this period differed in its specifics from what had occurred in English Canada, but, in the final analysis, the result was the same. The existence and characteristics of class struggle in the industrial system were obscured by an emphasis on ethnic and religious differences. The process of transfer of class struggle into ethnic and religious conflict was facilitated by a certain correspondence between position in the burgeoning capitalist economy and ethnicity.

Throughout the nineteenth century, a sizable Francophone wage-labour force emerged in Quebec. Initially, these workers were attracted to New England textile mills and industrial centres. Soon, however, the promise of cheap labour and a large profit margin drew British and American, as well as Canadian, capital to the province. In the process, the structure of class relations and the resulting social inequalities were confused and complicated by religious and ethnic divisions which coincided with those between capital and labour. In effect, since the source of capital determined that control and management of the major commercial, financial and industrial enterprises would remain with the Anglophone minority in the province, the Francophone majority was largely confined to the role of skilled or unskilled labour. Thus, from the outset of industrialization, the effects of inequalities caused by the workings of industrial capitalism could be attributed to relations between ethnic and religious groups.

Industrialization quickly spawned a union movement in Quebec, but, from the beginning, it differed from that of English Canada. Trade unions appeared in Montreal and Quebec City as early as the 1820s and 1830s and these were soon followed by a scattering of Catholic *syndicats*, principally isolated in one-industry towns. Independent labour activity in partisan politics was discouraged by the Catholic Church which, at the time, opposed anything that could be interpreted not only as socialist but even as liberal. The possibility that organized labour would enter politics in any major way to challenge the existing relations of authority was ruled out almost from the start. The opposition of the Church, given its position in Quebec's traditional social structure, was too pronounced. Not only did this influence block the organization of labour's criticism in partisan politics, but it also significantly reduced the ability of the labour movement to improve the conditions of the workers within the capitalist system. In this way, the Roman Catholic Church was an important ally of the bourgeoisie. It was an ally with economic and political as well as obvious ideological effects.

Labour organizations were, from the beginning, viewed with trepidation by the Church, church leaders and lay nationalists. In particular, they feared that Francophone workers, organized by "alien" trade unions, would lose their traditional ties of culture, language and religious beliefs. Perhaps even more importantly, trade unions from outside of Quebec were secular, and, thus, they were seen as a threat to the control of the social order maintained and jealously guarded by religious authorities.

The Knights of Labor were the most important secular and "alien" organization to challenge the Church's dominance over the Quebec labour movement before the turn of the century. They had a significant impact on the organization of labour because their method of bringing together workers by locality rather than by craft was particularly well-suited to the situation and requirements of Quebec labour. Craft unions were impractical, for the most part, because industry was widely scattered and few workers were skilled craftsmen. The Knights were successful in setting up branches in Quebec, but, in contrast to their practices in the other provinces, they were immediately prevented from undertaking partisan political activity. The Roman Catholic hierarchy in Quebec initially banned its adherents from joining the Knights. Later, Catholics were permitted to join the movement, but this came only after the leadership of the Knights succeeded in convincing the ecclesiastical authorities that the movement was untainted with socialism, or other undesirable political characteristics.[34] Thus, the Knights neither developed a party in opposition to the Liberals and Conservatives in Quebec nor did they provide any real challenge to the dominance of the Church in that province. After the expulsion of the Knights of Labor from the TLC, the Church regained virtually full control over the organizational and ideological development of the labour movement in the province.

The Church's relationship with labour was less one of organizer than one of ideological mentor and conciliator between worker and capitalist. To this end, the Boot and Shoe Strike of 1900 in Quebec City represents a significant turning point for trade unionism in Quebec. The Church's intervention ensured the subordination of labour to capital in industrial disputes for almost half a century. It established a precedent for labour relations, the form of which was adopted later by the federal state. In essence, the Church set up a mechanism for the conciliation of industrial disputes. It placed itself in the centre as the 'neutral arbiter' between the employers, who made up the Board of Conciliation, and the workers, who were the Board of Complaint.[35] Yet, the process, inspired by the papal encyclical, *Rerum Novarum*, was less than neutral with relation to the interests of labour. In fact, the ideological biases of this conciliation process assured the continuation of the existing class relations.

The constraints it placed on labour are clear. First, it presupposed a hierarchy of human beings, based on function performed and arising from Divine Plan. Obviously, something derived from a source such as this must both be proper and non-conflictual.[36] Thus, a religious view of the world, substituting harmony of function for the socialist view of class conflict, dominated the ideology of the Quebec labour movement. In addition, the Church could retain control more directly over the trade unions of the faithful because it demanded and received the acceptance of a union chaplain, named by the religious authorities, to take part in their meetings. Finally, in stressing harmony and co-operation between the worker and the capitalist rather than conflict, little legitimacy was granted to labour militancy, strikes, or independent political action. Indeed, the ideological constraint came, in subsequent years, to act as a barrier to co-operation between English and French trade unions as much as did language itself.[37]

Thus, although the early years of the Canadian union movement had seen some influx of radical politics and critical ideologies, this did not continue within the organizationally dominant segment of the movement. The radical critiques were increasingly moderated as time passed. The Knights, in order to maintain their position as organizers of the working class of Quebec, had to adopt a particular and restricted analysis of capitalism. They were increasingly confined to a political discourse within the boundaries acceptable to the bourgeois political parties and, in particular, to the political party that the Catholic Church strongly supported for much of this period, the Conservatives. As a result the Knights gradually began to take on the appearance of nothing more than another location for the contest between the two parties. Over time, more and more party politicians were incorporated into the organizational hierarchy of the union, and, therefore, the Knights provided a convenient point of access for these politicians into the TLC. This infiltration aroused the hostility of members of other unions and the TLC. One goal of the union movement became the escape from the organization of labour activity as an adjunct of the political activity of the bourgeois parties. By 1902, the expulsion of the Knights from the TLC could be seen as a way of doing this and, thus, as a progressive step. Their expulsion was seen as a way of ridding the trade union movement of excessive attachments to bourgeois parties.[38]

The craft unions, particularly as collected together in international unions affiliated with the AFL, also, over time, became less radical in their political analysis. Their strategy, called "independent labour representation," had initially carried the implication that the trade union movement should not align itself in a continuing way with any of the parties that represented the forces and power of the capitalists. Such a permanent alignment, with either the Liberals or the Conservatives, would weaken the ability of labour organizations to make demands. In addition, certain trade unionists' personal links with one or other of the parties could potentially divide that movement into factions—to its detriment. However, the concept of "independent representation" came quickly to mean that the trade union movement should not undertake independent action so far as to establish or provide substantial support for the establishment of a labour party. In other words, the evolution of the strategy came to imply that the unions or the central bodies should look only within the existing two-party system to find the "friends of labour."

In the particular conditions of the Canadian labour movement of the time, this strategy evolved into opposition, at times violent opposition, to the idea of providing support for the various socialist and labour party formations that were coming into being. The struggling parties lost, as a result of a continuing series of resolutions similar to that of the 1902 Berlin Convention, their natural ally in the other major institution that spoke to workers as workers. The 1902 Convention defeated a proposition which would have had the Congress endorse the Socialist Party of Canada. There were several reasons for this decision, including differences of ideology between labour militants, calculations of methods to maximize trade unions' effectiveness and the reduction of the influence of rival labour organizations. All these factors together, most of which were internal to the labour movement itself, resulted in a failure to nurture allegiance to a party of the working class. While the lack of trade-union support did not preclude the emergence of socialist parties during this period, it so weakened their potential that they evolved into factionalized and uninteresting political alternatives.

In the final analysis, both in Quebec and in English Canada, the fate of organized labour as a nation-wide independent political actor was set by the beginning of the twentieth century. In Quebec, class cleavages were weakened and obscured by the activities of the Church, which stood between the worker and the capitalist in conflict and which propounded a harmonious view of relations within capitalism. In eastern Canada, by 1902, the activities of the trade unions were confined, for the most part, to questions of wages, working conditions and, only as a last resort, concessions to be extracted from the state. In both cases the discussion of what politics was about, the definition of the political, lacked any notion of class struggle or the possibility of the organization of workers to contest elections as workers. Both French and English workers were left to be organized into party politics on the basis of other criteria.

The trade unions were not alone in their concern for the partisan allegiance of the new voters. Social organizations as well as political parties shaped the context within which federal partisan politics was conducted. For the workers, the way that their daily bread was or could be earned represented only one aspect of existence. There were also the non-work hours which, as a result of one of labour's most important campaigns (for the nine-hour day) were increasing, and, most obviously, there was Sunday. Therefore, the effect that the experience of work and work conditions would have on the political activity of workers was the prize to be won by hard-fought ideological and political competition. If religious associations like the churches or the several associations which existed beside and which were supported by the churches, could draw workers into a world view that described the relations of capitalist and worker as something coming from the hand of God, the task of a labour union or a socialist party attempting to "demystify" the laws of economic development would be that much more difficult. Similarly, if ethnic associations could explain the relative wealth and status of different individuals in terms of the language they spoke, someone else, offering a competing explanation, had first to account for the question of language. If political parties could promise and evoke the limitless possibilities of the "national dream," an organization attempting to demonstrate that the laws of that dream were biased and unfair had strong competition. This was a time of great competition for the allegiance, both partisan and ideological, of the Canadian working class. What was at stake was its political and partisan existence.

The years from 1867 to 1905 are a history of struggle about the importance of class-based inequalities, about the existence of costs in the operation of the new economy, about who should and would pay these costs and about the possibilities of transformation of all of these relationships. Neither the political parties, the ethnic and religious associations nor the trade unions were free to or capable of imposing answers. It was a contest, a contest about ideology and about possibilities.

By 1905, the influence of ethnic and religious associations and the political parties was given a push forward by the withdrawal of the trade union movement from much of the competition. In English Canada they had decided not to attempt to substitute for the ideology of the bourgeoisie, a language of class which described politics as class struggle. In essence, they withdrew from the task undertaken by the union movement in much of Europe at that time, to organize a class cleavage into politics, through competition in the party system. Up to that point, the possibility had not really existed in Quebec because of the overwhelming influence of the Church. Moreover, the challenge to the Church's reading of class relations, which did eventually come, was postponed about half a century.

The churches and the myriad secret societies and voluntary associations were crucial ideological influences. They provided an alternative explanation of inequality, and they made strong and effective claims for the affection of workers. Their impact was to downplay the ideas of class conflict and to emphasize religious and ethnic differences. One of the effects was that these cleavages began to assume great importance in the electoral process. The following condemnation of the notion of class and class-based struggle, developed after the Toronto Printers' Strike by a Presbyterian clergyman, illustrates that the parties were not alone in their struggles to define the political as something other than class conflict.

> No man ever rose above a lowly condition who thought more of his class than of his individuality. In this new country where every man who strives may advance in social power and rank, to teach men subordination to class movements is to deprive them of those noble opportunities for personal advancement which are the particular glory and advantage of this continent.[39]

The Protestant churches, generally, did not challenge the ideology of economic liberalism before the turn of the century. In addition, voluntary associations based on religious allegiances reinforced the social isolation of Roman Catholics and Protestants and, by extension, that between French and English. They did this by fostering a sense of separateness from persons of the other group. They provided a network of contacts and benefits without which the individual would have been in difficulty in a world with few state-provided social services.

The Orange Lodge of Ontario is an appropriate example of how the social organizations of the period helped to consolidate the stratification of the electorate on the basis of religion and ethnicity rather than class. Although this organization was an expression of militant Protestantism in Ireland, it had become a familiar part of the Ontario landscape and acquired a large following of native Canadians and Protestant immigrants, even those of non-Irish backgrounds. Orangemen were primarily skilled workmen and farmers, although this was seldom reflected in the Lodge's typically upper class Tory leadership. Beyond fellowship and society, the Orange Lodge provided much-needed welfare similar to that provided by "sick and death-benefit" societies organized by socialists in Continental Europe. It was on this basis that the bonds between the worker and the religious-based voluntary association were particularly strong. Orangemen were responsible for the well-being of one another and of each other's families. At the very least, membership would assure a decent burial.[40]

Yet, along with the tangible benefits came a world view, based on identification with a religious group. The centrality of religious differences embodied in the philosophy of the Orange Lodge and the Catholic Church, helped to cut across similarities of class experience. Catholic and Protestant workers were separated by a gulf that was constantly reinforced by the dogma of their respective religious associations. In essence, these associations served as a bridge between the classes and as an alternative organization of workers. They also helped to incorporate the workers into the Liberal and Conservative ranks, because these parties gradually began to realize that an emphasis on differences of religion and/or language could be a useful way to attract an electorate and postpone, if not eliminate, the threat of a partisan socialist or labour challenge to their hegemony.

These parties could not afford to ignore the changed social structure created by the National Policy. They found the electorate to be increasingly composed of people who earned their living by working for wages. The same workers were also beginning to organize themselves collectively. Not unexpectedly, the two parties made strong and explicit efforts to manipulate early manifestations of class conflict to turn these struggles to their own partisan advantage. One strategy, used with some success, was to trivialize the discussion and to draw the workers into partisan ranks on the grounds that class differences were more apparent than real. The Toronto Printers' Strike stands as an illustration of the bourgeois parties' tactics. This strike and organized opposition to the jailing of the strike leaders, was sufficiently impressive to convince Sir John A. Macdonald, the leader of the Conservative Party, of the need for remedial legislation. This relief from the historical restrictions on trade union organization came in the form of the Trades Union Act of 1872. It recognized the right of unions to organize, registered them as the legitimate representatives of labour and freed them from criminal liability arising from their activities.[41]

Whether the Act was necessitated by class conflict, motivated by enlightened liberalism, or the result of a calculated electoral manoeuvre is not clear. However, the fact that the strike was directed against a newspaper, *The Globe*, owned by a prominent and powerful Liberal politician, George Brown, lends considerable weight to the third of these possibilities. For Macdonald, the Trades Union Act provided irrefutable evidence of the Conservatives' responsibilities as "friends of labour" and of their willingness to carry out these responsibilities. In fact, the Act served as a timely introduction to the serious electoral wooing which was to follow in the 1872 federal election campaign. The strategy of trivialization of class-based conflict was abundantly evident during the strike.[42] Trivialization was to serve as an important ingredient in the scramble for votes with the Liberals, who had been scarred seriously because it was one of their own who had provided the motivation for the Act.

> I ought to have a special interest in this subject [of the legislation] because I am a working man myself. I know that I work more than nine hours every day, and then I think I am a practical mechanic. If you look at the Confederation Act, in the framing of which I had some hand, you

will admit that I am a pretty good joiner; and as for cabinet making, I
have as much experience as Jacques and Hay themselves.[43]

The co-opting of labour spokesmen also served to gather the labour
vote into the Liberal and Conservative folds and it discouraged organized
labour from undertaking its own independent political activity. It was
always possible to point to the "real working men" in Parliament and to
argue that they provided a sufficient voice for labour. However, only a
handful of candidates with a background and identification with workers
and their organizations were co-opted directly into the ranks of the
Liberal and Conservative parties. Labelled Lib-Labs or Tory-Labs, they
were typically hybrid candidates, sponsored so as to satisfy the yearning
of the labour organizations and their members for a minimum representation in the political structures.[44]

Being the "labour friends" of the bourgeois parties had both positive
and negative consequences for the influence of workers in the parliamentary democracy. On the one hand, labour did gain a voice, although a
muffled voice, in Parliament at a time when organizational difficulties,
small memberships and limited funds mitigated against strong, independent action by the unions. On the other hand, these same candidates,
because of their visibility as elected representatives, helped to fasten the
partisan loyalties of the workers to the two bourgeois parties. Therefore,
the practice of co-optation was an obstacle, although never an insurmountable one, for the socialist parties which also aspired to win the
loyalties of the workers.

This was the economic and social context within which the federal
party system took root. The Fathers of Confederation had designed a
federal state which, armed with the National Policy, could exploit the
new nation's abundant resource potential and industrialize the central
provinces. Yet, the resulting changes in the class structure were not
clearly articulated in the emerging system of partisan relations. The
language of class conflict had been ruled out of partisan politics by the
actions of ethnic and religious organizations, the two national parties, and
the trade unions themselves. Thus, partisan debate was not occupied
with class relations but, rather, became increasingly preoccupied with
cultural questions. The entrenching of the bicultural cleavage in the
federal system of partisan alignments will be the final concern of this
chapter.

The Development of Cultural Conflict as the Basis of Partisan Differences

It was not obvious in the first elections after Confederation what the
elections would be about. The pre-Confederation period had been

characterized by political debate over a series of issues, several of which were no longer relevant because they had been settled by the new arrangements. Other issues could now come to the fore. A second reason was that the partisan divisions within the electorate were not firmly established. The organization of opposition to the founding coalition of Macdonald and Cartier required some political sagacity. It was not clear from where that would come. The one side, the pro-Confederation side, had a clear position to advance and defend.[45] However, the opposition consisted of a variety of possibilities. These ranged from anti-Confederationists of the Maritimes, to free traders, to the Grits of Ontario, to a miscellany of people who had no place in the Conservative Party and therefore, by definition, could only be in the opposition. The political and partisan history of this period is the history of the fashioning of a coherent and a sufficiently threatening opposition—the Liberal Party. By 1905, two national parties existed, and they had well-tried, reliable electorates. It took the Liberals longer than the Conservatives to create a national coalition, and part of the reason for the tardiness was that they had to discover their particular issues. They had to find a viable way of distinguishing themselves from the Conservatives, a way that would allow them to win and to keep winning. They had to define and create their electorate.

Partisan lines were not firmly drawn during the first elections primarily because of the form of the electoral system. The early electoral practices discouraged stable partisan alignments within the electorate. They were designed to maximize the potential for voter and candidate mobility between coalitions and for using the vote as a favour, sold in exchange for payoffs of several kinds. These procedures were finally changed, partially because the Conservatives thought that they could "trust" the voters in a particular area and partially because of some politicians' efforts to "clean up" electioneering.

The two most important voting practices retarding partisan development were non-simultaneous elections and open voting. Non-simultaneous elections allowed the government party to call an election in what were considered to be safe seats and then gradually work outward to the more uncertain constituencies some days or weeks later. In this way, they could seem to be riding on a tide of victory which would induce voters in later elections to support the obvious winner. Candidates were encouraged to remain uncommitted to a political party until the complexion of the new government was certain, so that they could be on the side of the winners; a useful position in the days of widespread patronage. As a result, voters were oftentimes faced with one ambiguous alternative, between two parliamentary candidates who opposed the trailing party.

Open voting also tended to discourage the growth of stable voter alignments. Like non-simultaneous elections, it discouraged long-term identification with a candidate or party. In addition, it generated hostility to the idea of elections because voters were placed in a very difficult position of double jeopardy. Anyone wanting favours from the government could not vote against the government party. However, a vote for the government, if the opposition managed to win, led to an equally unhappy fate. In other words, when everyone knew how a particular person voted, it was always necessary to somehow end up on the side of the winner. This conflict was particularly acute in the early years of Confederation because patronage constituted the major currency of exchange between the voter and the politicians. Both procedures were manipulated to advantage by the Conservatives in the early elections. Macdonald put together creative coalitions of "loose fish" to support his ideology and politics of national development. Within a decade these practices led to the nationalization of the Conservative Party in the four original provinces so that the party no longer had to depend on the effects of the electoral law but instead could defeat the Liberals by appealing to national unity. They did this in 1872 and again in 1882. However, open voting and non-simultaneous elections were retained in the western provinces for a considerably longer period.[46] By doing so, the Conservatives could continue to count on a western electorate which saw nothing to be gained from federal elections unless they could align themselves with the government.[47] As a result, non-partisanship continued in the West long after it had disappeared in the East.

In the immediate post-Confederation elections there was not much discussion of cultural questions. The early partisan debate largely revolved around issues of national development and the particular form that it would take. These discussions were often flavoured with allegations of corruption and patronage. With time, however, the Liberals realized the electoral potential of religious and ethnic allegiances, as a basis for formation of voting support. They discovered this at the same time that they abandoned their fundamental objection to the goals of the union and accepted the strategy of economic development implied by Confederation. Macdonald had recognized the need to defuse cultural differences by forging strong links with the leadership of Quebec, through Cartier, and with the hierarchy of the Roman Catholic Church. The combination of a strong spokesman for French interests in the governing party and the intervention of the Church on the side of the Conservatives assured the Conservatives of political domination for many years. However, this formula could not survive the competition that followed the emergence of cultural disputes in electoral politics and adoption of the NP development strategy by the Liberals.

For the Fathers of Confederation, concerned about building a national economy, the existence of two linguistic groups and two cultures in the same territory was an inescapable fact but not something to be allowed to get in the way of the project. Sir John A. Macdonald was careful to assure his support base in Quebec not only among the Montreal merchants but also within the upper ranks of the Roman Catholic Church. He won the Church's co-operation primarily by agreeing to leave it in control of cultural, linguistic and educational development in Quebec. Indeed, this accommodation was built into the British North America Act itself, assigning as it did cultural questions to the provinces and the mechanisms for economic development to the federal government, thus freeing it to pursue its national development goals unhindered.

However, the plan did not work exactly as conceived. The Liberals soon discovered that Quebec was an extraordinarily important source of voters. If they could not break the Conservatives' electoral strangle hold on that province, any hopes of victory would be dashed. One way to break Quebec away from the Conservatives was to emphasize ethnicity. The Conservative Party, put together to sustain the Confederation project, could not deal with cultural differences. It was an amalgam of Ontario Protestants and French Catholics from Quebec, a coalition which threatened to collapse once cultural questions appeared on the scene. If the fundamental ethnic division could be made to count, the contradiction of the Conservative coalition would become evident. This tendency was encouraged by the near-total lack of challenge to an ethnic and religious language of politics, given the lack of a large, well-organized labour movement and the abandonment by the Liberals of an anti-Confederation position.

Tensions between the French and English had been aggravated by the Riel affair. The treatment of the demands of Riel and the Métis for the formation of a new province west of Ontario, which culminated in the Manitoba Act of 1870, provides a useful example of the way in which ethnic questions have been used in Canadian politics. The indigenous population of the "Hudson Bay Territories," led by Louis Riel, sought provincial status so that they could retain their habitual rights and protect their lifestyle in face of the very obvious threat from the development strategy of Confederation. The invasion of the railroad, bringing with it huge numbers of settlers to farm the same land, spelled doom for the Métis. Their uprising was the first real challenge to the project put in place in 1867. If the West was to be a real hinterland of the eastern provinces, the project of railroad-building and immigration obviously could not be replaced by another form of land use, one not integrated into the capitalist commercial system. The pro-Confederation alliance was mobilized to protect their project from the conflicting vision of Riel and his followers. This was the first but not the last time that the federal state would resort to coercion when its strategy was threatened.

Riel made three demands, some more threatening than others. First, he sought the immediate entry of the entire Northwest into Confederation as a single province. Second, he claimed that public lands should be controlled by the new province. Finally, there was the proposal that a system of confessional schools in the West, replicating those of Quebec, be established.[48] Clearly, the first two demands were a grave threat to the plan to develop the Northwest as a colony of the East. These lands, so crucial for the development of a northern market and for the exploitation of their natural resources could not be surrendered. Therefore, faced with these proposals and the need to settle quickly, a compromise was made—the first two demands were refused, and the third was granted.[49] In this way, the new, and small, province of Manitoba acquired a system of bilingual and bicultural institutions and rights. The controversy over the development project of the West was redefined, by the compromise, as an ethnic and religious dispute. Riel was classified according to his language and religious projects, rather than his views on land tenure and development.

This compromise shifted to Manitoba the same type of political debate as that of the East. And it guaranteed that, up until the First World War, a series of controversies would reinforce the interpretation of Canadian politics as ethnic politics. In addition, and ironically, it was the introduction of this question in this form into western partisan politics which would eventually destroy the remarkable string of successes of the Conservative Party.[50] In 1896 the leadership of the Conservatives would not be able to overcome the contradictions in its own Confederation-building coalition of Orange Ontario and French Quebec. It would be defeated by Laurier.

Despite efforts by the Conservative Party to dampen cultural dispute by emphasizing national unity, the grass roots organization of the party, particularly members of the Orange Lodge in Ontario, was such that anti-French and anti-Catholic rhetoric began to enter electoral debate and campaigns. The Conservatives became increasingly identified as the defenders of Protestantism and the British connection. This image damaged the Conservative Party in Quebec and made it easier for the Liberals to make inroads in that province in the 1890s.

It was under these conditions that the western situation festered and reached crisis proportions. The forces of national development were strong, and in 1887 the Liberals, under Greenway, came to power in Manitoba. The provincial Liberals had succeeded in convincing the Manitoban electorate that Premier Norquay was allied with the federal Conservative government which repeatedly supported the policy of a railway monopoly in that province. The provincial Liberals had simply taken up the cry against the unpopular federal policies and set themselves up as the champions of provincial rights.[51] However, shortly after their election, the provincial Liberals found themselves caught in a dilemma. They had come to power with a promise to reduce the monopoly position of the Canadian Pacific Railway. They agitated for lower freight-rates for western farmers, but the federal government and the railroads were unwilling to accede to such a demand to alter the structuring effects of the NP. Politically embarrassed by this, "to divert attention from their failure, the Liberals had already determined to take up the amendment of the separate school system."[52] Once again, Canadians were plunged into the politics of culture to avoid a confrontation over the costs of the national development strategy.

It was on the wave of this controversy that the federal Liberals finally succeeded in finding their issue, creating their electorate and forging a national party. They would secure the Quebec electorate by satisfying the nationalists in Quebec at the expense of the Manitoba Catholic hierarchy.[53] At the same time, the nationalizing bourgeoisie would have to shift its support to the Liberals because only that party could smooth over the threat to their project that the current violence, although not the existence, of the ethnic controversy implied. Only the Liberals could guarantee an electoral coalition large enough to keep the wheels of the NP turning. 1896 represents a shift not only of voting support from the Conservatives to the Liberals, but also a shift in the support of the bourgeoisie from the tattered Conservatives to the ascendant Liberals.[54] The Conservatives, after the death of Macdonald, were in disarray over the search for a new leader and how to deal with the "hot potato" bequeathed them by Macdonald.[55] In this way, the Liberals could become the party of the national dream and the tariff, a position solidified by the fact that 1896 marked the beginning of a huge economic boom which continued almost until the First World War. The Liberals had little to do but point to the prosperity and continue to garner the votes of the newly-created coalition. Such was their strategy in the 1900 and 1904 elections.

However, by insisting upon the importance of linguistic and religious factors as the substance of politics, the Liberals were also nurturing a force which would haunt them—perhaps even to this day. The Conservatives had been caught by the growth and incorporation into their party politics of a militant Protestantism which eventually alienated their Quebec allies. Similarly, nationalists, first led by Honoré Mercier and later Henri Bourassa, would develop a constituency in Quebec. As a result, the Liberals too would find themselves forced into difficult electoral situations because of the need to appease nationalists and nationalism, a need induced, at least in part, by their own emphasis on ethnic politics. However, they had by 1896 captured the winning position of representing the "national interest" of the nationalizing bourgeoisie. This was a position to be guarded.

Conclusion

The result of this pattern and timing of structural change, organizational growth and partisan history was that the two-party system of the East was established by 1905. The division of support between the parties, the basis of this support and the language to describe it was well in place. The new industrial workers had been integrated into electoral politics on the basis of their language and religion. Their own organizations both supported this ethnic-based party system and opposed the substitution of any other form of electoral organization of the relations between classes. Thus, between 1867 and 1905 conflict between the bourgeoisie and the workers—class conflict—was defused and lacked electoral expression. It lacked access to the party system, except to the extent that it constituted no demands for the modification of existing relations of capital and labour. Instead, the party system was organized by the parties themselves along with the ethnic and religious organizations that appealed to and explained Canada to the voters.

NOTES

[1]Vernon Fowke, *The National Policy and the Wheat Economy* (Toronto: University of Toronto, 1957), pp. 4-5.

[2]Paul Phillips, "National Policy, Continental Economics, and National Disintegration," in David Jay Bercuson, ed., *Canada and The Burden of Unity* (Toronto: Macmillan, 1977), p. 25; G. W. Bertram, "Economic Growth in Canadian Industry, 1870-1915," in W. T. Easterbrook and M. H. Watkins, eds., *Approaches to Canadian Economic History* (Toronto: McClelland and Stewart, 1967), p. 75.

[3]Obviously, the term 'staple-based economy' does not imply that staple production for export is the only form of economic activity. What it does imply is that it is the motor for economic growth. Thus, says Bertram, "Throughout Canadian economic history the familiar succession of export staples initiated increases in productivity and income expansion." In other words, the staple trade was a growth inducing factor. See Bertram, *Ibid.*, p. 76.

[4]An obvious comparison can be made between the fur trade and wheat production. The development of the fur trade did not require a large labour force, nor did it encourage a settled population. It required little transportation infrastructure or technological advances before it could be profitable. Dissimilarly, the production of wheat required the opposite conditions. *Ibid.*, p. 76.

[5]Canada's agricultural industry, particularly wheat milling, was dealt a debilitating blow in 1846 when Great Britain repealed the Corn Laws. Previously, the British gave preferential tariffs to Canadian wheat and flour ground in Canada. After 1846, however, it became clear that Canada would have to improve its competitive position *vis-à-vis* the United States to maintain the British market. See Edgar McInnis, *Canada: A Political and Social History* (Toronto: Holt, Rinehart and Winston, 1969), pp. 287-288.

[6]Many of the Fathers of Confederation had direct links with railroad companies

and major banks. See Patricia Marchak, *In Whose Interests* (Toronto: McClelland and Stewart, 1979), p. 103.

7After the repeal of the Corn Laws, merchants, particularly those in Lower Canada, had little faith in Canada's ability to maintain economic autonomy in the absence of imperial protection. The idea of a new state to promote an independent economy was rejected by some because it implied that concessions would have to be made to the French. Thus, rather than face that prospect, a section of the Tories preferred annexation to the United States. The Annexation Manifesto was issued by a group of Montreal leaders in October 1849. Its promoters hoped annexation would provide high farm prices, lower import costs, new sources of credit and access to American capital to build up industry and transportation. However, the response to the proposal was disappointing among the English and vigorously opposed by the French. McInnis, *op. cit.*, p. 289.

8Fowke, *op. cit.*, p. 6; Phillips, *op. cit.*, p. 20; R. T. Naylor, "The rise and fall of the third commercial empire of the St. Lawrence," in Gary Teeple, ed., *Capitalism and the National Question in Canada* (Toronto: University of Toronto, 1977), pp. 13-25.

9See Fowke, *op. cit.*, pp. 34-37. This new strategy of independent development on the part of the colonies was supported by the evolution of capitalism in the United Kingdom. Once industrialization had taken off there, British capital needed locations for investment, and active overseas connections provided that. Thus, British imperialism, led by investment, began to replace the colonialism of the earlier period. For a further discussion, see A. Dubac, "Le fondement historique de la crise des sociétés canadiennes et québécoises," *Politique aujourd'hui*, vol. 7-8, 1978, p. 32.

10During the Confederation debates, this theme was often struck. For example, A. Galt said ". . . it is in the diversity of employment that security is found against those sad reverses to which every country, depending mainly on one branch of industry, must always be liable . . ." as quoted in Fowke, *op. cit.*, p. 34. Strength would come from combinations which would bring diversity and self-sufficiency.

11See for example, P. Phillips, *op. cit.*; Tom Naylor, *The History of Canadian Business*, vol. 1 (Toronto: Lorimer, 1975), especially pp. 27-30.

12See Glen Williams, "The National Tariffs: Industrial Underdevelopment Through Import Substitution," *Canadian Journal of Political Science*, vol. 12 (1979), pp. 333-368.

13Fowke, *op. cit.*, p. 3.

14J. M. Beck, *Pendulum of Power* (Scarborough, Ontario: Prentice-Hall, 1968), p. 2.

15See Frank H. Underhill, *In Search of Canadian Liberalism* (Toronto: Macmillan, 1960), especially Part I, Chapter I, "Some Reflections on the Liberal Tradition in Canada."

16*Ibid.*, pp. 24-27, 28, 47, 56.

17Beck, *op. cit.*, pp. 4-7.

18When introducing the tariff in 1878 Macdonald said, "I believe that, by a fair readjustment of the tariff, we can increase the various industries which can interchange one with another and make this union a union in interest, a union in trade and a union in feeling. We shall then grow up rapidly a good, steady and mature trade between the provinces, rendering us independent of foreign trade, and not, as New Brunswick and Nova Scotia formerly did, look to the United States or to England for trade, but look to Ontario and Quebec—sending their products west, and receiving the products of Quebec and Ontario in exchange. This is the great policy, the National Policy, which we on this side are advocating. . . ." See Williams, *op. cit.*, see also, Fowke, *op. cit.*, p. 64. Protection was advocated by the commercial community which feared the effects of a continuous downturn of the economy on their trade. See also, T. W. Acheson, "The Maritimes and 'Empire Canada'," in Bercuson, *op. cit.*, p. 91.

[19]Donald Smiley suggests that there are three dominant definitions of the National Policy. The first refers only to the tariff modifications of 1878. The second view, which is accepted in this analysis, was initially put forward by W. A. Mackintosh. His contention was that the National Policy consisted of three policy goals: settlement of the frontier, transportation infrastructure and industrialization behind tariffs. The third interpretation, provided by V. Fowke, has a much broader perspective. It suggests that the NP represents the attempts of successive governments to shape a national economic and political unit. See Donald Smiley, "Canada and the Quest for a New National Policy," *Canadian Journal of Political Science*, vol. 8 (March, 1975), pp. 40-62.

[20]Vernon Fowke, *Canadian Agricultural Policy: The Historical Pattern* (Toronto: University of Toronto, 1938), p. 261.

[21]The farmers were not self-sufficient. Great demands were placed on industry to equip them with tools and consumer goods. This captive market provided significant investment opportunities in both the pre- and post-Confederation period. See Fowke, *The National Policy and The Wheat Economy, op. cit.*, p. 66.

[22]The expansion of the home market, consequent on the rise of wheat export and national policies, reoriented a large sector of Canadian industry and induced further expansion. British Columbia's lumber industry, hitherto dependent entirely on export, became dependent for 70 to 75 per cent of its greatly enlarged market on prairie demands. . . . [Manufacturing] expansion was to a greater extent in some cases than others dependent on direct sales to the prairies and other exporting regions. Indirectly, however, the expansion of exports was the dynamic force behind their growth. The relation of the growth of the agricultural machinery industry is particularly direct. Iron and steel expansion was the direct result of railway and other building demands deflected by the tariff and government purchasing policy to home industry. See W. A. Mackintosh *The Economic Background of Federal-Provincial Relations* (Toronto: McClelland and Stewart, 1964), p. 50.

[23]*Ibid.*, p. 45.

[24]For example, in 1867, there were not more than 50,000 labourers employed in all the cities of the four provinces while over 50% of the population of all the four provinces in 1871 worked as farmers, lumbermen or fishermen. See Donald V. Smiley, ed., *The Rowell/Sirois Report: Book I* (Toronto: McClelland and Stewart, 1954), pp. 15, 24. However, after 1867 there was a rapid increase in industrial workers so that by 1901, their proportion of the population reached 26%. See F. A. Angers and P. Allen, *Evolution de la structure des emplois au Canada* (Montreal: Ecole des Hautes Etudes Commerciales, 1954), p. 37.

[25]Bertram, *op. cit.*, p. 78.

[26]*Ibid.*, Table 1, pp. 82-83.

[27]For more detailed discussions of the developments within the trade union movement in Canada before the turn of the century see H. A. Logan, *Trade Unions in Canada* (Toronto: Macmillan, 1948); H. A. Logan, N. J. Ware and H. A. Innes, *Labour in Canadian-American Relations*, (Toronto: Ryerson, 1937), Chapters 1-4; Charles Lipton, *The Trade Union Movement of Canada, 1827-1959*, 3rd ed. (Toronto: NC Press, 1973); Stuart Jamieson, *Industrial Relations in Canada* (Toronto: Macmillan, 1973), Chapter 1; Martin Robin, *Radical Politics*

and *Canadian Labour, 1880-1930* (Kingston: Industrial Relations Centre, 1968), Chapters 1-5; Robert Babcock, *Gompers in Canada* (Toronto: University of Toronto, 1974); A. R. McCormack, *Reformers, Rebels and Revolutionaries* (Toronto: University of Toronto, 1977).

28Jamieson, *op. cit.*, p. 14.

29The TLC took that name only in 1892, but it has direct antecedent links to the Dominion Trades and Labour Congress which met annually from 1886-1891. Jamieson, *op. cit.* and E. A. Forsey, "Unions and Co-operatives," in J. M. S. Careless and R. C. Brown, eds., *The Canadians* (Toronto: Macmillan, 1967), pp. 492-93.

30McCormack, *op. cit.*, pp. 18-34.

31Horowitz, in his search for the Canadian roots of socialism, argues that the following distinction is possible between the political philosophy of the TLC and AFL but that the practical differences are non-existent.

"The TLC's political philosophy was not like that of the AFL, a *positive* policy of support for capitalism *against* socialism. Gompers Canadianized is not an atheist, but an agnostic; not an anti-socialist, but a non-socialist susceptible to socialist influence; not an opponent of labour and socialist parties, but an opponent of *union* involvement in their activities. . . . The TLC's non-partisanship did not mean a preference for Liberals and/or Conservatives against socialists. It meant no preference for anyone; 'no politics' *at all*." G. Horowitz, *Canadian Labour in Politics* (Toronto: University of Toronto, 1968), p. 181.

32See Babcock, *op. cit.*, pp. 14, 34 and especially Chapter 7, "The Berlin Victory."

33At this time in England, industry-wide and 'general' trade unions were being organized. It was precisely out of this organization that the leadership of the movement for independent labour representation came. See E. Hobsbawn *Labouring Men* (London: Weidenfeld and Nicolson, 1964).

34For a discussion of the clerical opposition to the Knights see P. Sylvain, "Les Chevaliers du Travail et le Cardinal Taschereau," *Relations industrielles/Industrial Relations*, vol. 28, no. 3 (1973).

35Henry Ferns and Bernard Ostry, *The Age of Mackenzie King* (Toronto: Lorimer, 1976), p. 69.

36See Clinton Archibald et K. Z. Paltiel, "D'un Passage des Corps Intermédiaires aux Groupes du Pression: La Transformation D'une Idée Illustrée Par Le Mouvement Coopératif Desjardins," *Recherches Sociographiques*, vol. 18, no. 1, (1977), pp. 59-64, *passim*.

37Robin, *op. cit.*, pp. 20-23.

38*Ibid.*, pp. 68-69.

39Quoted in K. A. MacKirdy *et al.*, *Changing Perspectives in Canadian History* (Don Mills, Ontario: Dent, 1967), p. 110.

40See C. H. Senior, "Orangeism in Ontario Politics, 1872-1896," in Donald Swainson, ed., *Oliver Mowat's Ontario* (Toronto: Macmillan, 1972), *passim*. A close study will demonstrate that Orangeism offered to workers a profoundly ambiguous heritage—a set of traditions which, on the one hand, aided them in their struggle to exist in the industrializing city but which, on the other hand, led them on occasion into the streets in riots against their fellow workers. See G. Kealey and P. Warrian, eds., *Essays in Canadian Working Class History* (Toronto: McClelland and Stewart, 1976), pp. 13-21.

41Almost identical legislation was introduced in Great Britain in 1871. The Trades Union Act essentially removed the grounds for charges of legal liability against union leaders if the union was officially registered. See Canada, Department of

Labour, *Labour Legislation in Canada* (August 1945), p. 6.

[42]*The Globe* reported during the strike that:

It can hardly be said that in this country there is such a thing as a capitalist class, much less, like that of England, a capitalist class socially separated from the working man, closely united with a territorial aristocracy, and, in conjunction with that aristocracy, wielding overwhelming power. . . . Oppression of the working class is in Canada morally impossible. The only thing that here threatens the kindly relation between employer and the employed, and the industrial prosperity of the country, is the gratuitous introduction from the old country into Canada of those industrial wars which were the natural consequence of the antagonism of classes and the depressed condition of the working men of England but which have no justification here.

Quoted in Frank Underhill, "Political Ideas of the Upper Canada Reformers, 1867-78," in *In Search of Canadian Liberalism, op. cit.,* p. 80.

[43]Sir John A. Macdonald as quoted in Donald Creighton, "George Brown, Sir John A. Macdonald and The Working Man," *Canadian Historical Review,* XXIV (1943), p. 375. Jacques and Hay was a furniture company located in Toronto.

[44]Robin, *op. cit.,* p. 7.

[45]For example, in 1872 and 1882, the Conservatives emphasized national unity appeals designed to defeat the Liberals. For detail see Beck, *op. cit.,* Chapters 2-6.

[46]The federal franchise has a complicated history. Nevertheless, simultaneous elections and the secret ballot were introduced in the provinces east of Manitoba in 1878. Open voting was reintroduced for the first two federal elections held in the Northwest Territories (Saskatchewan and Alberta after 1905) in 1887 and 1891. Simultaneous elections were not established until 1882 in Manitoba and 1908 in the remaining Prairie Provinces. See David Smith, *Prairie Liberalism* (Toronto: University of Toronto, 1975), especially p. 5.

[47]Beck, *op. cit.,* p. 18 for an explanation of why the western electorate tended to support the eventual winning party.

[48]See D. Creighton, "John A. Macdonald, Confederation and the Canadian West," in Canadian Historical Readings, *Minorities, Schools and Politics* (Toronto: University of Toronto, 1969), pp. 3-6; G. Stevenson, "Federalism and The Political Economy of The Canadian State," in Leo Panitch, ed., *The Canadian State: Political Economy and Political Power* (Toronto: University of Toronto, 1977), p. 77.

[49]Creighton, *op. cit.,* p. 6.

[50]Beck, *op. cit.,* p. 74.

[51]W. L. Morton, *Manitoba: A History* (Toronto: University of Toronto, 1957), p. 120.

[52]W. L. Morton, "Manitoba Schools and Canadian Nationality," in Canadian Historical Readings, *Minorities, Schools and Politics, op. cit.,* pp. 10-11.

[53]R. Cook, "Church, Schools and Politics in Manitoba, 1903-1912," in Canadian Historical Readings, *Minorities, Schools and Politics, op. cit., passim.*

Laurier could, by his insistence on the maintenance of provincial rights, guarantee the original Confederation bargain with the Catholic Church in Quebec. Only with provincial rights would that institution satisfy itself that it could have unhindered access to the cultural development of its flock in Quebec. Therefore, with Laurier's guarantee most of the Church could overcome its objections to "liberalism" and suggest that good Catholics could support the Liberals. Despite the reluctance to abandon the Catholics of

Manitoba, which Laurier's "sunny ways" implied, the Quebec bishops did not, in their collective *mandement*, condemn the Liberals.

[54]As Creighton argues, the "Laurier Plutocracy" was composed of the same "bankers, engineers, corporation lawyers, railway builders, mining promoters, pulp and paper producers and public utility entrepreneurs." D. Creighton, *Canada's First Century* (Toronto: Macmillan, 1970), p. 108.

[55]Beck, *op. cit.*, pp. 72-76.

Chapter 3

1905-1917—Exporting the Party System Westward

Introduction

In the years from 1905 until the outbreak of the First World War, Canadians saw, at one and the same time, fruition of the national economic strategy begun by the Fathers of Confederation and a mounting tide of protest against it. It was a period of fundamental change which was rich in controversy. By 1905, the National Policy of railroad-building, increased immigration and industrial development behind protective tariffs began to realize its intended effect. The next decade was to see its culmination with almost explosive success. Wheat production for export reached unprecedented levels. Grown by the thousands of immigrants to the western provinces, it filled the cars of a myriad of railway lines. The westward returning trains were filled with more immigrants, not only farmers, but also construction workers, miners and loggers. They would build and work the sites of the new industries extracting the bounties of the rich frontier made accessible by the railways. The same trains carried manufactured goods produced in the East to western consumers. The integration of the national economy finally seemed to be accomplished. The metropole had developed its hinterland, not in its own image but in the image of what it wanted. However, it was not long before political confrontations raised doubts as to whether the National Policy could be kept in place and functioning.

This period, then, represents a story of success and stories of increasing conflict. The strategies of "development by staple export" and "industrialization for the domestic market" carried with them certain dangers, costs and consequences. The conclusion that was drawn from the first forty years of Confederation by the leaders of both bourgeois parties was that the primary division between them, that which distinguished them for the electorate, was their appeal to the different language and religious groups. This cleavage, between French and English, Protestant and Catholic, had been nurtured by the parties in the heat of partisan battles over ten elections. Whether Canada was created as an outpost of the British Empire or as a more or less independent country in North America, whether it was a nation of several languages or only one, and the proper status of these languages in the country as a whole but particularly in the new areas were the questions which divided the parties. One or the other of the myths of nation-building were the only real choices available to the electorate. This debate dominated the electoral contests of the period.

The parties continued to be occupied by differences over concepts of nation-building until the 1917 election led to a disastrous division, a new partisan alliance and, ultimately, a realignment of electoral forces in the West. The federal politicians with their roots in the East, had attempted to export and implant their definition of politics and their concept of nation among the new western voters. However, this version fell on stony ground. The transplant did not take. The farmers and the workers of the West had their own critiques of the "national dream." By the time the First World War broke out, these criticisms resounded loudly and aggressively throughout the West. New parties based upon another definition of politics were taking form, preparing to step onto the stage for the 1921 federal election.

In recognition of the problem posed by developments fostered by their own previous strategy and programmes, the Canadian political elite adopted a set of tactics designed to win the 1917 election and control the dissent in their midst. The effects of these decisions can still be seen in partisan alignments. This chapter will document the conflicts leading up to the 1917 election, account for their creation and demonstrate their impact on the form and resolution of electoral conflicts in Canada. The primary focus is the effects of the particular economic development of the period, the organization of relations within and between classes and the effect these relations had on subsequent political manifestations of class relations.

The Political Economy of the Wheat Boom and Industrialization in "Canada's Century"

First and foremost, this was a period of economic boom. Wheat production and export, primarily to the United Kingdom and other parts of Europe, surpassed previously imagined levels. The value of this crop to the Canadian economy reached $279 million by 1920 from a level of $14 million in 1900 and an insignificant figure in 1890.[1] In addition to the wheat staple, there was increasing development of other natural resources and industries connected with them. Exploration and technological change, as well as railroad-building, held potential for the successful exploitation of new resources of the Canadian forests and mountains.[2] Thus, new staples, which would eventually replace wheat, began to make their mark on the thriving staple-based economy and in so doing, seemed to justify the efforts of the railroad-builders and politicians.

Rapid population growth provided further evidence of the viability of the National Policy. Population increased by over 60% in the first two decades of the century with almost equal numbers going to the three Prairie Provinces and to Quebec and Ontario.[3] Moreover, there was a good deal of internal population shift, as people left the farms of the East to move to the cities or to take up lands further west. The very rapid pace of urbanization meant that living conditions in the cities grew increasingly harsh.

This growth of population seemed to satisfy the second goal of the NP. The country was now sufficiently settled, not only in numbers but also in territorial dispersion, that encroachment by American authorities could not occur as it had in the past. In this way, the concept of a Canadian interprovincial market was realized. With tariffs firmly in place, the growing population provided the market for the products produced by the corporations of an increasingly industrially-oriented bourgeoisie.

One of the reasons why this population could be sustained and high rates of immigration maintained was that protected manufacturing was expanding, and new jobs were being created. The value of secondary industry had an average yearly growth rate of 6.0% in the first decade of the century. This rate exceeded any period before World War Two.[4] Moreover, the low cost of labour ensured high capital returns and, thus, further capital investment. Wages were kept low because many in the labour force were new immigrants who were both willing to accept low wages and difficult to organize into trade unions. Thus, again, the successful expansion of the industrial sector can be attributed in large part to the National Policy, specifically to the immigration and tariff policies.

As a consequence of the rapid population growth, cities mushroomed in size. All regions experienced rapid urbanization, but it was in the cities of Ontario, Quebec and the Maritimes that most of the population increase (40% of the total) occurred. Montreal and Toronto, in particular, increased dramatically in size. Both reached the half-million mark by 1921. This growth of the central cities reflected the metropole-hinterland effects of the National Policy. These two centres,

> . . . were the focusses of the economic integration of the country. In them the highly specialized banking and financial services, and the specialized distributive services found their centres. As they developed they proved a magnet for the lighter manufacturing industries in the location of which the pull of the market was the chief influence. . . . The existence of these great centres was not based by any means wholly on provincial resources and provincial industry; they were the result of the knitting together of the entire country and as financial and mercantile markets they belong to the entire country. Other metropolitan centres, Vancouver, Winnipeg, Saint John, Halifax, were essentially regional. . . .[5]

Thus, the proponents of the East-West pattern of economic development could look with some pride at their product and the increased revenues to them, their firms and their political parties.

However, all was not as bright as it might be. The first cloud on the horizon was the result of the inherently unstable policy itself. Staple trade was subject, by its nature, to the vagaries of international markets. If the price of wheat fell, if new products were substituted, if markets were closed by political actions, the Canadian economy, dependent on exports, would be in difficulty. This is, in fact, what threatened to happen just prior to the First World War. To understand this threat, it is important to recognize that the boom years of the early twentieth century in Canada were not solely the result of foresight and good planning on the part of the makers of the NP. That policy represented a strategy of development which could only succeed under quite specific international economic conditions. The economy was dependent on the import of capital to finance railways, industrial development and resource exploration and exploitation. In addition, many of the manufactured goods required by the consumers and by industry (capital goods) were imported rather than produced domestically. In this way a balance of payments deficit was likely, unless exports could be maintained at an increasingly high level to counterbalance the effect of importing capital and goods. If the price of exports fell, the economy was in difficulty.

The painful effects of the worldwide depression of the 1870s had led to the NP. However, this policy was not sufficient, in itself, to overcome Canada's difficult international position, and its first years were disappointing.[6] But by the mid-1890s the international situation improved dramatically, and it was then that the promise of the NP seemed realizable.[7] However, while Canada's position in the international economy meant that prosperity could be easily taken away by an unfavourable conjuncture of international conditions, the domestic changes derived from years of prosperity and the organization and reorganization of classes and class relations, could not be similarly removed. The consequences of such a development strategy were to reverberate through the Canadian social fabric for decades.

The Canadian economy was threatened in 1913 but revived again with the outbreak of the First World War. The reorientation of borrowing and the demand for Canadian goods during the war put the balance of payments into a healthier condition. However, this momentary salvation was not without its costs. The inflation which had been postponed in the first decade-and-a-half of the century could no longer be avoided. The inflationary costs of fighting a war and saving the balance of payments by massive exports coincided with the already grim effects of twenty years of booming industrialization and urbanization. The price of consumer goods rose progressively throughout the war years. These increases fuelled the already long litany of complaints against the Canadian strategy of economic growth and ultimately threatened to overwhelm the government preparing to face the electorate in 1917. As we shall see, the bourgeois parties diverted this threat but only by using extraordinary measures. The period from 1905 until the war was one of mounting discontent.

Nevertheless, it was not only the effects of the international economy which provided the substance of political struggle in this period. The structural and regional inequalities nurtured and sustained by the National Policy were increasingly recognized and resented. The umbrage of those who felt themselves penalized by the mechanisms of the staple economy eventually resulted in separate partisan activities. Most of the dissent was organized by western wheat farmers, but there were also important contributions from eastern farmers and from workers' organizations, especially those in the West.

The tariff and freight-rates were at the centre of the western protest. These were the two particular political mechanisms which maintained the National Policy's design of specialized regional economic activity. Whereas in the nineteenth century the most important export products originated in all areas of the country, by the beginning of the twentieth century regional differences were clear. The pattern was a fairly simple one. The West exported to the rest of the world while the East, particularly the central provinces, exported to other regions within the country. British Columbia's economy was primarily an exporting one—sending primary products outside of Canada. It bought more from other regions than it exported to them.[8] However, in the Prairies the pattern was the clearest.

> The Prairies stood out as the great export region, which provided an expanding home market for the other regions. . . . Thus the investments of the great expansion had built up a greatly magnified exporting economy in which exporting regions were more specialized than formerly and provided larger markets for imports or the products of other regions. The dominance of one exporting region had given the Canadian economy for the first time a marked interdependence. Wheat was not merely the largest export and the product of a new region, it was the central dynamic and unifying force of the expansion. The fortunes of regions with declining exports depended on their ability to share in the home market, to integrate themselves with the expanding export regions.[9]

This integration fuelled industrial growth in Ontario and Quebec as they began to sell more and more to the western hinterland. Of course, their ability to sell in this way was much enhanced by the NP, whose effects were, largely, regionally specific, benefiting firms which were active in the centre of the country. With protection from international competition, domestic industries were encouraged to expand and proliferate. This expansion was largely contained in Quebec and Ontario partially because discriminatory rates for shipping freight made it more profitable to ship manufactured goods from East to West than the reverse. By 1911, four-fifths of manufacturing output was produced in these two provinces.[10]

The tariff and freight-rates policies gave neither incentive for competition among the Canadian bourgeoisie nor assurance that eastern industry would be developed by indigenous capital. Rather, the opposite appeared to result. Generally speaking, protection and the virtual absence of legislation regulating capitalist enterprise allowed the large eastern industries to dominate the market with combinations and price-fixing agreements.[11] With a protected market, unrestricted profits based on monopoly practices, principally price-fixing, were almost assured. In addition, because corporate profits depended on costs, particularly the cost of labour, it was increasingly commonplace for employers to form national and oftentimes continental associations for the express purpose of influencing the state, holding the line against trade unions and their wage demands, or even reducing wages on an industry-wide basis. The membership of one of these organizations, principally comprised of Toronto manufacturers, pledged in their initial declaration of purpose to protect each other from the unjust demands of labour, to protect the right of employers to determine working conditions, to refuse to arbitrate with workers on strike and to maintain open shops.[12]

An additional characteristic of industrialization during this period was that it was increasingly either financed directly by American capital or operated under licensing arrangements.[13] The relationship between the protective tariff and the infusion of American capital into Canada, particularly in the form of branch plants, was predictable if not purposive, as capital and profits could flow back and forth unrestricted by the tariff walls while goods could not. Therefore, branch plants became increasingly prevalent during this period, particularly in those sectors which required a substantial outlay of capital and were in the forefront of a modernizing economy.[14]

In this way, the proliferation of combines and the extension of American industrial influence northward significantly reduced the potential, if not the rationale, for competitive capitalism in Canada. Moreover, Canadian manufacturing was not only concentrated and often monopolistic, but also primarily geared for the domestic market.[15] For a variety of reasons, Canadian manufacturers at first made few efforts to capture markets outside the country, and later they could not. As the previous chapter pointed out, the industrialization component of the NP was primarily designed to substitute Canadian-made goods for those previously imported.[16] Therefore, Canadian manufacturers concentrated on making only what the home market could consume. Consequently, they were extremely dependent on the maintenance of that market and could allow nothing to happen that might cost them the loss of their domestic consumers.

The retention of this market was guaranteed by careful manipulation of political levers—the protective tariff and discriminatory freight-rates. The politics of tariff-setting was a very complicated matter, not only because of objections to the tariff itself, but also because manufacturers were divided in their own needs. Moreover, the tariff on consumer goods and machinery, especially farm machinery, produced conflict between the metropolitan centre and the hinterlands. Increasingly, it was evident that the failure to export, to seize possibilities for selling abroad, necessitated the maintenance of a protected domestic market. But this market itself clearly saw that the structure was artificial and of little benefit to itself. Not only did the captive consumers earn most of the foreign exchange which kept Canada's international position in some semblance of balance, but they were compelled to spend that money to buy, not the cheapest goods, generally those available from the United States, but, rather, more expensive goods produced in eastern Canada. In addition, they were compelled to do so according to the trading conditions set in that same region. Credit, finance and transport were increasingly concentrated in Montreal and Toronto. Under such conditions, the outbreak of opposition to the tariff is not surprising.

There was an additional issue around which political conflict was concentrated and which challenged the hegemonic dream of economic development. Transportation expansion was, as we saw in the previous chapter, a major component of the NP. The East-West economy could only be achieved by linking the isolated areas to the centre with railway lines. Therefore, the costs for the use of these networks was of obvious concern. These costs, or freight-rates, became one of the levers used to create and maintain the patterns of economic dominance and dependency so crucial to the success of the NP. The freight-rates were prices for use set by the railroads and approved by the federal government. Thus, as important political, as well as economic, levers they became a focus for dissent.[17] In essence, without exploring a long history and the technical details of rate-setting, the federal government, as part of its policy of encouragement of and support for railroad-building, initially allowed the railways to discriminate against the western users. They did this by setting different rates for the same amount of freight carried the same number of miles but differing in destination. In the East, especially around the St. Lawrence where there was strong competition from other modes of transportation, the rates could be set below cost because whatever losses accumulated there could be recovered by charging a higher rate elsewhere. Obviously, the higher rates were charged where competition was lower, specifically, where the CPR had been granted a transportation monopoly. This was in the West. The practice called "fair discrimination" began as early as 1883 when the first western rate schedule was published by the CPR.

While the particular rates were presented as necessary to balance costs and meet other corporate needs, they were clearly decisions motivated by criteria other than cost efficiency. They were based on the desire for an all-Canadian transportation network to escape the competition of

American routes which would have diverted trade from eastern Canada to the United States. These were the needs of that fraction of the bourgeoisie which had first proposed Confederation, and the federal government continued to meet these needs for as long as it could. Thus, the East-West route was created and maintained by a federal government policy which first, enabled the railroads to be built; second, allowed the rate-setting practices described; and third, banned competition by prohibiting any rail links from the Canadian West southward.[18]

However, these rates could not be expected to go unchallenged. Political agitation, threats and unilateral action by the Manitoba provincial government resulted in some readjustments, both in the rates and in the level of competition. The Crow's Nest Pass agreement of 1897 was negotiated to alleviate some of the dissent arising in the West, and it reduced the differential between rates. Nevertheless, even these more "favourable" rates did not eliminate the discrepancies.[19] Furthermore, because freight-rates were a product of an "agreement" between the federal government and the railways, there were constant tensions and demands for renegotiation. The freight-rate was a political question which involved a definition of politics radically different from that of the predominant ethnic controversies. Like the tariff, it raised the question of who should pay the costs of Confederation.

In addition to the effects of the international economy and the regional structures of the domestic economy, other changes with great political potential also became evident in this period. The very rapid transformations in the Canadian economy brought changes in the social structure and serious social tensions. The rapid growth of the secondary manufacturing sector and the proliferation of new resource-extraction industries placed strains on the prevailing social order and systems of class relations. The traditional rural lifestyle crumbled as the demands for a skilled and unskilled labour force attracted more and more people to the urban centres. Indeed, the proportion of Canadians living in urban areas mushroomed from 14% of the population in 1881 to over one-half of the population in 1918, and one-half of these were wage-earners.[20] The industrial centres, however, were ill-equipped to provide tolerable living conditions for the new urbanized workforce. Adequate housing was virtually unavailable for those unable to buy or build their own accommodation. Rents were high, and crowding was common.[21] The cost of most other essentials rose, and inflation spiralled upwards.

Wages failed to keep pace, and the trade union movement, although growing in numbers and increasingly strike-prone throughout the period, could not alter the disparity between the cost of living and the average wage as conditions of life and work deteriorated. The trade unions did not develop into strong collective bodies able to force concessions from employers for a number of reasons which the next section documents. The new labour force grew more and more miserable by the year. These changes did not occur without their effects being felt in the elections of the period. Aspects of these policies were constant sources of conflict, and the resulting accumulation of resentments led to increasing militancy and radicalism. The National Policy seemed about to turn on its originators.

Resentment and anger first festered and then bloomed into political organization and opposition. What was challenged, in a series of electoral confrontations, was the continued dominance of the "nation-builders." Increasingly, appeals to national unity and debates about the definitions of the Canadian nation fell on deaf or disgruntled ears. Farmers and workers eventually would come to realize the possibilities of an alliance against the bourgeoisie and its supporters. Our task here is to explain how conditions evolved, within the bourgeoisie and the subordinate classes, to make that alliance viable, to cause it to take the form that it did, with the policies it propounded and to account for its subsequent failure.

The Labour Movement—Growing Divided

The rapid growth of the wage-labour sector, poor working conditions, difficult living conditions in both cities and new mining, railway and logging camps, plus the consolidation of the bourgeoisie, were all factors which favoured the organization of the labour movement. However, and paradoxically, the realization of an integrated national economy and the growth of a wage-labour sector did not foster a strong socialist or labour party. Such a development was hindered by a number of things: the regional concentration of workers; different types of work and workers; the dominance of craft unionism; the state's role in industrial conflict and conflict within the labour movement itself. As a result of these factors, electoral politics remained under the organizational control of a self-protective bourgeoisie and parties which organized elections around questions of national development and national unity. Labour grievances, notably, the right to collective bargaining, closed shop regulations, the use of strike-breakers and the immigrants' place in the labour force were not treated as partisan questions. There was some acceptance of labour's demands for regulation of the conditions of work, but, for the most part, these demands were defined as a threat to the national interest. Hence, the temporary resolution of class conflict was often left to the coercive apparatus of the state. However, its activities would not guarantee that the two-party system would survive unscathed.

During this period, the collective organization of workers in Canada went forward at a great rate. In 1897, the number of trade union locals was approximately 320; by 1903 it had reached 1133.[22] Similarly, the number of workers organized in trade unions rose from 133,000 in 1911 to 176,000 in 1913 to 205,000 and 249,000 in 1917 and 1918, respectively.[23] Throughout this period, radicalism and militancy increased. Industry-wide strikes occurred in Toronto in 1903, in Montreal in 1904, in Winnipeg in 1906 and in Vancouver in 1911. Not only did strikes proliferate but they were often violent and uncontrolled. Between 1901 and 1913, fourteen large strikes involved extensive property damage, death, the reading of the Riot Act and/or the proclamation of martial law.[24] However, despite these levels of conflict and violence, militancy led to few concessions either from employers or government. The long and bitter disputes frequently ended in a total rejection of labour's demands and the dismissal of strikers or, more frequently, strike leaders. The rights of collective bargaining, in the meantime, remained unrecognized. How could this happen? What were the conditions that produced these defeats, which, in turn, had a major demobilizing effect on the labour movement itself? Finally, what discouraged labour from playing the role of midwife to a viable socialist movement as it had in much of Western Europe?

These outcomes resulted from a complicated interaction of several factors. Among these, state action rendered labour's only weapon, the strike, ineffective. However, partly as a cause of the state's activity and partly as its consequence, the labour movement was divided over questions of ideology, organization and political activity. Thus, throughout this period it became increasingly factional with one set of unionists often pitted against another. A repressed and fractured trade union movement, as well as splits within the socialist movement, effectively doomed any potential for organizing a socialist alternative to the hegemonic bourgeois parties. The organization of workers, as workers, in the federal party system was, to a major extent, circumscribed by their lack of cohesion and organization in the workplace.

The unionization of an expanding labour force is a difficult task, even under the most favourable conditions. The early Canadian trade unions were confronted with many obstacles because of the pattern of industrialization and the rapid expansion of the population. To the usual controversies over the best form of organization for workers in the extractive and industrial sectors were added complications arising from the isolation and geographic concentration of certain types of workers and a constant expansion of the number of unorganized and unskilled workers due to immigration. These latter two factors allowed two quite distinct ideological and organizational tendencies to grow up and, ultimately, collide within the labour movement. In the process, they also nurtured regionally specific reactions to the state and to conceptions of political activity.

Immigrant labour was a central point of contention among trade unions, the state and employers for much of this period. Immigration policy was used by the state, and immigrants by the employers, to effectively weaken the union movement's organization and ability to collectively challenge employers through strike action. Employers took advantage of an open immigration policy to maintain production by employing large numbers of immigrant workers who, without any other means of subsistence, were willing to take low-paying jobs. In addition, labour was imported by employers at certain crucial points in time with the specific purpose of breaking strikes.[25] This was possible through the use of loopholes or the outright violation, sometimes with the concurrence of the federal government, of the Alien Labour Law. In the uncommonly strike-prone mining sector, for example, Orientals were frequently imported for as little as ten dollars a head by employers confronted with an organized strike.[26] This type of immigration both deflated the cost of labour, as only those willing to work at minimum rates were hired, and rendered the strike weapon impotent.

More generally, immigrant labour also weakened the labour movement's efforts to organize the workers. There was a constantly increasing supply of new and unorganized workers. In addition, the workers were divided from each other because of hostility toward the immigrants on the part of the English-speaking or Canadian workers. Consequently, cohesive organizations were difficult to achieve and economic struggles were obscured by differences of race and language.[27]

Be that as it may, the more effective and blatant obstacles confronting militant labour during this period were those constructed by the state. Throughout the period, state machinery was tuned and refined to maintain production even during industrial conflict. The intensification of labour strife was countered with increased reliance on state repressive mechanisms. The militia, for example, was mobilized in civil strife eleven times for a total of seventy-one days between 1895 and 1905 and seventeen times for a total of 1232 days between 1905 and 1914. Almost all these interventions involved a strike, and almost invariably the troops were used to protect non-strikers or imported strikebreakers from those who had stopped work.[28] In other words, the militia acted to maintain production and make the strike futile.

Coercive action formed only part of this process. The bulk of the state's intervention in the reproduction of class relations involved legislation. Initially the state assumed a role similar to that which the Roman Catholic Church had adopted in industrial disputes in Quebec and which also responded to new theories of management.[29] The state set itself up as mediator and conciliator between the workers and the owner, and the regulation of labour disputes by the state became incrementally more with each piece of legislation passed between 1900 and 1907.[30]

The legislation largely displaced industrial relations from the realm of partisan debate. In fact, the Minister of Labour, seeking endorsement for the Industrial Disputes Investigation Act (IDIA) in Parliament, argued,

> The principle involved in the Bill is too vital and too important a one to be made a party issue. It is, indeed, essentially a national issue which in these days of organized capital and organized labour, should command the hearty cooperation and sympathy of everyone who takes an interest in industrial questions. I contend, Mr. Speaker, that this is both a Liberal and a Conservative measure.[31]

The Conservatives apparently accepted this assessment and welcomed the Liberals' initiative.

All of these state actions, however, did not completely block the development of the trade union movement. Organization went ahead, under conditions which also created problems for the development of a class cleavage in electoral politics and for co-ordinated action by the labour movement. The bourgeoisie had by this time developed an ideological advantage in that it had been defined as the nation-builders and thereby was able to identify the particularistic interests of one class as the national interest. But its strength was not merely ideological. The bourgeoisie was the force behind the creation of the country. Canada was a bourgeois project. This dependence on the bourgeoisie for the national existence and the dependence of some parts of the labour force on this creation also made the organization of a challenge to this same bourgeoisie by a united labour force and socialist movement difficult. It was this reliance on a particular development strategy which to some extent blocked the organization of a class cleavage into partisan conflict. This left a space open for another form of dissent—dissent based upon another class in a regionally-based formula.

Workers in the East and West had different conceptions of capitalism and of Canadian capitalism in particular. The reason for these differences was the location of the two sets of workers, particularly those organized into trade unions. The eastern workers were concentrated in manufacturing in factories and workshops. This condition was coupled with the fact that only workers with an identifiable skill, a craft, were eligible for membership in the trade union central, the TLC. Moreover, craft workers, because of their relatively advantageous position *vis-à-vis* the labour market, have tended to be the most conservative and least critical trade unionists. Having a craft to sell in a labour market in which skilled labour was in short supply, enabled them to bargain for higher wages and better working conditions when other workers could not. Thus, eastern workers were the most economistic. They were also the most involved in manufacturing, which in Canada meant the production of goods for the domestic market.

The first policy implication of this location was that trade union demands could focus on improvements in wages, working conditions and other benefits, improvements which could be obtained from capitalists without challenging the existence of capitalism itself. Workers of this type realized that they were in a position to make demands and expect results from the capitalists because they were not easily replaceable. These conditions did not lead easily to the development of a radical critique of capitalism.

A second implication was that these unionists were dependent upon the maintenance of a certain market and economic structure for their jobs. Their interests were not divorced from the system of metropolitan dominance and hinterland dependency. The workers of eastern Canada needed the captive consumers of the West as did the Canadian entrepreneurs and branch plant managers. Their own jobs depended on the National Policy which located the manufacturing sector in Quebec and Ontario.

This reliance on the industrialization strategy meant that a wedge was driven between eastern and western workers and, perhaps as important, between eastern workers and their available allies, the farmers. The alliance which was possible and obvious between western workers and farmers around issues of eastern capital domination was more problematic if eastern workers were included. They depended on precisely the government policies which the farmers and western workers vehemently opposed.

An additional factor dividing western and eastern workers was their work experience. The major concentration of workers in the West was in sectors producing primary products. Miners, loggers and fishermen, along with the farmers, were all involved in producing staples for export. They were dependent upon the maintenance of a staple-based economy but not necessarily one with a high level of industrialization. Moreover, the workers in these industries were generally unskilled or semi-skilled. They lacked the advantages of the craftsmen in the labour force because they could be easily replaced with cheaper and often immigrant labour.[32]

The craft-based unions did not organize these workers. In 1914, of the half-million workers in manufacturing, the 246,000 in the building trades, and the 100,000 in the forest and mining sectors, an unimpressive 160,000 were organized.[33] This inability of the TLC to absorb the new workers opened the way for more radical competing labour unions as well as new forms of industry-wide organization. It was in the West that the strongholds of industrial unionism were found. They had been driven out of the East by the dominance of the TLC, but they grew up again to challenge that body.

It was under these conditions that cleavages within the labour movement concerning the form of its own organization continued to develop. Since the conflict corresponded, for certain objective reasons, to a regional division, the labour movement was divided for much of the period into a western and an eastern wing, each of which had very specific views of labour and its "proper" political activity. The decision in 1902 of the Trades and Labour Congress to affiliate with the American Federation of Labor did not settle the conflicts between the advocates of craft-based organizations and those who saw industry-wide unions as more likely to meet the needs of the new industrial work force. The "Berlin Decision" which, it will be recalled, was taken partly to eliminate the influence of the non-craft union, the Knights of Labor, meant that the TLC, in affiliation with the AFL, would permit within the congress only those unions organized along craft lines. Due to the distribution of productive activity, with manufacturing concentrated in the centre and resource extraction and primary industry in the northern and western peripheries, these cleavages over organization and eventually ideology, were concentrated in specific areas. Artisans and skilled workers, organized under the auspices of the TLC, were concentrated in central Canada, while unskilled and semi-skilled workers, particularly those in the West, remained ineligible to participate in that congress.

The resulting organizational vacuum was filled by the more radical industrial unions from the United States which had themselves broken away from the AFL. The industrial unions, beginning with the Western Federation of Miners and continuing through the American Labor Union and the Industrial Workers of the World (Wobblies), were committed to greater labour militancy. Their itinerant organizers moved from isolated mining camps to mobile railway construction sites with the intent of organizing workers, many of whom were immigrants, to demand higher wages and improved working conditions. The organizational task was immense. The potential recruits, for example, often did not speak the same language and feared the reprisals of the employers. The employers' power over all workers, not only the immigrants, employed in the primary sector was great. The owners controlled much of the worker's life, providing both the conditions of work and often, the worker's food, housing and any leisure facilities that might exist.

However, it was these conditions which facilitated the growth of industrial unions. The workers, lacking skills which might provide job security and high wages, recognized the need for a new form of organization. Their conditions of work, isolated as they were and separated from their families, meant that the workers lacked the opportunity to diversify their social activities, their interactions, with social organizations such as religious or ethnic societies. The work life was the most pressing condition, and workers were receptive to those who could promise to improve their lot. Thus, while western workers were receptive to politicization, the task was facilitated by the fact that although the primary-sector labour force was composed of many nationalities, the workers' mutual class position was potentially less obscured by the question of ethnicity than was the case with the French and English workers in the East. This was particularly the case when the IWW began to organize among the several ethnic groups in their own language.[34] Second, and more importantly, class domination was readily visible to the workers in the resource industries and railways of the West. Indeed, the fundamental stratification between worker and owner was harsh and real. Miners and loggers were generally located in company towns far from any urban centre. Their existence was stripped of cultural outlets. They were housed by the company and spent their wages in the company store. They slept, woke and ate in the common pattern dictated by the company siren. In short, the nexus between their life experience and socialist doctrine required little illumination.[35]

Given the failure of real wages to rise during the pre-war years and the decline during the war, the stark relevance of class analysis and the syndicalist tactics of the Wobblies, it is not surprising that throughout the war years strike activity in the western mines far outweighed that in any other sector. In 1916, for example, British Columbia, followed closely by Alberta, accounted for 30% of all national time lost due to strikes. The same trend continued in the following year.[36]

The success of the industrial unions, particularly the IWW was not left unchallenged, however. The unions were eventually broken by a combination of state intervention, employer repression (supported by the state) and a tacit alliance between the TLC and the state. This alliance was made because the state supported the TLC in its offensive against the challenges to its hegemony arising from the industrial unions. The state had an obvious interest in buttressing the less threatening, more pliant TLC against the more militant and socialist-influenced industrial unions which were launching serious disruptions in the production process in the West.

The Wobblies in particular challenged the strategy and tactics of the conservative craft unions because they stressed the need for an organization of all types of workers in a central body, the desirability of direct strike action and the socialist theory of the inevitability of class struggle. The IWW achieved almost immediate success in the West. By 1912, only six years after coming to Canada, the Wobblies had recruited 10,000 members in British Columbia alone. The Wobblies organized itinerant workers, such as miners, loggers, harvesters, longshoremen and construction workers.[37] At first, the IWW did not move into the TLC's jurisdiction, but the organizational success of the IWW gradually gave them access to urban trade and labour councils in western cities. There they began to act in concert with the representatives of TLC affiliates on local issues. This co-operation radicalized the TLC affiliates and encouraged them to advocate more militant tactics within the TLC itself. The struggle within the TLC about industrial unionism became more intense after 1906.[38] By 1910, the British Columbia Federation of Labour declared itself in support of industrial unionism, and this spread within a few years to other areas where the Wobblies were influential.[39]

Immediately prior to the war, the union movement was divided on questions of proper organizational strategy and goals. However, it was the war and conscription that ultimately magnified the split within the movement and provided the spark for the conflict between labour and the state. During the war years, the alternative strategies of organization for electoral conflict or for general strikes were debated, encouraging divisions within the movement which were not conducive to a united front for political action. The industrial unions, particularly the IWW, tended to be militant but syndicalist, advocating direct action against the employers, usually in the form of a general strike, rather than through electoral organization.[40] The TLC feared the obvious power of the state and the militancy of the socialists, who were often associated with the western unions. When the incidents of class conflict in this period are examined, the distinct regional tendencies within Canadian organized labour are clear. The most turbulent strikes were concentrated in the West in sectors with few TLC-organized workers.[41] In consequence, much of the state's repressive activity was directed against workers organized outside the TLC. This concentration of conflict coincided with a regional malaise which was already being organized by the agrarian movement. Thus, the conflict was partially interpreted as a regional rather than as a class problem and maintained divisions within the labour movement rather than uniting it against the bourgeoisie.

The regional divisions within the labour movement, as previously noted, can be partially attributed to the effects of the National Policy. Western workers, producing goods for export, saw few benefits and many costs to an economic structure which maintained manufacturing in the East at their expense. On this question they were much closer to the analysis of the western farmers. Both saw the enemy in the East. For the farmers, the enemy was the capitalists who controlled credit and the railways, as well as the manufacturers of the more expensive Canadian-made goods. For the workers, it was capital, which organized the extractive industries and with increasing frequency the financial and transportation sectors as well. While in the beginning some capitalists did originate in the regions on the periphery, increasingly, with the merger and monopoly movements, the centre of concentration moved East. Thus, the construction of an alliance between farmers and western workers was conceivable, and this alliance often advocated reforms which contradicted the demands of the eastern workers. It would take several decades and a fundamental transformation of the Canadian economy before this division within the labour movement, based on region, would work itself out.

In the meantime, because of divisions over the NP and, more importantly, because of the split within the movement and pressures coming from affiliation with the AFL, the TLC accepted the help of the state to break the industrial union movement.[42] The help was given in an environment which was hostile to labour. Even though the environment was hostile, the TLC managed to gain a number of concessions for its members—but they were concessions gained at great cost. The first cost was the demobilization of a large portion of the labour force by confining union organization to craft bases. The second was a reinforcement of the position that labour should not develop independent political organizations. The final one, clearly a function of the previous two, was that the workers remained tied to the bourgeois parties on bases other than their position as labour. When the TLC accepted the prevailing notion that political action by workers, as workers, was inappropriate, it failed to challenge the bourgeois parties' conception of "nation-building" partly because it was itself implicated in the maintenance of the structures of that "nation." In so doing, it left the field open to the activities and ideas of other organizations appealing to workers as members of ethnic or religious groups or residents of particular regions. It meant that, when the TLC did change its position during the war, the task of organizing a constituency, neglected for years, was immense.

Nor was the ideological hegemony of the bourgeoisie much threatened by the socialist movement of these years. Throughout this crucially important time of rapid changes in the social structure, the socialist movement, particularly in the West, was highly sectarian, divided and averse to parliamentary activity. The various small socialist parties were self-styled revolutionary parties and adopted a line against participation in elections. Their claim was that any gains from Parliament were merely reformist and illusionary if not destructive of the socialists' goals. Therefore, elections should be contested only as ends in themselves, for educational purposes and not because the elections of socialist candidates could lead to meaningful change.[43] Thus, while socialists did contest and were sometimes successful in elections, a goodly portion of the influential socialists described the action as unnecessary. Even though the socialists were not without influence in the trade unions, particularly in the West, the ideological and organizational interface was not utilized to draw an alternative definition of the political into the partisan sphere. Moreover, the socialist parties tended to criticize the trade unions as reformist, or inappropriately syndicalist.[44]

In sum, even though during this period there was considerable growth in the wage-labour sector and the trade union movement, as well as a proliferation of small socialist parties, the partisan organization of the class cleavage remained illusive. This statement, issued by the

Canadian Manufacturers' Association in 1908 perhaps best summarizes the status of the labour vote in these years.

> The truth is, there is no such thing as a labor vote at all. . . . The labor vote which the leaders refer to is the union labor vote, and even that, if it were united, which it is not, is only a mere fraction of the total vote cast by labor.[45]

Notwithstanding this rather complacent observation, the regional specificity of labour unrest, radical organization and state repression were integral to the crisis that was to break the two-party system in 1921. However, the opposition which did come was to be defined in regional terms as much as class ones.

The Effect of the Partisan Organization of the West

The independent commodity producers, the farmers, represented a class position by no means the same as that of the workers who were later to become their allies. It was for this reason that the alliance between workers, particularly western workers, and farmers was so difficult to achieve and maintain. In the earlier periods, particularly before the 1917 and 1921 federal elections, the farmers differentiated the interests of their own class position from that of the workers. In fact, many of the farmers' organizations and leaders feared the workers and their unions, especially militant western industrial unions and those involved in the 1919 violence of the Winnipeg Strike.[46] Moreover, the workers' parties did not make appeals to the farmers who, for the most part, sought a return to earlier and less centralized, less monopolistic capitalism rather than a transformation of society in the direction of socialism. It would be another decade before the agrarian movement divided and the more radical position within it allied with the workers on the basis of a common analysis of the weaknesses of capitalism.

This difference in class position which distinguished independent commodity producers from workers entailed a different indictment of the capitalist system. The activity of independent commodity producers was crucial to the existence and development of the country, but, at the same time, their future was threatened by the growth of industrial capitalism. Farmers were different from workers because they owned their means of production and did not sell their labour. In contrast, the workers owned nothing in the production process but their own labour which they sold for a wage. Thus, the farmers viewed mature capitalism from a different perspective than did the workers. The farmers saw the increasing effects of mergers and monopoly practices among those who organized the production of the goods consumed on the farm. Food, consumer goods, agricultural implements, transportation and credit were provided by larger and less accessible corporations. These corporations were felt to have a hammerlock on the small producer, the farmer, who could not compete with them in any contest. Thus, the goal of the farmer was to make this competition more equitable, to return to previous less concentrated capitalism or to pre-capitalistic conditions of co-operation among producers outside of the market. The farmers' movement advocated co-operative organizations, both consumer co-operatives and collectives for the sale of their products. They advocated control of credit, more equitable transportation costs and devices like marketing boards to protect the farm producer from the immediate vagaries of the market. All these measures were pursued because they offered the independent commodity producer protection from maturing capitalism, but this was not a socialist analysis.

Not only did the class position of the farmers differ substantially from that of the workers, but their political strength and potential influence was greater than the workers' in the prewar period. The strength of the independent commodity producers arose from the same set of factors which made political organization outside of the compass of the existing two-party system almost a foregone conclusion. As we have seen, this period realized an unprecedented expansion of agricultural production, primarily western wheat. This meant that wheat producers had a particular position of importance in the Canadian polity. They could not be ignored, nor could their complaints be left unresolved. The motor for the growth of the staple-based economy was wheat, and Canada needed its farmers in place and producing. Thus, it was crucial to the maintenance of the economy that the farmers be organized into the existing system of partisan relations.

It was under these conditions that the eastern politicians attempted to extend the politics and partisan relations which had been familiar and successful in the East to the new voters in the West. This meant that politics should be characterized by consensus about national growth and development while the parties divided the electorate along lines of ethnic, religious and language differences. The initial transfer of the party system to the West was quite successful in Manitoba, where, from the beginning, the two parties split the electorate largely according to language and religion. The Conservatives were the electoral home of the English-speaking, British immigrants, that is immigrants either from the "mother country" or from Ontario. The traditions of Orangeism were strong in the early years of Manitoba's history, as the experience of the school conflicts well illustrates. The non-British immigrants and the substantial number of Francophone residents were left to the Liberals.[47] It seemed, then, that the voting cleavages of the East would be reproduced in the West.

By 1905, the two-party system appeared successfully transferred, and the results of the 1908 elections only confirmed this conclusion. The previous election of 1904 had seen the reaffirmation of the Liberals as the representatives of the national development strategy. The 1908 election was, therefore, an election dominated by the usual exhortations of development and national unity.[48] The Conservatives supported the same development goals as the Liberals and could not find a strong issue around which to conduct an election. They reiterated their belief in the NP and suggested that preferential trade with the British Empire might be instituted. Nevertheless, there was really only room for one party of national unity, and this was, for the moment, the Liberals. Under Laurier's leadership they need do nothing but point to their achievements and claim they were obviously "good for the country." After all, it was the middle of an economic boom. In this vein, Laurier offered:

> . . . these years will be remembered in the history of Canada. In them Canada has been lifted from the humble position of a humble colony to that of a nation. . . . In 1908 Canada has become a star to which is directed the gaze of the whole civilized world. That is what we have done.[49]

The Conservatives could only argue that they would do the same thing but better or that the ruling Liberals were tainted with scandals. The 1908 election remains the quintessence of Canadian federal elections, pitting the two bourgeois parties against each other, with no differences but scandals between them.[50] The electorate, of necessity, had to fall back on traditional loyalties to make a choice. Once again, the ethnic and religious divisions differentiated the parties' supporters.

Table 3:1 displays the relationship between ethnicity and party support in the 1908 federal election.[51] It strongly supports our description of the characteristics of the early party system, showing that partisan alignments in the East were well defined by the bicultural cleavage.

Table 3:1
**THE 1908 ELECTION: CORRELATION OF PARTY VOTE AND
ETHNICITY BY REGION**
(Pearson's r)

	English	French	German
East			
Conservative	.45*	−.44*	.12
Liberal	−.41*	.41*	−.10
West			
Conservative	.39*	.05	−.08
Liberal	−.24	.22	.52*

* p < .05
Source: See Appendix A.

Table 3:2
**THE 1908 ELECTION: CORRELATION OF PARTY VOTE AND
CONSTITUENCY TYPE BY REGION**
(Pearson's r)

	Urban	Rural
East		
Conservative	.01	−.04
Liberal	−.07	.12*
West		
Conservative	.02	.00
Liberal	−.10	.03

* p < .05
Source: See Appendix A.

Constituencies with large English populations aligned with the Conservative Party and those with large numbers of French with the Liberal Party. In the West, this pattern of partisan support was repeated in 1908. As in the East, the more English the constituency, the higher the support for the Conservatives while the more French or non-charter the population, the stronger the alignment with the Liberal Party.[52]

That federal voting behaviour in 1908 was founded on an ethnic cleavage is also supported by the correlation coefficients shown in Tables 3:2 and 3:3. They indicate that there is no relationship between support for the two major parties and the constituency type (urban/rural) in either the East or the West. The pattern remains even after the effects on the party vote of the ethnic composition of the constituency are held constant with statistical controls. In other words, rural ridings did not systematically differ from urban ridings in terms of their party preferences. This perhaps is not surprising given that, as we have seen, neither

Table 3:3
**THE 1908 ELECTION: CORRELATION OF PARTY VOTE AND
CONSTITUENCY TYPE CONTROLLING FOR ETHNICITY, BY REGION**
(3rd order partial)**

	Urban	Rural
East		
Conservative	−.03	.06
Liberal	−.07	.03
West		
Conservative	−.09	.05
Liberal	.07	−.09

* p < .05
** controlling for English, French, German, Austro-Hungarian.
Source: See Appendix A.

of the two major parties offered policies to appeal to the subordinate classes whether they were in rural or urban contexts in 1908. The failure of both the labour movement and the farmers' organizations to inject a class cleavage into electoral politics is confirmed here. There were no national parties challenging the hegemonic conception of the "national dream" which was propagated by both the major parties. Thus, even though the workers and western farmers were involved in very real class-based conflicts in the years leading up to the 1908 federal election, these questions were not debated in the federal party system. The workers in the East remained tied to an ethnic view of the political world while the West responded predictably to party "packages," the set of partisan options carried from the East for them. Western voting behaviour in 1908 firmly revolved around the partisan vocabulary developed in the East years before, in which ethnic identity rather than class position was deemed to be the basis of political choice. By all indications, the politics of ethnicity appeared to have been successfully transplanted in the West.

However, a number of factors made this transfer imperfect and the partisan division less than stable in the West. The eastern-based definition of the political, emphasizing nation-building and the religious and ethnic composition of the new country, were largely out of tune with the western social fabric. A substantial proportion of the western electorate was neither English nor French and could not help but be divorced from the charter-group debate. While the mean proportion of those of British origin in eastern and western constituencies was 55% in 1911, 27% of the average western as compared to 6% of the average eastern constituency were of "other" European, non-charter origin. Thus, the original party system dividing along a bicultural cleavage found its genesis and dynamic in a legacy of bicultural conflict that did not correspond to the realities of the West.

The class biases contained within the two traditional parties would create tensions between the western electorate and the imposed party system. Both parties, almost exclusively relying on the economic elite of Montreal and Toronto for financial support and largely recruiting their leadership from the same select group, consistently pursued policies that benefited the eastern financial and commercial interests at the expense of the independent commodity producers of the West.[53] It was difficult to maintain widespread support in these areas for the idea that national development based on the NP was the best and only possible strategy. It implied that these areas should bear the costs by paying higher prices for goods brought to them on monopolistic railroads from protected eastern corporations while they saw their products marketed with a maximum of uncertainty and competition among a large number of small producers. The independent commodity producers had only to compare their prices for farm machinery and other goods with those paid by their neighbours in the western United States to realize that they carried the costs of the National Policy. Opposition movements grew up which refused to break along the familiar ethnic and religious cleavages. The British-born, the Anglophone Canadian, the eastern European farmer all criticized the eastern-based political party which refused to consider their interests in partisan debate. Whether that party was named Conservative or Liberal did not make a great deal of difference after a certain point. The Conservative Party had been the originators of the NP but this programme had been continued by the Liberals in the 1890s.

Much of this history of political activity in western Canada is a history of organization by farmers to overcome the structural effects of the National Policy. This activity was co-ordinated by farmers' organizations which began as non-partisan self-help bodies concerned solely with occupational issues. These were gradually transformed into institutions providing support for independent political activity under the aegis of a farmers' political party. The success of their activity, which came to fruition in 1921, was partially due to the cohesiveness of these organizations. The contrast with the divided labour movement is clear.

The farmers' organizations first tried to achieve their demands within the two-party system. However, they soon found this strategy brought few successes. The 1911 election marks a turning point. Prior to that election they tried for redress within the Liberal Party. Indeed, the tactic was encouraged by Laurier's statements which, as early as 1894 in Winnipeg, denounced the policy of tariff protection as "bondage in the same manner in which American slavery was bondage."[54] Nevertheless, after the Liberals took office the tariff remained essentially intact, although reformed. Demands for its abolition reached potentially disruptive peaks immediately prior to the 1911 election.

The farmers' organizations collectively developed a pro-reciprocity "Farmers' Platform" in 1910, and, whether by design or coincidence, Laurier advocated reciprocity as part of a joint programme with the United States in 1911. Free trade appealed to the western electorate, allowing the farmers to import less costly American manufactured goods, particularly agricultural implements, and promising to break the eastern-based control over western production costs. However, reciprocity was not equally popular in other parts of the country and for other classes. The Liberals found themselves in a difficult position in the 1911 election because they seemed to be fighting two issues at the same time in different areas. The first of these was the naval question, which threatened to push Quebec, under the leadership of the nationalist Henri Bourassa, into a coalition with the Conservatives. The second was reciprocity, which was the favoured policy in the West and almost nowhere else. As a result the Conservatives managed to end the Liberals' fifteen years of uninterrupted rule.

The development of the nationalist issue in Quebec has been

described in the previous chapter. Laurier's capture of that province, based on a careful nurturing of the sense of nation, rebounded against him later because it provided fertile ground for the more nationalist position of Bourassa, who was a nationalist because he was an anti-imperialist. His view of the Canadian nation was that it was independent from the British Empire and any obligations of colonialism. He and his supporters saw in Laurier's proposals for a Canadian navy a threat to that independence. Therefore, Bourassa withheld the support that he had given to the federal Liberals in 1904 and shifted to a position of "neutrality" in 1911.

In essence, however, this neutrality was not what it claimed to be. First, if the Liberals lost seats in Quebec, either to the Conservatives or to the Nationalists, the possibility of forming a government was much reduced. They counted on Quebec to give the slight edge in the tight contest with the Conservatives elsewhere. Therefore, by not supporting the Liberals, Bourassa was, in essence, aiding the Conservatives. However, there were more tangible links between Bourassa and the Conservatives. Bourassa had been an ally of the provincial Conservatives and the organization and financial support of this alliance was transferred to the federal level in 1911. Bourassa was so crucial to the Conservatives because he represented a way to assure defeat of reciprocity which, if implemented, would challenge the intent of the National Policy. Thus, at this time, Bourassa's newspaper, *Le Devoir*, was at least partially financed by St. James Street financial interests. It was these interests which were most threatened by reciprocity and which could afford and indeed were willing to see nationalism in Quebec if it meant that the Liberals and their campaign promise of free trade with the United States could be defeated.

> . . . "protectionist and imperialist big business (proceeded) to use the nationalist movement to defeat reciprocity." Big business poured funds into the Nationalist war chest and financed hundreds of additional subscriptions to *Le Devoir* . . . English-speaking Conservatives who had previously denounced the Nationalists as "rebels" and "traitors" suddenly discovered Bourassa to be the true patriot.[55]

Despite the seeming contradiction of an alliance between the anti-imperialist Bourassa and the imperialist Borden, these allies won twenty-seven seats in Quebec in the 1911 election and six were in ridings which had largely English-speaking populations.[56]

The anti-reciprocity campaign in the rest of the country was based on the negative employment possibilities of reciprocity as well as an appeal to the loyalty of Canadians, threatened with the possible loss of independence to the Americans. Over and over the loyalty argument was invoked against the western farmers who hoped to buy more cheaply in the US and to sell their goods more profitably. The campaign was conducted by the most prestigious of Canadians.

... Sir Edmund Walker, President of the Canadian Bank of Commerce and a Liberal, told a protest meeting of the Toronto Board of Trade that the proposals put continentalism ahead of the British connection. Four days later eighteen prominent Toronto Liberals issued a manifesto calling the proposals the worst blow ever to threaten Canadian nationality. ... Sir William Van Horne, the former president of the CPR, declared that he was "out to bust the damned thing." Within days the country's business, financial, manufacturing, and transportation interests had generally arrayed themselves against reciprocity.[57]

In this way the Liberal party split, losing not only Quebec voters but also much of the Montreal and Toronto business community which, since 1896, had supported Laurier as the heir to Macdonald and the protector of the NP. When that policy was threatened, party loyalty was unimportant. It was a policy loyalty which motivated the bourgeoisie, no matter what the partisan label and no matter what ethnic affiliation the label implied. As in Manitoba in the 1870s and 1890s and in the wartime election, nationalism and ethnicity were used to obscure the threat of changing the National Policy as it had evolved at this point into primarily a protective policy for an increasingly corporate bourgeoisie.

The negative impact of Bourassa's Nationalist Party on Liberal Party support among French-speaking constituencies in the East can be observed in Table 3:4. The ethnic correlates of the 1911 vote show that the strength of the relationship between proportion of the population of English origin in the constituencies and the Conservative vote remained stable across the two election periods. However, the relationship between proportion of the population of French origin in the constituencies and Liberal Party support was reduced considerably. Thus, the traditional bicultural cleavage between Liberal and Conservative party supporters was less pronounced in 1911 with the emergence of a specifically French nationalist party in Quebec. In contrast, in the West, the bi-ethnic cleavage endured and even strengthened across the two elections.

Table 3:4
THE 1911 ELECTION: CORRELATION OF PARTY VOTE AND
ETHNICITY BY REGION
(Pearson's r)

	English	French	German
East			
Conservative	.38*	−.34*	.02
Liberal	−.21*	.24*	−.11*
West			
Conservative	.52*	.09	−.61*
Liberal	−.50*	.12	.55*

* p < .05
Source: See Appendix A.

Table 3:5
THE 1911 ELECTION: CORRELATION OF PARTY VOTE AND
CONSTITUENCY TYPE, BY REGION
(Pearson's r)

	Urban	Rural
East		
Conservative	.12	–.05
Liberal	–.22*	.13*
West		
Conservative	.28*	–.28*
Liberal	–.37*	.25*

* p < .05
Source: See Appendix A.

Nevertheless, Table 3:5 indicates that there was an additional dimension to the 1911 election. Unlike 1908, the Table shows that the agrarian community, especially in the West, responded positively toward the Liberal Party's campaign promise of reciprocity. In other words, while the major cleavage in the East remained ethnic, a division between urban and rural interests emerged in the West.[58] This pattern remains when the effects of ethnicity on party vote are controlled. The partial correlation coefficients displayed in Table 3:6 show that, even when the effects of the relationship between ethnicity and the vote are taken into account, the Conservative "protectionist" party remains an urban-supported party. Although the Liberals in the East have no distinct identity among rural constituencies, in the West the Liberals clearly maintain their rural support after the effects of German, French and German, Austro-Hungarian voting patterns are taken into account.[59] The western farmers had responded as farmers to the Liberal Party's

Table 3:6
THE 1911 ELECTION: CORRELATION OF PARTY VOTE AND
CONSTITUENCY TYPE CONTROLLING FOR ETHNICITY BY REGION
(3rd order partial)**

	Urban	Rural
East		
Conservative	.12*	–.00
Liberal	–.15*	.04
West		
Conservative	.19	–.25
Liberal	–.26	.29*

* p < .05
** controlling for English, French, German, Austro-Hungarian.
Source: See Appendix A.

policy of freer trade arrangements with the United States. Reciprocity promised to improve their position as independent commodity producers, and Laurier had offered them a clear partisan alternative which spoke to their class interests.

This election, then, split the country regionally and saw the beginning of class-based voting patterns in the West. When the Liberals met defeat in 1911, the western electorate became even more convinced that the party system which they had inherited was but a tool of eastern manufacturing interests.[60] It confirmed their suspicions that they could count on neither of the two major parties for redress. Thus they were further propelled into their own organizations. If they could not capture one of the bourgeois parties as a national vehicle to legislate according to their needs, another tactic would have to be developed.

The farmers' organizations began to transform themselves from educational organizations and self-help bodies, non-partisan by long tradition, into institutions which could undertake a new form of political activity—the development of a political party based upon the interests of farmers as producers. The transformation was a long and conflictual one. It required hard work to convince the farmers both that the old parties would not change and that the farmers must, therefore, ignore their traditional party loyalties and often deeply felt antagonisms to other ethnic and language groups in order to work together as farmers. This was a long process which reached its culmination only in 1921. It was helped along by a series of crises which disrupted the federal party system and set loose partisans from the two bourgeois parties.

The defeat of reciprocity intensified and clarified the analytic understanding of class relations of the independent commodity producers. This process is discernible in the progressive radicalization of the Farmers' Platforms. For example, in 1910 the Platform read:

> We bear with us no feelings of antipathy towards any other line of industrial life. We welcome within the limits of Canada's broad domain every legitimate form of industrial enterprise, but in view of the fact that the further progress and development of the agricultural industry is of such vital importance to the general welfare of the state that all other Canadian industries are so dependent upon its success . . . we consider its operations should no longer be hampered by tariff restrictions.[61]

However, the endorsement of the complementary location of the independent commodity producers and capital in mature capitalism was to become a condemnation of dominance by 1916 when the Platform was reformulated. The events of 1911 were not negligible in stimulating this analysis.

... the Protective Tariff has fostered combines, trusts and "gentlemen's agreements" in almost every line of Canadian industrial enterprise, by means of which the people of Canada—both rural and urban—have been shamefully exploited through the elimination of competition, the ruination of many of our smaller industries and the advancement of prices on practically all manufactured goods to the full extent permitted by the tariff ... thereby building up a privileged class at the expense of the masses, thus making the rich richer and the poor poorer.[62]

Conclusion: The Crisis Conditions of 1917

The 1911 election underlines the ability of the federal Liberal Party to learn from its mistakes. Never again would it harken back to the "old Grit" free-trade position, despite pressures from the West. Reciprocity was a losing position and the Liberals would, in the future, offer nothing more in that direction than minor tariff modifications and adjustments. But 1911 also indicates that new partisan relations might develop which encompassed the effects of class formation and organization described in this chapter. This possibility was recognized by the bourgeois parties and produced the reaction to the crisis which arose prior to the election of 1917. The early war years saw the culmination and acceleration of many of the pressures for change in partisan and political relations that the chapter has documented. The farmers, particularly those in the West, were increasingly dissatisfied with the two-party system which they had inherited. This two-party system, based upon the partisan organization of differences between cultures and in which campaigns turned on questions of nationality with an accepted and unchallenged framework of national development did not suit them. For the farmers, other issues, particularly their class position in the staple-based Canadian economy, were crucial and they wanted to see this organized into the system of partisan relations. They hoped for parties offering definitions of politics which proposed readjustments in the relations between classes. The experience of the election of 1911, however, led these independent commodity producers to believe that such a change would not, and could not, come from within the existing two-party system precisely because of the existing balance of class forces. This election had produced for the first time a split in the basis of electoral choice in different regions of the country. It would take one more election, one more experience with the existing bourgeois parties, before the farmers' organizations could both organize themselves on a basis other than that of ethnicity and convince the electorate to follow them. They would finally, in 1921, fracture the two-party system forever.

The workers, too, were coming to the realization that a new partisan activity was essential. The war would be the catalyst. Not only the workers of western Canada with their traditions of radicalism and militancy, but also the more conservative eastern workers organized by the craft-based TLC, would come to see that the two-party system organized around ethnic rather than class cleavages, could not speak to or resolve their differences with capital. Their own parties, again a different form of political discourse and appealing to workers on the basis of their occupational positions, would be created.

Thus, the war brought unrest and dissatisfaction which amplified the already existing conditions of the struggle between classes which the past decades of economic development, organized under the rubric of the National Policy, had brought into being. This dissatisfaction centred on questions of how the costs of the war would be distributed and what the effect of the war would be on postwar class relations. And, suddenly, there was an example from abroad of what would happen, what might happen, if a means of coping with this dissatisfaction was not found by the bourgeoisie and the state. The lesson of the Russian Revolution was not lost on the Canadian bourgeoisie and the federal state.

Dissent and dissatisfaction threatened to bring about a major reorientation not only of class relations, but also of the organization of Canadian economic development. This reorientation threatened to come, not from the bourgeoisie, but from the subordinate classes. In the face of these crisis conditions, the bourgeois parties undertook an extraordinary strategy in response to what they saw as extraordinary conditions. This response was organized within the existing system of partisan relations and its effects on the party system reverberated for years.

NOTES

[1] W. A. Mackintosh, *The Economic Background of Dominion-Provincial Relations* (Toronto: McClelland and Stewart, 1964), p. 46.

[2] Mining, for coal in Nova Scotia and British Columbia, for nickel and other rare minerals in northern Ontario and even for gold in the Klondike, promised increasing investment possibilities. Logging became an ever-expanding industry, pushed forward by the immense demand for newsprint in the increasingly industrial and urban United States. See *ibid.*, pp. 41, 46.

[3] *Ibid.*, p. 40.

[4] G. W. Bertram, "Economic Growth in Canadian Industry, 1870-1915: The Staple Model," in W. T. Easterbrook and M. H. Watkins, *Approaches to Canadian Economic History* (Toronto: McClelland and Stewart, 1967), p. 83.

[5] Mackintosh, *op. cit.*, p. 55.

[6] In the early 1890s, the volume of exports, per capita, was still at the level of the 1870s. The rate of immigration was not as high as had been hoped for, and the debt charges paid by the federal government for infrastructural improvements were rising. *Ibid.*, p. 37.

[7] Transportation costs fell because of the increasing number of railways, steamships and other less expensive modes of transporting goods; the cost of manufactured goods fell because of decreased production costs in those countries that had undergone an industrial revolution; interest rates fell and capital could be more cheaply borrowed; the price of agricultural goods, in contrast, rose. These conditions, caused by events outside of Canada, were perfectly suited to

the needs of a country such as Canada for capital and imported goods in exchange for agricultural exports. *Ibid.*, pp. 38-39.

[8]*Ibid.*, p. 52.

[9]*Ibid.*, p. 47.

[10]Wallace Clement, *The Canadian Corporate Elite* (Toronto: McClelland and Stewart, 1975), p. 79.

[11]Between 1909 and 1911, for example, 196 firms were absorbed by 41 combinations. The government introduced the Combines Investigation Act in 1910, but the measure was largely without substance as it required complaints by affected individuals before any investigation could be initiated. See Edgar McInnis, *Canada: A Political and Social History* (Toronto: Holt, Rinehart and Winston, 1969), p. 455.

[12]R. Babcock, *Gompers in Canada* (Toronto: University of Toronto, 1974), p. 34.

[13]De facto cartelization in the United States provided pools of capital in search of profitable but controlled outlets. The protective tariff of Canada guaranteed such a profitable investment frontier. The multinational presence in Canada, therefore, is as old as the national economy itself. See Paul Phillips, "National Policy, Continental Economics, and National Disintegration," in David Jay Bercuson, ed., *Canada and the Burden of Unity* (Toronto: Macmillan, 1977), p. 31.

[14]American financiers, for example, initiated the formation of the Algoma Steel Company in 1901 and the Steel Company of Canada in 1910 while General Electric, Westinghouse, American Locomotive, Singer, American Asbestos, and Goodyear, among others, established branch plants in the environs of Montreal, Toronto and other southern Ontario cities. Indeed, the practice was so prevalent that by 1909 Toronto alone could boast of no fewer than fifty American branch plants. Only three years later, Canada, with approximately two hundred such industries, gained the dubious distinction of harbouring more American branch plants than any other nation. See Babcock, *op. cit.*, p. 31.

[15]Mackintosh, *op. cit.*, pp. 34-35; T. W. Acheson, "The Maritimes and 'Empire Canada'," in Bercuson, *op. cit.*, p. 93.

[16]Glen Williams, *Getting to the Moon by Railway: The Political Economy of Why Canada Can't Export Manufactured Products* (Toronto: McClelland and Stewart, forthcoming 1981).

[17]T. D. Regehr, "Western Canada and the Burden of National Transportation Policies," in Bercuson, *op. cit.*, p. 115.

[18]The federal government repeatedly used its constitutional powers, in particular the right to disallow provincial legislation, to prevent competitive railways from being built. Manitoba attempted to sponsor such a construction but the charter granted to a company desiring to build south from Winnipeg was revoked by the federal government. For a discussion, see *ibid.*, p. 121.

[19]See *ibid.*, p. 126; Mackintosh, *op. cit.*, pp. 61-62.

[20]Henry Ferns and Bernard Ostry, *The Age of Mackenzie King* (Toronto: Lorimer, 1976), p. 324.

[21]*Ibid.*, p. 325.

[22]Babcock, *op. cit.*, p. 52.

[23]John Crispo, *The Canadian Industrial Relations System* (Toronto: McGraw-Hill Ryerson, 1978). p. 164.

[24]Stuart Jamieson, *Industrial Relations in Canada*, 2nd ed. (Toronto: Macmillan, 1973), p. 81.

25A. Ross McCormack, *Reformers, Rebels and Revolutionaries* (Toronto: University of Toronto, 1977), p. 9.

26*Ibid.*, pp. 39, 40; Babcock, *op. cit.*, p. 115.

27McCormack, *op. cit.*, pp. 9, 10; Ferns and Ostry, *op. cit.*, p. 77.

28Desmond Morton, "Aid To Civil Power: The Canadian Militia in Support of Social Order," in M. Horn and R. Sabourin eds., *Studies in Canadian Social History* (Toronto: McClelland and Stewart, 1974), p. 429.

29The role of the Church in Quebec is described in Chapter 2. In addition, "Mackenzie King, Minister of Labour under Laurier and later Prime Minister, promoted a new role for the state that augmented the new management strategies of industry (scientific management). Thus under a facade of concern for the workers came the federal Department of Labour, The Labour Gazette, the Industrial Disputes Investigation Act (IDIA), and, in general, a whole new theory of the role of the state in industrial relations. The state became the supposedly neutral arbiter ruling in the interests of the 'public'. The working class response to these innovations varied from an initial grudging acceptance to overt hostility after they perceived that the 'public,' as interpreted by the courts and the government seemed to have precisely the same interests as the capitalists." See C. Kealey and P. Warrian, eds., *Essays in Working Class History* (Toronto: McClelland and Stewart, 1976).

30The legislation from the Conciliation Act of 1900 to the Industrial Disputes Investigation Act of 1907 (IDIA) stands as an index of reaction to the intensification of class conflict. The former defined the state as a facilitator, authorizing the Minister of Labour to appoint conciliation boards at the request of either party. It was followed by the Railway Disputes Act of 1903 which provided mechanisms for arbitration. As labour unrest intensified the notion of arbitration was expanded in 1906 and finally made compulsory for coal miners and railwaymen in 1907 with the IDIA. Inspired by the then-Deputy Minister of Labour, Mackenzie King, in reaction to the coal miners' strike in western Canada, the legislation disallowed any work stoppages until a tripartite board of conciliation and investigation had gathered testimony and heard evidence about the dispute. See Jamieson, *op. cit.*, Chapter 5, *passim*; Ferns and Ostry, *op. cit.*, pp. 67-99.

31*Ibid.*, p. 74.

32The whole industrial structure was growing rapidly at this time, with the most rapid rate of growth being for the workers without a craft—unskilled labour. Thus the percentage of craft employment within manufacturing enterprises declined from 91% in 1881 to 78% in 1891 to 41% in 1911. This decrease marked both the reduction of importance of craft workers in the active population and the introduction of other forms of employment in the manufacturing sector, for example, semi-skilled and unskilled workers, office employees and technicians. See F. A. Angers and P. Allen, *Evolution de la structure des emplois au Canada* (Montreal: Ecole des Hautes Etudes Commerciales, 1954), *passim* and especially pp. 23, 43-45.

33Of the 160,000 in these sectors that were unionized, 80% were organized in the TLC. Edgar McInnis, *op. cit.*, p. 455.

34McCormack, *op. cit.*, p. 102. For a more detailed description of the industrial union movement and its organization see Chapters 3, 6.

35N. Penner, *The Canadian Left* (Scarborough, Ontario: Prentice-Hall, 1977), p. 32; Walter Young, *Democracy and Discontent* (Toronto: McGraw-Hill Ryerson, 1969), p. 69.

36M. Robin, *Radical Politics and Canadian Labour* (Kingston: Industrial Relations Centre, Queen's University, 1968), p. 154.

37*Ibid.*, p. 150; McCormack, *op. cit.*, p. 101.

38"From 1906 onward Gompers was troubled by the possibility of the IWW making gains in western Canada, and the AFL and TLC organizers fought what they perceived as the 'dual union' heresy. C. O. Young, the AFL's organizer in British Columbia, considered the Wobblies 'lawless brigands' and did whatever he could to retard their propaganda." McCormack, *op. cit.*, p. 111.

39". . . the TLC's 1911 convention, which because it was held in Calgary was dominated by western delegates, passed a Vancouver resolution calling upon workers to organize by industry, because craft unions had demonstrated their inability 'to successfully combat the present day aggregations of capital.' TLC bureaucrats were unable to block the western resolution, but the following year, when the convention was safely back in Ontario, an eastern majority returned the congress to Gompersian orthodoxy." *Ibid.*, p. 114.

40It also organized those workers for whom elections were of little importance, since they tended not to be enfranchised. *Ibid.*, p. 105.

41Of the fourteen strikes in which extensive violence occurred, six were in BC. Further, the coal miners emerge as the most radical of industrial workers. Although comprising only 2% of the non-agricultural work force, they accounted for 5% of all strikes, 24% of all strikers, and 42% of all time lost due to strikes in the period 1901-1913. Jamieson, *op. cit.*, pp. 81-82.

42The strike of the United Brotherhood of Railway Employees (an affiliate of the ALU, which had been founded in the United States to wage war on the AFL) against the Canadian Pacific Railway in 1903 provides a case in point. The TLC's role in the strike almost ensured its failure. It not only ordered affiliated unions which had acted in sympathy to go back to work but also helped the CPR organize scab workers to replace the striking UBRE workers. The strike was eventually broken, but it, plus numerous others, were of sufficient impact to lead to the appointment of a Royal Commission to investigate what was seen to be an industrial crisis in BC. The Minister responsible for labour affairs thought that "perhaps it would assist to disillusion [the workers] if an intelligent commission . . . were to point out the injuries that have come to them because of the interference of the American unions." In accordance, the Royal Commission recommended that the ALU and its affiliates be declared illegal. This was clearly a case in which the TLC was willing to co-operate with the employers in order to break a threatening organization and to accept help from the state, even if it meant restrictions on the activity of labour. See McCormack, *op. cit.*, especially pp. 47, 42-51.

43There was a conflict within the movement in these years ". . . between the gradualists, who contended that while the coming of the revolution was assured by history it was only practical for socialists to work for the relief of the working class under capitalism, and the so-called impossibilists, who argued that not only was the reform of capitalism impossible but that efforts to achieve reform could only delay the advent of the co-operative commonwealth by diverting the proletariat from the class struggle." For a discussion of the intricacies of the debate see McCormack, *op. cit.*, Chapter 2, p. 25; for further details, see Penner, *op. cit.*, p. 32.

44*Ibid.*, p. 55; Penner, *op. cit.*, pp. 27, 51.

45Quoted in Babcock, *op. cit.*, p. 182.

[46]W. L. Morton, *The Progressive Party in Canada* (Toronto: University of Toronto, 1950), p. 242; W. Young, *The Anatomy of a Party* (Toronto: University of Toronto, 1969), p. 14.

[47]See T. Peterson, "Ethnic and Class Politics in Manitoba," in Martin Robin, ed., *Canadian Provincial Politics* (Scarborough, Ontario: Prentice-Hall, 1972), pp. 69-115, *passim*.

[48]M. Beck, *The Pendulum of Power* (Scarborough, Ontario: Prentice-Hall, 1968), p. 97.

[49]Quoted in *ibid.*, p. 107.

[50]The condition of Canadian partisan politics at the turn of the century was described by the touring French political scientist, André Siegfried, this way: "Originally formed to serve a political idea, these parties are often to be found quite detached from the principles which gave them birth, and with their own self-preservation as their chief care and aim. Even without a programme, they continue to live and thrive, tending to become mere associations for the securing of power, their doctrines serving merely as weapons, dulled or sharpened, grasped as occasion arises for use in the fight. . . . This fact deprives the periodical appeals to the voting public of the importance which they should have. . . . Whichever side succeeds, the country it is well known will be governed in just the same way; the only difference will be in the personnel of the Government. . . . Canadian statesmen . . . undoubtedly take longer views. They seem, however, to stand in fear of great movements of public opinion, and to seek to lull them rather than to encourage them and bring them to fruition. . . . The existing parties are thus entirely harmless. The Liberals and Conservatives differ very little really in their opinions upon crucial questions, and their views as to administration are almost identical. . . . They have come to regard each other without alarm: they know each other too well and resemble each other too closely." In Underhill, *op. cit.*, pp. 9-10.

[51]For the construction of Table 3:1 and subsequent tables like it see Appendix A. The use of correlation procedures with aggregate data may be misleading when the distribution of a specific ethnic group within the constituency is very small. This poses no problem with the use of the English category as the mean constituency distribution of those with British origin is 54.8% in the East and 55.4% in the West. The mean distribution of those with French origin is 35.6% in the East and 5.2% in the West. The respective frequencies for the German category which also includes Austro-Hungarians and Bulgarians are 4.5% and 17.1%. A growing ethnic population in the West, but less so in the East during this period was the Eastern Europeans. According to the 1911 census, the mean constituency distribution for those of Polish or Russian origin was .3% in the East and 3.7% in the West. The correlations between Eastern European population and party vote in the west in 1908 were -.16, $p > .05$ and $.29^*$, $p < .05$ for the Conservative and Liberal Parties respectively.

[52]By "non-charter group" we mean ethnic groups which are of neither British nor French origin.

[53]C. Winn and J. McMenemy, *Political Parties in Canada* (Toronto: McGraw-Hill Ryerson, 1976), p. 19.

[54]Morton, *op. cit.*, p. 20.

[55]Beck, *op. cit.*, p. 131.

[56]*Ibid.*, p. 125.

57*Ibid.*, pp. 122-23.

58The relationship of support for the Liberal Party in rural constituencies in the East in both the 1908 and 1911 elections was largely isolated outside Quebec. When constituencies in Quebec are not included in the analysis of the East, the correlation coefficient between rural ridings and Liberal Party support is .24 ($p < .05$) in both 1908 and 1911. The bicultural cleavage was of overriding importance in that province.

59The correlation between Eastern European distributions and party vote in the West in 1911 was .39 $p < .05$ for the Conservatives and .40 $p < .05$ for the Liberals.

60Morton, *op. cit.*, p. 31.

61*Ibid.*, Appendix A, p. 297.

62*Ibid.*, Appendix B, p. 300.

Chapter 4

1917-1921—Two Parties in Crisis

Introduction

The events of the First World War and the immediate post-war years form a unity in the history of partisan relations in Canada. There is an intimate connection between the two elections because the fundamental change resulting from the 1921 election was prepared and set in motion by the conditions of the 1917 campaign. The 1921 election represents an outbreak of protest by a subordinate class demanding to be heard electorally. However, this incursion into the bourgeois parties' guarded domain was not guided by the workers' organizations nor did it include a viable coalition between the two subordinate classes whose development we have been tracing. Even though this period experienced widespread and major confrontations between the workers and the bourgeoisie a strong and cohesive political arm for labour was not realized. The combined forces of the nationalizing bourgeoisie first used the opportunities for inter-election activity to contain the most pressing source of opposition to their strategy. The organized dissent of the farmers could be dealt with later. That of the workers, since it extended beyond single industries and regional boundaries, was more challenging. These years witnessed successful efforts to break working class radicalism. It primarily involved the state and the employing class, but support was also forthcoming from some elements of the trade union movement itself. The techniques employed against the radicalism were coercive and ideological, and their effects were far-reaching.

The offensive against radical labour was organized on a complex combination of fronts. However, it most fundamentally involved the translation and the transformation of class-originated and class-based dissent into issues of ethnic conflict. Ideology of war, involving as it seemed, a conflict between nations, was evoked, and workers were persuaded to place the "national interest" before "narrow" class interest. Where appeals to nationalism failed, the representatives of working class interests were treated as conspirators and "enemy aliens" or harbingers of "non-Canadian" subversive world views which would reap havoc for all. With such accusations, the state legitimized its coercive offensive against the radicalism of the union movement. In the end, the hegemony of the less militant component of the trade union movement was re-established. Moreover, the workers, as a class, were so intimidated that the unions retreated from the party system that they had hesitantly entered in 1917.

As we shall see in this chapter, the war was disruptive of the two-party system. The social tensions of the previous decade and the pressures of the war effort gave crisis proportions to social cleavages between East and West, workers and owners and French and English. However, the two bourgeois parties initially proved unwilling or unable to adjust their definition of the political, namely cultural conflict, to accommodate the emerging cleavages in the national society. Thus, opposing definitions were organized outside the two-party system. The Union Government responded to the challenge to its authority with a series of mechanisms: propaganda, co-optation, legislative repression and physical coercion.

In the end, however, the efforts to turn the mounting tide of dissatisfaction were only a partial success. While the radical challenge was overcome, the two-party system was broken. Canada emerged in 1921 with a regionally-fractured federal party system, one aligned around the opposition between the petite bourgeoisie, of the West in particular, and industrial capital. It was not, therefore, organized or reorganized around the usual cleavage of industrial capitalism, that is, an electoral cleavage between workers and capitalists. That possibility had been made highly unlikely, for the moment, by the state and capital's reaction to the radical stance adopted by labour during and immediately after the war and by divisions within the labour movement itself.

Not all dissent, however, was neutralized by this offensive. The independent commodity producers used the same situation, the breakdown of partisan identities under wartime conditions, to insert their own party into the federal system. Space was created for them within the electorate by the destruction of the traditional division of partisan relations during the 1917 Unionist campaign and by the War Time Elections Act. They moved into the space and, by moving, brought about a fundamental realignment of partisan forces. They did this, however, at a time when their political influence and importance as a class was on the wane. The measure of influence guaranteed them as producers of the staple gradually eroded as wheat and other agricultural exports declined in importance. Increasingly, in the next two decades, Canada would become a modern industrialized country. The more far-sighted of the bourgeoisie recognized the implications of this transformation, and it was for this reason that the dissent organized by the workers, and not necessarily the farmers, had to be circumscribed and broken. A workers' revolution was, ultimately, a greater threat than a farmers' revolt. It was this perspective which formed the backdrop to these five years and which led to a strategy of repression and ideological reorganization which delayed the electoral organization of workers, as workers, for many years. The workers' parties and unions were not strong at the beginning of the war, and they emerged from the postwar experience in a profoundly weakened condition. The bourgeoisie had recuperated its power to organize electoral relations around ethnic divisions. It would take another decade before there was sufficient force to begin again to reconstitute the workers' political organization and to institute the alliance with the other subordinate class, the farmers.

Re-structuring Within a Wartime Economy

Just on the eve of the "war to end all wars," the Canadian economy suffered a dramatic reversal of the optimistic trends of the previous decade, a reversal which reflected the fundamental weakness of the economy. As an exporter of primary products and an importer on a massive scale of goods and services, Canada was extremely vulnerable to the slightest fluctuations in international conditions.[1]

The previous stimulus for economic prosperity, the growing western frontier, weakened because that expansion was largely accomplished. By 1913, after an influx of approximately 400,000 new immigrants, the flow of new Canadians began to dwindle.[2] Transcontinental railway systems linking the western hinterland to its eastern source of supplies and services were set in place, and the production process which had created these systems began to wind down. The boom finally reached its logical conclusion, and, by the winter of 1913, increasing numbers of the new urban work force found themselves out of work.[3] Canada, having just entered the second decade of "its" century, was enmeshed in an economic recession.

While the outbreak of war in Europe the following year stimulated economic recovery, it merely postponed the difficulties that were inherent in the nation's economic order. The war opened an immense market for Canadian cereal grains and redirected the industrial sector from production for internal consumption to supplies destined for the European front. However, just as had been typical of the period of western expansion, the re-activated industry located in the East.[4] The growth in the industrial sector principally benefited southern Ontario, but in Quebec, as well, manufacturing's contribution to the provincial economy grew from a mere 7% in 1900 to 38% in 1920.[5] Such was not the case in the West. Because the nation's resources were redirected from national development to production for external use, the service and construction industries which had grown for western development virtually ground to a halt during the war years. The war brought economic boom, but once again, the benefits, except those accruing to agriculture, were concentrated in the centre of the country.

World War I acted as a very important stimulus for the already active manufacturing sector. The total annual value of both manufacturing and steel capacity doubled in the period 1910-1920.[6] The transition from an agricultural to an industrial economy, which had begun in the previous decade (manufacturing output had surpassed that of agriculture in 1910), was accelerated. Significant changes were also evident within the primary sector.[7]

The shift in the pace and focus of the production process increased tensions and dislocations in the relations between classes. The combined demand for factory workers and troops placed labour at a premium. Resentment rumbled through the farm communities of rural Ontario which, at first heartened by the seemingly insatiable market for their products, witnessed the evaporation of the agrarian work force as high wages pulled more young men and women into the urban and industrial work force.[8]

In contrast, in the West, because of the slowdown of development, countless workers were unemployed and left to return to agriculture or to join the army. The great demand for industrial workers was in the East and even those western workers who were employed generally received a lower pay than their eastern counterparts.[9]

Moreover, what might have appeared to be attractive wages were soon eaten away by inflation. Food prices alone increased 65% between August 1914 and December 1917.[10] Shortages of other essential products such as fuel for heating and transportation and basic foodstuffs grew to be extreme after 1916. Indeed, the gap between the need for goods for domestic use and the supply was so great that it was not until the economy was drastically deflated in 1921 that real wages returned to their 1913 recession level.[11] Yet, even with equitable wages, the burden of inflation would have been heavier for the West, where freight-rates amplified the price of the already costly goods. The western workers' and farmers' condition suffered in comparison to both the dominant class and the workers in the East.

The 1917 Election

By 1916, the combined effects of inflation and opposition to the war swelled the ranks of the trade union movement, which doubled from 166,000 members in 1914 to 378,000 in 1919.[12] The opposition to rising prices and falling real wages sparked a host of industrial disputes, and strikes became increasingly prevalent, especially in the West. In 1917, the time lost because of strikes was four times greater than in any other war year; one million man-days, 86% of which was in the West.[13] Western unemployment remained high into 1915, and, by the next year, economic anxieties and hardships were such that radical leadership and programmes gained widespread credibility.

Nevertheless, despite increased membership, all was not well with the trade unions. The first concern was the maintenance of the rights and position of trade unions during war. The war economy, with its strict regulation of labour and loss of traditional rights, threatened the very basis of union organization.[14] However, conscription, and the reaction to being forced to fight a war not of their own choosing radicalized the labour movement which in turn threatened the government's war effort. This issue revealed the extent of the gulf between organized labour in the West and the East. The western unions, even those affiliated with the Trades and Labour Congress, were more militant, having been influenced for almost a decade by the syndicalism of the International Workers of the World. Their analysis of capitalism led many western unions to advocate a general strike to break the government's conscription policy and to affect the conduct of the war. However, this direct approach to the resolution of labour's grievances, by-passing the parliamentary process, was not acceptable to the more conservative leadership of the TLC, which dominated the eastern unions.

Therefore, despite the increased politicization of the TLC and despite its organization for the first time in many years for direct political action, the split between the eastern and western components of the union movement was not to be bridged. A cohesive labour party would not emerge. The political initiatives of the TLC were insufficient to weld together the two regional wings of the movement. The result was that workers were not provided with strong leadership and consistent explanations of the burdens they bore because of the war. Mutual hostility and distrust rather than common action still characterized the labour movement.

Before and during the early years of the war, there was little division within the ranks of organized labour, or at least its leadership, on the question of compulsory military service. Opposition was the norm.[15] Overwhelmingly pacifist in principle, as early as 1911 the TLC passed resolutions at annual conventions condemning conscription of labour for military service. Influenced not only by socialist principles but also by Christian ethics, the leadership defined the war as one between imperial powers fought with the lives of the working people. However, the leadership of the labour movement was not sufficiently influential among its own rank and file to reproduce this opposition on a large scale. In fact, the earlier failure to develop class-based thinking and analysis within the working class challenged the labour movement itself, as the men put race and nation before class and volunteered for service.[16] However, as the war dragged on and the discrepancy between its costs to the workers and the unregulated profits accruing to the manufacturers of wartime materials grew more apparent, support gathered for the unions' campaign in favour of "no conscription of manpower without conscription of wealth."

Conscription was also opposed by the trade unions because it struck at the very heart of the rights and procedures of collective bargaining.

Conscripts could not make contracts because they were, by definition, not free labour. Additionally, troops had already been used to break strikes, and it was feared that the state would continue to use conscripts to maintain production. Thus, mobilization of manpower into the armed forces was taken to mean the potential for a further weakening of collective organizations of labour.[17]

The generalized belief, particularly among the western radicals, that conscription was on the horizon, was confirmed in 1916 when the Borden Government initiated, by Order-in-Council, a programme for registration of the work force. According to the government, the sole purpose of the registration programme was to determine the location and distribution of labour to aid in the contingencies of wartime production. It adamantly denied that it was a preliminary step toward the institution of compulsory service. Organized labour was suspicious, however, and initially was united in its opposition to the programme. Nevertheless, as the possibility of conscription became daily more certain, a rift developed between eastern and western organized labour both within the TLC itself and between that congress of craft-based unionism and the industrial unions. The dispute was over the type of defensive strategy to be adopted. Despite initial unity in hostility to the registration programme, when the government went ahead without any support from the labour movement or any consultation with it, the TLC leadership finally recommended that its members comply with the registration campaign. This "capitulation" infuriated the western unions. The labour councils of several western cities where TLC affiliates had sat for almost a decade with the IWW-organized unions, led the opposition. They censured the TLC leadership and began to mount an anti-registration campaign with great fervour. This reaction was, in turn, termed "inexplicable" and "deplorable" by the national leadership of the TLC.

In the spring of 1917, the fears and suspicions of western labour leaders were confirmed, when conscription was finally instituted. At that point, they began to prepare for a general strike that they hoped would force the end to compulsory service, bring about the conscription of wealth and introduce the nationalization of industry. When the TLC met in conference the following September, the distance between the western plans and what the eastern unionists were willing to do to manifest their opposition became clear. The general strike tactic was proposed by the western unionists, and it was rejected by the Congress as a whole. The TLC leadership had successfully convinced the majority attending the convention that the law, and conscription was now the law, must be obeyed.

At the same time, however, in the eyes of the more conservative leadership and the eastern unions, especially those in Ontario, the time had finally come for the TLC to launch a labour party to challenge the government in the electoral sphere. But, even the TLC's decision to encourage the formation of the Canadian Labour Party and the final acceptance of co-operation with the Socialists (something that had been repeatedly rejected up to that point) was not sufficient to bridge the gap across the regions. By this time, the two factions were sharply divided over questions of strategy, principally whether it would be more effective to confront the government by direct action through a general strike or by political action in the form of a labour party. By 1917, the support for a labour party had shifted to Ontario while the West adopted the more syndicalist position.[18]

Moreover, there was not unanimous support within the TLC. Of particular note is the opposition to direct partisan action that came from the AFL leadership. Despite the fact that prominent TLC officials were actively involved with the Labour Party, in opposition to Unionist candidates, the president of the AFL, Samuel Gompers, made a personal visit to the Toronto area to campaign against the CLP candidates. He pleaded with labour to back the government and, presumably, the Unionist candidates, because a war was on and democracy was at stake.[19]

In this way, the conscription issue, which might have united the labour movement and forged a class cleavage into electoral politics, only further split the movement into factions. The effect of a split on the partisan situation became clear as, once again, Canadian workers and the population received confusing and sometimes contradictory interpretations of the situation. The effect was debilitating for the organization of a class cleavage into partisan conflict.

This long-term effect was not obvious at the time to the government. It found itself confronted with a level of opposition and growing civil strife which it thought perhaps uncontrollable.[20] The conscription issue appeared to have opened the floodgates for a major confrontation between the state and labour, a confrontation which could threaten the war effort and the life of the Conservative government itself. The sense of urgency and apprehension which flooded the offices of Prime Minister Borden and his cabinet ministers in the early months of 1917 could only intensify with the realization that labour was not the only subordinate class that had lost confidence in the government.

The farmers too were beginning to organize as a result of both the war and the lessons learned in 1911. Farmers, just as labour and French Canadians, were not immediately enthusiastic about the war. Their publications reveal they were "frankly isolationist and accepted Canadian participation reluctantly," which is not surprising, given the mixed loyalties that must have been felt by new Canadians of non-British stock who saw former homelands now at war with the Empire.[21] In addition, the experience of war made their lives difficult as anti-alien feeling reached some astonishing peaks.[22]

Farmers were anti-conscriptionist for some of the same reasons as the labour movement. They too saw injustice in conscripting only manpower and not wealth. For example, farmers' candidates in the 1917 election:

> . . . were committed to conscription, provided it was conscription, not only of men, but also of wealth, by means of income and excess profits, taxes, and national control of every industry affected by war conditions.[23]

Prior to the 1917 election, farmers were wary of conscription and the ideology of "win the war at any cost" which called them to put aside their traditional objections to the effect of the tariff and other aspects of national development policy. As their post-1911 position radicalized they began to organize for farmers' candidates in the 1917 election, and the idea of a third party, sponsored by farmers' organizations, began to gather grass-root support.[24] The Conservative Party could hope for little support among class-conscious farmers, both because of its image as the protectionist party and its failure to make accommodations to the West during its period in office. Unless there were dramatic change in the electorate, Borden faced the probability of losing in the West in the forthcoming election.

The Conservatives were well aware that they could not afford to lose seats in the provinces west of Quebec if they were to remain in power. They could not rely on Bourassa's Nationalists in 1917 as they had in 1911 to reduce the Liberals' support in Quebec. Participation in the First World War aggravated, once again, relations between the founding cultures. Unlike many of those born in Britain who demanded little persuasion to rally to the call for the "defence of the Empire," the Canada-born Francophones, long cut off from France and with little feeling for a homeland other than Canada, were not enthusiastic about fighting "Britain's war."[25] Understandably, then, when conscription was enacted despite Borden's previous assurances to the contrary, Quebecers felt themselves betrayed by the Conservative Party. Laurier's adamant opposition to compulsory service only served to reinforce and reaffirm the traditional bicultural cleavage in the East.

The Conservative government seemed to be surrounded by opposition and confronted with almost insurmountable obstacles prior to the 1917 election. Moreover, Laurier was successful in courting organized labour's support in the West by jointly sponsoring some labour candidates and adopting favourable policy positions.[26] In addition, although farmers were not optimistic, they might have been willing to listen to another offer of changes in the tariff from the Liberals.[27] The war and conscription threatened to produce a Liberal coalition of the disgruntled, namely, the French, the farmers and a substantial number of workers.

A final threatening factor for the government was the international situation. Events abroad had already produced a situation which became of increasing importance as a justification for actions of the Unionist Government. The lesson of the Russian Revolution was not lost on the Canadian bourgeoisie. In Canada, as well as elsewhere, the wave of sympathy and enthusiasm that greeted that event provoked numerous fears. 1917 would go down in history as a difficult year.[28]

Seemingly confronted with a hopeless situation, the Borden government attempted to avoid an election in 1917. It undertook a daring strategy to save the situation by proposing to share its power with the Liberals in a Union government. This coalition of formerly hostile partisans would put aside their differences and campaign to elect a nonpartisan government to win the war. Laurier and many Liberals turned down the offer in June. After this failure, Borden, the next month, attempted to extend the life of Parliament, apparently in order to avoid a wartime election. Again the Liberals, justifiably feeling close to victory, rejected the idea out of hand.[29] Then, having failed to win the support of the Liberals, Borden and his colleagues undertook initiatives to break the potential opposition coalition and to reduce the number of likely Liberal voters in the electorate. First, they manipulated the conscription issue to split the pro- and anti-war forces in the Liberal Party. This isolated the Laurier Liberals in Quebec. Next, they disenfranchised many of the potential and usual Liberal voters in the West where dissent was great. Finally, and for good measure, they began a systematic campaign of harassment of dissenters which continued well into the postwar period.[30] In this way, the government assured itself of power in the face of crisis; it served its narrow partisan goals, and continued the definition of Canadian electoral politics as being primarily about ethnicity.

To deal with the strength of the Liberal Party among non-British voters of the West, the government developed a solution which constitutes one of the most lamentable if not despicable episodes in the history of Canadian elections. Since the government could not be assured of the votes of new Canadians in the West, it simply denied them the right to vote. In September 1917, the rules of the electoral game were changed. Under the provisions of the War Time Elections Act, the federal franchise was manipulated so that "every British subject naturalized after March 31, 1902, who was born in an enemy country or was born in any European country whose natural language, otherwise described as 'mother tongue' was a language of an enemy country" was denied the right to vote until the end of the war. The Act further extended the franchise to any woman who could claim to be "the wife, widow, mother, sister or daughter of any person, male or female, living or dead, who served in any of the military forces of Canada or Great Britain in the present war."[31] While the Act applied across the nation, the greatest weight of exclusion fell on the non-charter groups in the western provinces. Specifically, the Germans,

Austro-Hungarians, and other eastern Europeans were defined by the federal legislation as "alien." An impression of the differential impact that the Act might have cross-regionally can be gleaned from Table 4:1. While an imprecise measure, the data suggest that disenfranchisement by ethnic criteria was at least five times more likely in western than eastern provinces. The partial enfranchisement of women, on the other hand, gave additional electoral force to the pro-conscriptionists and those of British origin, because it was predominantly these men who had joined the armed services.[32]

Table 4:1
MEAN PER CENT ETHNIC POPULATION IN EASTERN AND WESTERN CONSTITUENCIES

	East	West
Total Charter Population	90.4%	60.5%
British	54.8	55.4
French	35.6	5.1
Major Non-Charter* Population	6.4	26.8
German; Austro–Hungarian	4.6	16.7
Scandinavian	.1	5.3
Western European	1.3	1.2
Eastern European	.3	3.6

*Totals do not include native or Asian population. Calculated from per cent distributions of ethnic populations within the 1917 constituency.
Source: 1921 Census data, see Appendix A.

The War Time Elections Act was, in some ways, a work of genius. Its object was to disenfranchise as many voters as possible who might be expected to support Laurier and to enfranchise and control the votes of as many as possible who might be expected to accept the government's claim that conscription would "bring the boys home by Christmas"—the female next of kin of men in the armed forces.[33] Arthur Meighen, the Secretary of State and the architect of both the conscription legislation and the War Time Elections Act admitted that the intent was to "shift the franchise from the doubtful and anti-British of the male sex and extend it at the same time to our patriotic women."[34] The final detail needed to secure maximum vote potential for Unionist candidates was to give farmers the assurance that their sons working on the farm would be exempt from conscription.[35]

This withdrawal of the right to vote from new Canadians proved a solution for the government in at least three respects. First, it left, as almost the only basis for stratification of the electorate, the linguistic division between French and English as it isolated the bulk of the anti-conscriptionist vote in Quebec. Many anti-conscription labour votes in the West were disenfranchised (recall the ethnic composition of the labour movement) and farmers were bought off with exemptions. The conscription question was transformed and redefined as an ethnic dispute. Second, given the hostility and hysteria of wartime, repression of the "alien" minority promised to draw little public protest of the Act's unprecedented violation of the rights of citizenship. That the attitude toward the immigrants had often been one of suspicion and hostility, was clear from the way the immigration issue had excited the labour unions. These historical reactions could be re-activated or played upon with legislation like the War Time Elections Act. Thus, the effect of the Act was to fuel aggressive wartime nationalism and to diminish opposition to conscription. Finally, the Act propelled Liberal members in favour of conscription to desert the Liberal Party and join the ranks of the Union government. Ontario Liberal candidates began to trickle one by one into the coalition as opposition to conscription became identified as a cultural issue. They were followed in October by the western Liberal members who were faced with the disenfranchisement of their previous supporters, the non-charter groups.[36] The foundations for a bitter electoral confrontation between French and English Canadians had been firmly established.

In this context, the threat of a national labour party did not materialize. The Canadian Labour Party was launched, with TLC support, only three months before the election. In that short time-period, frantic efforts were made to fill a labour slate but only ten labour candidates were put forward in Ontario, principally in Toronto and its environs and in Northern Ontario. In addition, as described above, the labour movement was divided on the question of political action. The AFL influence undercut the CLP, by advocating support for Unionist candidates. The western labour movement went forward with alternative actions. Such divisions could only have the potentiality of driving the untested labour vote back into the traditional bicultural cleavage.

The 1917 election campaign reverberated with harsh and extreme animosity between the two founding cultures. In Quebec, the few French Canadian Unionist candidates were often mobbed or sometimes threatened with lynching. The Nationalists were united behind Bourassa's view that the Unionist government was "the synthesis of all we detest, of all we despise, both in men, ideas and tendencies in both parties."[37] Wisely, Borden decided to stay out of Quebec throughout the campaign. In electoral terms, Ontario was a great threat to the Conservatives unless the issues around which labour and farmers had been organizing could be altered. The early opposition to conscription in the ranks of farmers and labour was defused by isolating the opposition to the war in Quebec. If the election could become concerned with the need to "win the war at all costs" and if the opponents of such a victory could be shown to be concentrated in Quebec, specifically among the French Canadians, then there might be some hope that Ontario would swing behind the

Table 4:2
THE 1917 ELECTION: CORRELATION OF PARTY VOTE AND ETHNICITY BY REGION
(Pearson's r)

	English	French
East		
Government	.86*	-.87*
Opposition	-.87*	.88*
West		
Government	.26*	-.15
Opposition	-.32*	.28*

* p < .05

Tories. The old division of ethnicity would be re-activated. Thus, in Ontario, a vote against a Unionist candidate was portrayed as a treason of the most insidious sort. Indeed, on election day, the *Toronto Globe and Empire* declared that "a vote for Laurier was a vote for Bourassa; a vote against the men at the front, the British connection and Empire; a vote for Germany, the Kaiser, Hindenburg, von Tirpitz and the sinking of the Lusitania."[38]

Given this context, the correlations shown in Tables 4:2 and 4:3 are hardly surprising. Table 4:2 shows that in the East the bicultural cleavage was much stronger than in either 1908 or 1911. In the West, too, the constituencies with large English populations gave more support to the Union government. However, this tendency was far less pronounced than it was in the East. Furthermore, as Table 4:3 indicates, rural support for the opposition, while seemingly intact in the East, eroded in the West.[39]

The correlations displayed in Table 4:4 show more clearly the effects of the abnormal circumstances surrounding the 1917 campaign. When the effects of ethnicity are held constant, it appears that the Liberals retained a certain measure of rural-based support in the East. However,

Table 4:3
The 1917 ELECTION: CORRELATION OF PARTY VOTE AND CONSTITUENCY TYPE BY REGION
(Pearson's r)

	Urban	Rural
East		
Government	.08	-.21*
Opposition	-.08	.21*
West		
Government	.09	.16
Opposition	-.11	-.16

* p < .05

in the West, the rural constituency that the Liberals developed in the 1911 campaign disappeared entirely. In fact, the government candidates emerged with a statistically significant rural constituency in the West in 1917 when the relationship between ethnicity and constituency type are held constant. Conversely neither the opposition nor the Conservatives appeared to have an urban constituency in 1917. The election was clearly conducted along other than rural and urban dimensions. The conscription crisis, the disenfranchisement and the demobilization of the radical labour movement guaranteed that considerations of nation would be of primary importance in stratifying the eligible voters. The cleavage based on economic rather than ethnic identity which had blossomed with the reciprocity issue in 1911 was overwhelmed by appeals to nationalism in combination with a skilfully manipulated electoral law. In the end, the pro-conscription forces gained 57% of the popular vote and 153 of the

Table 4:4

THE 1917 ELECTION: CORRELATION OF PARTY VOTE AND CONSTITUENCY TYPE CONTROLLING FOR ETHNICITY, BY REGION
(3rd order partial)**

	Urban	Rural
East		
Government	.08	-.20*
Opposition	-.13	.15*
West		
Government	.03	.27*
Opposition	-.17	.06

* $p < .05$
** controlling for English, French, German, Austro–Hungarian.

235 seats in Parliament. Only in the Maritimes did the two-party system survive this onslaught. The Unionists were predominant in Ontario and the West and virtually non-existent in the province of Quebec.[40]

However, this integrated response to crisis had certain profound, and no doubt unexpected, consequences for subsequent partisan developments. The Liberals were isolated in Quebec, seemingly confined to the bare bones of their traditional constituency and without a partisan identity elsewhere. The appearance of differences between the two parties was lost. It was readily apparent to everyone that the two bourgeois parties could act as one when threatened. In the West, a further result was that the Liberals disappeared as a distinguishable party and possible contender for support in the region, and the Conservatives had already been much discredited by the reciprocity issue in 1911.[41] All these losses of partisan distinctiveness had the effect of dislocating supporters of the bourgeois parties from their traditional attachments. The western electorate came out of the 1917 campaign with much weakened party loyalties. It had undergone a political emancipation and the old ties of party were to remain permanently weak across the West. This dislocation, in turn, provided the necessary audience and gave credibility to the criticisms increasingly developed by farmer and labour organizations. It opened the space for a new party within the electorate, a party which was to come into being in the next election, a party which found its strength with the conditions and discontents described here. It found its support among groups most affected by the National Policy and the events of the wartime election.

The Inter-Election Years

The Conservatives stayed in power, transformed into a Union government, but their re-election had not suppressed the several currents of opposition which had been mounting on all sides before the election. This opposition only grew more and more inflamed and determined as the Union government's term went on. Moreover, western labour lost all patience with the conservative elements of the TLC, as the TLC convention in Quebec City in September 1918 made apparent. Here, at one of the most divisive conferences in Canadian labour's history, the radical wing of the movement made a desperate, but ultimately unsuccessful, attempt to mobilize the TLC against the Unionist government. Resolution after resolution, condemning the National Service Act, craft unionism, the use of Asiatic labour, the loss of civil rights, and the TLC's participation on the National Registration Board, were introduced by the radicals and defeated on the convention floor. The conservative elements within the TLC rose to defeat the challenge to their influence. The president and vice-president of the TLC, both socialists and somewhat sympathetic to the grievances of the West, were voted out of office. The former was replaced by an international unionist and a personal friend of Samuel Gompers. In the end, the western unions were defeated but not subdued.[42] Initiatives were immediately taken to hold an independent Western Labour Conference as early as possible in 1919. Regional divisions around questions of ideology and tactics and strategy within the TLC were to be solved by separation.

The events of Quebec City and the promise of a breakaway syndicalist union movement in western Canada were, needless to say, a cause for great alarm for the government.[43] It was clear that a limited rapprochement of the Union government and the officers of the TLC unions had not subdued nor contained within acceptable bounds the rising current of protest generated by the registration and conscription crises, the spiralling cost of living, and national mobilization for war. Co-optation and propaganda appeals to labour's patriotic role in the war effort had failed to rally the western unions behind the cause. All of these currents of protest, both organized and latent, threatened to disrupt not only the production process, but governmental authority as well. An alternative strategy was needed and, therefore, as in the previous decade, the government prepared to mobilize the state's coercive forces to contain the western revolt.

Immediately after the 1917 election, the Union government developed a series of measures designed to gain the co-operation of labour and to avoid the type of industrial conflict which threatened the production process. These measures were at first largely symbolic and then increasingly restrictive, in the form of legislation and prosecution. The symbolic action began with the recognition, at last, that labour or its organizations should be consulted in the policy process. The failure to bring trade union leaders into the wartime council of government, particularly with reference to conscription, had offended organized labour leaders and was another reason for discontent. Therefore, after the 1917 election the Union government attempted to make amends. Gideon Robertson, a former union member and supporter of conscription, was made Minister of Labour. Shortly after, Samuel Gompers, the president of the AFL, returned to Canada to address a joint session of Parliament. Copies of his speech, which emphasized the theme that the war was "the most wonderful crusade ever entered upon by men in the whole history of the world," were sent to every union in Canada, with the compliments of the Ministry of Labour.[44] Finally, the government designed a policy to hold industrial conflict in suspension for the duration of the war. It proposed an agreement between government and labour, whereby the government would take measures to support the workers' demands for the right to organize, equal pay for women workers and the improvement of working conditions. In exchange, labour would refrain from strike action.

These efforts by the government to win labour's co-operation through co-optation and promise, however, had a limited, if not negative, impact on the industrial unions in the West. Conscription and the peculiarities of the 1917 federal election had damaged the credibility of both the government and the TLC among the western activists. The craft-based unions appeared to be working in concert with the government against the expressed positions of western labour leaders. Finally, any hope that industrial unions and western TLC affiliates would be reconciled to and co-operate in the war effort was shattered in 1918 when a vice-president of the British Columbia Federation of Labour was killed by a police bullet while attempting to avoid the draft, and the president of the same organization was jailed under charges of aiding draft evaders. The incident became a *cause célèbre*, motivating sympathy walkouts by unionists throughout western Canada.[45]

The volatility of relationships between the state and the industrial unions posed a difficult problem for the Borden government. On the one hand, any repressive action which visibly discriminated against labour and against industrial unions in particular would certainly only further politicize and, perhaps, even mobilize the dissidents against the government. Yet, on the other hand, if left unchecked, western revolt remained a looming eventuality. Thus, the government undertook to legitimize the struggle with the unions using its powers to control sedition given under the War Measures Act. In this way, ethnicity, once again, became the visible problem.

The intention of the state to mobilize its coercive mechanisms against the unions and especially the IWW was evident as early as February 1918. The Minister of Labour approached the Minister of Justice to request co-operation in the collection of evidence and the prosecution of agents of the IWW for "attempting to spread sedition and foment industrial unrest in British Columbia." However, after a "thorough and exhaustive investigation" during the spring of 1918, the Chief Commissioner of Police reported that he could find no trace of such activity by the IWW and its officers. Then, in May, Borden appointed a new commission, headed by a corporation lawyer, to locate any seditious groups which might obstruct the war effort. Specifically, the body was charged with the search for subversion carried out by aliens. Again, no evidence could be reported to suggest that "alien" associations were involved in anti-government activities. Rather, the lawyer reported that the social unrest appeared to be related to the growing belief that the Union government was failing to deal effectively with the financial, industrial and economic problems growing out of the war years and mobilization.[46]

Apparently undaunted by evidence contrary to its own analyses, the government introduced an Order-in-Council in mid-September 1918 which enlarged the scope of mandatory alien registration. It required the registration of every alien over the age of sixteen. In addition, by the end of September, the designation "enemy alien" was extended to cover Russians, Ukrainians and Finns. According to the official rationale for these policies, it was these ethnic groups which were receiving IWW literature in the mining areas of British Columbia, literature which advocated the destruction of all property rights. A rash of more discriminatory and repressive Orders-in-Council followed. Meetings in alien foreign languages were prohibited. The use and publication of material in alien foreign languages was forbidden. Fourteen associations, including the Social Democratic Party, were declared illegal. Authorities were also given the power to declare, at a later time, *any* association to be illegal. Finally, on October 11, 1918 an Order-in-Council was issued revoking the right to strike.[47]

Given the pervasive hostility toward the "enemy alien" German and Austro-Hungarian community during the war and the later development of public fears of the effects of the 1917 revolution in Russia, these actions were rationalized as part of the war effort.[48] However, the effects of these restrictive measures were not equitably distributed. Because of the concentration of alien ethnic groups in the western provinces, each of the measures effectively separated the western from the eastern trade unions and suppressed the activities of those organizations which challenged the hegemony of the TLC within the labour movement. Common practice in the West, particularly in mining areas, was to conduct union business and meetings in several languages, depending on the ethnic background of the membership. This was a way for the unions to gain access to an immigrant population which found itself isolated from the mainstream of Canadian society. However, as a result of the government's actions this practice had to be curtailed. IWW union leaders, who were in the habit of publishing their union literature and pamphlets in the languages of their membership found themselves threatened with prosecution for the possession and distribution of their material. Finally, the measures reinforced the already pervasive antagonisms toward immigrants and succeeded in maintaining ethnic divisions within the working class.[49]

Soon a letter-writing campaign was begun to the Prime Minister demanding more repressive measures, such as forced work programmes for immigrants. Returning soldiers, confronted with difficult demobilization conditions, began to demand access to jobs held by "aliens." Reports of ugly racial incidents between workers became more common. For example, in Manitoba unemployed veterans attacked "bohunks" on the street, forcing them to kneel and kiss the Union Jack.[50]

The restrictions on the right to strike, not unexpectedly, aroused the protestations of both eastern and western labour officials. However, while the new president of the TLC only issued a warning to the government and a demand that it remove "some of the obvious injustices before it was too late," unions in the West began preparations for a general strike. In Winnipeg, 92% of the union membership voted for strike action, while, in Vancouver, unionists threatened to call a general strike if the ban on alien language publications were not lifted.[51]

The Western Labour Conference convened in March 1919, under conditions of extreme polarization, and delegates clearly recognized the implications of the government's actions. Resolutions calling for the release of political prisoners, the removal of censorship of union publications, the collection of funds for members arrested for the possession of banned literature and the abolition of craft-based unionism were all passed with little opposition. In addition, and most alarming to both government and TLC, there was the decision to call a referendum among the western union membership on the question of the formation of One Big Union (OBU). Such a union was conceived of as an organizational form to maximize effect in modern industry. The OBU would group together all workers, whether skilled, unskilled, craft or service, into a single body and then use the general strike to force its demands for social reform and reorganization and to gain attention and solutions from the authorities. Referendum ballots for the OBU were soon issued, and by the end of May 1919, 188 of the 258 unions west of Port Arthur had voted in support of the idea.[52] Clearly, the government's attempts to suppress industry-based union organization had turned against itself, and, instead of industrial unions, it was now to be confronted with a single representative of all labour. A major confrontation seemed imminent.

However, the confrontation which did occur did not involve the OBU. Instead, what is now seen as one of the greatest incidents of class-based conflict and violence in Canadian history, the 1919 Winnipeg General Strike, began before the organizational efforts of the OBU were either in place or effective. It arose over locally generated issues of the right to collective bargaining. However, the "confrontation at Winnipeg" represented in the eyes of many a "rehearsal for the real revolution which was to follow."[53] Because of the intense emotions attached to this event, there was a tendency to link together as "causes" of the strike everything to which any of the actors, on either side, were opposed. Therefore, there was, within government and business discussion and opposition to the general strike, a tendency to identify it as an OBU and Bolshevik (they often used the two terms interchangeably) conspiracy.[54] The "Red Scare" that reverberated throughout the western world after the 1917 Revolution and the rash of sympathy strikes throughout western Canada and in particular in Vancouver in support of actions in Winnipeg, seemed to provide support for the conspiracy theory. However, later investigations found little evidence of OBU involvement in the Winnipeg dispute and none that it was the result of international agitation.[55] Indeed, the federal government's official investigation of the general strike, the Robson Report, dismissed the conspiracy theory. Instead, it listed the causes of the strike as the high cost of living, poor working conditions and the continued refusal of the employers and the state to recognize the right to collective bargaining.[56] In short, the OBU and the Winnipeg General Strike grew separately out of the same malaise.

Nonetheless, there seemed to be determination to use this incident as an opportunity to repress radical unionism and its consequences. This involved a large amount of military and legislative action. The resulting violence was considerable as numerous strikers were killed or injured while others were deported without trial. However, the government's actions after it had actually suppressed the strike best illustrate the existence of a longer-term objective. They intended to break the influence and position of the radical unions generally and the OBU specifically.[57] Thus, although the Robson Report dismissed the idea that the strike had seditious motivation, the government amended the Criminal Code and broadened the interpretation of sedition. As a result of the change in legislation, all but one of the strike leaders were jailed.[58] At the same time, the 1910 Immigration Act was amended so as to restrict the entry of foreign workers into British Columbia, in the hope of reducing or limiting some of the labour agitation endemic to that province.[59] Finally, in 1920, legislation was introduced into the federal Parliament requiring all workers eligible to become members of the United Mine Workers to do so. This was, in essence, legislative intervention to establish a closed shop for an international union, in an industry where the OBU had previously been strong.[60]

In the final analysis, this orchestrated attack on the western unions had an important effect. The state had overpowered the radicals' ultimate weapon, the general strike. The syndicalists were discredited. Radical unionists, if not jailed, were tainted with the hint of conspiracy, which isolated them at last from the moderate elements of the labour movement in the West and from the farmers as well. By late September 1919, the OBU membership had dwindled to fewer than 3,000.[61] The TLC immediately initiated a massive and largely successful organizational drive in the West to recoup its lost position now that an organizational vacuum seemed to exist. However, without a strong industrial union presence, the ranks of the trade union movement immediately began to shrink from 374,000 in 1920 to 313,000 in 1921 to 277,000 in 1922.[62] The crisis of the postwar period had been resolved in a way that strengthened the position of the craft-based unions again and disorganized, in the process, those institutions which offered to workers another, an alternative, interpretation of Canadian conditions in the post-World War I period.

The 1921 Election

The triumph of the TLC over the OBU and radical unionism did not change the hostility of the labour movement toward the Unionist administration. The registration and conscription legislation, wartime shortages and inflation, postwar recession and massive unemployment resulting from the demobilization of thousands of soldiers, all convinced organized labour of the necessity of independent political action. However, because of the disorganizational effects of the campaign against western unions, provincial variations in ideology and coalition potential with the increasingly active farmers' groups, a national labour party was still unrealized on the eve of the 1921 election.[63] As a result of wide variations in provincial conditions, history and practice, a potpourri of provincially-specific labour parties such as the Ontario section of the Canadian Labour Party, the Federated Labour Party of British Columbia, the Independent Labour Parties of Saskatchewan, Manitoba and Alberta all existed at the time of the 1921 election. They were not ready to coalesce into a nation-wide political entity and this unco-ordinated and disjointed movement produced only twenty-seven labour candidates in 1921.[64]

The socialist parties were also incapable of organizing a national partisan alternative for 1921. Although they had been extremely active in the TLC, by the end of the war, there was a fundamental rift between them and the union movement. The socialist parties had been invigorated and encouraged to become active in the trade union struggle by two developments within the international socialist movement. The first was the success of the 1917 revolution in Russia, and the second was the adoption of a socialist programme by the British Labour Party. However, these two events also carried the seeds of division for the Canadian socialist movement. As in the previous decade, it was split into factions over the question of appropriate political action in the Canadian milieu. Drawing from the example of Britain, the leadership of the Social Democratic Party (SDP) and other moderate elements favoured a coalition with the labour unions. They argued that it was possible for "one strong working class party to embrace trade unionists, socialists, co-operators, Fabians and farmers."[65] Conversely, those within the SDP and the Socialist Party of North America (SPNA) committed to the Bolshevik strategy, vehemently opposed any coalition which would compromise the struggle to abolish the capitalist system. The fear was that an alignment with the trade unions, concerned as they were with wresting benefits for their members from the capitalist system, would lead to a weakening of the revolutionary thrust of the socialists. Between the two strategies there was little common ground.

Thus, a period which began on a crest of militancy and radicalism in the labour movement, unprecedented before that time, ended with a splintering of the movement into radical and reformist elements.[66] In consequence, the SDP and the SPNA emerged from the wartime restrictions against their activities only to disband. The remaining Socialist Party of Canada was significantly reduced in influence and numbers.

In the final analysis, however, public attitudes rather than internal fractional struggle were a greater barrier to a viable socialist electoral presence. The socialists, like the OBU, were the casualties of the government's efforts to restrain what it saw as challenges to its authority and the economy from an organized Left. The SDP, after suggesting the possibility of a grand coalition of dissident positions, had been declared illegal by Order-in-Council in 1918. This event, coupled with the continuous reports of the trouble in the post-revolutionary Soviet Union, turned many of the potential voters after the war away from a position which challenged the right to the accumulation of private property. By and large, popular opinion, as supported by the dominant ideology, excluded the socialist parties as a viable alternative. Instead, they faced suspicion and hostility. Thus, the labour movement faced the 1921 election in a weaker condition than in 1917. This dearth of viable mechanisms to mobilize discontent meant that no new or consistent "re-definition of the political" emerged. There was little organized opposition from a divided and weakened labour movement, whether acting in the economic sphere as trade unions or politically as an organized party. The bicultural cleavage remained the major dividing line between parties, except in those areas where farmers organized their class-based electoral activity. The farmers and their organizations were strong, and 1921 was their election. Their party was the Progressive Party of Canada, essentially a farmers' movement with minor labour support tacked on. It won seats and broke forever both the two-party system and the hegemonic definition of the political which described electoral politics as referenda on cultural relations.

The farmers' decision to organize was not taken easily and, in fact, was resisted for some time, by the leadership which had ideological and pragmatic reservations about forming a farmers' political party.[67] Indeed, the leadership of the farm organizations tried repeatedly to escape the formation of an alternative party, preferring rather to secure concessions from the bourgeois parties.[68] After 1917, however, the Liberals failed to demonstrate responsiveness to the aspirations of western farm organizations, neither electing the pro-reciprocity candidate, W. S. Fielding, as leader nor making any significant concessions on the tariff issue. The actions of both the Liberals and the Union government dashed any hopes of the leadership of the Canadian Council of Agriculture (CCA) that their demands would be accommodated within the existing party system.[69] Thereafter, the movement for an independent party spread rapidly. At the head of the movement was the *Grain Growers' Guide*, the official publication of the farmers' organizations, which kept "whooping it up for independent action."[70]

The impressive victories of farmers' candidates in federal by-elections and provincial elections in Alberta and Ontario only intensified the rank and file's eagerness to launch a farmers' party for the forthcoming 1921 federal election. This party unfolded its banner officially in February 1920 when T. A Crerar, a former Unionist cabinet minister, and ten other farmer MPs formed the National Progressive Party. The best-known analyst of the Progressives offers this description of the process which led to the emergence of a third party in the federal party system:

> The creation of the Progressive party was complete [by 1921]. It had been forced from below by the spontaneous action of the rank and file of the members of the organized farmers in Ontario, Alberta, Manitoba, and indeed throughout the movement. Resentment of the

victory of the eastern wing of the Liberal party in the convention of 1919 and the growing unpopularity of the Union Government and of its successor the Meighen administration, had contributed to the demand for independent political action. The action of the agrarian leaders in the Council of Agriculture and in the associations in respond-ing to the pressure from below had been slow and hesitant. They had in the majority preferred to try to influence the policies of the existing parties rather than to embark on political action. The failure of the old parties to frame platforms and find leaders acceptable to the aroused farmers had forced their hand. By the end of 1920 the agrarian leaders were committed to leading in the attack on the tariff and the party system forces which they had been unable to control.[71]

Organizational sponsorship was crucial because, as we shall see in the next chapter, the withdrawal of this support contributed, in no small way, to the Progressives' rapid demise during the twenties. However, the farmers' organizational resources were largely concentrated in the Prairie Provinces and Ontario. Although the United Farmers had established branches in all provinces in the period 1917-1920, eastern branches had not secured the grass-roots support that characterized the West.[72]

Hence, on the eve of the 1921 election, the scenario for a sectional class party had been set. During the campaign, the farmers provided a thoroughgoing critique of the effects of the National Policy. The focus of this critique was, irrevocably, the tariff. The tariff had emerged as the key for the Canadian bourgeoisie, which was transforming itself from a commercially-oriented group to one intricately involved in corporate capitalism. Industry, not trade and the railways, was now the basis of their strength, and the tariff was the means of creating and maintaining it. Once again, as these words of Prime Minister Meighen, the leader of the defensive attack on the Progressives, show, it was to be packaged in terms of the national interest. Therefore he told the farmers of Ontario:

> Surely if we have learned anything from the days of the sixties to the days of the twenties, we have learned that, situated as we are on this continent, the young beside the old, the small beside the big, the scattered beside the colossal, the Canadian beside the American, *we must guard the industrial structure and integrity of our country*, and there is only one way to do it.
> It can be done by a tariff system and it cannot be done without a tariff system—a tariff system made by the Canadian people for the Canadian people, made on a clear, sound and impregnable principle, and that system must not rest on the insecure foundation of arrange-ments with the United States.[73]

For him, the crucial fact was that the electors of Canada must learn to recognize the enemy. Who was this enemy? It was not the Liberal Party, which would not challenge the National Policy. It was the Progressives:

> The real challenge comes from another quarter. A new party has arisen in this country. It took its birth in Western Canada. There it flourished

and there it has its stronghold still. By adroit organization, by special periodicals, and by propaganda, by class appeal, misinformation has been scattered, prejudice has been imbedded, and the harvest is a political party whose set purpose is to reverse the fiscal policy of this country.[74]

In this way, the battle lines were drawn between petit bourgeois farmer and industrialist. The full strength of the opposition was raised against the farmers; the appeals to national loyalty were made.

The new leader of the Liberal Party, Mackenzie King, also criticized the Progressives' attempt to introduce a class-based analysis into the federal partisan debate. In his view, during the campaign:

To support the Government of today is to endorse reaction; to experiment with class in matters of government is to invite the unknown. The Liberal Party . . . offers a means of escape from both extremes, neither of which is in the national interest.[75]

Throughout the 1921 campaign, the Liberals could chart the middle course. They could count on the support of the Montreal-based bourgeoisie and the electoral support of nationalist Quebec and thus, made only a few concessions to the class-conscious independent commodity producers in the West.[76] They would rely on a bicultural cleavage in two ways. The first was to simply recall to Quebec memories the part that Conservatives and, in particular, their new leader, Arthur Meighen, had played in the conscription crisis. The second was to offer to reduce the imperial connection, a policy which was also of interest to the corporate elite.[77]

The statistics of Tables 4:5 and 4:6 demonstrate that in 1921 the two bourgeois parties were able to maintain the bicultural cleavage in the East while the Progressives introduced a class cleavage in the West. In the East, once again, as Table 4:5 indicates, the Conservative vote increased with the proportion of English in the constituency. The same was found for the relationship between the Liberal vote and the French population. In the West, as well, British constituencies disproportionately supported Conservative Party candidates. However, the Liberal party was not disproportionately supported in constituencies with large non-charter group representation as had been the case earlier. These groups had been forced to be passive bystanders in the previous election, and 1921 provided their first opportunity to register their anger and electoral rejection of the two bourgeois parties. The correlation coefficients suggest that constituencies with large non-charter group populations supported the new third party alternative, the Progressives.[78]

Nevertheless, the real story of the 1921 election can be seen in Table 4:6. In the East, an urban-rural cleavage did not develop.[79] In the West, however, the statistics show a cleavage between the urban and rural constituencies' support for the Progressives which is strong and deep.

Table 4:5
THE 1921 ELECTION: CORRELATION OF PARTY VOTE AND ETHNICITY BY REGION
(Pearson's r)

	English	French	German Austro-Hungarian
East			
Conservative	.69*	−.66*	.03
Liberal	−.77*	.78*	−.17*
Progressive	.32*	−.37*	.22*
West			
Conservative	.52*	−.33*	−.65*
Liberal	−.10	.06	−.03
Progressive	−.17	.04	.22*

* p < .05

Table 4:6
THE 1921 ELECTION: CORRELATION OF PARTY VOTE AND CONSTITUENCY TYPE BY REGION
(Pearson's r)

	Urban	Rural
East		
Conservative	−.04	−.03
Liberal	−.02	.13*
Progressive	−.17	.05
West		
Conservative	.32*	−.32*
Liberal	.17	−.24
Progressive	−.70*	.52*

* p < .05

Table 4:7
THE 1921 ELECTION: CORRELATION OF PARTY VOTE AND CONSTITUENCY TYPE CONTROLLING FOR ETHNICITY BY REGION
(3rd order partial)**

	Urban	Rural
East		
Conservative	−.01	−.01
Liberal	.13*	−.04
Progressive	−.24*	.17*
West		
Conservative	.19	−.20
Liberal	.19	−.30*
Progressive	−.71*	.51*

* p < .05
** controlling for English, French, German, Austro-Hungarian.

These constituencies rejected outright the eastern-based parties and mobilized behind their own party. In the end, the Conservatives won no seats in Manitoba, Saskatchewan or Alberta, and the Liberals held only two seats. The Progressive Party of Canada had managed to capture twenty-four seats in Ontario and thirty-nine seats in the western provinces from the two bourgeois parties that had dominated elections since Confederation.

The data displayed in Table 4:7 only reinforce the conclusions gleaned from Tables 4:5 and 4:6. With the effects of ethnic voting controlled, the Progressives emerge in the East and much more strongly in the West as an agrarian party. Unlike 1917, there is no indication that the Conservatives appealed disproportionately to a rural or urban constituency in either the East or the West. The Liberal Party also failed to regain its traditional appeal in both regions. Unlike previous elections, the Liberals no longer benefit especially from rural support in the East while in the West they were markedly unappealing in rural constituencies.

The legacy of 1917 was the emergence of a federal party which spoke to the interests of the farmers and which brought severe dislocations to the federal party system of the West. The tenuous ethnic cleavage seen in 1908 competed with a rural-urban cleavage in 1911. Moreover, in both years, party support, whether structured along ethnic or class considerations, was divided between the two bourgeois parties. After 1921 the predominant cleavage in the West was structured along class lines, and, in addition, the rural vote was firmly beyond the grasp of the two major parties.

This election represents both a vast migration of independent commodity producers from the hegemonic definition of politics and a realignment of electoral forces in the West. The two bourgeois parties would be unable to fully re-establish the politics of ethnicity in federal elections. The Progressives had created a space for the debate of class issues among the western electorate, a space which the Liberals and Conservatives would, thereafter, have to take into account. The Progressives succeeded because they were ready to take advantage of a two-party system discredited by the Unionist adventure. The voters dislocated from previous and traditional partisanship and those who had been the victims of disenfranchisement and other anti-ethnic attacks during the war were available for mobilization. Over several elections, these voters had lost any hope that one of the bourgeois parties would reform itself and abandon the National Policy of economic development, the costs of which they paid. The Progressives could take advantage of these conditions because they were ready with well-developed and self-conscious organization to move into the gap in the electorate left by the virtual absorption, in 1917, of the Liberals and Conservatives into a single party.

However, as we shall see in the next chapter, the farmers were unable to reproduce the Progressives' victories of 1921. The success of the farmers' party proved short-lived because these voters occupied an ambiguous class position. As petit bourgeois they could not stop or turn around advancing capitalism. They were principally concerned with improving the independent commodity producers' condition within the prevailing system of class relations, and they could never be sufficiently strong to mount a national challenge against the two major parties. The Progressive experience was also short-lived because the obvious strategy of an alliance with western workers, which did develop later in Parliament in the form of the "Ginger Group," did not materialize in the electorate.[80] Both the farmers' distrust of workers and the divisions within the labour movement blocked the growth of a class analysis which would indelibly alter the vocabulary of Canadian federal politics. Because of the fundamental acceptance of capitalism by many farmers and without a new class vocabulary, the Progressives proved vulnerable to assimilation into the bourgeois parties, specifically the Liberal Party, after concessions on tariff and freight-rates were offered to the farmers.

Largely because of their rapid demise, the Progressives have been viewed as an episodic and sectional deviation from the two-party system. While, on the surface, this is an accurate observation, they nonetheless left two distinct legacies in the West that are conspicuously absent in the East. First, they represent a significant departure from the prevailing definition of federal politics because they challenged the cultural definition of politics. This is not to say that elections were never fought on economic issues before the Progressives appeared. Clearly, as previous chapters show, they were. However, the Progressives challenged the central thread running through both bourgeois parties' economic analysis, namely the National Policy. Unlike the two old parties who maintained that industrialization was in the "national interest," the Progressives and the farmers' organizations backing the party argued that this version of the "national interest" was a myth. They drew into the electoral sphere a striking indictment of Canadian industrial capitalism that was conspicuously absent from electoral rhetoric in the East. Specifically, they identified the eastern capitalists and their parties as the beneficiaries of the protective tariff. In short, the Progressives offered the western electorate a re-definition of the political and fostered a realization that western economic grievances could find a voice in the party system only by mobilizing a third party. Finally, the electoral success of the Progressives produced a certain sense of "efficacy" among western farm organizations, a feeling that the bourgeois parties could be beaten at their own game. The Progressives thus kept open a support market of voters available to a new political formation when the capitalist system collapsed in the thirties. The Progressive Party of Canada would all but disappear by 1926, but its legacy would endure as an integral component of Canadian politics.

NOTES

[1]"The most direct cause of the depression of 1913 was the latest in a series of power struggles centred in the Balkans. The wars of 1912 and 1913 channelled the heavy flow of British investment capital away from Canada and the millions of pounds of sterling which had financed railways, towns, industries, and grain elevators were converted into machines of war." See David J. Bercuson, *Confrontation at Winnipeg: Labour, Industrial Relations and The General Strike* (Montreal: McGill-Queen's, 1974), p. 22.

[2]Roger Graham, "Through the First World War," in J. M. S. Careless and R. Craig Brown, eds., *The Canadians: 1867–1967* (Toronto: Macmillan, 1967), p. 173.

[3]See Barbara Wilson, ed., *Ontario and the First World War* (Toronto: University of Toronto, 1977), p. xxi.

The unemployment problem was not resolved until mid-1915. Thus, in the interim period, recruitment to the armed forces was much enhanced by 'hunger-scription,' that is, the jobless joined the army to gain a pay-cheque. See A. Ross McCormack, *Reformers, Rebels and Revolutionaries* (Toronto: University of Toronto, 1977), pp. 121.

[4]Canada was a major producer of both light and heavy munitions during the First World War. In fact, one-third of her industrial capacity and a labour force of approximately three hundred thousand were absorbed in war production, turning out munitions to the value of over $10 billion. See Edgar McInnis, *Canada: A Political and Social History* (Toronto: Holt, Rinehart and Winston, 1969), p. 489.

However, this industrial development was concentrated in central Canada. Western cities such as Winnipeg, for example, were "not important to the nation's war production. . . . The city, the third largest in the Dominion, actually placed thirtieth among all Canadian localities in the output of war materials, although its total was second for areas west of Thunder Bay. Western Canada was at a serious disadvantage in comparison with Ontario and Quebec since its industrial capacity was lower and it produced shells at higher cost due to the greater shipping distance." Bercuson, *op. cit.*, p. 35.

[5]D. Postgate and K. McRoberts, *Quebec: Social Change and Political Crisis* (Toronto: McClelland and Stewart, 1976), p. 27.

[6]Bercuson, *op. cit.*, pp. 25-26; Graham, *op. cit.*, p. 193.

[7]There was a shift in the balance of exports, away from agricultural products to the new staples of pulp and paper and minerals. However, wheat remained a crucial export into the 1930s. The class composition of the country also changed radically. Control of industrial enterprises began to shift to those capitalists who could, at one and the same time, manipulate the financial and commercial markets and participate in manufacturing production. In these years, "the effect of the merger movement and organization of production through corporate capitalism was for increasing participation by the dominant Canadian commercial interests in manufacturing but at the ownership and control level through consolidation, and not in entrepreneurial activity." See Wallace Clement, *The Canadian Corporate Elite* (Toronto: McClelland and Stewart, 1975), pp. 79-81 and especially p. 75.

[8]In Ontario, where industry exerted its greatest pull, rural depopulation was most pronounced and most resented. The 1919 provincial election platform of the United Farmers of Ontario (UFO) placed it first among the reasons for the farmers entering politics. See W. L. Morton, *The Progressive Party in Canada* (Toronto: University of Toronto, 1950), pp. 72-75.

9Graham, op. cit., p. 193.

10Ibid., p. 122.

11Martin Robin, Radical Politics and Canadian Labour (Kingston: Industrial Relations Centre, 1968), p. 158.

12McCormack, op. cit., p. 123; John Crispo, The Canadian Industrial Relations System (Toronto: McGraw-Hill Ryerson, 1978), p. 164.

13Bercuson, op. cit., p. 57; McCormack, op. cit., p. 123.

14McCormack, op. cit., p. 118.

15For a detailed discussion of the trade unions' activities during WWI see Robin, op. cit., especially Chapters VIII-XII. See also McCormack, op. cit., pp. 118-136.

16McCormack, op. cit., pp. 120-123.

17"As early as January 1917 the TLC had expressed the fear that industrial conscription might be introduced. Although seldom given priority in public discussions, this ghost continued to haunt labour's consideration of military conscription. . . . If military conscription were put into effect, they believed industrial conscription would follow and workers would lose the right to strike. Labour, therefore, thought conscription of manpower for military purposes was connected with and would lead to conscription of manpower for industry." See Bercuson, op. cit., p. 41.

18Robin, op. cit., Chapter X; McCormack, op. cit., p. 132.

19Robin, op. cit., p. 135.

20"The labour movement's truculence in the summer of 1917 alarmed the federal government. Borden and his colleagues, who were coming under increasing pressure because of the workers' militancy, were anxious to improve the situation for which they were in part responsible. . . . Despite their concern, then, Borden and his colleagues were unable to quiet the workers' protests, and by the end of summer Bennett, Director-General of the National Service Board, admitted that the situation in the West was 'more or less acute'." See McCormack, op. cit., p. 130.

21Morton, op. cit., p. 40.

22After the sinking of the Lusitania in 1915, German Canadians were increasingly subject to discrimination, in both the public and private spheres. In Ontario, for example, they were detained for the slightest of provocations while Toronto civic employees of German origin were dismissed and street names with German associations were changed. See Wilson, op. cit., p. lxxi.

23Morton, op. cit., pp. 57-58.

24Ibid., p. 44.

25In the initial call for volunteers for the armed forces, men born in the British Isles living in Canada showed the greatest eagerness to join. Even as late as October 1917, this group represented just under one-half of the Canadian volunteer force. See McInnis, op. cit., p. 486.

26"When the Liberal leader issued his election manifesto, which contained several planks sympathetic to trade unionists, labour acceptance of the proffered help was assured. Fred Dixon told Laurier, 'your opposition to Conscription has encouraged many radicals who had begun to fear that democracy was doomed in Canada'." See McCormack, op. cit., p. 133.

27Morton, op. cit., p. 58.

28That the workers of Russia could, through united action, overthrow the Czar, was greeted with enthusiasm in Canada not only by Ukrainian socialists, but also leaders of the IWW and socialists in general. Western radicals took measures to forge new labour parties during 1918 and to further radicalize the rank and file. However, their efforts met considerable resistance. Strikers were denounced as unpatriotic, criminals or traitors by the press and business and the IWW was infiltrated by government law-enforcement officers. See McCormack, *op. cit.*, pp. 143-157; Bercuson, *op. cit.*, p. 43.

[29]J. M. Beck, *Pendulum of Power* (Scarborough, Ontario: Prentice-Hall, 1968), p. 139.

[30]McCormack, *op. cit.*, p. 131.

[31]*Statutes of Canada*, 1917, 7-8 George V, Chapter 39. The War Time Elections Act was given royal assent in September, 1917; Henry Ferns and Bernard Ostry, *The Age of Mackenzie King* (Toronto: Lorimer, 1976), p. 231.

[32]The government's rationalization that the enfranchisement of some women merely substituted votes for those soldiers unable to vote at the front was hardly supportable in so much as the voting period for the military extended over a twenty-seven day period. See Beck, *op. cit.*, p. 139.

[33]Ferns and Ostry, *op. cit.*, p. 231.

[34]As quoted in Beck, *op. cit.*, p. 138.

[35]Ferns and Ostry, *op. cit.*, p. 231.

[36]Both Skelton and Graham are certain that the Act propelled the conscriptionist Liberals into a coalition. Despite Laurier's rejection of Borden's advances, negotiations with other Liberals had continued for four months, unfolding slowly "like a great crowded swirling ballet (as) various Liberals boldly approached and coyly retreated, until finally some of them joined their hands to [Borden's]." Beck, *op. cit.*, pp. 139-140.

[37]As quoted in Beck, *op. cit.*, p. 142.

[38]As quoted in *ibid.*, p. 143.

[39]When Ontario is not included in the analysis of the eastern constituencies, the urban-rural distinction between the Conservatives and the Liberals largely disappears. The rural correlation for Liberal Party support is reduced to .15 and is not significant at $p < .05$

[40]The government elected only three candidates in Quebec and achieved only 24% of that province's popular vote. Beck, *op. cit.*, p. 148.

[41]Morton, *op. cit.*, p. 60.

[42]See McCormack, *op. cit.*, pp. 131-132; Robin, *op. cit.*, pp. 131-3.

[43]This split within the trade union movement occurred at a time of rapidly increasing union membership which grew from 205,000 in 1917 to 249,000 in 1918 and 374,000 in 1919. Crispo, *op. cit.*, p. 165.

[44]Gompers was requested to return to Canada after he had campaigned against CLP candidates in 1917. This was the first time in Canadian history that a labour leader addressed Parliament. C. D. Robertson, Minister of Labour, suggested at the time that the Privy Council's invitation to Gompers would have "a pleasing effect on organized labour in Canada and indeed be popular in the public mind generally." Borden agreed that "under the circumstances it is fitting that Parliament should give distinctive recognition to Mr. Gompers' high purpose and of his patriotic service in the cause of the allied nations." As quoted in Robin, *op. cit.*, p. 139.

[45]*Ibid.*, p. 152.

[46]*Ibid.*, p. 165.

[47]*Ibid.*, pp. 165-167.

[48]"An irrational anti-socialist hysteria seemed to have gripped the Federal Cabinet when in April 1919 it despatched an urgent telegram to Borden in Versailles, asking him to get the British to station a cruiser off Vancouver as a 'steadying influence' against 'socialism' and 'Bolshevism' which were rampant in Vancouver, Calgary and Winnipeg." N. Penner, *The Canadian Left* (Scarborough, Ontario: Prentice-Hall, 1977), p. 70.

[49]*Ibid.*, p. 166.

[50]T. Peterson, "Ethnic and Class Politics in Manitoba," in Martin Robin, ed., *Canadian Provincial Politics* (Scarborough, Ontario: Prentice-Hall, 1972), p. 80; Bercuson, *op. cit.*, p. 86 ff.

[51]Robin, *op. cit.*, p. 168.

[52]*Ibid.*, p. 179; Bercuson, *op. cit.*, p. 97.

[53]In Vancouver, sixteen thousand workers walked off their jobs in sympathy for the Winnipeg strikers and remained out for thirty days. See Walter Young, *Democracy and Discontent* (Toronto: McGraw-Hill Ryerson, 1969), p. 51.

[54]"The Citizens' Committee of 1,000 was created by businessmen and other anti-strike people in Winnipeg. It focussed its attack on the OBU and developed a definition of the Winnipeg Strike as primarily about the influence and position of the OBU rather than the issue of collective bargaining or organization of industrial unions."

"The Committee of 1,000 was instrumental in pushing the issue of alien participation in the strike to the fore, in an effort to tie Winnipeg to a world Bolshevik conspiracy and to arouse . . . popular prejudice. . . ." See Bercuson, *op. cit.*, pp. 123, 135.

[55]The strike was in progress before the OBU had its founding meeting, and while socialists were active in both events, no members of the Winnipeg General Strike Committee attended the inaugural convention of the OBU. See Penner, *op. cit.*, p. 53.

[56]See Young, *op. cit.*, p. 31; Bercuson, *op. cit.*, p. 137.

[57]The Minister of the Interior and the Minister of Labour were at least as interested in preserving the status quo in labour management relations as they were in countering a revolution. They wanted to nip the One Big Union movement in the bud, shore up the position of the international unions and ensure the survival of craft unionism. They were willing to see the strike end peacefully as long as there was no recognition of the Metal Trades Council, but if this could not be accomplished the strike must be decisively crushed. Bercuson, *op. cit.*, p. 185.

[58]Robin, *op. cit.*, p. 32.

[59]This provision also was extended to restrict the entry of enemy aliens or immigrants who had been enemy aliens during the war. See Warren Kalbach, *The Impact of Immigration on Canada's Population* (Ottawa: Census Monograph, 1970), p. 15.

[60]Robin, *op. cit.*, p. 191.

[61]*Ibid.*, p. 189.

[62]Crispo, *op. cit.*, p. 164.

[63]Movement toward a national labour party was also hindered by provincial variations in class relations. Although farmer-labour candidates managed to poll 32% of the popular vote in the Nova Scotia provincial election of 1920, in

the Maritimes in general, organizations of farmers and workers were too weak to challenge federal Liberals and Conservatives. Quebec labour was less restless than in some provinces because the Laurier Liberals, by opposing conscription, maintained their position. Great strides were made in Ontario in 1919, when a coalition of the Independent Labour Party and the United Farmers of Ontario captured the provincial government. Alberta labour too recognized the electoral advantages of coalition and co-operated with the United Farmers of Alberta in federal by-elections and the 1921 provincial election. In contrast, where farm organizations were embittered and frightened by the Winnipeg General Strike, there was no coalition between the two subordinate classes of Manitoba. In British Columbia farm organizations were too weak to have any appreciable effect on the electoral activity of labour. See Robin, *op. cit.*, pp. 199-206.

[64]Penner, *op. cit.*, p. 68; Beck, *op. cit.*, p. 160.

[65]Penner, *op. cit.*, p. 63.

[66]*Ibid.*, p. 68.

[67]This resistance was principally in the Albertan wing of the Canadian Council of Agriculture, the United Farmers of Alberta. On the one hand, political mobilization stood as a direct contradiction to the organization's professed belief that the party system was inherently decadent and hence, capable of corrupting even the best-intentioned farmers' party. This ideology of non-partisanship reflected strains of both the American Non-Partisan Movement and guild socialism. Resistance also stemmed from practical observations of the experiences of the American populist experiment of the 1890s. In particular Wise Wood, the UFA leader, was convinced that the creation of a third party of organized farmers would lead to the defeat and destruction of the farmers' organizations themselves. See Morton, *op. cit.*, p. 89.

[68]Initially, the farm organizations both sought accommodation and were courted by the Liberal Party. After the 1917 election, the Canadian Council of Agriculture continued to revise and reissue the "Farmers' Platform" which repudiated the National Policy and called for substantial reductions in the tariff. Its leadership hoped to convert the Liberal Party to its point of view. The Liberals, in turn, attempted to draw the disenchanted farmers back into their fold and specifically invited the CCA to send a delegation to the 1919 Liberal leadership convention to help choose a successor to Laurier. The CCA did not choose to send any delegates but rather sent their "Farmers' Platform" and specified that its adoption by the convention was a precondition for its support of the Liberal Party. Beck, *op. cit.*, p. 105; Morton, *op. cit.*, p. 80-82.

[69]The farmers failed twice to gain tariff reductions from the bourgeois parties in 1919. In June 1919, T. A. Crerar and nine other western Unionists withdrew their support from the Union Government because it refused to respond to the farmers' demands. Beck, *op. cit.*, p. 151.

[70]*Ibid.*, p. 150.

[71]Morton, *op. cit.*, p. 106.

[72]*Ibid.*, p. 103.

[73]Quoted from a campaign speech given in London, Ontario in 1921, *ibid.*, pp. 113-114. Emphasis added.

[74]*Ibid.*, p. 114.

[75]*Ibid.*, p. 122.

[76]Bourassa observed in 1921 that the difference between the two major parties in

the tariff question was that Meighen wanted a tariff for protection that would also provide revenue, and King wanted a tariff for revenue that would also supply protection. Beck, *op. cit.,* p. 153.

[77]Graham suggests that in Quebec in 1921 there was a "kind of Meighen phobia" which gripped the people and made them anathematize him more bitterly than any public man since Confederation. Moreover, as Rumilly recounts, voters in the Quebec ridings were told that in the event of a Conservative victory, Orangemen would "pilfer the consecrated wafers in the churches and feed them to the pigs which they lead in the streets on July 12th. And the author of this sacrilege is Meighen, the father of conscription, the anti-Christ." As quoted in *ibid.,* p. 155; see also Penner, *op. cit.,* p. 22.

[78]There were reasons for the non-charter groups and the disenfranchised to support the Progressives in 1921. First, many were farmers. Indeed, as late as 1931, the Official Census of Canada (Vol. VIII, *Agriculture*) noted that 35.9%, 43.0% and 49.4% of the farm operators on occupied farms of Manitoba, Saskatchewan and Alberta, respectively were of non-charter group origin. Furthermore, the Grain Growers published their Guide in German from 1908 until 1918 when they were forced by federal legislation to discontinue the practice. Finally the Farmers' Platforms, specifically, protested the disenfranchisement of this group.

[79]When Quebec constituencies are not included in the analysis of eastern constituencies, the correlation between rural constituencies and the Progressive vote is .24 $p < .05$.

[80]See Morton, *op. cit.,* pp. 221-224, for an account of the "Ginger Group."

Chapter 5

The 1920s—The Pursuit of "Normal Politics"

Introduction

This decade was caught between two great events which struck at the very heart of western capitalism—the First World War and the Depression. In contrast to these shattering international events, the twenties appear to be marked by economic recovery and political calm. Although the decade began in recession, the economy recovered, only to collapse along with international capitalism at the decade's end. In these years of recovery and calm there were fundamental changes in the economy and class structure which represent the culmination of forces which have been described in previous chapters. These changes were essential components of the recovery from postwar recession, and it was during the twenties that the shape of the modernized economy became clear. The project of Confederation had succeeded to the extent that Canada was more industrialized and seemed better able to compete in world markets. But long-term costs and structural effects of the project were still to be realized. The decade would witness the increasing importance of manufacturing, particularly in Quebec and Ontario; the reduction, but not yet the elimination, of the wheat economy as the motor for development; the gradual replacement of wheat by new staples which contributed to the rapid growth of the industrial labour-force and considerable adjustment, in reaction to political pressure from the West, to the instruments of the National Policy, adjustments which de-industrialized the Maritimes.

Although set in motion by the war, the economy moved from an agricultural to an industrial foundation during the twenties. The manufacturing sector expanded, and there was a shift away from the wheat economy toward mineral extraction, production of hydro-electric power and pulp, as well as industrialization resulting from some processing of these materials. All of these factors encouraged profound changes in the social formation and in the distribution of electoral and political power. The geographical determinants of Confederation shifted to the centres of mineral extraction and hydro-electric production—to the barren and rocky Canadian Shield in Quebec and Ontario. These two provinces joined British Columbia as the new locations of production for export.

The new staples required a very different form of economic organization. Export production was no longer organized by hundreds of thousands of independent commodity producers, but rather by corporations with financial resources large enough to undertake massive construction projects. Resource-extraction industry required greater numbers of wage labourers. The mine, the pulp mill and the power project began to replace the Prairie farm as the motors for economic growth. This new staple production was often organized by already prospering American-based corporations, and, during the decade, they came to control much of industrial production, not only for the domestic market, but also for export to world markets.

The complexion of the Canadian bourgeoisie also changed dramatically during these years. It became increasingly corporate, less commercially-oriented and more dependent on manufacturing enterprises which had direct links to the growing American industrial empire. The influence of the agricultural producer was in decline in the economy as a whole while the other subordinate class, the workers, grew in numbers. It was the workers' political organization and activity which would be increasingly and carefully monitored. In the meantime, the central provinces retained, if not enhanced, their commanding position as their domination within Confederation became almost self-maintaining. Economic development was less dependent on the most gross and most obvious mechanisms of stimulation used earlier, such as the discriminatory freight-rates. The centre could now be developed and sustained without resort to blatant political intervention, and dissent from the western provinces could be accommodated somewhat, because their actions no longer fundamentally threatened the direction of national development.

In the electoral sphere the federal parties attempted to re-establish the "normal politics" which had sustained them in power before the 1921 debacle, and, for a few years, their efforts appeared to be rewarded. The Liberals succeeded in defusing the Progressives' challenge in Parliament, but any hopes that the politics of class had been dislodged from the federal sphere were short-lived. By the decade's end, another organized class opposition threatened on the horizon. However, the decade, by and large, was marked by political calm. After an unpredictably successful rendezvous with federal politics in 1921, the farmers' movement turned its attention to provincial politics where it remained until the late twenties. Elements of this movement would return to federal politics a few years later, even more radicalized and committed to the idea of a united class-based opposition than it had been in 1921. A similar fluidity characterized the political activities of the socialists and the labour movement. The socialist movement fractured into social democratic and communist factions, never again to reunite in a political party. At the same time, the TLC, after reviving its national labour party in 1921, disavowed its legitimacy as the decade drew to a close, not to return to federal politics for thirty years.

The 1920s, thus, represent a time of both reinstatement and fundamental change. It was a time when the old and the new struggled for ascendancy, to prepare and consolidate Canada's new place in the international economy. This struggle between the new and the old was also acted out in the federal party system. The two major parties attempted, largely successfully, to quiet the farmers' revolt and re-establish the "normal politics" of earlier years. The class-based analysis of the Progressive Party which challenged the hegemonic definition of national development, would be, gradually but surely, overwhelmed by partisan debate about corruption, constitutional crisis and minimal tariff adjustments. It is, perhaps, because there were so few reverberations of the controversies of the previous decade that the twenties are passed down to us as uneventful years in Canadian politics. However, in many respects, they constitute a watershed in our partisan history. The legacy of this decade can hardly be overestimated, for, during these years, the federal parties learned to cope with organized class opposition from the West without disturbing the more stable ethnic alignments in the East. This chapter examines how the economic, political and ideological adjustments unfolded and set the stage for the definition and practice of federal politics in the next decade and in many more to follow.

The Political Economy of the Twenties

Canada tumbled into the twenties with accelerated eastern industrialization and urbanization inflating the costs of essential goods and services. The war boom had strained domestic supply, and prices for basic commodities spiralled beyond comfortable or even competitive levels. As we have seen in the previous chapter, inflation aggravated discontent in the immediate postwar period, but it also promised unwelcome long-term consequences. Canada was pricing itself out of the world market at precisely the same time that the demand for wheat to feed the allied armies and replace supplies previously acquired from Russia was abating. International conditions had changed in the postwar world, and Canada had to adjust to the new economic order.

Recognizing the negative consequences of an inflated economy, the federal government took steps to force the economy to correct itself. The mechanism was deflation, which required the government to withdraw from its wartime intervention in the economy and the banks to retard growth by limiting credit and escalating interest rates. The federal government abolished the Wheat Board which had guaranteed farmers high prices for wheat, and the banks, by tightening credit, brought "the whole hurtling trade cycle to a grinding, shuddering halt."[1] The year of deflation, 1920, realized its logical consequences in 1921, with high unemployment and falling wheat prices. Deflation dealt its most debilitating blow to the farmers who saw the price of their products drop by 50% between 1920 and 1923.[2]

Nevertheless, the period of deflation, which, in no small way, influenced the results of the 1921 election, proved short-lived for most sectors of the economy and for all regions except the Maritimes. By mid-decade, fears of deflation were replaced by expectations of continued growth and prosperity. The manufacturing sector was again expanding, and wheat production rose to record levels. The promise that the twentieth century would belong to Canada seemed once again within reach. However, the remarkable recovery which occurred after 1923 was based on quite different factors than the pre-1913 boom. The wheat economy of the Prairies revived, but this, in many respects, was an illusory boom, based upon unique international conditions.[3] The importance of agriculture was fundamentally reduced in this decade so that, despite expansion due to favourable growing conditions, mechanical harvesting, and other technological innovations, agriculture was soon overshadowed by other types of productive activity.[4] The contribution of the western agricultural frontier to economic development had reached its logical conclusion. The Prairies were full, and the benefits to be gained from outfitting and transporting huge numbers of immigrants and building railways had been realized.[5] By 1930 it would become clear that agriculture was no longer the most vital or determinant component of the economy, and the farmers were left to face the exigencies of the international market alone, relying only on the political power they could muster to protect their interests.

The economic recovery of the 1920s was, in large part, stimulated by two factors: the increased exploitation of new natural resources and modern technology, which was implanted in central Canada during and after the First World War—often by American branch plants. The interaction of the two encouraged considerable growth by mid-decade. Between 1920 and 1929 the population grew by one-sixth, new investment increased by $6 billion, and the real national income rose by one-half its previous value.[6] Moreover, while the economy of the twenties was export-based, it relied upon more products, not only wheat, but also hydro-electricity, pulp and paper, non-ferrous metals and gold.[7] By the end of the decade Canada had, despite its relatively small population, become the world's fifth-largest trading nation, exporting 30% of total national production. Canada provided 32% of the world's export trade in wheat, 63% of the newsprint, 31% of the aluminum, 14% of the copper and 12% of the lead and zinc. With the ascendancy of the new staples came a shift in the relative importance of the export regions in Canada, with Quebec and Ontario providing most of the newsprint, wood pulp, base metals and gold.[8]

These new industries were also financed by new sources of capital. In the early years, abundant foreign capital had been needed to finance railways and to construct and operate manufacturing enterprises. Most of this capital came from Britain, but the war and other costs associated with an increasingly threatened Empire forced British lenders to with-draw capital from Canada.[9] Money had to be found elsewhere, more and more often in the United States.[10]

The increasingly popular type of investment coming into Canada during the twenties was also different from that of previous years. Most prewar investment had been portfolio investment, which meant that, while the capital was borrowed, direction and control over its use were retained in the hands of the Canadian entrepreneurs who had solicited the money. Contrastingly, the postwar style—direct investment—enabled the investor in a specific project to maintain control of its opera-tion.[11] Instead of Canadians going abroad to obtain capital to finance their adventures, capital was brought into the country by foreigners who either built factories or purchased the rights to explore and exploit Canadian natural resources. In other words, they did not use Canadian intermediaries but were direct participants in the economy, and, by so doing, they retained control of enterprises located in Canada.[12] The increasing reliance on direct rather than portfolio forms of foreign investment was to have profound effects on the Canadian economy and polity.

A second factor promoting changes in the structure of the Canadian economy was technological innovation. Both the recovery from the post-war recession and the long-term restructuring and modernization of the economy were stimulated by growth of new technology. With the war, Canada crossed the threshold into an economy of electricity and gasoline motors. This conversion also signalled more intensive interaction with the United States. Canadian consumers demanded the products of American technology such as electrical appliances and motor cars, in essence, all the symbols of industrial "modernity." Farms were mechan-ized and electrified; cities grew and residential suburbs began to sur-round the largest cities, as street cars and automobiles made escape from inner-city living a possibility for many. Similarly, factories employed production methods which were as modern and technologically advanced as the goods they produced. Simple production techniques and quasi-artisanal labour, typical of earlier periods, were replaced by the elaborate technology of mass production and the assembly line. These methods had been first introduced in the United States, but they were quickly adopted by Canadian industry.

The logic of the Canadian tariff was not lost to American industrial-ists eager to reap the profits of their new technology in markets outside of the United States. The promise of a protected domestic market and easy access to the Empire encouraged American industry to locate in Canada. In fact, the number of American-owned industries arriving each year in Canada grew progressively from seventeen in 1918 to ninety-seven in 1930.[13] These branch plants produced the same goods with the same production methods as did parent companies in the United States. Moreover, financing in manufacturing, even more than in the resource industries, was by direct investment and control over production, and profits, rested with the parent corporations.

The establishment of these branch plants had a very important effect on the location of the manufacturing sector. Reinforcing the already-strong regionalizing tendencies, begun by the National Policy, manufacturing activity was increasingly confined to the central provinces while the Maritimes were eliminated as industrial competitors of Ontario and Quebec. What was the process behind this centralization? With the locus of American industrial activity already on the eastern sea-board west to the lower Great Lake states and Chicago, there was a certain "natural" logic to locating branch plants in areas adjacent to these industrial states. There were great economic advantages because trans-portation and communication costs were reduced by minimizing the physical distance between the branch plant and the parent company. Moreover, the centripetal tendency of geographical proximity was but-tressed by the existing transportation and communication links between Canada and the United States. One of the results of "industrialization by branch plant" was that manufacturing activity became more concentrated in the centre of the country and especially in southern Ontario. By 1931 73% of all factories were in Ontario or Quebec (42% and 31% respectively) but of the American-owned plants, 66% were located in Ontario and 16% in Quebec, or 82% in the central provinces. Moreover these industries were largely concentrated in Toronto and southern Ontario border cities.[14]

The locational advantages of central Canada for American-based corporations, plus the legacy of the National Policy, concentrated industry in central Canada. However, there were several important differences between the structural effects of the National Policy and direct foreign investment. First, the early National Policy brought industrialization to the "East" based on the stimulation of the wheat economy of the "West." In contrast, the postwar period saw the rapid expansion of the "Centre" and the decline of industrial activity in the Maritimes, which returned to a resource-extracting economy.[15] Second, the prewar economic develop-ment was based on the stimulation of these regional effects, largely by railway, immigration and resource policies which maintained the western provinces in a less-than-equal position within Confederation. With the virtual completion of Prairie settlement, the effects of these policies on the direction of national economic development declined. Moreover, new motors for growth were available in the resource industries located, for the most part, in Ontario, Quebec and British Columbia.[16] The stimula-tion of differences was no longer really essential. The differences became almost self-maintaining.

Increased manufacturing and resource extraction brought changes to the social formation. As manufacturing and resource extraction replaced wheat export as the source of economic development, the bourgeoisie relied less on the organization of transportation and export for profit and began instead to invest in other forms of economic activity. However, they did this primarily as financial capitalists rather than as manufacturers or industrialists.[17] In essence, new industries were organized, almost from the beginning, as large enterprises with members of the financial and commercial elite sitting as corporation board members. This overlap of membership between transportation, financial, extractive and manufacturing interests became increasingly common, especially as industry and production became more and more concentrated. The movement toward concentration and monopolization began at the end of the nineteenth century, but it accelerated during the war and the period of postwar deflation.[18] Many smaller businesses could survive neither the competition with corporations aggrandized by war contracts nor the period of "tight money" which followed the war. Many failed, only to be bought up by large corporations, often American branch plants, undertaking either vertical or horizontal integration (and sometimes both) of the production process.[19] With their market and technological advantages, it was easy for these corporations to convince Canadian entrepreneurs that the future lay with amalgamation and integration into the American industrial structure. Thus, the automobile industry and many other of the most modern industries in the manufacturing sector, were dominated by foreign interests.

These two forces, concentration and direct investment, led to profound changes in the Canadian bourgeoisie. It became involved in more diversified capitalist activities, through the organization of manufacturing by the financial fraction of the bourgeoisie. It also began to contain more and more people who were involved in some way, as managers, investors, or corporate lawyers, in the activities of American capital in Canada. The NP's goal of East-West economic development was less important to these entrepreneurs. A domestic market, protected by tariffs, was still sustained, but, increasingly, that market could be located elsewhere than the farms of the West. The Prairie farmers, as consumers, lost some of their importance for the bourgeoisie.

The De-Industrialization of the Maritimes

Not all provinces benefited from the optimistic economic trends of the twenties. In fact, as mentioned previously, this decade was a watershed in the economic development of the Maritimes, for they were transformed from a participant in the National Policy's industrialization strategy to a staple-producing region, similar in many ways to the Prairies. It is often forgotten that the Maritimes have not always been the "poor cousins" of Confederation. They acquired their dependent status after political and structural factors, both conducive to Maritime de-industrialization, coincided in the twenties. The following section provides a brief account of the economic developments and political decisions which effectively transformed these provinces into a hinterland region producing and consuming for the benefit of the central provinces. It also explains why the political protest movement which developed out of this changed status was less successful than its counterparts in the West in gaining popular acceptance and success. The protest of the Maritimes was not led by a subordinate class, as was the case in the West.

Up until the 1870s the Maritimes were a classic example of a staple-based economy with industries shaped by export demand for timber and fish, abundant in the area.[20] In this way, shipbuilding for fishing and transportation became an important manufacturing industry, and, for some time in the mid-nineteenth century, it made Maritime sailors famous.[21] This economy, as in other colonies, was dependent upon the vagaries of the international economic system. For example, the shipbuilding industry collapsed with the arrival of steam and iron ships, and the prosperity of the lumber and fish trades vacillated with the needs and demands of the British fleets and the West Indian colonies.[22] However, shortly after Confederation and specifically with the adoption of the National Policy, the economy of the Maritimes began to respond to the creation of a Canadian domestic market. Despite initial reluctance to join the political union in 1867, Maritime capitalists soon began to participate in the larger economic unit that Confederation made possible. One of the principal motives behind Confederation had been the unification of the four colonies to create a larger and more self-sufficient market, and one of the structures necessary to assure this wider market was the Intercolonial Railway, linking the Maritimes to Montreal. The construction of this line was negotiated when the Maritimes entered Confederation.[23] Its construction brought an abundant flow of trade between the Maritimes and the centre which sustained the new economy while the mechanisms for westward expansion—the other goal of Confederation—were put in place.[24] There is no evidence to suggest that the Maritimes were initially conceived as a hinterland of central Canada. Rather, the expectation seems to have been that all four original provinces would participate in the colonization of the West. Indeed, in 1867 the occupational structure of the four provinces was very similar, suggesting that each sector of economic activity (whether primary, manufacturing or service) was of equivalent importance in each province.[25]

Few factors militated against Maritime industrialization after the National Policy was set in place. Capital, primarily in the hands of the merchants who had organized the staple trade, was available for industrial activities. After the recession of the seventies and with the recovery of the eighties and nineties, this capital moved into manufacturing. As in the central provinces, many import-substitution industries grew and prospered behind the protection of the tariff wall.[26] Only ten years after the introduction of protective tariffs the industrial output of Nova Scotia increased at a rate higher than that of Quebec and Ontario.[27] Moreover, the growth of manufacturing continued into the first two decades of this century such that the increase in manufacturing was more than two-and-a-half times that of its population increase, while Ontario and Quebec doubled their output compared to population growth.[28]

Textiles and iron and steel were the important areas of growth. The iron and steel industry was principally founded on Cape Breton Island coal reserves, and the rapid expansion of railways in the West provided a market for its products, as it did for most of the Canadian iron and steel industry of the time.[29] In this way, a stable market nurtured by the federal tariffs made Nova Scotian industry a viable and attractive investment, and it expanded in response. The Maritimes as well as Quebec and Ontario relied on the continuation of the National Policy for ongoing industrialization.

The transportation policy of the federal government, in general, and the structure of the freight-rates, in particular, also nurtured the manufacturing sector in the Maritimes. Its entrepreneurs, as manufacturers, hoped to follow the American example and locate the industrial system in the East of the country.[30] To realize this ambition, the obstacles of geography had to be overcome, largely by modifying transportation structures and policy. Quite obviously, without some special arrangements, Maritime industry could not successfully compete with the central provinces for the western market. Railways had to be built and western farms equipped, and, under normal circumstances, goods could travel to the West more economically from Toronto or even Montreal than from Halifax. A way to overcome the liabilities of distance had to be found so that goods manufactured in the Maritimes could compete, in price, with those from the central provinces. The solution was a complicated series of adjustments to the Intercolonial Railway freight-rates. Throughout the post-Confederation period special freight-rates served as a catalyst for industrial development in the Maritimes. Maritime goods remained competitive because the Intercolonial offered rates cheaper per mile than the rates prevailing in the rest of the country, for goods carried over long distances and particularly to Montreal.[31] These rates

> . . . enabled the secondary manufacturers in the Maritimes to penetrate markets in Western and Central Canada to obtain the sales volume necessary for competitive production. With such encouragement, capital invested in manufacturing in the Maritimes quadrupled between 1900 and 1920.[32]

Obviously the "special" treatment afforded Maritime manufacturing was not popular with the western farmers who already felt unduly penalized by the freight-rate structure. Nor was it popular among the competing manufacturers in central Canada.[33] The rates were disputed and the Maritimes were exposed to pressure for consolidation, pressure which was alleviated by adjusting the Maritimes' freight-rates upwards. These increases began before World War I and after the war they were increased until freight-rates were finally "equalized" across the country in the twenties.[34]

A further difficulty for the Maritimes was that the federal government did not guarantee that Canadian goods for export to Europe would pass through Canadian winter ports. In 1867, Maritime merchants anticipated that all European trade would be channelled through their ports. This business was expected to provide major growth of the region and to make Maritime cities regional metropolises. In the process, some of the increasingly important service sector jobs would locate in eastern cities rather than being attracted to the central provinces. However, except for abundant shipping activity during the war years, exports from the West and the centre of the country generally continued to move through the ports of the American eastern seaboard. These ports were linked to Canada by rail lines, in particular, the Grand Trunk Railway. Thus, despite earlier promises by federal politicians, especially Prime Minister Laurier, an exclusively Canadian route to the Atlantic did not materialize.[35] Any hopes for strong eastern Canadian shipping centres withered away when the rates on the Intercolonial were raised and the federal government took over the Grand Trunk in the railway mergers of the twenties. "With it, the Canadian Government inherited a strong vested interest in the commercial success of Portland [Maine]."[36] This interest eroded the hopes of the Maritime merchants that Atlantic Canada would grow into a major commercial and service centre. Moreover, as Canadian exports were redirected from Great Britain to the United States in the interwar years the very importance of an Atlantic port was diminished. Both of these obstacles to Maritime economic development—the withdrawal of special freight-rates and the attrition of the winter ports—were, in part, amenable to political solutions, but none was forthcoming in the twenties. The pleas of the Maritime merchants for a greater proportion of the export trade fell on deaf ears. Similarly, demands for the re-establishment of favourable freight-rates were not heeded.

There were other factors in addition to political failures which served to accelerate de-industrialization in the Maritimes. The operation of the National Policy and the changes which it induced in the Canadian economy after World War I were of greater long-run importance. As a result of a reorientation of the Canadian economy, Maritime entrepreneurs lost their individual initiative and succumbed to the leadership of the central Canadian financial and manufacturing elite. This came about, for the most part, because the Maritime manufacturers accepted the National Policy as the charter for national economic development.[37] In accepting this definition, they were not prepared to resist the regional disparities which were inherent in the policy itself. Increasingly, these disparities would fall on the eastern regions themselves.

The method of financing industrial ventures was one of the changes in the manufacturing sector which had detrimental consequences for the Maritimes. After the 1890s, industrial capital came increasingly not from individual entrepreneurs but from joint stock companies which were firmly attached by overlapping directorships to the banking and financial system. Capital had been readily available in the Maritimes after Confederation, and, indeed, the area was a net exporter of capital to the rest of the country.[38] However, the region lacked its own financial structures to support large corporate activity and became increasingly dependent on outside financiers to organize and subsidize large-scale corporate ventures. After the 1890s, the industrial activity of the country was largely organized as corporate capitalism which used the stock market as a mechanism for financing ventures. With this form of organization, the direction of the Maritime economy began to pass out of the hands of indigenous capitalists into the orbit of the Canadian financial elite, especially the Montreal group.[39] This financial fraction of the bourgeoisie was, as has been indicated, moving more actively into manufacturing activities but principally as financiers rather than as entrepreneurs.

At the same time and, for some of the same reasons, industry moved toward corporate concentration. A process of rationalization was taking place, reducing the number of firms operating in the country, and the competition within the domestic market, which, since there had never been an emphasis on exporting manufactured goods, was the only market. This movement toward rationalization and concentration, the "merger movement" as it is sometimes called, responded to the goals of the NP and the federal government's industrial strategy generally. This was to supply the domestic market and to engage in export activity only in special cases.[40] The reasons behind this strategy are too complicated to explore here, and they have been discussed in previous chapters. What is crucial to note is the effect of this strategy on manufacturers during periods of reduced demand. The Canadian corporations' response to an unfavourable market was simply to reduce their losses by limiting competition and the number of competing firms. In essence, the strong absorbed the weaker.

> The tariff served to increase the number of mergers, particularly in textiles, where many small manufacturers gave way to two giants by 1892. With the tariff and increasing entry of US firms into the domestic market, concentration proceeded to consolidate the multitude of small

firms. These developments should be placed in the context of dominance of commercial interests over industrial entrepreneurs and the effect they had on the under-development of an industrial base in Canada.[41]

The Maritime textile industry, in particular, was affected by this process. Textiles had been one of the most important industries in the Maritimes, as these provinces imitated the development strategy of the New England states, often with the same technology. Numerous textile factories were built in Nova Scotia and New Brunswick to produce for the Canadian domestic market. However, with the recession of the 1890s, control of this industry passed from Maritime entrepreneurs to a national syndicate of textile manufacturers centred in Montreal and Quebec. How did this happen?[42] Prior to the recession, the cotton manufacturers of Canada produced enough to meet the needs of the domestic market. During the recession, however, American manufacturers began to dump their products in Canada, selling at a price so low that they slipped under the tariff wall. The Canadian producers were undersold, and their market soon retracted. There were three possible solutions to the dilemma: reduce the price of Canadian-made goods by lowering railway rates; increase the tariff and block the Americans; or regulate output, so that only goods which could be sold at a competitive price would be produced. The third option, the regulation of output, was chosen, an option which also provided an opportunity to eliminate some of the competitors and "chaos" of competition in the industry. A syndicate of "Montreal interests" gained a steering role in the industrial activity of the Maritimes by forging an agreement and an association of Quebec and Maritime textile manufacturers. The membership agreed to abide by the rules of the syndicate and limit production, thereby limiting areas of independent action. A similar procedure was followed in almost all sectors of the regional economy.[43]

Thus, although the National Policy initially brought industrialization to the Maritimes, it also brought, as part of the same policy, de-industrialization. Maritime entrepreneurs were fully integrated into the "national" design, and, as part of this plan, they followed the same processes of development and change as did capitalists in the central provinces. They took part in the same merger movement, and, as a result, by 1895, almost all mass consumption industries in the Maritimes had passed to interests outside the Maritimes.

However, added to these common effects were several other factors which fell disproportionately on the Maritimes. Rationalization, as part of the merger movement, had, in itself, no regional or locationally specific effects. Only when the extra costs of long-distance travel and the centralizing effects of American investment were added to the equation, did the weakness of the Maritimes become clear. The profound consequences of these factors coincided in the twenties, eliminating the Maritimes as full participants in the transformation of the Canadian economy taking place at the time.[44] As a result, this region began to take on the characteristics of an unmodernized economy.

The de-industrialization of the Maritimes was a consequence of the integration of Maritime and central Canadian capitalism, part of the strategy of Confederation and the National Policy. This integration, as we have seen, ultimately reduced manufacturing activity in the Maritime provinces. However, it did not come about because of a conscious effort by "Montreal interests" to take jobs from the Maritimes and give them to their province. Rather, the financial and manufacturing structure of the Maritimes and Montreal were integrated in such a fashion that, with all the impersonality of a "business" decision, once the costs of Maritime production became too high, Maritime industry was curtailed or allowed to wither away. These costs became too high when the political costs of the special post-Confederation freight-rates were too great and when the centralizing effects of branch plant development appeared. Manufacturing in the Maritimes was sacrificed partially because of the pressures that the Progressive revolt of 1921 placed on the federal party system. But the freight-rates and political accommodations to the West are only partial explanations. The de-industrialization of the Maritimes was even more pronounced because, as we have seen, the new industries of the decade were predominantly located in the central provinces adjacent to American industrial heartland. Thus, both de-industrialization and non-industrialization reduced growth in the region during this period.

The Maritime provinces, then, provide a counter-example to the experience of the Prairie Provinces. This region had entered Confederation as a full participant in the strategy of economic development nurtured by the National Policy, but by the 1920s it slid back into a hinterland status, similar to that of the Prairies. Also, similar to the experience of the West, a protest movement would grow out of these conditions to object to the Maritimes' declining status in the national economic order. The Maritime Rights Movement challenged the dominance of the central provinces within Confederation and demanded adjustments from the party system of the 1920s. However, unlike the farmers' protest, the Movement was absorbed by the two-party system. Nonetheless, while a new party did not materialize in the East, disenchantment with the federal arrangement in the Maritimes proved to be an obstacle inhibiting the return to "normal politics" that the two major parties struggled to achieve throughout the decade. The Movement was another indicator that there was profound dislocation all across the country during the twenties.

The Labour Movement of the Twenties

Many of the changes in the occupational structure which became visible before and during the war were accelerated by technology and the manufacturing and resource-extraction activities of the twenties. By and large, there were three major changes in Canada's class structure which held important political potential and, in fact, affected the political organization of class relations during the twenties. Of primary importance was the drastic reduction in the percentage of the population involved in agricultural production, which fell from 46% in 1891 to 33% in 1921 and 29% in 1931.[45] This steady reduction was fundamentally relevant to the partisan organization of class relations. By the thirties, the petite bourgeoisie could no longer dominate the organization of political protest, and it would not again shake the foundations of federal politics as it had in 1921. The implications of this situation are discussed in the next section of this chapter.

Unprecedented growth in the "tertiary" or "service" sector of the workforce was the second important alteration in the occupational structure that occurred in these years. There was a rapid expansion of the number of occupations providing supportive services to the new industrial structure. This growth could be seen in the rising number of Canadians employed as office workers, as clerks, in banks, in department stores and, increasingly, in government offices—all those "white collar" jobs which appear in a mature industrial economy. These jobs differed in several important ways from those involved in construction, mining or manufacturing. First, the conditions of work were different. It was not manual labour in a noisy factory, or even a workshop. Neither did it require descending into a dangerous mine. Rather, it was often work in offices separated from the factory floor by distance, if not set above the work floor itself, or it was work in offices, in banks, in stores, in government buildings and other places which were far removed from the centres of industrial or extraction activity. Moreover, it was "clean work" which often required higher levels of education, increasingly a high school diploma, but it was not a craft or a trade with specialized skills. More and more, it was work done by the unskilled, the unorganized or women.[46]

The development of these new kinds of occupations, variously described as "white collar" or "tertiary sector" jobs, changed the occupational structure of the country drastically. The percentage of the population in the tertiary sector increased by 16% between 1891 (23%) and 1931 (39%).[47] The most dramatic growth within the tertiary sector itself was among the clerical sub-sector, although all types of service occupations increased steadily.[48] Moreover, these changes created a situation which was not quickly grasped by labour organizations. These new types of employees provided a challenge for the craft-based labour movement but it did not attempt to deal with them until well after the Second World War. The challenge of organizing white collar workers involved the question of whether these workers had any place in the trade union movement. The trade union movement's initial response to this question was negative. Not only was the craft-oriented trade union centre unable to see a similarity between white collar and blue collar workers, but most white collar workers themselves were uninterested in throwing in their lot with the blue collar workers. Office workers, store clerks and government bureaucrats seemed to share more with management than with the other workers. They seemed, because of the working conditions, education levels, responsibilities, if not their apparel, to resemble the bosses or, at least, their managerial representatives. In advancing capitalist economy where more and more functions of capital are carried out by hired managers and directors, the employee, paid by the month or the week rather than hourly, seemed to have a higher status than the workers on the factory floor. Thus, white collar workers often did not even consider unionization. In turn, the fact that so many of the more menial white collar tasks were performed by women only reinforced the tendency of the existing union movement to ignore the organizational potential of this new workforce.[49] In consequence, this group of workers was beyond the reach of those organizations which might have offered them another language of electoral politics and another view of class relations.[50] Their numbers were increasing, but their potential support of a class-based political movement was unrealized.

The modernization of industry and the sophisticated technology of mass production which demanded a different type of worker also held out the possibility of profound changes in the partisan organization of class conflict. Fewer and fewer craft workers were necessary for modern industry which required, instead, workers who could perform a repetitive task on the assembly line; a task which sometimes required job experience but did not demand a trade or the acquisition of a skill through a process of apprenticeship. By the twenties, the proportion of traditional craft jobs within the labour manufacturing sector in Quebec and Ontario had been reduced to about 40% (from 78% in 1891). Even within this two-fifths of the workforce there had been a change in the meaning of "craft" as the term now applied to those who performed skilled labour in the partial fabrication of a product whereas, previously, a "craft" worker manufactured the complete product.[51] Increasingly, other kinds of workers, whether they were semi-skilled or unskilled labourers, were employed in the manufacturing sector. The Canadian workforce had undergone significant and irreversible changes.

This shift from craft to semi-skilled and unskilled work had been acutely felt in the West, where the lumbering and mining industries had made similar labour demands earlier in the century. There, this type of labour force had created problems for the trade union movement's choice of form of organization. By the 1920s, the question of organizational format was widely debated in both the East and the West. Modern manufacturing, and particularly the growth sectors of chemical, electrical and automobile industries, increased the demand for semi-skilled workers in the centre of the country. These workers remained outside the jurisdiction of the TLC and its craft-union affiliates.

Such alterations in the workforce meant that industrial unionism became an even more obvious strategy for the union movement. However, the organization of industrial unions, and their leadership, had been immobilized by attacks mounted against them after the Winnipeg General Strike. Much of the potential of almost thirty years of industrial unionism in the West had been destroyed. Organizations were eliminated; leaders were jailed and/or deported; or they were just recently released from jail. The TLC co-opted some of the newly disorganized workers into its craft-based industrial structures but many more were left unorganized. Although other industrial unions, and even new centrals, began to develop during this period, the going was hard. The lack of organization was exacerbated by the TLC's continued inability to adapt to the new conditions. It maintained its hard-line position against industrial unionism throughout the decade and thereby fostered the development of union strife and division around this question in the thirties.

As a result of these conditions, the proportion of the labour force organized by unions did not increase during the twenties. Union membership and strike activity declined throughout the decade. More workers were organized, both in absolute terms and as a percentage of the civilian labour force in 1920 than in any other year of the decade.[52] Labour lost any unity that it had developed during the war, and improved economic conditions in the twenties only compounded the movement's organizational and political difficulties. Because of the boom in resource extraction and manufacturing, there was a great demand for workers, which kept wages high.[53] However, renewed immigration and rural-to-urban migration sharpened the competition for jobs. Many of the new jobs appeared in "new and largely unorganized industries and/or in older industries that had successfully resisted unionization."[54] Most growth industries, such as automobiles, electrical, steel, chemicals, heavy machinery, mining, logging and smelting remained unorganized. This weakness was compounded by the fact that employers were successful in co-ordinating open-shop campaigns against those workers who did attempt to organize. Competition for jobs, as well as a labour movement uninterested in the massive organization of either unskilled or white collar and service workers reduced the potential for major class confrontations during this period.

Labour was also affected by a gradual erosion of federal power and the ever-increasing strength of the provincial governments. For example, the federal government lost its steering role in the field of labour legislation when its constitutional right to determine the conditions for labour for the country as a whole with legislation such as the Industrial Disputes Investigation Act (so crucial in earlier conflicts between labour and capital) was declared *ultra vires* by the Judicial Committee of the Privy Council in 1925. The Privy Council's decision applied only to the question of jurisdiction; that is, whether the provincial or the federal government had the right to legislate in labour matters. When the court ruled in favour of the provincial governments, each province was free to relax wage levels, safety regulations and workmen's benefits and/or strengthen restrictions on strikes or unions to better compete for labour-intensive industry.[55] As a result, the Privy Council's decision only aggravated the already persistent tendencies in the labour movement to "regionalize" their demands. Moreover, it necessitated that organized labour adopt a fully federal structure which, in turn, implied even greater potential for inter-provincial conflict on goals and strategies and lessened the possibility for a united political front in the federal sphere. The partisan impact of the labour movement was further reduced and the field was, once again, left to other political actors.

The Privy Council's decision, of course, only served to reinforce the existing divisions within the labour movement; it did not create them. As we have seen in previous chapters, a strong national labour identity had been impaired by different traditions in organization, ideology and, not the least, language and religion. A striking example of the potentialities of such balkanization is seen in the organization of the workers of Quebec. Unlike the other provinces, a considerable measure of consolidation was achieved among Quebec workers early in the decade. Yet, the organizational vehicle which emerged neither forged a class consciousness among Quebec workers nor promoted co-operation with trade unions in the other provinces. In fact, the ideology which characterized the labour movement in Quebec in the 1920s only served to encourage nationalism and reinforce the bicultural cleavage in Canadian politics.

As will be recalled, the Roman Catholic Church in Quebec took initiatives at the turn of the century to organize and educate Quebec workers about their collective condition because it was concerned that secular and American unions would compromise the Quebec workers' cultural and religious identity. The Church's intervention in the labour movement was ideological and practical. It emphasized co-operation rather than conflict with employers, and parish priests both led labour discussion groups and acted as mediators between workers and employers during industrial disputes. The Church's compatibility with, if not tacit support of, the existing system of class relations successfully isolated Quebec from radical trade unionism, and the Church's guidance over social relationships in the province remained secure. However, by the early twenties this control was threatened by changes in the type and location of the occupational structure. The new economic order was rapidly transforming a Quebec society of the farm and the parish to one of the mine, the lumber camp and the factory, as population left farms in increasing numbers for unskilled jobs in New England, Montreal, or isolated one-industry towns in the interior of the province. The Church's influence over these workers was maintained to a degree by small Catholic trade unions (*syndicats*) which sprang up in various locations, but these were largely isolated from one another. To re-establish its guiding role, the Church organized an amalgamation of these small and dispersed unions under the auspices of the Confédération des Travailleurs Catholiques du Canada (Canadian and Catholic Confederation of Labour, CCCL) in 1921.

Although the CCCL unified the trade unions, it promised neither to radicalize nor change the condition of the Quebec worker. When the CCCL did oppose industrialists, it was not so much because they were capitalists but that they were *les étrangers*, English Canadian or American rather than French Canadian. [56] The coincidence between ethnicity and class seemed to confirm this nationalist world view in Quebec in the twenties. English was the language of business and for Francophones seeking economic mobility, knowledge of that language was a requisite. American, British, and English-Canadian monopolies dominated the industrial and extractive sectors. Likewise, those in positions of authority, owners, managers and white collar workers, were overwhelmingly Anglophone, while the Francophones assumed subordinate roles in the production process. This translation of class antagonisms into ethnic hostilities encouraged economic and political consequences which pervaded Quebec for years. However, in the short run, in the absence of critical labour organizations, Quebec workers generally earned less for their labour than their counterparts in the rest of Canada. In 1924, for example, the average yearly wage for Quebec workers in manufacturing was $883.00 compared to $1,039.00 in Ontario. [57] In effect, the ideology of the CCCL complemented partisan organization along the bicultural cleavage. [58] Lacking their own ideology and basis for political action, classes could only express their discontent, opposition or aspirations by altering the equilibrium between the bourgeois parties through electoral support for one or the other.

Of course, workers outside Quebec also had limited partisan alternatives. However, the absence of a strong working class party in the 1920s was certainly not due to a lack of awareness of its necessity or even, initially, for a lack of trying. [59] The organization of a challenge to the major parties again fell prey to conflict within the labour movement as, once again, in order to maintain the existing craft-based organization, direct partisan activity, in this case a labour party, was abandoned. On the eve of the 1921 election, as the previous chapter described, the TLC revived the Canadian Labour Party (CLP) which it had founded in 1917.[60] The CLP organizers envisioned a national party to link numerous small labour parties competing at the provincial level. The flaw in the design was the TLC's stipulation that no industrial union could directly affiliate with the CLP. This requirement, clearly in the interests of craft unions, led the Dominion Labour Party (DLP) and the Independent Labour Party (ILP) to rebuff the CLP and in doing so, reduce the potential influence of the CLP from the beginning.[61] The provincial parties refused to abandon some of their allies who did not belong to the craft-union centre and they were unwilling to give up their autonomy in federal elections to the moderate leadership of the TLC. Nevertheless, in view of the farmers' successful entry into federal politics in 1921, the idea of a national labour party was revived in earnest in 1923. Renewed interest in the CLP came principally from the Communists and their Workers' Party, who decided to affiliate with the CLP.[62] The decision to join forces with the CLP, by that time little more than a paper organization in Ontario, was tied to the Communists' commitment to the tactic of influencing the working class by "boring from within" the existing trade union organizations. They focussed on the CLP because of its relationship with the TLC and because they saw little possibility of mobilizing a national political party by themselves or with the DLP or other small labour parties. Therefore, the Ontario, British Columbia and Alberta sections of the CLP accepted the affiliation of locals of the Workers' Party.

However promising the future of the CLP may have appeared in 1924, conflict between moderate and radical elements within the TLC shattered any hope that a labour-based party would mobilize in the federal elections of the 1920s. The conflict in the TLC between the Communists and moderates was similar to the experience of British and American trade unions during the same period. At the heart of the tension was the moderate leadership's resentment, suspicion and fear of the Communists' growing influence within the labour body. Communists had assumed positions of authority in unions, and they were gaining an important ideological leadership through ongoing programmes such as the Trade Union Education League (TUEL). In light of this challenge from within the trade unions, the moderates followed the course adopted by their American and British counterparts and expelled the Communists from the international unions, or, in effect, from the TLC. With this refusal to accept Communists, the TLC tacitly divorced itself from the CLP, the labour party it had created as a working class partisan alternative in federal elections. The brief period of union harmony and direct political action had ended. Once again struggles within the labour movement diminished its political potential and initiative.

The TLC's actions placed the Communists in a paradoxical dilemma. Because they sought to build a unified workers' movement, they had rigorously defended the TLC and actively encouraged dissenting unions to join forces with the TLC. After their expulsion from the international unions, however, the Communists had little alternative but to promote an organization outside the auspices of the TLC or to lose contact with organized workers.[63] Therefore, Communists helped organize the All-Canadian Congress of Labour (ACCL) in 1926. The ACCL was largely comprised of breakaway unions from the TLC, such as the Mine-Workers' Union of Canada, the Canadian Brotherhood of Railway Employees and the Electrical Communications Workers' Union, as well as remnants of the OBU. With an affiliated membership of 40,000 (compared to the TLC's 130,000) the ACCL represented a threat to the central craft-based organization.[64] The TLC was prompted to condemn the Communists, the ACCL, and finally the CLP, arguing that the party no longer represented labour. By 1927, all the TLC's ties with the CLP were severed, and that union central claimed to be the only legitimate spokesman for Canadian labour.[65]

In this way, the primary organization of labour abandoned the electoral organization of working class dissent in federal politics, not to return wholeheartedly, or united, to a labour party for almost three decades. Thus, the labour movement did not threaten the dominant position of the Liberals and Conservatives during the twenties nor did it provide an interpretation of class relations to challenge the ideological hegemony of the two major parties. It was, instead, the farmers who continued to organize dissent and obstruct the return of "normal politics."

The Political Movement of the Farmers

If the major parties' efforts to restore "normal politics" in the federal sphere was not greatly inhibited by the labour movement, defusing the class demands of organized farmers required considerably more political skill and fortuitous circumstances. The election of sixty-five Progressives in 1921 had underlined deep divisions over the issue of national development strategy, and the National Policy became the focus of political dissent. With their dissent the Progressives injected class-based demands and arguments into electoral politics and challenged the existing assumption of federal electoral politics, that a government policy promoting the interests of the dominant class also secured prosperity for all. They successfully discredited the supposition that the National Policy benefited all classes and all regions. In essence, the dominant definition of the political had been rejected by a substantial proportion of the western electorate when the Progressives demanded that the class interests of western petit bourgeois farmers be recognized and accommodated. Their demands required attention in Canada's first minority Parliament because, if they were ignored or left unattended, the Progressives could refuse to support and, thereby, defeat the governing Liberal Party. Thus, after 1921, the fate of Mackenzie King's government was in immediate peril unless and until the *status quo* was somehow adjusted.

This change in the basis of electoral discussion, in the content of claims, this emphasis on farmers as a class with their own interests was of profound importance for subsequent electoral politics. It was the first time that any group had successfully argued that the operation of existing partisan politics was based upon the promotion of a small group's self-interest.[66] In other words, this movement of farmers altered the previously predominant world view of electoral politics, and they talked about and criticized "the interests," domination, patronage and corruption.

However, the farmers' movement, precisely because of its own class composition, was in a contradictory position. It was a class-based movement but that class was the petite bourgeoisie. As the previous chapter has shown, the movement did describe a fundamental societal division between industrialists and financial capitalists and farmers. This was a conflict between one class, steadily transforming the economy into an industrial one, and another class which represented the old ways of the pre-industrial past. The farmers wanted to improve their lot by adjusting, if not eliminating, the tariffs and discriminatory freight-rates and by arresting the drain of farm labour into the mines of the north and the factories of the cities. Their fundamental objection was that they were expected to finance their own subordination through their production of wheat for export and their consumption of goods produced in the East. They provided the financial and commercial bourgeoisie with profit and, thus, much of the capital needed to exploit the new resources and operate the factories. The injustice of this situation was sufficient to unite the farmers in opposition during a time of economic crisis.[67] However, because they were a petite bourgeoisie, and, therefore, not fundamentally critical of capitalism but only its most advanced manifestations, they attacked concentration, monopolies and their effects.[68] The farmers' movement and its party, the Progressives, argued that if big business, power, corruption and the two-party system were eliminated, co-operative group government could be instituted. They talked of classes but classes which could co-operate in the exploitation of Canada's potential and not classes necessarily in conflict with each other in the capitalist production process. They were not sufficiently radical in their analysis to sustain an enduring opposition among farmers or to forge an alliance with the working class. These weaknesses were evident in the Progressive movement from its conception.

One need only to consider the farmers' reaction to labour's demand for an eight-hour day to perceive the difficulties involved in building a political alliance between the two classes. The United Farmers of Ontario (UFO) was derisive of this demand, arguing that they, as farmers, some of whom occasionally employed farm workers, could never think of working only eight hours. Neither were the interests of the farmers and some elements of organized labour compatible with respect to the tariff. The protectionist ILP and the TLC were at odds with the anti-protectionist farmers.[69] Moreover, the Manitoba Progressives, deeply suspicious of the labour movement, and the socialists in particular, after the 1919 Winnipeg General Strike, refused to make an alliance with labour party candidates.[70] Agrarian distrust of organized labour permeated the other provinces as well.

A second hindrance to full mobilization of the farmers around a class-based analysis was the appeal of the hegemonic ideology to the petite bourgeoisie. Most farmers understood that "something" was wrong with the present economic arrangements and that the politicians and political parties were, at least, partially responsible. However, the farmers' remedy did not constitute a fundamental challenge to capital, especially during the 1920s, when there was a shift away from the wheat economy as the essential lever of economic development. This left farmers open to the manipulation of the Liberals who recognized that the Progressives would be reluctant to defeat the Liberals in Parliament only to find them replaced by the even more protectionist Conservative Party. The Liberals' tariff policy and its budgets reflect an understanding of the trap within which Progressives found themselves caught.[71]

The Progressives' line of division concerning the political expression of their class analysis was reflected by their actions in Parliament and, more specifically, by their decision not to accept the role of official opposition to which their electoral success entitled them. The Alberta wing of the party was a strong supporter of the concept of group government, a scheme of occupational representation and non-party government. However, this conception of the "ideal" government could not be easily superimposed on the existing parliamentary arrangement, based as it was on cohesive parties. They proposed to replace the existing system of one-party cabinet government with one based on proportional representation of all groups present in the House. These groups would represent occupational rather than geographical interests in Parliament. The goal of the Progressives was to break the old party system and caucus and thus eliminate much of the influence of the "interests" which they argued manipulated both major parties with their campaign funds.[72] It was in this way, speaking as the representatives of farmers against the "interests," that the language of class conflict entered the Progressives' vocabulary. Obviously, the position of official opposition in the House of Commons, determined as it was by party standing and disciplined party voting, contradicted the concept of group government.

The Manitoba Progressives, on the other hand, were less enamoured of the theory of group government and concentrated on achieving concrete adjustments to the National Policy. Their real hope was to win back the Liberals to a low tariff position and to reinvigorate the Liberal Party with a "spirit of rural democracy." The post-1896 Liberals, especially as embodied in the Montreal capitalists, were not to the liking of the Manitoba Progressives.[73] They hoped that the open revolt in which they had participated would force the Liberals to concede to their demands. For them, too, the role of official opposition was less than acceptable. The goal of gaining concessions from, if not transforming, the Liberal Party had little chance of success if they stood in direct and formalized opposition to the government.

Thus the Progressives could be diminished in influence and number if the Liberal Party could absorb those who appeared to be little more than "crypto-Liberals." This group became the focus of Mackenzie King's "opportunistic politics." This is Morton's term for what most simply consisted of keeping things as they were in Quebec while, at the same time, attempting to win back former Liberal voters of the Prairies and Ontario.[74] The Liberals were aided in this strategy by the Conservative Party which continued to be uncompromisingly protectionist. The Progressives were confronted with a choice between what Conservatives would give them—which was nothing—and whatever the Liberals might offer. The politics of opportunism was essentially limited to a series of adjustments in the freight-rates and the tariff. In 1922 freight-rates were lowered for grain and flour moving out of the Prairies. In the same and the next year, rates on grain moving to the Pacific were also reduced, but rates on commodities moving westward to the Prairies were not reduced. However, the higher price for goods moving to the Prairie consumer was partially obfuscated by the timely alterations in the tariff structure. While there was no general change in the tariff policy until 1930, substantial reductions were made on farm machinery duties in 1922 and 1924. Preferential tariffs were terminated and intermediate and general tariff rates on tillage equipment were reduced by one-half. To further demonstrate that the Liberals had mended their ways, the government concentrated its railway expansion in Saskatchewan and Alberta during the period.[75] These minimal changes were sufficient to expose the fissures within the Progressive Party and to win over the Manitoba group to the Liberal Party.[76]

These divisions within the party were clear to all only one year after the 1921 election. At the conference of the Progressive MPs in 1922,

> . . . the lines were clearly drawn between those who wished to make the Progressive movement a democratic party of reform, purged of the evils of party patronage and "professional" politics, and those who denied that the traditional party system admitted of reform and sought

to replace it by the representatives of occupational groups. Both sides had much in common, the representation of agrarian interests, the cleansing of political life, a dislike and distrust of the "interests." Both feared the consequences of a split in the movement. The conflict, however, was fundamental.[77]

One result of the expression of these differences, muted as they were, was that the Canadian Council of Agriculture began to withdraw its support and to cease to act as the central organization of the party. These actions, which came the following year, meant that the characteristic which had distinguished the farmers from labour, that is strong and consistent support from an occupational organization, was no longer present. Without the organizational help of the farmers' groups, the Progressives lost much of their grass-roots strength. By 1926, they lacked both the funds and the organization to continue, and the party disintegrated completely by the end of the decade.[78]

The return to prosperity in the 1920s in no small way accelerated the collapse of the farmers' protest party. The worst of the hard times appeared to be over by 1924, and conditions steadily improved until 1927. Thus, much of the passion of dissent was dissipated. Although wheat prices did not return to wartime highs, they did improve from the deflationary low of $.65 a bushel to $1.25 in 1925. In addition, financial gains denied by price were more than offset by much higher yields.[79] New varieties of wheat extended the area of cultivation, and automotive technology reduced the farmer's labour per acre as productive areas were expanded.[80] Tractors, combines and trucks appeared on the Prairie landscape as symbols of wealth recovered. If all discontent was not eliminated by these conditions, it was at least muffled, and, by the eve of the 1925 election, the combined pressures of recovered prosperity and the "opportunistic politics" of the Liberals split the Progressives into two clearly defined groups. Some re-entered the Liberal Party while others remained independent and increasingly co-operated with labour representatives. This latter group, coined the "Ginger Group," began to co-operate with the labour representatives elected in 1921.[81] However, little could threaten the Liberals after the fragile unity of the Progressives was broken, and the farmers lost their will to struggle with the bourgeois parties. Persistent strength in Quebec could only be buttressed by an anticipated flood of Prairie and Ontario farmers back to the Liberal Party fold.

With the western farmers appeased, only the Maritimes threatened to deprive Mackenzie King of a majority government in 1925. The Maritimes had not recovered from the deflation of 1920 but rather because of corporate mergers and increased freight-rates, as well as changes in national development strategies, continued to lose jobs and industry to the central provinces. The Maritime Rights Movement, comprised largely of Nova Scotia businessmen, arose prior to the 1925 election to protest the region's reduced status in Confederation. However, while a potential support market for a Maritime protest party might have developed, disaffected voters were contained within the two-party system. Neither in 1925 nor 1926 would the major parties be threatened by an eastern protest party similar to the one which arose in the West in 1921.

The failure of the Maritimes to produce a third party option was related both to the nature of the organization and its choice of allies. Unlike the western experience, the Maritime Rights Movement did not permeate grass-roots occupational organizations but, rather, was largely comprised of local businessmen and entrepreneurs. Their grievances were not directed against industrial capitalists in Central Canada as capitalists but against federal policies which abridged local initiative and hampered industrial development in the Maritimes. These entrepreneurs wanted a greater share of Canadian industry, particularly the American branch plants which proliferated in southern Ontario.[82] They did not clearly understand that it was these branch plants themselves and the development strategy so heavily reliant on them that was a source of their problems. They objected to the increased rail costs and demanded that concessions be offered to Maritime manufacturers. Because of the nature of the demands, the Movement had little alliance potential outside of its own region. It identified the other major protesters of hinterland status in Confederation, the western farmers, as the cause of part of their frustration. In their view, Maritime manufacturing had been sacrificed to quell the protests of western farmers demanding equalized freight-rates across the country. Western farmers were equally uninterested in supporting the analysis and goals of the Maritime Rights Movement, with a social base among the manufacturers who relied on the protective tariff for their existence. The question of freight-rates and tariffs militated against a movement uniting the peripheries against the centre. The Progressives challenged the old NP while the Maritime Rights Movement wanted it continued.

The Movement chose from the beginning to make an alliance with the Nova Scotia Conservative party. This strategy proved successful, at least at the provincial level, when, after forty-three years in opposition the Conservatives mobilized this discontent and took the provincial government in 1925. However, while the election of the provincial Conservatives afforded the Movement a committed provincial voice, the alliance with that party did not guarantee that the Movement's radicalism would be clearly articulated in the forthcoming federal election. The provincial party could not dominate the federal one. In fact, the intimate connection between the provincial and federal Conservatives actually militated against the Movement's independent political action. Thus, although the provincial leader of the party wanted an immediate referendum on the question of separation from Confederation, the party quickly dispensed with the secessionist issue and focussed on economic injustices. As a result, the Movement did not grow into a full-blown repeal crusade, and the discontent was, instead, successfully moderated and contained within the two-party system.[83] New definitions of the political would not be forthcoming from the Maritimes in the twenties.

Nevertheless, the federal Conservatives under Meighen were not prepared to leave the pervasive discontent against the federal government unharnessed for the 1925 campaign. In many respects, they took the Maritime Rights Movement as their own.[84] Meighen stood staunchly in support of the tariff in 1925 and held out an electoral "plum" which was designed to appeal to both the East and the West. The Conservatives, if elected, would establish a system of compensatory freight-rates funded by the Dominion treasury. Otherwise, there was no clear-cut issue in the 1925 campaign.[85] King expounded the merits of his government's record and his "common sense" tariff and pleaded with the electorate to return to a "reintegrated nation" under the direction of a majority Liberal government.[86] At the same time, the Liberals continued to stress bicultural issues in Quebec, particularly Meighen's association with wartime conscription.

Despite these efforts, "normal politics" was not fully recovered in 1925. In fact, the electorate once again returned a minority government and a Parliament rife with regional peculiarities. While the Progressives retained twenty-four seats in the House, their popular vote fell from 23% in 1921 to 9% in 1925. They had lost many voters in Ontario and Manitoba. In addition, the Conservatives appeared to have finally recovered some of their traditional constituency. They made an impressive comeback in Ontario and captured no less than twenty-three of the twenty-nine seats in the Maritimes. Overall, the Conservatives won seventeen more seats and 7% more of the popular vote than the Liberals. Lack of attention to discontent in the Maritimes had proved a costly oversight for the King government. Nevertheless, neither party had made a successful appeal to all areas of the country, and a minority Parliament once again sat in Ottawa.

The Conservatives had defeated the Liberals, but they had not gained a majority so Mackenzie King chose not to resign, as was his right in a minority situation. He tenaciously clung to power, with the support of the remaining Progressives, the Independent Labour Party and Independent Members of Parliament. From this position of uncertainty, he undertook to enhance the Liberal Party's popularity among the disenchanted electorate, especially that of the Maritimes. The Royal Commission on Maritimes' Claims (The Duncan Commission) was initiated and instructed to find a solution for the region's grievances immediately after the election. However, before the Commission had time to report back to Parliament the country was once again thrown into a federal election, one which dramatically reintroduced the politics of national unity and reopened the debate about Canadian nationhood.

The "King-Byng Affair" provided the major fuel for the 1926 campaign. The electorate was asked to choose between the Liberal and Conservative Parties on the basis of a constitutional issue which touched at the heart of Canadian nationhood, specifically, whether the Governor General, the appointed representative of the King, had the right to refuse the elected Canadian Prime Minister an election. The very complicated controversy arose when King attempted to avoid a motion of censure in the House by dissolving the House and calling an election. Given that Parliament had sat less than a year, Lord Byng, the Governor General, refused the Prime Minister's demand. King reacted in an unprecedented fashion by resigning forthwith, thereby leaving Byng without a Prime Minister or a Ministry. The Governor General then approached the Conservatives to form a new Cabinet. Meighen accepted but his government survived only three days before it was defeated in the House.

In the ensuing election King translated the affair into an issue of primary importance relating to the integrity of Canada as an independent nation free from the interference of the Imperial connection. All other questions were subordinate to that of the nation's existence and independence. With the issue defined in this way, his actions could hardly be rebuked, especially in Quebec.[87]

Thus, in neither the 1925 nor 1926 campaigns was the electorate confronted with a class-based analysis or a national alternative to the major parties. Labour had forfeited its electoral role while organized farmers, with the return of prosperity, withdrew from federal politics leaving their partisan expression, the Progressives, vulnerable to complete disintegration. The correlation coefficients in Tables 5:1 and 5:2, which measure the relationship between party support and constituency type, suggest that class-based voting was less important in the 1925 and 1926 campaigns than in 1921. In the East, neither the Liberal nor Conservative Parties had a special identity among urban or rural constituencies. In the West, support for the protectionist Conservative Party continued to be strongly related to constituency characteristics—a positive relationship in urban and a negative relationship in rural ones. The Progressives manifested a class-based pattern, but support for the party declined dramatically in 1926, to 5% of the popular vote. Thus "normal politics" appeared almost, but nowhere completely, recovered after the elections of 1925 and 1926.

The 1926 election decimated the Progressives, but this did not mean that the organized farmers were no longer a potential threat to the two-party system. The few Progressives who did remain outside of the

Table 5:1
THE 1925 ELECTION: CORRELATION OF PARTY VOTE AND CONSTITUENCY TYPE BY REGION
(Pearson's r)

	Urban	Rural
East		
Conservative	.12	−.16*
Liberal	−.02	.08
Progressives	−.20*	.19*
West		
Conservative	.31*	−.50*
Liberal	.05	−.13
Progressives	−.55*	.66*

*p < .05

Liberal Party continued their co-operation with the Labour representatives. Outside of Parliament, farmers' organizations remained active at the provincial level, and, as the price of wheat plummeted in the final years of the decade, they moved step by step closer to renewed federal electoral activity.[88] Yet, their second venture into federal politics would not be into untested waters as had been the case with the Progressive experiment. This time the farmers would actively seek out labour allies and create a federated party structure building upon the strengths of diversified provincial components. Moreover, they would be committed to a reconstruction of Canadian society on socialist principles. While the party which later became known as the Co-operative Commonwealth Federation did not contest the 1930 election, the eventual character of the new party of the thirties was largely determined by organizational strategies of the twenties.

The thrust for class-based action gained momentum after 1926 in Saskatchewan when the Farmers' Union and the Saskatchewan Section of the Grain Growers' Association (GGA) formed the United Farmers of Canada (Saskatchewan Section) [UFC (SS)]. The inclusion of the predominantly socialist Farmers' Union brought new determination and new ideas to the more conservative GGA membership. The new organizational efforts were primarily focussed on direct economic action rather than on partisan activity. The goal was to break the marketing monopoly for grain and cut out the middleman by organizing co-operative marketing (through wheat pools) by farmers themselves.[89] Within a year the new organization called meetings throughout the province to generate grass-roots support for a Farmers' Wheat Pool. The ordinary farmer, however, was relatively unmoved by the initiatives toward wheat pools during the twenties, as good times favoured the moderates in the movement.[90] Nevertheless, when the wheat market crashed the

Table 5:2
THE 1926 ELECTION: CORRELATION OF PARTY VOTE AND
CONSTITUENCY TYPE BY REGION
(Pearson's r)

	Urban	Rural
East		
Conservative	.28*	−.12*
Liberal	−.10	−.02
Progressives	−.13*	.11
West		
Conservative	.28*	−.46*
Liberal	−.16	−.02
Progressives	−.30*	.49*

*$p < .05$

farmers were attracted to the idea of a wheat marketing co-operative and rapidly mobilized for collective action in the 1930 election.

As in 1921, a faltering economy motivated the hesitant farmers to reconsider independent partisan action. Although the real tragedies of the Depression were yet to be realized, agricultural incomes in 1929 and 1930 previewed what was to come in other sectors in the following decade. The national agricultural income dropped from $820.3 millions in 1928 to $691.4 millions in 1929 to $399.3 millions in 1930. And, the most dramatic decline was witnessed by Prairie farmers. While in the 1928 to 1930 period agricultural income dropped by 50% in Ontario, it plummeted by 64% in Manitoba, 75% in Alberta and 85% in Saskatchewan. The collapse of the agricultural sector was also reflected in considerable declines in wages and salaries paid in those provinces.[91] As their profits evaporated, and in the face of growing economic uncertainty, the UFC (SS) in 1929 declared its support for a socialist movement among organized farmers. The national convention of the UFC of that year adopted a motion stating that the farmers were "in favour of the abolition of the present system of capitalist robbery and the establishment of a real co-operative social system controlled by the producers."[92] Nevertheless, convention delegates were not prepared to enter partisan politics to achieve this goal, debating and rejecting independent political action.

If the UFC was still not ready to step into the electoral arena, urban socialists moved closer to forming a cross-provincial social democratic party the same year. The first Western Labour Conference drew representation from western socialists, labour, and organized farmers. The Independent Labour Parties of Manitoba and Saskatchewan were most prominent in this alliance. Because it had done much educational work in both the urban and rural areas, the ILP maintained a high profile in the West, despite the paucity of numbers.[93] By 1929, the ILP in both provinces prepared to form a closer union between themselves and with farmers. The Western Labour Conference of 1929 agreed that the ILP in Saskatchewan would establish locals throughout the province and work to collaborate with the local UFC lodges.[94]

This murmur of revolt against the two traditional parties in Saskatchewan was not replicated in the central and eastern provinces on the eve of the 1930 election. The Depression had not yet dealt its crippling blow to their more diversified economies.[95] Salaries and wages had not declined alarmingly, and unemployment was not as visible as it soon would be. The effect of this lack of an organized class-based opposition to the analysis provided by the major parties is indicated by the positions and solutions for economic ills suggested in the 1930 election campaign. No radical solutions were offered. This is not to say that the electorate did not hear discussion of economic issues in the campaign. The question of how to remedy Canada's declining export income and rising unemployment was central to both the Liberal and Conservative platforms. Both parties advocated a specific cure but the alternatives were ranged along the same continuum, albeit at opposite points. Both parties claimed that the solution to the economic ills was enlightened tariff-tinkering. The Liberals advocated an extension of Imperial Preferences to revive export markets while at the same time erecting mild retaliatory tariffs against the Americans' recent and onerous tariffs. By contrast, R. B. Bennett, the new leader of the Conservative Party, promised a more daring approach to revive prosperity. He proposed a new and aggressive National Policy which would, at one and the same time, protect the home market and "blast a way into the markets of the world." Bennett sensed the gravity of the economic situation in 1930 and modified his platform to appeal to specific target groups. The Maritimes were assured larger federal subsidies; dairy farmers in Quebec and Ontario were promised tougher restrictions against New Zealand butter, recently dumped on the Canadian market; workers were promised jobs.[96] Of the major parties, the Conservatives were clearly the most prepared to respond to the new economic reality. Mackenzie King showed little awareness of the severity of the economic crisis or little concern. Indeed, as his diaries later revealed, he apparently did not recognize the economic problem at all. Two months after his election loss, he recorded that the country was happy and contented, manufacturers and labour alike. The only criticisms were those due to electoral propaganda.[97] In effect, the Liberals lost the election almost by default.

As in 1925 and 1926, there was little reason to expect widespread class-based opposition to the bourgeois parties. The only group that continued to be attuned to the biases inherent in the dominant vocabulary of federal politics was that of organized farmers, and they had not yet reorganized an alternative partisan expression. Nor did they reaffirm their support for the Progressives, divided and weakened by Parliamentary manoeuvring. Thus, as Table 5:3 indicates, the voting patterns of urban and rural constituencies in 1930 in both the East and the West were very similar to the patterns evident earlier in the decade. The West, dissimilar to the East, continued to manifest a rural-urban cleavage. The Conservatives were again disproportionately rejected by the rural constituencies in the West. The Liberals, however, had neither a particularly urban nor rural support base in either region. Only the Progressives remained a predominantly rural party but they offered only twenty-two candidates in 1930, only two of whom contested the election in Ontario.

The Conservatives won 49% of the popular vote compared to the Liberals' 45% with the Progressives reduced to a mere 3%. The Progressive Party had been successfully absorbed by the two old-line parties less than a decade after it rocked the two-party system and the prevailing "classless" conception of politics. Nonetheless, the West continued to manifest a rural-urban cleavage. The Progressives may have disappeared as a party but their conception of politics, as being founded on other than ethnic criteria, remained partially visible in 1930. The 1930 election campaign spelled out the major themes of the decade to follow. The Liberal defeat revealed that the country was not content to endure the Depression nourished only on the same promises and solutions, and memories of prosperity. In the West, organized class opposition was rising to challenge the dialogue of "normal politics" of the bourgeois parties. However, for most of the population, alternatives had not yet appeared; voters wishing to register their anger and frustration had little choice but to shift their support from one of the major parties to the other.

Thus, while the old-line parties may have appeared to regain their monopoly in the federal sphere, their hegemony would not survive the

Table 5:3
THE 1930 ELECTION: CORRELATION OF PARTY VOTE AND CONSTITUENCY TYPE BY REGION
(Pearson's r)

	Urban	*Rural*
East		
Conservative	.11	−.12*
Liberal	−.08	.03
Progressives	−.06	.12*
West		
Conservative	.15	−.36*
Liberal	−.24	−.08
Progressives	−.26*	.52*

*p < .05

economic collapse of the thirties. The Depression would make it painfully obvious to everyone that the bourgeois parties had defaulted on their promise of "prosperity for all." The Progressive Party had faded into history but its legacy, an electorate disengaged from the "bicultural" vocabulary of federal politics, would once again be mobilized. This partisan expression, arising out of the Depression, would be less easily absorbed by the bourgeois parties. This time, the opposing analysis would be founded on social democratic principles and a coalition of farmers, workers and socialists. This party would challenge the very foundations of the capitalist system and not simply the National Policy. Its emergence would mean that political discourse in federal politics would less easily be confined to different conceptions of the nation and to the politics of biculturalism.

NOTES

[1] W. L. Morton, "The 1920's," in J. M. S. Careless and R. Craig Brown, eds., *The Canadians* (Toronto: Macmillan, 1967), p. 208.

[2] National unemployment rate rose to 16.5% in 1921, and in hardhit NS it reached 27%. When the federal government gave up its wartime powers and abolished the Wheat Board, and with it the western farmers' assurance of a stable market price, the price of wheat fell 60% between 1920 and 1922. In Saskatchewan, for example, the price per bushel fell from $2.32 in 1919 to $.76 in 1921, and it continued to drop. S. M. Lipset, *Agrarian Socialism*, revised and expanded edition (Los Angeles: University of California, 1971), p. 46, and W. A. Mackintosh, *The Economic Background of Dominion-Provincial Relations* (Toronto: McClelland and Stewart, 1969), p. 71.

[3] For details see Mackintosh, *op. cit.*, pp. 89-90.

[4] There were important shifts in the sources of national income. Agriculture declined relatively in importance and, despite abundant crops, the decline was most marked in the later years. Contributing 41% of the national net production in 1920, the statistic was 40% in 1925, 36% in 1928 with bumper crops, and 26% with the poor yields of 1929. *Ibid.*, p. 81. See also, pp. 50-52.

[5] Walter Young, *The Anatomy of a Party* (Toronto: University of Toronto, 1969), p. 19.

[6] Vernon C. Fowke, *The National Policy and the Wheat Economy* (Toronto: University of Toronto, 1957), p. 287.

[7] *Ibid.*, and Wallace Clement, *The Canadian Corporate Elite* (Toronto: McClelland and Stewart, 1975), p. 80.

[8] See J. B. Brebner, *North Atlantic Triangle* (Toronto: Ryerson, 1945), p. 288; Mackintosh, *op. cit.*, pp. 79-80.

[9] At the beginning of the century, Canada had the highest concentration of British portfolio investment of any major area of the world. See Kari Levitt, *Silent Surrender: The Multinational Corporation in Canada* (Toronto: Macmillan, 1970), p. 61.

[10] From 1914 to 1929, American investment abroad increased almost fivefold, and Canada was the single most important target of this direct investment. See Wallace Clement, *Continental Corporate Power* (Toronto: McClelland and Stewart, 1977), p. 67 ff.

[11]"The distinction between the import of foreign capital by the sale of bonds or debentures or non-controlling equity stock, and the intake of direct investment in the form of subsidiaries and branch plants controlled by externally-based parent corporations is crucial. In the former case control remains with the borrower; in the latter it rests unequivocally with the lender. Liabilities incurred by debt borrowing can be liquidated by the repayment of the loan. Direct investment creates a liability which is in most cases permanent." Levitt, *op. cit.*, pp. 58-59.

[12]In many cases, American corporations stepped up their investment in Canada after World War I, in order to satisfy "demands for access to secure supplies of strategic natural resources." See J. Laux and M. Molot, "Multinational Corporations and Economic Nationalism: Conflict Over Resource Control in Canada," *World Development*, vol. 6 (1978), p. 838. The effect of these efforts is seen in the pattern of investment. In the years of the wheat boom, from 1900 to 1913, although Canadian indebtedness increased dramatically, $3080 of the $3850 millions was portfolio investment, almost all of it British. By 1926 the proportion of direct to portfolio had increased to 30% (a 10% increase since 1913) while American investment had become 53% of all foreign investment compared to 22% in 1913. The increase in American investment in the 1913-1926 period stands out as the highest absolute increase, until after the Second World War. Levitt, *op. cit.*, pp. 66-67.

[13]Herbert Marshall *et al.*, *Canadian-American Industry* (Toronto: McClelland and Stewart, 1976), p. 21.

[14]*Ibid.*, pp. 220-222; Paul Phillips, "National Policy, Continental Economics and National Disintegration," in D. J. Bercuson, *Canada and The Burden of Unity* (Toronto: Macmillan, 1977), p. 28.

[15]See Mackintosh, *op. cit.*, pp. 82-87.

[16]Vernon C. Fowke, *Canadian Agriculture Policy: The Historical Pattern* (Toronto: University of Toronto, 1946), pp. 8-9.

[17]Clement, *The Canadian Corporate Elite, op. cit.*, pp. 70, 85.

[18]*Ibid.*, pp. 67-69.

[19]See *ibid.*, pp. 82-85, especially Table 2, p. 84; Stuart Jamieson, *Industrial Relations in Canada* (Toronto: Macmillan, 1973), pp. 5-6.

[20]Donald V. Smiley, ed., *The Rowell-Sirois Report*, Book 1, (Toronto: McClelland and Stewart, 1963), p. 17.

[21]Carman Millar, "The Restoration of Greater Nova Scotia," in Bercuson, *op. cit.*, p. 50.

[22]T. W. Acheson, "The National Policy and the Industrialization of the Maritimes, 1880-1910," *Acadiensis*, vol. 1 (Spring, 1972), p. 3.

[23]In fact, when the Fathers of Confederation met to debate the Quebec resolution, construction of the Intercolonial was one of the principal demands. See Edgar McInnis, *Canada: A Political and Social History* (Toronto: Holt, Rinehart and Winston, 1969), p. 354.

[24]E. R. Forbes, "Misguided Symmetry: The Destruction of Regional Transportation Policy for the Maritimes," in Bercuson, *op. cit.*, p. 64.

[25]Smiley, *op. cit.*, p. 15, especially Table 1.

[26]Acheson, *op. cit.*, p. 3ff.

[27]Forbes, *op. cit.*, p. 56.

[28]It should be noted that the population increased much more in other provinces than in the Maritimes. However, the growth which did occur in the Maritimes

was in manufacturing, whereas, the Prairies, for example, concentrated their growth in farm investment. Therefore, the Prairies, with a 40-45% increase in population, had a smaller rate of increase in manufactures than did the Maritimes. See Mackintosh, *op. cit.*, p. 49.

[29]For discussion, see Acheson, *op. cit.*, pp. 20-23.

[30]Clement, *The Canadian Corporate Elite, op. cit.*, pp. 66-67.

[31]For details, see Forbes, *op. cit.*

[32]E. R. Forbes, "The Origins of the Maritime Rights Movement," *Acadiensis*, vol. 5 (Autumn, 1975), p. 56.

[33]*Ibid.*, p. 57; Acheson, *op. cit.*, p. 15.

[34]C. D. Howell, "Nova Scotia's Protest Tradition and a Search for a Meaningful Federalism," in Bercuson, *op. cit.*, p. 183.

[35]Acheson, *op. cit.*, p. 13.

[36]Forbes, "The Origins of the Maritime Rights Movement," *op. cit.*, p. 58.

[37]Acheson argues that freight-rate improvements along with export support might have saved the industrial structure of the Maritimes. However, he offers these two factors as alternatives to consolidation or mergers. In other words, the mergers, which were what destroyed the independence of Maritime industrialization, might have been avoided with better railway policy. This is where we disagree with him and argue that independence was lost because of the Maritime capitalists' participation in the national development strategy, which in the twentieth century turned against them. See Acheson, *op. cit.*

[38]Mackintosh, *op. cit.*, p. 53.

[39]Acheson, *op. cit.*, pp. 7, 23-24.

[40]The most obvious special case was exports by American branch plants producing goods in Canada for sale in countries of the British Empire, which were markets closed to American-made goods by the system of Imperial Preference.

[41]Clement, *The Canadian Corporate Elite, op. cit.*, p. 69.

[42]For a fuller discussion, see Acheson, *op. cit.*, p. 6 ff.

[43]*Ibid.*, pp. 19, 25-26.

[44]David Frank, "The Cape Breton Coal Industry and the Rise and Fall of The British Empire Steel Corporation," *Acadiensis*, vol. VII (Autumn, 1977), p. 6.

[45]P. Allen, *Tendances récentes des emplois au Canada* (Montreal: Ecole des Hautes Etudes Commerciales, 1957), Table IV, p. 34. In Ontario the percentage of the population in agricultural occupations fell from 41 to 23 for the 1901 to 1931 period. *Ibid.*, Table XII, pp. 51-52. See also Leo Johnson, "The Development of Class in Canada in the Twentieth Century," in G. Teeple, ed., *Capitalism and the National Question in Canada* (Toronto: University of Toronto, 1972), pp. 141-183.

[46]See Janice Acton, *et al.*, eds., *Women at Work: Ontario 1850-1930* (Toronto: Canadian Women's Educational Press, 1974), Tables F and G., pp. 280-281.

[47]Allen, *op. cit.*, Table IV, p. 34.

[48]See Johnson, *op. cit.*, Table 10, p. 165.

[49]For an account of union activity among women production workers, see Acton, *et al.*, *op. cit.*, pp. 331-361, and especially pp. 354-56.

[50]The low level of unionization of these new workers is indicated by relative rates of unionization in several sectors. While in 1931, 39% of all paid workers in mining, 24% of construction and 59% of railway workers were unionized, only

6% of the service workers were in unions. Thus, although they were rapidly increasing in number, they were not being integrated into the union movement. This partially accounts for the low levels of unionization until the Second World War. See *Union Growth in Canada, 1921-1967* (Ottawa: Department of Labour, 1970), p. 17, Table VIII A, p. 85, and Table VI-A, p. 78.

[51]François-Albert Angers and Patrick Allen, *Evolution de la structure des emplois au Canada* (Montreal: Ecole des Hautes Etudes Commerciales, 1954), pp. 42-45.

[52]John Crispo, *The Canadian Industrial Relations System* (Toronto: McGraw-Hill Ryerson, 1978), p. 165.

[53]The Department of Labour's wage index shows salaries for skilled trades at 180 in 1925, compared to 100 in 1913, although this was a decline from the postwar high of 198 in 1920. See Mackintosh, *op. cit.*, p. 78; Jamieson, *op. cit.*, especially Chapter 3.

[54]Jamieson, *op. cit.*, p. 86.

[55]Between 1925 and 1932, all provinces except Prince Edward Island passed legislation similar to the IDIA. See *ibid.*, p. 120.

[56]H. Quinn, *The Union Nationale: A Study in Quebec Nationalism* (Toronto: University of Toronto, 1963), p. 41.

[57]*Ibid.*, p. 33.

[58]For a discussion of the class biases of nationalist ideologies in Quebec see G. Bourque and N. Laurin-Frenette, "Social Classes and National Ideologies in Quebec," in G. Teeple, *op. cit.*, p. 23; *passim.*

[59]See Martin Robin, *Radical Politics and Canadian Labour* (Kingston: Industrial Relations Centre, 1968), pp. 199-278.

[60]Norman Penner, *The Canadian Left* (Scarborough, Ontario: Prentice-Hall, 1977), pp. 32-33, 130.

[61]Robin, *op. cit.*, pp. 242, 252, 265.

[62]*Ibid.*, pp. 254-256; Penner, *op. cit.*, p. 130.

[63]Robin, *op. cit.*, pp. 260, 268.

[64]Penner, *op. cit.*, p. 131.

[65]*Ibid.*, p. 134; Robin, *op. cit.*, pp. 247, 253-254, 259ff, 262-263.

[66]To one part of the Progressives, most generally the Albertan representatives, ". . . it increasingly appeared that a mere sectional realignment could not heal the ills of the body politic and economic. The evils of metropolitan domination would work in a free or a protected economy. They increasingly saw the cleavage in society, not as one of sectional alignment, but as one between classes. The cleavage might be closed by a new economic order, in which co-operation would replace competition and inaugurate a commonwealth in which the state would render economic justice to all classes in all sections." W. L. Morton, *The Progressive Party in Canada* (Toronto: University of Toronto, 1950), p. 201.

[67]Morton describes the Progressives as transitional, with the Manitoba wing representing the old order and the Alberta wing moving toward a demand for state intervention and nationalization which were demands similar to those being made by social democrats at the time. "At this point, there came to the surface the transitional character of the Progressive movement. It was itself an expression of the transition from the era of laissez-faire to the era of the managed society." *Ibid.*, pp. 201-202.

[68]Robin, *op. cit.*, p. 241; Penner, *op. cit.*, p. 174.

[69]Robin, *op. cit.*, p. 243.

[70]Young, *op. cit.*, p. 14.

[71]The Minister of Finance in 1922, argued that a "moderate" tariff was as low as the country could bear, and stability of tariffs was also essential. "Moderation was, indeed, the condition which alone could give stability. The policy of a moderate tariff was itself conditioned by a standing offer of reciprocity of trade with the United States. Thus the ancient Maritimer, with debonair, old-world deftness, offset the concession to industry of a stable tariff by holding out the prospect of reciprocity with the US, long desired by the continental West and the Maritime Provinces. It was to balance a fact with a hope, a deed with a delusion; apart from that, Liberal tariff policy had come to rest dead centre between the protectionist followers of Meighen and the agrarian low-tariff men." Morton, *The Progressive Party, op. cit.*, p. 183.

[72]For a more detailed discussion of these ideas see *ibid.*, pp. 162-163.

[73]*Ibid.*, p. 147.

[74]Morton, "The 1920's," *op. cit.*, p. 215.

[75]Mackintosh, *op. cit.*, pp. 101-104.

[76]Morton, *The Progressive Party, op. cit.*, pp. 191-192.

[77]*Ibid.*, p. 164.

[78]*Ibid.*, pp. 165, 175ff, 263, 269.

[79]Lipset, *op. cit.*, p. 46.

[80]Mackintosh, *op. cit.*, p. 87.

[81]For the formation of this group see Morton, *The Progressive Party, op. cit.*, p. 194ff.

[82]C. D. Howell, *op. cit.*, p. 183.

[83]*Ibid.*, p. 184.

[84]J. M. Beck, *The Pendulum of Power* (Scarborough, Ontario: Prentice-Hall, 1969), p. 169.

[85]The following discussion of the 1925, 1926 and 1930 campaigns is drawn largely from *ibid.*, pp. 163-205.

[86]Morton, *The Progressive Party, op. cit.*, p. 238.

[87]See Beck, *op. cit.*, pp. 185-186 for a discussion of how ethnic divisions were also important in the West.

[88]For a survey of this activity, see *ibid.*, p. 274.

[89]*Ibid.*, pp. 277-290.

[90]Fowke, *The National Policy and the Wheat Economy, op. cit.*, pp. 91-92. For a discussion of wheat marketing, see pp. 198ff and 256 ff.

[91]Mackintosh, *op. cit.*, pp. 124-131.

[92]Lipset, *op. cit.*, p. 103.

[93]J. S. Woodsworth, the ILP member from Winnipeg, co-operated with some of the more radical western farmers' representatives, like W. Irvine of Alberta, in the impromptu "Ginger Group" in the House of Commons. In Saskatchewan, M. J. Coldwell, who topped the aldermanic polls in Regina in the civic election of 1926, conducted weekly educational radio broadcasts on the subjects of socialism and economics. See Young, *op. cit.*, p. 55ff.

[94]*Ibid.*, p. 24.

[95]The Employment Index for Manufacturing Industries had only dropped moderately from 120.3 in July 1929 to 111.2 in July 1930 (1926 = 100), Mackintosh *op. cit.*, p. 115.

[96]Beck, *op. cit.*, p. 192.

[97]The Liberal Party's problems in 1930 extended far beyond King's myopia. As a party biographer indicates, the Liberal Party organization was in shambles in every province except Quebec. Unlike the Conservatives, who depended heavily on funds from their millionaire leader and his corporate allies, the Liberals were nearly bankrupt. Furthermore, their literature was often distributed late, the speakers' itineraries were poorly organized, and, throughout the campaign, the Conservatives seemed to outdistance the Government Party. See Reginald Whitaker, *The Government Party* (Toronto: University of Toronto, 1977), p. 13; and H. Blair Neatby, *William Lyon Mackenzie King: The Lonely Heights* (Toronto: University of Toronto, 1963), pp. 301-302.

Chapter 6

The 1930s—The Depression Election

Introduction

Unlike the previous decade, which masked the major currents of economic and social change with seeming continuity and which attempted to avoid readjustment by returning to "normal politics," the 1930s brought yet another challenge to the dominant definition of federal politics in Canada. These were years of crisis, disaster, realignment and reform. During the "depression years" old assumptions were questioned, and new strategies came to the fore to reflect the developments in the economy and polity of the previous three decades. The collapse of the international economic order forced Canada to accept a new place in the world economy and increasing dependence on American capitalism. The British and Imperial connection was less appealing as an alternative focus. Similarly, the party system and the state had to adjust to a new organization of class relations. Several new parties were born in the midst of the Depression and they would not go away as easily as had the Progressives. But these new parties were not the only changes in the system of class relations of the 1930s. The state, especially the federal state, was increasingly called upon to assume new responsibilities to cushion the ravaging effects of capitalism for the workers. In addition, the union movement could no longer avoid organizing non-craft workers. The dominance of the craft-based TLC was broken and new partisan initiatives began to appear in the labour movement.

Thus, the 1930s were a time of political change, but the changes were responses to trends that had become visible much earlier. The Depression acted as a catalyst. It made obvious, with stark and painful clarity, some of the contradictions in both the existing political organization of class relations and the development strategy which, with adjustments and modifications, had characterized the post-Confederation years. The Second World War, coming at the end of the decade, would push the country into a new position in the international economy and into a new strategy for growth. In the meantime, the rationalization for politics without class dialogue, namely growth and prosperity for all, evaporated in the face of global depression. The traditional parties as proponents of this world view and the capitalist system itself lost credibility in the eyes of a large portion of the electorate. The boom of the late twenties had come to an abrupt halt. The economy could generate neither jobs for industrial workers nor commodity prices sufficient to sustain agricultural producers. The Depression denied hundreds of thousands of Canadians a means of providing the barest essentials for themselves or their families. Meanwhile both the provincial and federal states, without appropriate ideology, policy or legislation to cushion the effects of the prevailing economic order, practised only minimal intervention.

The failures of the capitalist system precipitated a disintegration of traditional party loyalties. These loyalties, which sustained the major parties and minimized class-based dialogue in partisan debate, began to dissolve as one group interest after another became conscious of its grievances and mobilized its own partisan expression. The "normal politics" which appeared at last recovered after the Progressives' foray into federal politics was once again in peril.

The new parties in the 1935 general election arose to protest the prevailing economic order, but none purported to represent a single class, and none emerged directly out of the ranks of organized labour. Nevertheless, a peculiar socialist party did emerge from a coalition of workers, farmers, intellectuals and socialists. This party set about challenging the major parties and their definition of the political. It was an alliance led by those advocating the interests of the workers. The independent commodity producers would also be critically important in the formation of this new party and later as voters, but it was meant to be, from the start, not only a farmers' party, but also a workers' party and a social democratic party. However, the contradictions within the party which such a birth implied haunted it for years.

The Co-operative Commonwealth Federation was conceived in the depths of the Depression. Similar to the Progressives, this party manifested the organized farmers' disdain for the prevailing economic order and its two political parties. Yet, the CCF differed from the Progressives in several important respects. It sought to eradicate not merely the National Policy, but the entire capitalist system. To achieve this goal, it sought the support of, and represented itself as the party of, farmers and workers alike. Nevertheless, while the Depression allowed this coalition, the CCF, from its conception, housed class contradictions which would act upon its support base and its socialist doctrine when economic conditions improved. In essence, the Depression made a social democratic party comprised of fundamentally different class interests possible, but it could not ensure that the coalition would be a durable one. These contradictions explain the outcome of the 1935 election, but, perhaps more importantly, they help to explain the subsequent strategies of all the parties in the federal sphere and the underdevelopment of the socialist option in Canadian politics.

The failure of the CCF to mobilize the electorate behind it sufficiently to ensure success in federal politics was, once again, as with other socialist parties throughout Canadian history, the result of the interaction between the prevailing class composition of the country, the mobilization potential of the labour movement, the influence of other political ideologies and the strategic decisions of the party itself.

The Political Economy of the 1930s

Canada's ability to weather the Depression was only partially in its own hands. As previous chapters have described, the development strategy of the National Policy with its heavy reliance on export trade, left the country vulnerable when customary markets closed and new ones failed to materialize. The Depression of the 1930s involved a collapse of the international system of trade. Most countries, and particularly Canada's major trading partners, tried to deal with the crisis by drawing in on themselves.[1] Economic isolationism ensured that their products would dominate their home market and thereby provide them some shelter from the full impact of the Depression. This movement toward self-sufficiency, in turn, amplified the economic crisis in countries whose economies were very dependent on export trade.

For countries where only a small proportion of national income depended on foreign trade, this was, in the short run, a strategy for survival. However, for a country where almost a third of production was exported, such a strategy was disastrous because when the others became isolationist, Canada lost its markets.[2] Isolationism was an impossible option for Canada because the domestic market could not consume the products which had been habitually exported. Buyers for wheat were essential, as were markets for fish, pulp and paper, non-ferrous minerals —all those products produced in Canada for consumption elsewhere.

The only hope for Canada was that the other countries would realize economic isolationism could not work in the long run because modern capitalism required an abundant interchange of products across national boundaries.[3] With the recognition of this necessity by the United States in 1934 and the reduction of tariff barriers that had been erected in 1930, Canada could again begin to anticipate recovery, which would only be realized fully during World War II.[4] This recovery brought with it a new place in the international economy, as the Depression effectively ended Britain's leadership of the international capitalist system and marked the end of Canada's original National Policy.[5] Increasingly, the trends of the 1920s would become the norm, and the Canadian economy would be enmeshed with the production process of the United States.[6] The development of the economy, class structure and political organization of class relations would respond not only to the international economic system but more and more to decisions taken in the United States, in cities such as Detroit, Chicago, New York or Pittsburgh.[7] This was the legacy of the

"Great Depression." In the meantime, the thirties had to be endured. What was this crisis? In the economy, it soon became apparent that Canada's problems would not be solved by "blasting a way into markets" as Prime Minister Bennett had promised in 1930. Export markets had not faltered momentarily; they had collapsed. Canada's traditional trading partners had bolted their doors, and therefore, export and commodity prices plummeted. In turn, jobs in the manufacturing and service sectors were lost by hundreds and then thousands, as the production process ground to a halt. The chance of securing employment grew increasingly illusive for an alarming proportion of the population. Year after year, unemployment defined uncharted extremes in poverty and despair.

Although popular demands for new forms of state action multiplied, the requisite mechanisms for economic recovery were largely beyond the reach of the Bennett government. The simultaneous and global collapse in manufacturing and agriculture and the isolationism of its trading partners forced Canadian decision-makers to make choices which only aggravated the already abused condition of the industrial workforce and western farmers. With the collapse of the international wheat market, manufacturers in Quebec and Ontario could no longer depend upon demand from the hinterland to keep their enterprises buoyant. At the same time, high tariff walls denied the manufacturers the option of seeking markets outside the country. Not only did the Canadian domestic market collapse but the tariffs established by Great Britain and other Commonwealth countries removed an incentive for Americans to manufacture in Canada. Without the stimulus of the preferential tariff among Commonwealth countries, what little manufacturing export activity that did exist, usually by branch plants seeking a way into the Commonwealth markets, fell off.[8]

The floundering economy clearly required some form of state intervention, but few policy alternatives were available, and none promised to serve the needs of the manufacturing and exporting sectors equally. On the one hand, there was a call for retaliatory tariffs to protect domestic manufacturing from the dumping of cheaper foreign-made goods on the Canadian market. On the other hand, escalating retaliatory tariffs would only block the wheat producers' and other exporters' efforts to find markets abroad, as well as raise prices in Canada. However, there was really little choice. Alone, Canada could not reverse international trends. The Conservative government was forced to throw up tariff walls against other nations' products to protect the Canadian manufacturing sector.[9] Already steep tariffs were raised throughout the period 1930-1933 to guarantee Canadian manufacturers a domestic monopoly and to divert purchases to home-produced goods. As with all the post-Confederation tariffs, the strategy disproportionately benefited the capitalists and the workers of the central provinces.[10] Programmes for recovery, or at least survival, were directed toward the maintenance of production in the centre of the country.

This was, then, a policy of minimum innovation to assist the least vulnerable sector of the economy. Economic isolationism protected the very sector of the economy which was most able to defend itself. Although profits in the manufacturing sector dropped dramatically during the early years of the Depression, the logic of supply and demand afforded manufacturers some defensive mechanisms to minimize their losses. When market conditions demanded limits on production, profits could be maintained by reducing costs, for example, labour costs.[11] Thus, during the bleakest years of the Depression, when unemployment reached unprecedented levels, the manufacturing sector was profitable, albeit less than in the boom years of the 1920s.[12]

In contrast to manufacturers, farmers had few mechanisms to regulate their margin of profit or loss. Their position was in some ways similar to that of workers. Both were totally vulnerable to the dictates of the market. Yet, unlike workers, the farmers' production required continued expenditure of labour and capital, regardless of market conditions. By mid-decade wheat prices declined to approximately one-half of the 1929 level. To aggravate what seemed to be insuperable injustices stemming from the marketplace, the Prairie region also experienced a series of natural disasters. Extreme drought was followed by smothering dust storms, clouds of grasshoppers, and wheat disease.[13] Yields were so reduced and mounting debts so onerous that countless western farmers were forced off the land to join the ranks of the unemployed in swelling urban relief lines.

That the onus of the Depression fell disproportionately on the independent commodity producers of the West is clearly seen in Table 6:1. The average mean income for Prairie farmers plunged 94% in only five years. More generally, however, the table shows the differential impact of the collapse of world markets. In the agricultural sector, western interests, heavily dependent on the single crop, lost approximately 30% more income than the more diversified agricultural sector of the other provinces. For wage and salary earners a similar pattern emerges. The decline in income for employees in exporting industries and in growth-related industries, such as construction, was considerably greater than in the protected manufacturing sector. All told, those sectors most linked to the protected home market were shielded somewhat from the bleakest consequences of the Depression. The upward adjustments in the tariff apparently reached the intended clientele, while the exporting sector struggled despairingly against the maladies of the prevailing capitalist system.

Similar imbalances of effects between and within classes occurred in most advanced capitalist countries. However, in Canada, because of the

Table 6:1
DECREASES IN NET MONEY INCOME BY SOURCE OF INCOME
(1928-1933)

Source of Income	% change 1932–33 average mean income from 1928–29 average mean income
Agriculture (Prairie provinces)	-94
Fisheries	-72
Salaries and wages in construction	-68
Agriculture (other provinces)	-64
Salaries and wages in exporting industries	-50
Dividends received by shareholders	-40
Salaries and wages in protected industries	-37
Income of small businessmen and professionals, individual entrepreneurs	-36
Bond interest, property income from life insurance and interest on farm mortgages received by individuals	+13

Source: Report of the Royal Commission on Dominion-Provincial Relations, 1867-1939, Book 1, (Ottawa: Queen's Printer, 1940), p. 150.

past development strategies, these class differentials also implied regional disparities. As Table 6:2 indicates, decline in personal income between 1929 and 1933 was considerably more pronounced in the western than the eastern provinces.[14] The most striking contrast was between the industrialized central provinces and the wheat-producing provinces. Indeed, personal income in Saskatchewan dropped by 70% compared to approximately 32% in Ontario and Quebec. This disparity was due to two factors. First, the old staples were principally located in the periphery and the protected industries in the centres. Second, the economy of the

Table 6:2
PER CENT DECLINE IN PERSONAL INCOME, BY PROVINCE
(1928-1933)

	% Decline from 1928 to 1933
Prince Edward Island	45.4
Nova Scotia	34.1
New Brunswick	38.1
Quebec	31.9
Ontario	32.2
Manitoba	44.9
Saskatchewan	70.8
Alberta	55.0
British Columbia	60.5

Source: calculated from National Income and Expenditure Accounts, Vol. 1, The Annual Estimates, 1926-1974 (Ottawa: Information Canada, 1976), Table 35, p. 48.

Prairies was not as diversified as that of the East. The effects of diversification can be seen in farm incomes. The eastern farmers, generally involved in mixed enterprises producing for the domestic urban market, suffered far less than the export-oriented Prairie farmer whose income was almost totally dependent upon a revived wheat market. These patterns are the result of the development strategies of previous decades. The decline in wages and salaries between eastern and western workers was less marked, but regional differences were also evident. In the East, wages and salaries decreased by 36% during the period 1928–1933 while in the West the decrease was 44% for the same period.[15]

The Bennett government's tariff policy thus cushioned the effect of the Depression for specific economic interests and regions. This did not mean, however, that it was immune to demands from others. The farmers continued to have political weight which made some form of help essential. However, even more pressing was the need to revive a domestic market which would consume the products of the industrial system. Consumers were necessary. Dirt-poor farmers and unemployed industrial workers did not buy enough. Therefore, the state attempted to revive the economy and thereby, ensure a market for the manufacturing sector. However, the legislative tools available were hardly capable of meeting the task, and past practices and the prevailing ideology placed even greater restrictions on remedial measures. Nevertheless, throughout the Conservatives' term of office one makeshift policy after another, designed to improve the lot of the Prairie wheat farmer, was introduced.[16]

The urban unemployed had an equally pressing case for state assistance, but for them, even less was forthcoming from the state. Once again, the provision of relief was partially inhibited by confusion over constitutional jurisdictions and by the inability of some provincial governments to finance welfare programmes. However, there were also ideological barriers. In the past, the Canadian state had made few provisions for the urban unemployed. Before the widespread industrialization of the previous decade, unemployment was usually absorbed by the agricultural frontier or emigration to the United States; or the costs were assumed by the extended family. However, these alternatives were largely exhausted in the early thirties.[17] Thus unemployment occurred in an entirely different context, and, at the same time, the ranks of the unemployed swelled as never before.[18]

The state lacked mechanisms to cope with this immeasurable human tragedy. Even when the federal government came to the aid of the nearly bankrupt provinces and municipalities, spending by all levels of government was low and unimaginative. As the unemployed increased rapidly in number, the proportion of the national income spent on relief edged upward from 4.9% in 1931 to 6.6% in 1933 to the peak for the decade of 8.4% in 1935.[19] However, this spending did not significantly change the unhappy lot of the unemployed nor could it begin to justify the visible inequalities of the Depression for its victims.[20]

Although the federal state developed few mechanisms to improve the condition of unemployed workers, this did not mean that it was confident that the prevailing system of class relations would survive the crisis unaided. The Conservative government unveiled a variety of measures designed to anticipate and turn aside civil unrest. A two-pronged offensive was initiated. On the one hand, the government attempted to organize and control certain categories of the unemployed under the auspices of the state. On the other, it mobilized its coercive apparatus to monitor and suppress potential agents of dissent, particularly within the labour movement.

Unemployment touched all categories of workers, but one which was particularly hard hit and aroused the government's suspicions was single, homeless and unemployed young men. This group was very conspicuous. These young men could be seen swarming by the dozens around the infrequent 'help wanted' notices; they were strung one behind the other in relief lines; they covered the tops of railroad cars, moving along to yet another unrealized job possibility; or, they were simply huddled, day after day, around the rare construction site waiting for an accident or a firing to make work available. Their fate was the concern of government and public alike. Among the middle classes and clergy there was widespread demand for action, to reduce the risk that these young men might become irresponsible and irreverent citizens. For the government, they embodied the failure of the system and were considered a threat to civil and political stability. Indeed Bennett and the Minister of Labour, Senator G. Robertson, seemed convinced that these men were nothing less than political revolutionaries.[21] Moving quickly to bring this perceived threat under state control, work camps were set up in peripheral regions, and the promise of three square meals a day drew as many as twenty thousand young men off the city streets and to the remote interior of the country.[22] Yet, not even physical isolation was sufficient. When a strike of workers in British Columbia relief camps, organized by Communists and trade unionists, mushroomed into the "On-to-Ottawa" Trek in 1935, the RCMP stopped and turned back the otherwise peaceful march in Regina, amidst scenes of a bloody riot.[23]

The other prong of the government's offensive was directed toward ideological challenges and potential sources of radical criticism within the labour movement. Throughout this period Bennett made speech after speech condemning radicals and promising to stamp out "socialism, communism and dictatorship with the iron heel of ruthlessness."[24] The iron heel was largely legislative. In 1931 the Communist Party was outlawed, and eight of its leaders were immediately jailed. Section 98 of the Criminal Code, which gave an open-ended definition of sedition, was used frequently, in a manner reminiscent of the years immediately after the First World War. Books were censored and "aliens," some of whom had been in Canada for as many as twenty years, were arrested without warrant and deported without trial.[25] In addition to legislative action, the government converted the RCMP into what one author describes as a "private army of storm troopers."[26] These police operated either overtly to maintain social control, as in the 1935 Regina riot, or covertly to monitor the activities of trade unions.[27]

Yet, in spite of the anxious suppression of these perceived threats to the system, no amount of government activity could completely defuse the doubts which were aroused by the staggering economy itself. No one needed an "alien" conveying "subversive" ideologies to question the efficacy of the present-day capitalism. Nor was there need to censor literature. The failures of capitalism were experienced, albeit in varying forms and degrees, by all. It was manifest in relief lines, in the expropriation of family homes and farms and in business bankruptcies. It could be heard in tragic accounts of hard times by family members and neighbours. In effect, the Depression produced a loss of faith in stability and security.[28] As such, it precipitated a crisis in the dominant ideology. It acted as a catalyst for alternative definitions of the political and encouraged many social groups, especially those most affected by the economic crisis, to question old values and demand changes.[29]

This crisis in the dominant ideology undermined the faith that capitalism would provide a bountiful life for all. It was a crisis in the ideology of capitalist democracy which provided legal equality for all but brought state intervention on the side of the dominant class. It was a crisis in the ideology of classlessness which was vigorously defended by the major political parties. Thus, it was a crisis which created space for a political party with a new ideology, with a world view promising a different politics, a new state and another economic order. It opened the way for a coalition between subordinate classes and, hence, the possibility of re-making the face of Canadian politics.

Organized Labour During the Depression

During the 1930s the trade-union movement was ill-prepared to lead a challenge to the dominant ideology. A legacy of division, collaboration and suppression continued to weigh heavily on the movement. While the end of the decade would bring long overdue changes in the organization of workers, the state's coercive apparatus seems to have been mobilized against a threat that was more potential than real at the beginning of the decade. Economic conditions and the persistent disorganization of workers pre-empted the possibility of a workers' party emerging from the ranks of organized labour to challenge the two traditional parties and the faltering economic system. The League for Social Reconstruction perhaps best summarized the condition of organized labour in Canada when it wrote in 1935:

> The unskilled in all industries are largely unorganized. The only industries in which trade unions are really powerful are railways, printing, building, clothing, skilled metal-work, and musical entertainment. . . . Moreover, the unionists are divided among themselves. In Quebec 26,894, more than half of the total for that province, are [unions] completely controlled by the Roman Catholic hierarchy . . . [these unions are] . . . anti-militant, anti-class conscious and anti-socialist . . . 55,120 Canadian workers belong to "national" unions affiliated with all Canadian Congress of labor . . . a disproportionate amount of time and energy has been consumed in criticism and conflict between the All-Canadian and the American-affiliated Trade and Labor Congress groups. The smallest but most active group of unionists is the Workers' Unity League (21,253 members in affiliated unions) . . . Communist in its sympathies. . . . Their militancy at a time when most orthodox unions are in a state of coma has nearly doubled their membership in a year. . . . Most of the organized workers (167,720 or 58%) belong to the "international" unions . . . its leaders (in Canada) have been to say the least exceedingly cautious and its rank and file are not yet an effective political force, nor do they exert a unified influence on the labor market as a whole.[30]

Having been forced to surrender in the political and ideological sphere a decade earlier, organized labour was considerably weakened by economic crisis alone. It had few resources to bargain with employers or maintain solidarity within its ranks. Within the labour force, the numbers seeking employment far outweighed the number of positions open. Thus, for organized workers, without a tradition of radical political organization and without the protection of collective bargaining rights, there was little motivation to risk what little they had by engaging in militant trade union activity. For Canadian workers in the early thirties, the threat of being fired and replaced by the desperate unemployed was far too real.

Even more debilitating for labour solidarity was the lack of correspondence between the structure of the labour force and the organization of the labour movement. The dominant craft-based unions in the TLC were still refusing to organize the unskilled and semi-skilled. Therefore, competing industrial union centrals emerged and began to organize these workers on a massive scale. However, throughout the thirties the question of organizing industrial workers brought internecine conflict within the trade union movement and confusion over political strategies for labour, as well as competition for the right to "speak for labour."

The central labour organizations competing with the TLC, the Catholic Confederation of Labour (CCCL), the All-Canadian Congress of Labour (ACCL) and the Workers' Unity League (WUL) grew considerably. The number of workers organized in the above three national union centres nearly equalled the number in the TLC.[31] Thereafter, the number of trade unionists increased progressively from 323,000 in 1936 to the decade's high of 382,000 in 1938, which was, however, only 8% of the civilian labour force.[32] By far the most militant centre for industrial unionism during the early thirties was the Workers' Unity League. Formed in 1930 as the trade union arm of the Communist Party, the WUL was an extremely active political force despite its limited numbers.[33]

Consisting primarily of industrial unions in the mining, lumber and textile industries, the WUL also organized the unemployed, established unemployed workers' councils in the major urban centres and petitioned the government for a national non-contributory unemployment insurance scheme. The WUL was more willing than other centrals to strike against private industry and even against government, as exemplified by the "On-to-Ottawa" Trek, a massive protest by the unemployed which was organized by the WUL.[34] Obviously, however, the ability to translate these trade union successes into political activity was limited by the weakness of the Communist Party. A party without legal existence, it was forced to concentrate its actions and most of its efforts on the organization of trade unions, emphasizing immediate demands for the alleviation of the awful conditions of the Depression. This work could not be attributed openly to an illegal political party.

While the thirties mark the beginnings of real organization of industrial workers, this organization came about in such a fashion as to minimize the likelihood of any agreement on strategies for direct or even co-ordinated political action by labour. The CCCL worked so as to prevent, or at least inhibit political activity by the French Catholic workers. Ethnic conflict divided workers in Quebec, and the emphasis by the CCCL on cultural nationalism, founded in Catholicism and a horror of socialism, prevented any move toward a labour party.[35] The ACCL, the TLC and the WUL competed for recognition as the "spokesman for labour." The Communists, organizing in the WUL, could not directly engage in political activity and throughout the decade vacillated on strategy as the international communist movement changed its position on alliances.[36] Nor would the TLC, after the experience with the CLP in the twenties, countenance an unofficial alliance with the WUL. The ACCL, internally divided because it organized some of the most conservative as well as the most radical workers, was wooed by but not drawn into affiliation with the coalition which founded the CCF. In other words, the organizational divisions within the labour movement were not overcome so as to bring about participation in direct political action or to foster another party. That activity was left to a coalition forged by others. Organized labour stood aloof from the founding of the CCF and waited until succeeding decades to give it even minimal support. This had profound effects on the development of the new party.

The Founding of the CCF

The CCF was founded in 1933 with the merger of three left-wing currents which advocated direct political action and the formation of a new party. The first group, inheritors of the socialist traditions of party activity, was by 1933 clearly dominated by a social democratic analysis of capitalism and a parliamentary road map to socialism. The organized farmers of the West and Ontario comprised the second group, and professional intellectuals, an influence that had been conspicuously absent in the Canadian socialist movement to that point, were the third component of the coalition. The socialists and the farmers had, as we have described, a long and scarred history of electoral activity. Both had engaged in a series of internal struggles which had resulted in the dominance of one strand of each of their movements. We will briefly examine each of these currents as they came together in Regina in 1933 to found a new party.

However, a more general point to note is that, except for the intellectuals, the coalition was primarily a western one. The CCF arose out of the history and traditions of radicalism which upset the party system in 1921. This disruption, coupled with continued ideological work, challenged the definition of the political which prevailed in the rest of the country and maintained an electorate disengaged from the two-party system. The CCF moved into this space after 1933. It was the same opening which made it possible for the Social Credit Party, a party with a very different ideological complexion, to develop in Alberta at the same time. Thus, the electoral space available to the new parties was rife with contradictions. In one province, it could accommodate the populism of the Social Credit and in the next, the socialism of the CCF. The contradictions involved in aligning workers and farmers into a single party haunted the CCF for years and were only resolved much later by remaking the party.

The CCF was also a western party because this region was most severely affected by the economic collapse and the government's protection of manufacturing interests. If a catalyst is necessary for the organization of party, it was in the West that the pressures were the greatest. However, the nature of the party, the form it took and its electoral possibilities were shaped by factors other than the incidence of the Depression, factors such as the political and organizational history of the western region.

The Socialists

By the beginning of the thirties the socialist movement of the earlier years had been fractured into several distinct parts. One division was between the Communists and the non-Communists. After the formation of the Third International in 1921 a "choosing up" of sides took place within the ranks of Canadian socialists.[37] Prior to 1921, the socialist movement struggled with marxist and non-marxist analyses of capitalism and revolutionary and parliamentary strategies for the transition to socialism. However, with the polarization of the movement into the Communist Party and social democrats, the situation became much less complex. There were the Communists, who were wary of "reformist" initiatives and waited for the revolutionary seizure of power, and there were the social democrats, for whom capitalism was a system of class relations and exploitation to be eliminated by parliamentary reforms in the direction of social ownership, or "socialism." The theory and strategy of these Canadian social democrats were influenced by the British Labour Party, Fabianism and the Social Gospel. But, at the same time, the people who worked for the Regina coalition understood that the Canadian situation was not yet identical to that of Europe, or more particularly, Britain.[38] They had an understanding of the "peculiarities" of Canadian politics, especially the great importance of the independent commodity producers and the under-development of the industrial labour force and its organizations. Despite the goal of following the British Labour Party model, they were realistic enough in 1933 to know that it was not yet feasible. As J. S. Woodsworth said:

> I am convinced that we may develop in Canada a distinctive type of Socialism. I refuse to follow slavishly the British model or the American model or the Russian model. We in Canada will solve our problems along our own lines.[39]

Since, in Canada, there were neither enough workers nor strong enough unions to follow these models, Canadian socialism would be built by an alliance with another subordinate class, the farmers.

There was more than reformism in this national analysis. The CCF's Regina Manifesto contained a bald proposal for the overthrow of the capitalist system of production and called for the abandonment of the social relations of that system which had produced the agonies of the Depression. What it represents is a clear appreciation of Canadian conditions, class composition and organization and the possibilities of action, given this context. The Regina Manifesto was a document for its time, and the CCF was the party designed to implement the analysis.

The social democratic position was shared by the several labour parties which had emerged in the previous decade, most particularly the Independent Labour Party of Manitoba. It was also the position of the "Ginger Group," the minuscule, but vocal, labour group supported by dissident former Progressives, which had been in Parliament since 1921. It was this "Canadian" analysis which led to the first Western Labour Conference of 1929 and then culminated in the formation of the Co-operative Commonwealth Federation in 1933—a federation of labour, farmers and socialists.

The Farmers

The organized farmers had also been forced to choose sides in the 1920s, as the previous chapter has described. The Progressives had split into the "crypto-Liberal" faction, which eventually aligned with the Liberal Party, and the more radical farmers who demanded a fundamental reorganization of existing capitalism. A new agrarian party began to take shape in the early thirties, and the virtual collapse of the wheat market, coupled with a series of natural disasters, only hastened and intensified the move toward independent political action, including an alliance with labour against the "common foe," the Depression.[40] Thus, the new party, the CCF, would have a profoundly different character from that of the Progressive Party. If the organized farmers had gained anything from their previous encounter with federal politics, they learned that they must look for support outside the ranks of their own class. Thus, unlike the Progressives, these farmers actively nurtured an alliance with labour and the socialists.

The farmers also recognized that their position within the Canadian polity had changed. No longer were they so important to the economic growth of the country that the government had to react to, if not completely heed, their demands. With the changes of the twenties, they had lost much of their leverage in the balance of class forces and could only hope to be heard if their position were buttressed by an alliance. Although the farmers risked becoming the weaker partner in this new alliance, in 1933 the CCF seemed the "only game in town" for the drought- and Depression-struck farmers' organizations. They joined the labour parties and the socialists for yet another encounter with the federal Liberal and Conservative Parties.

The League for Social Reconstruction

The third, and new, current in the alliance was the intellectuals and specifically the League for Social Reconstruction. Previously, there had been little interaction between intellectuals, generally university professors, and the socialist movement. The reasons for the lack of interaction are complicated, but the effects were far-reaching.[41] The socialists had undertaken theoretical or educational work in the past, and, in fact, they had at times defined this as their principal task.[42] However, their educational work had been directed toward those who were already members of the parties or sympathizers with the movement. In other words, it was self-education. The LSR support added potential to the movement, in that they provided a way of contacting people not generally associated with the parties' cadres. The LSR published in periodicals such as the *Canadian Forum*; they gave radio broadcasts on the CBC, and they taught—principally at McGill and the University of Toronto. It was this ability to reach out to a wider audience that distinguished the CCF from the earlier and smaller socialist parties.

In addition, the LSR contributed much of the new party's programme. The League was formed in 1931 by a handful of left-wing academics from McGill University and the University of Toronto. Primarily socialist in outlook, they advocated the total restructuring of the prevailing order. But unlike the Communists, they were convinced that meaningful change could be achieved through existing political institutions. From its birth the League actively invited the public, largely through a series of CBC radio broadcasts and magazine articles, to consider the need for a new party with a radical approach to social problems.[43] Moreover, it contended that the emergence of a new party on the left was as much a question of ideology as of organization. Unlike previous political debates, the LSR objected to the Liberals and Conservatives not because of their particular religious, ethnic or regional biases but on the grounds that their political practice and conception of the national interest favoured the dominant class. In other words, the LSR sought to change the definition of the political rather than to create another political party with an ambiguous conception of the general interest. The primary objectives were programmatic, and, to this end, the members offered their support to any political party which would agree to embrace the LSR Manifesto of 1932 as its electoral programme.[44]

Needless to say, the Liberals and Conservatives were less than interested in the LSR's offer of conditional support. The LSR did not have a large enough membership to threaten either of the major parties electorally. Moreover, their Manifesto contained proposals such as public ownership and operation of transportation, communications and electric power; the nationalization of banks; full unemployment and health insurance, which were directly opposed to the interests of the financial backers and the personnel of the two bourgeois parties. Indeed, the major parties had every reason to dismiss the LSR's overtures out of hand.

The Coalition

In contrast, the LSR's ideas were welcomed by the organizations, located chiefly in Western Canada, already engaged in the building of a radical party of the left. The western Labour parties, already acutely aware of the electoral advantage to be gained from a coalition with the organized farmers, added the LSR as another component of their alliance. It was actually the labour parties which took the steering role in the creation of the new party. Representatives from the western agrarian movement were invited to the Western Labour Conferences of 1931 and 1932, and, together with the leaders of various socialist groups and provincial Independent Labour Parties, they agreed upon a new political formula. Farmers, workers and socialists would unite in a party committed to correcting the abuses of capitalism. At the same time, radical agrarian and labour Members of Parliament, commonly known as the "Ginger Group," forged an agreement among themselves to form a new "Commonwealth Party" to represent the subordinate classes in the federal party system.

In 1932 and throughout the winter of 1933, these forces converged, and the organizational and ideological profile of the new party was molded. Canada's socialist option would be a federated party composed of the small western labour parties, the LSR, the United Farmers of Canada originating in Saskatchewan, the United Farmers of Ontario and Alberta and a number of small socialist groups. The Co-Operative Commonwealth Federation (farmer, labour, socialist) represented a significant departure from previous political practice in the federal sphere. Its founders envisaged a new social order which would be brought into being by the electoral mobilization of all those dominated by the capitalist system. They were determined to take the parliamentary road to socialism, which, in the words of their Manifesto, would replace "the present capitalist system, with its inherent injustice and inhumanity, by a social order from which the domination and exploitation of one class by another will be eliminated. . . ."[45]

The CCF appeared to possess exactly those elements lacking in the Progressives, notably, a coherent programme and a potential support base outside the ranks of the organized farmers. Be that as it may, the strengths of the CCF in comparison to the Progressives were more potential than real and remained unrealized throughout the decade. Each element of the coalition, rather than reinforcing one another, actually precipitated centrifugal tendencies within the new party. In varying degrees, each current contradicted the others, posing one strategic dilemma after another for the party's leadership. Each contradiction placed a barrier between the party's aspirations for a new social order and the electoral strength it needed to achieve its goals, until finally a total restructuring of Canada's socialist option was undertaken in 1961.

The first contradictions which will concern us here existed between the party's predominant agrarian membership base and its socialist ideology.[46] The new party was a strange mix, in as much as its programme and ideology were basically socialist in principle while its organizational strength was not primarily working class but petit bourgeois. Of course, during the Depression, the western farmers could concur with a socialist analysis of the crisis. The collapse of the wheat market had placed the independent commodity producer in as uncertain a position as the unemployed worker. However, the farmer's position was never wholly analogous to that of the worker.

> In the thirties, the farmer's fight was against a progress in which he had no part and which seemed to be depriving him of his rightful share of

the world's goods. He was in the classical *petit bourgeois* position, neither bourgeois nor proletarian, and increasingly conscious of the disparity and anomaly of his position. Although he was able to join with labour parties making common cause against a common enemy, there does not seem to be any evidence that he really understood the problems of the industrial worker. Even in hard times the farmer is master of the productive process in a way the worker is not.[47]

The Depression made it possible for the farmers' organizations and the much smaller socialist and labour groups to converge to form the CCF. With economic stagnation, and being in the ambiguous position of the petit bourgeois, the farmers could accept a socialist prescription for change. Nevertheless, farmers were not workers, and, hence, their long-term interests were not wholly compatible with the CCF's more radical socialist prescriptions for restructuring capitalism. Although the party's leadership saw the CCF as a vehicle to correct the injustices imposed by capitalism on both the worker and the farmer, the majority of the farmers saw it simply as a means to improve the conditions of independent commodity production. In short, the objectives set out for the CCF did not entirely match the class interests of its organizational base.

This contradiction implied the existence from the beginning of a dilemma for the CCF, the full impact of which would not be realized until the economy recovered over the next decade. It implied that the radical tone of the Manifesto, particularly those elements concerning the nationalization of private property, might have to be modified to accommodate the interests of the petite bourgeoisie. At the same time, it also raised the possibility that the farmers, rejecting the socialist objectives, would desert the party once conditions improved.

That the CCF's doctrine disturbed the independent commodity producers was evident almost from the start. The United Farmers of Alberta, for example, were hesitant about the CCF's radical analysis of the capitalist system. They agreed to affiliate with the new party, but they retained their own name in Alberta. By doing so, they denied the CCF a visible presence in that province and inhibited the appearance of a new partisan option there at a time when all familiar loyalties were being questioned. Eventually, this tenuous alliance was ruptured when the UFA withdrew from the CCF in 1939. The coalition was even more short-lived in Ontario. The UFO affiliated with the CCF in 1933, but their commitment, at best, was uncertain. The situation of agriculture in Ontario, as we have seen, was not the same as in the West. Consequently, only two years after affiliating, the UFO withdrew from the coalition because the CCF was judged too radical. In 1935 the UFO transferred its organizational support to the Reconstruction Party instead. Only the organized farmers of debt-ridden Saskatchewan remained committed to the CCF at the end of the decade.

Thus, the contradiction between the CCF's policy and its organizational base left it more dependent on the electoral support of the urban workers than was initially anticipated. Herein lay the CCF's second strategic problem. The CCF saw itself as a party of farmers, labour and socialists alike. However, the presence of labour in the coalition was illusive, if not problematic, from the beginning. The founders of the new party presupposed that workers would vote for a socialist party without having first been organized *as workers*. In other words, the CCF assumed the political existence of a Canadian working class. Objectively workers existed but these workers did not, for the most part, recognize the political implications of their class position or accept their position within a single class. Workers who accepted the ideology of expanding capitalism benefiting everyone or who considered partisan politics to be merely a matter of ethnicity or religion could not be expected to support the CCF automatically. In effect, the dominant definition of politics reduced the potential flood of workers to the CCF to a mere trickle.

The CCF's difficulties were also related to the way workers were organized during the thirties and by whom they were organized. The low level of unionization, the divisions within the union movement as well as its position on direct political action weighed heavily on the CCF. The new party was more easily accepted by workers in British Columbia where the affiliated socialist parties had long been active mobilizers. Elsewhere, in its early years, the CCF made few overtures to draw organized workers into the party. Indeed, the CCF made no constitutional provisions for national unions to directly affiliate with the party. In addition, those most likely to engage in direct political action, notably the Communist-led unions, were rejected outright by the CCF leadership.[48] They feared infiltration of the CCF by the CP, via the unions. Therefore, the CCF rejected a Communist proposal for a United Front action in 1934, and the CCF leadership suspended the Ontario Provincial Council in the same year for co-operating with the CP.[49] The TLC, in its turn, maintained its rigidly non-partisan position, *vis-à-vis* all parties.

Thus, the CCF presented itself as a socialist party for the workers but did not actively seek trade union support, particularly if this involved co-operation with the Communists, or the possibility of alienating the TLC.[50] Nor would organized labour support be forthcoming from other labour centres favourable to direct political action, specifically the national unions. They simply did not consider the CCF a viable political alternative. The CCCL was opposed to the CCF as being both materialist and too centralist while the ACCL dismissed the CCF as being not radical enough. The ACCL publication, the *Canadian Unionist*, for example, mused about the CCF in 1933 in the following manner:

> . . . One is constrained to marvel at the confidence of those who undertake the regeneration of society by act of Parliament. . . .[51]

The newspaper was also critical of the CCF's reliance on the support of the farmers.

The CCF was at once too radical for the farmers and not sure enough of itself to actively work with organized labour. These contradictions limited the CCF's national electoral potential in at least two respects. First, hope for a strong agrarian vote was unlikely to be fulfilled, except perhaps in hard-hit Saskatchewan. Second, support from workers was unlikely to be realized except, perhaps, where the Independent Labour Parties were active and in British Columbia where the socialists had already developed a close relationship with the organized labour force. As a consequence of these two factors, then, rather than the promise of a socialist coalition of all subordinate classes across all provinces, the CCF held out the promise of being an agrarian petit bourgeois party in some provinces and a small urban socialist option in others.

Be that as it may, class contradictions at the heart of the CCF were not the only impediments to a widespread move to socialism. The CCF's possibilities were also shaped and limited by institutions both within and outside the party system. It had to survive confrontations with the prevailing definition of the political and compete with other new parties for that portion of the electorate detached from traditional party loyalties. The CCF's electoral strength was dependent both upon the success of forces based within the traditional ideology and upon the number and kind of new parties competing for an electorate disengaged from the two-party system.

The CCF met considerable opposition on both fronts prior to and during the 1935 federal campaign. Ideological resistance issued from most of the country's press which described the new party as a mixture of Bolshevism and impractical idealism. Similarly, most of the weeklies circulating among farmers attacked socialism and constantly tried to point out that farmers' demands for nationalization of certain industries potentially threatened their desire to own their own farms. Most religious institutions remained silent about the CCF, but the Roman Catholic Church denounced the party frequently as a dangerous movement resting on "a materialistic conception of the social order which precisely constituted the anti-Christian character of Socialism."[52]

The formation of two additional protest parties immediately prior to the 1935 election constituted more tangible ideological and organizational obstacles for the CCF in the electoral sphere. One party grew out of an essentially apolitical fundamentalist religious movement in Alberta while the other represented a splinter of the disintegrating federal Conservative Party. However, the relation of these two parties to the CCF was the same. Both constituted a partisan alternative to the traditional parties, and both weakened the claim of the CCF that partisan politics could be organized on the basis of class.

The first of these parties, Social Credit, emerged as a provincial party in Alberta in 1934. As did the CCF, it offered an explanation and a radical solution to Depression conditions. Nevertheless, its origins were entirely different. The Social Credit Party found its roots in religious fundamentalism and in the aspirations of its self-ordained prophet William Aberhart. Originally the Social Credit movement was as much a matter of theology as it was of partisan ideology and in many respects it was precisely this inter-relationship of religion and politics which gave it widespread credibility among the Albertan electorate. The contribution of the Prophetic Bible Institute to the Social Credit Party's meteoric conquest of Albertan provincial politics can hardly be underestimated. Of course, the dismal economic conditions and peculiar partisan experiences and disappointments rendered the Albertan electorate receptive to a fresh conception of the economic and political order, but it was William Aberhart and more specifically his Sunday afternoon radio broadcasts which determined that the new perspective would be embroidered with the tenets of social credit.

The Sunday afternoon broadcasts began in 1925, but only in 1932, when Aberhart himself discovered the virtues of social credit, did they focus on its teachings and propaganda and weave the doctrines of social credit into the fabric of religious fundamentalism.[53] Initially the doctrine was presented without partisan content, simply explaining that poverty in the midst of plenty could be eliminated by printing and distributing social dividends so as to keep the productive capacity in balance.[54] The movement turned to partisan politics only in 1934, after the United Farmer government and the UFA party convention refused Aberhart's request that they accept social credit economic policy as part of their platform. Rebuffed by the only viable political vehicle in Alberta, Aberhart and his assistant, Ernest Manning, travelled across the prairie provinces organizing constituency groups and intensifying the political content of the radio broadcasts.[55]

In August 1935, only two months before the federal election, the Social Credit Party swept to power in Alberta. This victory threatened the CCF's electoral potential in that province and, to a lesser extent, in Saskatchewan where Social Credit had also established constituency organizations. It provided the electorate with an alternative to the old-line eastern parties and proposed a solution to the independent commodity producers' economic crisis without arousing anxieties about socialism. In effect, the victory of the Social Credit Party denied the CCF space in the Alberta electorate, while the resounding defeat of the UFA provincial government, still affiliated with the CCF, diminished the CCF's organizational resources in the province.

The other partisan alternative which emerged to compete for those disillusioned and detached from the prevailing political order was more a product of political blundering than a vision of a restructured Canadian society. The Reconstruction Party was initiated by a former Conservative cabinet minister Harry Stevens, who resigned from the party after Prime Minister Bennett failed to enact legislation to protect small business from monopolistic practices. The party presented itself as an ambiguous class and, essentially eastern, alternative to the CCF. Not a radical departure from the traditional parties, it appealed to the more conservative of the disillusioned electorate by refusing to advocate "panaceas beyond the needs of the situation" or to "lend attraction to schemes of rigid state control of life or organization." Instead, the party promised to at last do justice to the forgotten groups of society which were identified as "the intellectual, the worker, the farmer, the small merchant, the small manufacturer and the organized clerical classes."[56] In other words, the Reconstruction Party criticized the two traditional bourgeois parties but did not promise a real departure from previous political practice. It sought to gather support from a variety of social categories without upsetting the existing system of class relations or economic exchange. It did, however, seek to gather together the discontented who were the target of the CCF.

Thus, the Depression acted as a political catalyst. The traditional definition of the political was challenged by a group of political parties seeking representation and resolution of class-related conflicts made blatantly obvious by a collapsed economy. Economic disaster had broken the politics of national consensus into an array of confusing and contradictory political solutions.

The traditional parties, and especially the governing Conservative party, were caught in a crisis of ideology—a crisis which threatened the latter's very survival. Lacking a class perspective to explain their hardships, most Canadians attributed the Depression to mismanagement on the part of the Bennett government. Indeed, the terms "Bennett" and "Depression" grew to be synonymous. The horse-drawn automobiles on the Prairies, for example, came to be known as "Bennett buggies," and the clusters of tar-paper shacks situated on the outskirts of urban centers were referred to as "Bennettburghs." As the 1935 election loomed closer, it was obvious to all that the Conservative Party would go down to defeat.[57]

However, the Conservative Party and Bennett did not accept this fate without attempting to turn it aside. The strategies of capitalists and particularly manufacturers began to change at this conjuncture of economic crisis and increasing labour and farmer militancy, which threatened a fundamental shift in the balance of forces in the economy if not the overthrow of capitalism itself. Part of the manufacturing fraction of the Canadian bourgeoisie recognized that the situation called for new strategies. The policy of repression and coercion of workers and their organizations, used at the turn of the century, during World War I, and in 1919 and in the early years of the Depression, was no longer adequate to quell the widespread militancy of the mid-thirties. Similar to what happened in other advanced capitalist countries, part of the Canadian bourgeoisie began to realize that some concessions would have to be made to the victims of the Depression. First among these concessions was unemployment insurance, which was seen for many reasons to be more efficient than the practice of direct relief.[58] Far-sighted businessmen saw numerous advantages to be gained from a state-administered social welfare programme. It could be financed through compulsory contributions from the employees' wages and thus free the provinces and the municipalities from the burden of financing direct relief while, at the same time, it would begin to control the rising wave of discontent among the workers.[59]

In view of these changing perspectives, Bennett laid aside his "iron heel of ruthlessness" and became the author of a "New Deal" for the subordinate classes. In January 1935, with all the zeal of the recently converted, he took to the airwaves to unveil his strategy for the revival of capitalism. The "New Deal" proposed five new acts—the Unemployment and Social Insurance Act, the Weekly Rest in Industrial Undertakings Act, the Natural Products Marketing Act, the Minimum Wages Act and the Limitations of Work Act—together with several lesser bills concerned with farm credit.[60]

In effect, on the eve of the Depression election, Bennett had, single-handedly, attempted to re-chart the course of the Conservative Party. However, this seeming about-face in the Party's position was incomprehensible only if the changes in ideas of how to control dissent are ignored. In essence, Bennett realized that if capitalism were to survive, the state had to protect the subordinate classes from some of the ravages of the Depression.[61] These programmes did not propose to redistribute income as the CCF and the CP demanded but rather were "forced savings" programmes which would be largely financed by the beneficiaries themselves. The state would administer the insurance-style programmes instead of leaving minimum subsistence up to private initiative.[62] This strategy would gather widespread support during World War II when the governing Liberal party would recognize the positive benefits of social security programmes and economic regulation. The following chapter will examine these developments in more detail, but the first evidence of this strategy appeared in the 1935 election.

Bennett's proposals for the reform of capitalism were not immediately understood or accepted by all capitalists or even voters. In fact, the "New Deal" legislation provoked fierce reaction from parts of the bourgeoisie and the old guard of the party. The Liberal Party also opposed the measures on the grounds that they interfered with "provincial rights."

More specifically, they interfered with the ambitions of the capitalist class well-entrenched in the provinces, the resource exploiters, who, throughout the thirties, showed themselves to be more amenable to strategies of coercion than compromise with their employees. These were the same capitalists who formed the backbone of the provincial Liberal Party in Ontario. Bennett's actions reaffirmed the resource capitalists' affinity with the Liberal Party. At the same time, they also drove many of the Conservatives' traditional financial supporters out of the party fold. Without them, the Conservative campaign machine could not function. As R. J. Manion, the Minister of Railways and Canals, lamented, "so far, this great Conservative Party, which is supposed to be the friend of big business, has not one dollar in its treasury." The well-tuned electoral machine that had won the 1930 election stood in shambles.[63]

In addition to the Conservative Party's financial and organizational troubles, there was widespread scepticism about Bennett's "Saturday night" conversion. The Conservative Party's shift in policy direction had been too rapid for much of the party's traditional constituency and for many campaign workers. As a journalist of the period recounted:

> The great asset of the Conservative Party ... has been that of reliability. The moment that the Rt. Hon. Mr. Bennett took the microphone for those all-shattering speeches in January, 1935 ... that priceless attribute disappeared in a veritable cloud of confusion, doubt and despair. The staunchest of party workers was blanched, the normally Conservative voter was dismayed, the great body of silent and unbiased electors wagged their heads.[64]

Thus, on the eve of the 1935 campaign, the Liberal Party appeared to be the only national partisan alternative situated between uncertainty and an intolerable status quo. Fortified by corporate financial support, the Liberals built a campaign strategy around this unique position.[65] They offered few accommodations to the prevailing mood of discontent and simply issued one campaign slogan, notably, "King or Chaos." As the only partisan option with a well-tuned nation-wide election machine, this simple slogan seemed to suffice.

When the last votes were tallied, it became clear that the Liberals had increased their popular vote in those provinces where party loyalties to the old-line parties had been most secure in the past. The proportion of the vote cast for the Liberal Party was particularly strong in the Maritimes, Quebec and to a much lesser extent in Manitoba. In contrast, as compared to the previous election, both bourgeois parties lost support in the West and to a lesser degree in Ontario. These parties lost voters in precisely those provinces which had previously voted along class lines and where alternative definitions of the political were widely circulated during the early years of the Depression.

Be that as it may, the strength of each third party alternative varied considerably from one province to another. The Reconstruction Party emerged as a weak eastern-based third party option while Social Credit represented a uniquely western and particularly Albertan phenomenon. The CCF also gained most of its support in the western provinces where it was less popular in Saskatchewan, its birthplace, than in the historically more class-polarized milieu of British Columbia.[66]

We have speculated throughout this chapter about the class alliances practised by each of the federal parties in 1935. We suggested, for example, that the Liberal Party attempted to aggregate all of the available electorate behind it. Similarly, the Social Credit Party made few direct appeals to particular subordinate classes or class fractions but rather attempted to gather cross-class support under the broad umbrella of religious fundamentalism and social credit doctrines. In contrast, the Reconstruction Party offered an ambiguous alternative to a mix of class interests but particularly to those located in urban environments in the East. Finally, we expected the CCF to obtain agrarian support in Saskatchewan but working class support elsewhere.

Data are not available to test the relationship between vote and either the occupational or ethnic composition of the constituency. Thus, as in the previous chapter, we will base our observations on the differences between the voting patterns of urban and rural ridings. Table 6:3 indicates that in both the East and West, the Conservative Party was neither a markedly rural- nor urban-based party. A similar pattern characterizes constituency support for the Liberal Party in the West. The Liberals did not develop a distinct urban or rural electorate but rather gained support from both. In the eastern provinces however, the Liberals appear to have been differentially supported in rural constituencies.

Table 6:3
**THE 1935 ELECTION: CORRELATION OF PARTY VOTE AND
CONSTITUENCY TYPE, BY REGION**
(Pearson's r)

	Urban	Rural
East		
Conservative	-.05	.11
Liberal	-.30*	.22*
CCF	.30*	-.36*
Reconstruction	.24*	-.22*
West		
Conservative	.02	-.18
Liberal	-.04	.10
CCF	.34*	.12
Social Credit	-.27*	.15

*p < .05
Source: See Appendix A.

The correlation coefficients in Table 6:3 also indicate that, as expected, the CCF and the Reconstruction Party had a distinctively urban support base. In the East and the West, the CCF was differentially strong in urban constituencies. The Social Credit, on the other hand, while a western partisan manifestation, appears to have an ambiguous identity.[67] Urban constituencies were not markedly supportive of the Social Credit and neither were rural ridings.

Our expectation that the CCF would also disproportionately gain agrarian support in the western provinces, and especially in Saskatchewan, was not strongly supported by our data. In order to determine whether agrarian support for the CCF in the West was largely isolated in Saskatchewan, this province was excluded from the analysis of the western vote and the relationship between party support and nature of the constituency was retested. The results confirm that the relationship between rural constituency type and the CCF vote is due to the impact of Saskatchewan. The relationship between the western CCF vote and rural constituency types becomes negative while the relationship between urban constituencies and CCF support in the West becomes considerably stronger when Saskatchewan is excluded. (-.26 $p > .05$; .44 $p < .05$ respectively). More broadly, however, the results of our analysis of the 1935 election suggest that the rise of the CCF and its particular interpretation of socialism also carried with it a demise in a particularly agrarian voting cleavage in the western provinces. The distinct rural cleavage that we have traced since 1911 remained only in Saskatchewan in 1935.

It was expected that the Liberal Party's apparent rural vote in 1935 might be attributed to the support given to this party by French-speaking rural constituencies in Quebec. However, Quebec support for the Liberal Party does not account for the rural cleavage in the East in 1935. In fact, the indicator of the distinctiveness of the rural vote actually improves in strength, in an analysis which does not include Quebec. (.34 $p < .05$).

Nor was the rural cleavage in the East confined to Ontario. The apparent relationship observed in Table 6:3 between Liberal Party support and rural constituencies in the East wholly disappears when only Ontario is considered (.01 $p > .05$). Thus, the relationship between rural constituencies and support for the Liberal Party, in the East, appears to be confined to the Maritimes, where the Liberals received the largest popular vote. In the more populous and diversified province of Ontario, their support-base was no more distinctly rural than urban. The Ontario "Grit" tradition does not appear in 1935.

In the end, the Liberal Party had, with its middle-of-the-road strategy, elected 173 candidates and gained 45% of the popular vote in 1935. The Conservative Party received the full brunt of the anger and despair of the Depression, managing to retain only forty seats and 30% of the popular vote. However, the anticipated socialist vote did not materialize. Moreover, while the CCF and the Social Credit secured approximately the same popular vote (8.7% and 8.8% respectively), the CCF elected only seven members to the House of Commons, ten less than the Social Credit which concentrated its efforts in Alberta. Thus, the election of 1935 had re-introduced multi-party politics into the federal party system but none of these new partisan options had developed sufficiently stable or encompassing coalitions to threaten the Liberals.

However, the Liberal Party's victory was, at best, only partial. If the mid-Depression election did not result in a decisive trend toward either socialism or social credit, neither did it demonstrate that the crisis of authority which spawned such a flourish of alternative political options had been resolved. Indeed, some 25% of the electorate, or slightly better than one in every four Canadians, had rejected both of the major parties in 1935. It is even more revealing that almost every second voter in the provinces west of Ontario voted for a new political party. In effect, the 1935 campaign did not demonstrate the efficacy of the Liberal Party's ambiguous conception of the political as much as it underlined the limitations of the brand new and fragmented opposition in the federal party system.

Conclusion

Shortly after the 1935 campaign, the Dominion Securities Corporation announced confidently to its American shareholders that the Liberal Party victory eliminated "the possibility of the introduction of unorthodox and experimental policies of government which were advocated by certain minority parties."[68] Nevertheless, the opposition arising in the Depression would not be turned aside as easily as in 1921. The major parties had been confronted with a class analysis of Canadian politics. Their prevailing notions of unity, growth and "prosperity for all" had been challenged by a sober critique of the capitalist system and the structure of social relations it reproduced. Nevertheless, this critique arrived somewhat prematurely for the vast majority of Canadian workers. Few were organized as workers and even fewer understood the political implications of their position in the production process. A political option for the urban worker, notably the CCF, had emerged from the despair of the Depression, but its electoral potential among labour was yet to be realized. Only a few years would rapidly change this situation. With the onset of another world war, the economy would recover and transform itself. There would be previously unimagined growth in the manufacturing sector and important strides made in the organization of industrial labour. Moreover, the state and the bourgeoisie would come to realize that the reproduction of class relations depended both on some regulation of capital and on the provision of some social welfare programmes. However, these changes would also agitate tensions within the coalition of the Co-operative Commonwealth Federation. Thus, after only one federal election, Canada's new socialist option was thrust into a situation which demanded rigorous self-evaluation and ultimately, redefinition.

NOTES

[1] For a general discussion of the economic policies of Canada's major trading partners during the early years of the Depression, see W. A. Mackintosh, *The Economic Background of Dominion-Provincial Relations* (Toronto: McClelland and Stewart, 1964), Chapter 6, *passim*.

[2] Canada's trade with the United States, for example, dropped from $1,372 millions in 1929 to $430 millions in 1933, 31% of the previous level. Canada's trade with Great Britain stood in 1933 at 43% of its 1929 level. See John B. Brebner, *North Atlantic Triangle* (Toronto: Ryerson, 1945), p. 292.

[3] *Ibid.*, p. 291.

[4] *Ibid.*, *passim*, pp. 289-309.

[5] Donald Smiley "Canada and the Quest for a National Policy," *Canadian Journal of Political Science*, VIII, no. 1 (March, 1975), p. 44.

[6] One basis of this enmeshing is seen in the mid-thirties with the American tariff relief, which improved the Canadian situation and helped pull the country out of the Depression. In 1934 the American Reciprocal Trade Treaties Act was enacted; the Canadian Parliament passed similar legislation the following year. "The more important effects of the Treaty were to make easier American sales to Canada of farm implements, automobiles, electrical apparatus, gasoline, and machinery; and Canadian sales to the United States of lumber, cattle, dairy products, fresh and frozen fish, whisky and potatoes." Brebner, *op. cit.*, p. 309.

[7] Wallace Clement, *The Canadian Corporate Elite* (Toronto: McClelland and Stewart, 1975), pp. 83-87.

[8] Thus, the number of American-owned companies establishing in Canada each year dropped progressively from ninety-seven in 1930, to forty-two in 1933, to thirty-four in 1934. See Herbert Marshall, Frank Southard and Kenneth W. Taylor, *Canadian-American Industry* (Toronto: McClelland and Stewart, 1976), p. 21.

[9] See Donald V. Smiley, ed., *The Rowell-Sirois Report*, Book 1, (Toronto: McClelland and Stewart, 1963), pp. 160-168.

[10] Mackintosh, *op. cit.*, pp. 154-71.

[11] For a discussion of cost-cutting strategies, see H. Blair Neatby, *The Politics of Chaos* (Toronto: Macmillan, 1972), pp. 29-30.

[12] Profits and other investment income in manufacturing declined from $280 millions in 1928 to $65 millions in 1932. See *National Income and Expenditure Accounts*, Vol. 1, The Annual Estimates, 1926-1974 (Ottawa: Information Canada, 1976), p. 40, Table 30.

[13] Saskatchewan suffered the largest losses among the western provinces during this period. The price of wheat fell from $1.03 in 1929, to $.47 in 1930, to $.38 in 1931, to $.35 in 1932. Yields fell from 23.3 bushels per acre in 1923 to as low as 8.8 in 1931. For documentation of both wheat prices and yields in Saskatchewan from 1900 to 1947 see S. M. Lipset *Agrarian Socialism*, revised and expanded edition (Berkeley: University of California, 1971), p. 46.

[14]As noted in Chapter 4, the Nova Scotia and New Brunswick economies were depressed before the 1930s.

[15]Agriculture figures calculated from *National Income and Expenditure Accounts*, Vol. 1, *op. cit.*, Table 39, p. 52. It was estimated that by 1932, two-thirds of the farm population was destitute. See W. Young, *The Anatomy of a Party: The National CCF, 1932-61* (Toronto: University of Toronto, 1969), p. 20. The wage and salary declines were calculated from Mackintosh, *op. cit.*, Table 13, pp. 124-131.

[16]In 1930, the Conservatives guaranteed the price of wheat. In 1931 market conditions were so bleak that a bonus of five cents a bushel on all wheat was added. In 1933 steps were taken to intervene in the market itself, and a selling agency was set up to buy and hold futures of the Winnipeg Grain Exchange until international markets improved. But the market did not turn around, and in 1935, the accumulated stock pile of wheat stood at no less than 205 million bushels. See Smiley, *The Rowell-Sirois Report, op. cit.*, p. 170.

In the final analysis, however, the federal government's limited action on behalf of the western wheat farmers was constrained by constitutional considerations. The BNA gave responsibilities for relief to provincial governments. Consequently, the actions taken to relieve the burden of the Depression varied from province to province, depending on the financial strengths and the balance of class forces and organization within each province. In the Maritimes and centre, for example, few measures were taken to protect agriculture or the fisheries. In contrast, the western provincial governments, who were wary of the sanctions on the organized farmers, took numerous and often costly initiatives to aid the debt-ridden agricultural sector. In Saskatchewan, especially, the provincial government supplied destitute farmers with seed grain, arranged for fuel and repair of farm machinery and paid doctors to remain in depressed areas. See also Neatby, *op. cit.*, p. 31.

[17]The agricultural frontier had largely been populated, the US had closed its borders even to Canadian immigrants, and urbanization had broken the links of the extended family.

[18]The numbers estimated to be without work grew from 107,000 in 1929 to 442,000 in 1931 to an unbearable peak of 646,000 in 1933, when the population of the country was only 10,300,000. See Walter D. Young, *Democracy and Discontent* (Toronto: McGraw-Hill Ryerson, 1969), p. 46; Pierre Camu, E. P. Weeks and Z. W. Sametz, "The People," in Bernard Blishen, ed., *Canadian Society* (Toronto: Macmillan, 1961), p. 24.

[19]Smiley, *The Rowell-Sirois Report, op. cit.*, p. 175.

[20]In BC, where class relations had traditionally been more clearly articulated along the worker-owner cleavage, specific programmes were designed to change the condition of the workers. Specifically, a Liberal government was elected in 1933 on a platform of job creation, progressive social welfare measures and state health insurance. Even in this case, however, few measures were actually put into legislation. See Kenneth McNaught, "The 1930s," in J. Careless and R. Brown, eds., *The Canadians* (Toronto: Macmillan, 1968), p. 256.

[21]Neatby, *op. cit.*, pp. 33-34.

[22]See McNaught, *op. cit.*, pp. 248-249.

[23]Young, *Democracy and Discontent, op. cit.*, pp. 47-48.

[24]Norman Penner, *The Canadian Left* (Scarborough, Ontario: Prentice-Hall, 1977), p. 136.

[25]McNaught, *op. cit.*, p. 249.

26J. M. Beck, *The Pendulum of Power* (Scarborough, Ontario: Prentice-Hall, 1968), p. 207.

27McNaught, *op. cit.*, p. 249.

28Neatby, *op. cit.*, p. 22.

29Within religious circles for example, the "Social Gospel," a doctrine which rejected ideas of an individualistic laissez-faire society and stressed the need for corporate Christian benevolence and action, gained widespread support, particularly in the West. The United Church in its place, publicly condemned the profit motive and called for state programmes for the unemployed and disabled. For the most part, however, the response of organized religion to the Depression was ideological rather than active and appeared as support for or influence on reform movements, rather than Church-initiated programmes or direct political action. A major exception was the back-to-the-land movement organized by the Roman Catholic Church in Quebec. See K. A. MacKirdy, *et al.*, *Changing Perspectives in Canadian History* (Don Mills: J. M. Dent, 1967), p. 316. For the role of the Social Gospel on the left in the thirties, see Penner, *op. cit.*, pp. 33-35, 178 ff.

30As quoted in Penner, *op. cit.*, p. 214.

31Irving M. Abella, *Nationalism, Communism and Canadian Labour* (Toronto: University of Toronto, 1967), p. 3.

32See John Crispo, *The Canadian Industrial Relations System* (Toronto: McGraw-Hill Ryerson, 1978), Table 1, pp. 164-165.

33Expelled from the TLC in the 1920s, the CP had been involved in the founding of the ACCL. However, the party soon became disillusioned with the tactics and activities of the ACCL and established an independent central union organization. Penner, *op. cit.*, pp. 131-133.

34Communist spokesman, Tim Buck, claimed that there were 86 strikes in 1931 and 189 in 1934. Of these, 109 were conducted under the leadership of the WUL and the only strikes that were won, 89 in all, were also led by the WUL. See *ibid.*, pp. 135-137.

35See E. Dumas, *The Bitter Thirties in Québec* (Montreal: Black Rose Books, 1975).

36Penner, *op. cit.*, pp. 138-139.

37*Ibid.*, pp. 78-79.

38*Ibid.*, pp. 174-175; Martin Robin, *Radical Politics and Canadian Labour* (Kingston: Industrial Relations Centre, 1968), p. 275.

39Quoted in D. Morton, *NDP: Social Democracy in Canada*, 2nd edition (Toronto: Hakkert, 1977), p. 3.

40See Penner, *op. cit.*, p. 194; Young, *The Anatomy of a Party*, *op. cit.*, p. 18.

41Penner, *op. cit.*, pp. 177-178.

42The socialists' writings and speeches tended to have an abstract and doctrinaire quality, repeating Marxist postulates over and over but giving little attention to the possible use of Marxism as an analytical tool for the critical study of Canadian society. *Ibid.*, pp. 42-45.

43The Research Committee of the League for Social Reconstruction, *Social Planning for Canada*, reprint of the 1935 edition, T. Nelson, ed., (Toronto: University of Toronto, 1975), p. vi.

44*Ibid.*, p. xi.

45Young, *The Anatomy of a Party*, *op. cit.*, Appendix A, p. 304. This Appendix reproduces the whole Regina Manifesto.

[46]Gary Teeple has also pointed out the contradictions in the Regina Manifesto in relation to workers. See "Liberals in a Hurry: Socialism and the CCF-NDP," in Gary Teeple, ed., *Capitalism and The National Question in Canada* (Toronto: University of Toronto, 1972), pp. 229-250.

[47]Young, *The Anatomy of a Party, op. cit.*, pp. 74-75.

[48]Penner, *op. cit.*, pp. 156-157.

[49]Young, *The Anatomy of a Party, op. cit.*, pp. 144-145.

[50]An example was the relationship between the CCF and the ACCL, a major competitor of the TLC in the early thirties. Initially, A. Mosher of the ACCL had been appointed to the provisional executive of the newly-founded CCF, but he withdrew after his presence on that body provoked consternation within the TLC. The CCF approached the international unions in 1938 to propose affiliation with the party (the Regina Manifesto provided only for the affiliation of union locals, not national bodies) and was rejected out-of-hand. Young, *The Anatomy of a Party, op. cit.*, p. 76.

[51]Young, *The Anatomy of a Party, op. cit.*, p. 77.

[52]Beck, *op. cit.*, p. 216.

[53]Young, *Democracy and Discontent, op. cit.*, p. 85.

[54]J. M. Careless, *Canada: A Story of Challenge* (Toronto: Macmillan, 1970), p. 254.

[55]They started a series of mid-week short plays. The central character of these home-styled dramas was the Man from Mars, a creature who could not understand why the people of Alberta had not already instituted social credit. Young, *Democracy and Discontent, op. cit.*, p. 88.

[56]Beck, *op. cit.*, pp. 210-211.

[57]Mackenzie King recounts the mood in Parliament in 1935, in his diary in the following vein:

". . . a sort of sadness seemed to pervade the chambers. It was quite plain that the Tories recognized they were defeated, and that nothing could save them."

Quoted in R. Whitaker, *The Government Party* (Toronto: University of Toronto, 1977), p. 83.

[58]As early as January 1934, Sir Charles Gordon, president of the Bank of Montreal and Dominion Textiles, the country's leading textile firm, wrote Bennett to urge him to adopt unemployment insurance as an alternative to direct relief. In his view, the burden of direct relief for many municipalities and even provinces was "threatening to strangle their general credit to the point where it would be difficult if not impossible to carry through refunding operations for any maturing issues, letting alone the finding of money for any new capital undertaking." Quoted in Alvin Finkel, "Origins of The Welfare State in Canada," in Leo Panitch, ed., *The Canadian State* (Toronto: University of Toronto, 1977), p. 349.

[59]*Ibid.*, pp. 349-350.

[60]McNaught, *op. cit.*, p. 261.

[61]The self-made millionaire who had sworn to crush the opponents of capitalism on countless occasions revealed to the entire nation that: ". . . The old order is gone. It will not return . . . I am for reform. And in my mind, reform means Government intervention. It means Government control and regulation. It means the end of laissez-faire." As quoted in Neatby, *op. cit.*, p. 65.

[62]As Finkel notes, "Insurance programs then were seen as a kind of forced savings by the workers for times of unemployment, old age, or infirmity rather than as

a means of increasing the relative overall income for workers." Finkel, *op. cit.*, p. 353.

[63]J. L. Granatstein, *The Politics of Survival: The Conservative Party of Canada, 1939-1945* (Toronto: University of Toronto, 1967), p. 7.

[64]As cited in E. Watkins, *R. B. Bennett: A Biography* (Toronto: Kingswood House, 1963), p. 220.

[65]In 1935, the Liberal Party received campaign funds from a variety of interests in Montreal and Toronto. However, motives for financing the Liberals were mixed. There were office equipment firms and construction contractors expecting government business, steel and manufacturing interests who may have been attempting to purchase access to the new Prime Minister and gold mining entrepreneurs who were upset with the bullion tax imposed by the Bennett government. The mining interests, although the second largest contributors to the Liberal Party coffers in Toronto, were first and foremost provincially-oriented and contributed far less than the federal party organizers had hoped for. The banks and financial institutions, who favoured Bennett's idea of a privately controlled central bank were also a disappointment to the Liberal Party in 1935. See Whitaker, *op. cit.*, pp. 66, 75-76.

[66]Beck, *op. cit.*, pp. 220-221.

[67]A single variable measures the vote for the Reconstruction and Social Credit Parties in the Blake data set in 1935. This poses no problem in relation to the analysis, since they were not in competition with each other in any province except Manitoba. Thus, this province is excluded from the analysis of the vote for these two parties in the West.

[68]As cited in Whitaker, *op. cit.*, p. 85.

Chapter 7

1936–1945—The Contest for Labour

Introduction

These were years of great growth and change in the Canadian economy and polity. They mark Canada's transition to a fully industrialized nation, with a concomitant evolution in the social structure, such as was experienced in all advanced industrial societies. These years also mark a major shift in policy direction, toward the "welfare state" as a mechanism for the management of capitalism. As industrial societies evolved, so did traditional state activities. To the encouragement of investment and subsidization of infrastructure were added major responsibilities for coordination of steady economic growth, high levels of employment, effective demand and new levels of social services. "Keynesian economics" were used to justify state intervention in the economy to modify investment incentives, to organize unemployment insurance and social welfare and to control levels of inflation and wages. Of crucial importance for Canada, was the fact that this role was developed in the context of integration of the Canadian and American economies.

The shift to a more active state occurred at the same time that the labour movement increased in size and radicalism. By the end of the 1930s, some of the divisions in the ranks of organized labour, although not all, were overcome. The Canadian Congress of Labour (CCL) organized mass-production workers into industrial unions, and the percentage of unorganized declined as more of the labour force was integrated into unions. The regional divisions which had existed in the earlier years were also overcome, except for the case of Quebec.

The labour movement was further altered with the declaration of war in 1939. Unlike the Depression years, when the mere threat of unemployment had discouraged direct political action by workers, the character of Canada's participation in the war enhanced the power of organized labour. Workers were needed for the war-related industrial expansion. Furthermore, the state's intervention in the production process and in regulation of the labour market turned workers' attention to the political arena. Canadian workers were at last in a position where they seemed able to force management to bargain collectively and the state to organize the removal of the worst abuses of the unregulated capitalist system. However, these reforms were only reforms, not a fundamental transformation of the economic system itself. Growth and investment were guided, not directed, by the state. Profits were still privately accumulated, despite the incentives for accumulation organized and paid for by the state. Workers were still subject to the decisions of capital, despite their potential power to demand, through the electoral process, that some of the profits as well as their own taxes be used to alleviate their working and living conditions and provide for their futures.

Nevertheless, there were reforms, even if the recipients of the new social programmes often financed the bulk of the costs themselves. The welfare state did reduce the possibility of repeating the awful conditions experienced by workers and farmers during the Depression. And, because these reforms were very similar to the policy demands of the youthful social democratic party, the CCF, the implementation of reforms by the Liberal government began to undercut some of the CCF's constituency. Facing a newly and only minimally radicalized union movement, with few traditions of class consciousness or socialist analysis and still reluctant to engage in direct political and partisan action, the CCF was hard pressed to explain why it was something more than a party of "Liberals-in-a-hurry." During this period, the CCF had to cope with the delicate balance implied by the contradictions of a socialist analysis grafted onto a farmers' revolt. Thus, as a party, it survived these years only with difficulty. The CCF leadership would come to realize that the future lay with the urban workers even though the present successes were with the farmers. This realization caused several crises within the party, which were resolved only with the party's reconstitution in 1961. However, by that time the social realities which not only the Canadian but all social democrats confronted were very different.

The Political Economy of 1936–1945

Undoubtedly welcome, but thanks more to international conditions than the policies of the government, the Canadian economy gradually climbed out of stagnation after 1935. In fact, economic conditions began to improve the previous year as world trade started to recover.[1] Capital trickled back into the production process, and wheat prices edged up from the abysmal lows of the early thirties until 1937 when the price per bushel actually reached the 1926 level.[2] Recovery remained sluggish, however, until the country entered the Second World War. The years of Depression taught the Canadian bourgeoisie and the state, as it did those of most advanced capitalist countries, that something more than traditional policies and economic levers were necessary to maintain economic stability in the future. Economies could collapse, capital accumulation virtually cease and social discontent become widespread when states remained aloof from the economy. Bennett's "New Deal" was a beginning, but very tentative, effort to stabilize the economy, to maintain effective demand and to aid capital accumulation. Unemployment and pension schemes were added to the repressive and anti-labour repertory.[3] Although there was resistance from business, indeed, often very strong resistance, the necessity of greater state activity was recognized by many.[4] Thus, as the Royal Commission on Dominion-Provincial Relations reported:

> Since the Great War, the Great Depression has been the chief stimulus to labour legislation and social insurance. The note sounded has been not so much the ideal of social justice as political and economic expediency. For instance, the shorter working week was favoured in unexpected quarters not because it would give the workers more leisure and possibilities for a fuller life but because it would spread work; and the current singling out of unemployment insurance for governmental attention in many countries is dictated by the appalling costs of direct relief and the hope that unemployment insurance benefits will give some protection to public treasuries in future depressions and will, *by sustaining* purchasing power, tend to mitigate these depressions.[5]

However, it would take not only the Depression but also the war to consolidate these ideas. The war brought rapid economic change, high levels of state intervention, and prosperity, as well as a great deal of labour militancy and challenge to the existing system of partisan relations. "The result was a rethinking among many businessmen of the proper relations between the state, industry and the people."[6]

The Second World War precipitated an economic and social transformation similar to the First World War. The production process which had operated at below 1929 levels until 1939 strained to a peak by 1943. In fact, in only five years the Gross National Product increased twofold.[7] Moreover, the character of economic growth departed radically from previous experience as Canada came of age industrially during the Second World War.[8] At the same time, the wartime co-operation of the Allies produced an integration of Canadian and American manufacturing, particularly in tools, electrical apparatus and chemicals, which were the modern industries with the greatest potential for growth. Under the direction of both governments, Canadian and American industry developed production-sharing, and, in turn, personnel and technology moved virtually unhampered back and forth across the border.[9]

The war necessitated direct state intervention in the production process, at greater levels than had ever been undertaken before. Demand for munitions and war supplies required massive capital outlays for new facilities and for the transformation of the old machinery and equipment. All told, some $4.5 billion were invested in the Canadian economy from 1939 to 1945, and much of this capital was provided by the federal government.[10] In addition, the wartime economy was organized by powerful state regulatory bodies—in particular the Wartime Industries Control Board, chaired by C. D. Howe, and the Wartime Prices and Trade

Board, under the direction of Donald Gordon.[11] However, the state did not enter into the production process to compete with capitalists. Private industry as a whole was pushed to peak production to provide for wartime needs and meet government contracts. The state undertook projects only where the private sector could not meet demand. In essence, the state worked in tandem with private enterprise to meet the requisites of war. The inducements provided by the state for production freed huge amounts of capital for expansion, and expand it did.

The war economy shaped the future as it overcame the conditions of the Depression and pushed the country into full industrialization. However, it was the reconstruction of the postwar years which was the topic of great concern during the war.[12] There was widespread apprehension that unemployment would result from the termination of wartime manufacturing and the demobilization of the armed forces. And, as the argument went, with unemployment would come radical politics and social dislocation. Organized labour seemed stronger and more united than it had during and after the First World War or the Depression. Therefore, the federal government was concerned to guarantee high levels of investment which would maintain jobs. As with the early years of the National Policy, it attempted to ensure both that the domestic market was maintained and that manufacturing took place in Canada rather than abroad. This involved a series of measures.

One set of these measures involved the encouragement of production under any conditions, including the widespread ownership of industry and resources by Americans. This set of programmes, however, was not put into operation until the state withdrew from active participation in the production process after the war. Therefore, it will provide the focus of the next chapter. Nevertheless, during the war, concern with postwar reconstruction and the rebuilding of capitalism, severely damaged by the experience of the Depression, led to a very different definition of the role of the state. The liberal notion that "that government is best which governs least" had patently given way, in the thirties, to the recognition that a much more active state was necessary. The ideas which had begun to filter through to the bourgeoisie and state officials during the thirties grew even more popular by the mid-forties. The Keynesian revolution had arrived, and the Liberal government and federal civil servants adopted its premises and programmes whole-heartedly.

The discovery that state regulation and prosperity could co-exist and the understanding that there was a link between the promotion of full employment and maintained demand and capital accumulation, were common to most states and national bourgeoisies. Part of the "postwar settlement" seen everywhere was full employment policies and a host of social services.[13] The legitimacy of the capitalist system had been severely threatened by the Depression, and there was a concomitant rise in socialist and social democratic party influence during the thirties but especially during and after the war.[14] Therefore, under pressure from organized labour and this left-wing analysis, if not directly implemented by social democratic governments, states began to adopt various tools for national economic planning. The rationale was that capital accumulation could continue even with, and perhaps only with, full employment and social programmes.[15]

Canada was no exception to the general trend. However, the Canadian state managed to pass more restrictive labour legislation, to spend less on social welfare while having higher levels of national unemployment.[16] The Canadian state could postpone the introduction of even minimum social welfare measures until the culmination of the war because of a number of factors, not the least of which was the organization (or disorganization) of the trade union movement.[17] As already discussed, workers, and specifically industrial workers, were neither adequately organized nor secure with collective bargaining rights during the early years of the Depression and thus, did not pose a sufficient threat to the balance of class forces to gain from the state reforms or special compensation favouring labour.[18]

Both the organization and militancy of labour intensified after 1935 but especially throughout the war years. However, even under these conditions, the state offered few concessions to labour. Indeed, the only significant legislation to appear in the 1935 to 1943 period was the Unemployment Insurance Act of 1940. Outlines of Canada's post-war settlement to labour began to appear in 1944, only after the trade union movement engaged in a bitter and strike-prone struggle for collective bargaining rights. The 1944 package included family allowances, mortgage-lending programmes and promises of massive postwar spending designed to avoid unemployment during the transition from a war to peacetime economy. These proposals were more fully embraced and embroidered the following year with the publication of the government's White Paper on Employment and Income.[19]

The Wartime Militancy of the Labour Unions

Rapid industrialization changed the composition of the labour force dramatically, and this, in turn, had an impact on political developments. The first change was that the percentage of the population engaged in agricultural occupations declined precipitously, to reflect the much-reduced importance of agricultural production and exports. Whereas in 1931, 29% of the active population was engaged in agricultural occupations, this fell to 26% in 1941. However, in the next decade, for the first time ever, primary occupations in general were in third place as generators of employment, and agricultural workers formed only 17% of the active population.[20] The rate of decline continued so that by mid-decade the farmers' place in the Canadian community was fundamentally different from what it had been before. Not only were there fewer farmers but agricultural exports provided a much smaller proportion of all exports. The contrast to the pre-Depression years is striking indeed.

Also important for its potential political effects was the major increase between the 1931 and 1951 census years in the proportion of the population employed in manufacturing occupations. In 1931, 13% of the active population held manufacturing occupations. By 1941, the proportion was 15%, and by 1951, reflecting the full extent of war-induced changes, it was fully 19%.[21] By 1945, manufacturing industries employed over 1.1 million people, about 70% more than in 1939.[22] Unlike the 1920s this change in the occupational structure took place in the context of an expanding and broader-based union movement. And, it was a union movement which was insistent on gaining some of the reforms that the Depression had made evidently necessary but that the war had postponed.

While manufacturing employment was increasing, it was not increasing, nor would it ever increase, at a sufficiently rapid pace to absorb all the workers no longer employed in primary industry. A third sector of the economy was rapidly expanding, and it reinforced a trend that was already occurring within industry—the trend, discussed previously, toward "white collar" work.[23] Modern industry required workers to perform expanded management functions and employed, for example, secretaries, clerks and public relations officers. However, not all these services could be provided by goods-producing firms themselves, and an expanded range of "service industries" came into being. At the same time, the state expanded its employment in the new social fields of welfare, education and other programmes to promote managed economic growth. Many of these state employees were also "white collar" workers.

Thus, the third major change in the labour force was the expansion of the service sector.[24] More and more employment was concentrated in the provision of services to industry and to the population. Commercial activities, financial services, research, education and government employment expanded to absorb that part of the population released from agricultural and other primary employment. This restructuring of the work force, due both to changes in advanced industrialization (declining agricultural employment, more white collar workers in industry, machines replacing labour in manufacturing, an expanded state sector) and Canadian patterns of economic development (fewer jobs in industry due to influences of foreign control) had crucial effects on the organizations of the labour movement. In particular, in the immediate postwar period, the decline in agriculture was felt, with a vengeance, by the social democratic party, the CCF.

During the war the unions and the parties recognized the huge push the war gave to the organization of industrial workers and the necessity of facing the always present weakness of the alliance strategy with the farmers. The labour movement had strengthened with the thrust toward industrial unionism which began as early as 1936. In 1935, changes in the Communist International led the Canadian Communist Party to dissolve the WUL and undertake united action with the non-communist labour movement.[25] Also in 1935, John L. Lewis of the United Mine Workers in the US founded the Committee for Industrial Organization (CIO) within the AFL, which ended the long neglect of industrial workers by that craft-dominated central. These two events complemented one another in the Canadian context. The CIO provided many of the disbanded WUL locals and organizers with a home, although some did move into the TLC. The WUL had been implanted among industrial workers and the unemployed, precisely those workers who were excluded from the TLC. Thus, the considerable organizational experience of the WUL was connected early to the CIO.[26] In the 1930s, this connection provided a basis for organizational success, but in the 1940s it grew into a basis for division within the whole labour movement.[27]

Canadian trade unionists were inspired by the considerable success of the CIO in the United States. Despite little support from overworked American organizers and no financial encouragements, a few Canadian unionists were determined to organize industrial workers independently. They adopted the CIO banner and began to establish industrial locals in Canada.[28] In very little time locals were established among Canadian industrial workers. Indeed, by the end of 1936, the CIO had organized 7,000 workers in the Amalgamated Clothing Workers, 16,000 in the United Mine Workers and another 3,140 in the Steel Workers Organizing Committee (SWOC).[29] Nevertheless, a full-scale mobilization of industrial workers, parallel to the American experience was hampered by lack of union rights and the extreme hostility of the provincial governments which faced the prospect of industrial unions in their jurisdictions.

Unlike the American CIO, Canadian industrial unions lacked the protection of collective bargaining rights in their formative years. Canadian legislation emphasized state intervention and coercion, and the absence of legislation similar to the American Wagner Act of 1935 proved a significant barrier for CIO organizers. Employers could, and did, refuse to negotiate with their employees collectively and in certain instances fired those involved in union activity. In a period of high unemployment this severely diminished the attractiveness of unions to potential members. It was only with the labour market conditions of wartime that this liability could be overcome and organization of industrial unions could take off.

Much of the responsibility for collective bargaining legislation rested with the provincial governments. However, the close relationship between the provincial administration and the owners of industries most likely to be organized by industrial unions, particularly in Ontario and Quebec, meant that collective bargaining legislation would not be achieved without a struggle. The continuing emphasis on coercion was nowhere more evident than in Ontario, where in 1937 Premier Hepburn personally intervened to try and block the organization of a CIO-inspired local in the General Motors plant in Oshawa.[30] What began as a typical conflict over wages soon grew into a struggle over the CIO's right to negotiate for the strikers and to organize in Ontario. Hepburn's intent was less to block the CIO from the auto plant than to stop its move into the province's mines, a sector controlled by his personal friends and a source of much of the provincial Liberals' funds.[31] Hepburn initially urged the federal government to send the RCMP against the strikers and to deport American organizers.[32] Unsuccessful in that request, the Ontario Provincial Police were mobilized against the strikers, and efforts were made to hinder the participation of CIO organizers in the negotiations with GM. However, the company was unwilling to engage in a long battle with the strikers, and the resolution of the dispute, in the midst of immense publicity, appeared to many to be a victory for the workers because of the CIO. As a result, more locals were organized and the membership grew from forty-six thousand in 1936 to sixty-five thousand in 1937.[33]

The provincial administration of Quebec also attempted to suppress industrial unions by relying on ideology and legislative repression. During the late years of the Depression, industrial unions which advocated a conflictual model of class relations began to organize in Quebec and made considerable progress at the expense of the essentially conservative Roman Catholic trade union centre, the CCCL. The proportion of CCCL membership among all organized workers in Quebec dropped from 74% in 1935, to 47% in 1939.[34] Premier Duplessis reacted to the growth of industrial unionism with the infamous Padlock Law. The legislation authorized locking up any premises used for the purpose of "propagating Communism or Bolshevism," the definition of which was left to the discretion of provincial law-enforcement officers and courts.[35] Their actions would suggest that the terms were often held to be analogous to industrial unionism. Numerous unions were raided and forced to disband. Thus workers in Quebec were not only denied collective bargaining rights but in some instances the right to organization in unions of their choice. This action was part of a general offensive by the provincial state which resulted, for a time, in the provision of low-wage labour in Quebec. There was a tacit alliance between the Church and the state which used pre-capitalist ideology to achieve its goals. Manpower was needed for pulp and paper and mining in northern regions. A provincial policy of "colonization" was developed to move workers into those areas and to make, in this way, inexpensive manpower (since it was supplemented by farming, unproductive as it was) available to enterprises. Thus, between 1931 and 1941 the number of farms in Quebec as a whole rose by 14% while the number in Abitibi went up by fully 21%.[36]

The federal government's response to industrial unions was somewhat ambiguous. On the one hand, it withheld the federal state's coercive apparatus during the Oshawa strike. On the other hand, it is apparent that King refused to disallow the Padlock Law supposedly out of respect for provincial autonomy, even though he was at the time disallowing one piece of Alberta Social Credit legislation after another because they interfered with the financial power of the federal state.[37] Yet whatever the federal government's predisposition toward industrial unionism was in the late thirties, it was clear during the war that the government could not ignore the increasing organizational influence of the new unionism.

In 1939 the CIO unions, on the urging of the AFL, were officially expelled from the TLC. The industrial union leaders set up a Canadian Committee for Industrial Organization and began an intense campaign to organize Canadian industrial workers.[38] The next year the ACCL joined forces with the CIO and formed the Canadian Congress of Labour (CCL). This new union centre was designed to provide industrial workers with an alternative labour centre to the TLC. Industrial unions remained on the margin of the labour movement until the Second World War changed the bargaining position of organized labour and conditions for industrial unionism ripened even more.[39] Starting in late 1939, the demand for workers for war-material production multiplied daily. The low profits and massive unemployment of the 1930s were quickly supplanted by peak production. Yet, the upswing in the economy and the demand for workers were not readily translated into either better wages or improved conditions of employment. Wage rates clung to Depression lows and employers, unresponsive to demands for better wages, would frequently refuse to negotiate with the new industrial unions.[40] In these conditions unionization pushed forward, and only two years after the CCL's formation it claimed a membership of no less than two hundred thousand industrial workers, a huge increase from the seventy-seven thousand of 1940.[41]

In normal times, conditions such as these undoubtedly would have generated a confrontation between employers and their employees in the form of strike action. However, these were not normal times. The federal state intervened to ensure that industrial conflicts did not slow down supplies to the front. With 60% of the employees in the manufacturing sector involved directly in the production of war materials, state control over the domestic labour force was considered necessary to ensure a maximum war effort.[42] The federal state legislated one condition of employment after another and, as a result, the state, rather than private capitalism, became the focus of union militancy. It was steady pressure from the state on the labour market, under wartime conditions of high employment, that generated union and then partisan militancy. Midway through the war the Liberals found themselves confronted with an enraged union movement and a developing alliance between it and the CCF. Something had to give. What resulted was new legislation about conditions of work and the beginnings of social welfare programmes long advocated by social democrats. These were seen as necessary if postwar capitalism were to continue.

The massive state intervention in and regulation of labour-market conditions began in 1939, when the Industrial Relations Dispute Investigation Act was applied to federal employees and all industries affected by the war.[43] In 1941, Orders-in-Council froze wage levels, permitted the use of troops in labour disputes, limited the right to strike and abolished the 1940 Unemployment Insurance Act.[44] Only a year later the National Selective Service Regulations, under the prerogatives of the War Measures Act, allowed the federal state total control over military and civilian movements within the labour force during wartime so that all hiring, firing, job-seeking and job-leaving had to be approved by the federal government.[45]

Not unexpectedly, the CCL resisted the state's intervention. From its beginnings, the CCL was more militant and critical of government policies than the TLC.[46] Much of the CCL's energy was spent on efforts to establish collective bargaining legislation and achieve recognition of industrial unions. However, few accommodations were made by the federal government until the CCL undertook strike action over the issue.[47] In 1943 the tensions induced by wage controls and the denial of collective bargaining rights erupted into a massive strike wave. Despite the prohibitory legislation, 1943 saw a nation-wide steel workers' strike and more labour unrest than even in the turbulent years following the First World War. However, unlike the postwar experience twenty years before when labour fought for higher wages in the face of rampant inflation, the major issue underlying the strikes of 1943 was union recognition and collective bargaining.

In the face of this militancy, and always concerned to keep up war production, the federal state conceded union rights but maintained the coercive aspects and state intervention of the post-1907 Canadian legislation. Thus, the labour victories were not complete.[48] However, the state was shaken by the militancy in the union movement, and the Liberals were to be even more shaken by subsequent developments in the party system. Midway through the war, the union movement was larger, more militant and more important to national development. Its allegiance was a valuable prize to any party that could claim it. All would try in the next years before the 1945 election to capture this newly-powerful and active social force.

The CCF: Farmer? Labour? Socialist? (1935-1943)

As the previous chapter describes, the CCF housed within it several contradictions which made it uncertain about ideology, strategy and tactics. While Woodsworth had posited that there could be a "Canadian road to socialism" different from that known elsewhere, it was not obvious in the early years of the party that the CCF was well launched on that road. A fundamental problem was the division over the commitment to socialism. The alliance forged in Regina in 1933 was a self-conscious effort to paper over cracks and contradictions so as to launch a new party capable of doing something about the awful effects of the Depression.[49] However, some of the farmers and their organizations which joined in the federation were neither committed to, nor rested comfortably with, the socialist ideology and language of the Regina Manifesto.

Throughout most of Canadian history, the only progressive alliance that seemed workable, given the economic relations and the occupational distribution, was a farmer-labour alliance. The balance of forces in the country, with the large role for the wheat economy and the economic structures of regional disparity, plus a divided trade union movement, all pushed this particular alliance forward. The Progressive outburst of 1921 made it seem even more feasible, as did the persistence of more dynamic and progressive politics in the western provinces. However, by the end of the 1930s, far-sighted and even not-so-farsighted Canadians could see that the balance of forces in the country was different. The wheat economy would never reassert its centrality in Canadian life. The proportion of the population engaged in agriculture was declining precipitously and, therefore, could not provide the expanding electorate that a new party needed. The social democrats in the CCF could see that their interest in a strong alliance with organized labour would have greater promise in the future, as the industrial sector expanded and the union movement began to grow and overcome some of its organizational failings.

There was a tension within the CCF. It was a tension due to uncertainties over self-definition and organizational focus. It was a crisis in the alliance which had brought the party into being, and the tension could not be relieved until much later when the party undertook to recreate itself and align more directly with another constituency, the union movement. In the early years, however, this fundamental contradiction was expressed as inner-party conflict, withdrawals of segments of support and increasing independence for the provincial wings of the party, especially in those areas with strong agrarian support for the CCF.

After 1933, there was an almost immediate shift to the East in the centre of gravity of the CCF. The leadership was in Ottawa, the LSR was centred in Montreal and Toronto, and there was, within the leadership of the party, an increasing emphasis on tightening the links with labour, especially in the industrialized and urbanized East. Thus, from the beginning the eastern, urban and intellectual leadership of the party de-emphasized its agrarian roots but, nevertheless, its parliamentary representation was from the West.[50]

The withdrawal of agrarian allies came quickly after 1933, when the United Farmers of Ontario withdrew in 1934 and the United Farmers of Alberta in 1939.[51] From the beginning, the Saskatchewan section of the party was strong and disproportionately contributed to the upkeep of the party. However, as early as 1936, this provincial wing adopted a new platform which contained no mention of socialism or the Regina Manifesto's plank calling for the nationalization of land. The party's contradictory internal workings and the process of disengagement of farmers from the party was speeded up by economic recovery, which revealed the petit bourgeois class position of the farmers.

Thus the crucial question for the CCF would soon become its relationship with organized labour. In the meantime, however, the effect of the existence of the two tendencies within the same party was a search for a "middle way." In this way the federal party, in its balancing act, began to shift its critique from one of the capitalist system itself to one of the distorting effects of monopolies, concentration and big business in general: the farmers' traditional complaints. By 1940, the blunt critique of capitalism which had reverberated throughout the 1935 campaign was already muffled in a party platform which envisioned only a modified and regulated capitalism in postwar Canada.

It would be incorrect to place all of the "blame" for this increased moderation on the farmers, however. With the change in the centre of gravity toward the East there was an increasing recognition that the future of the party lay with improved relations with organized labour. The recognition did not bring an immediate understanding of how to proceed. Trade unions, in the late thirties, were divided between the continued conservatism and craft unionism of the TLC and the more radical CIO. The CCF wanted to appeal to both wings of the union movement. This was a complicated task. In the early years of the party, the major risk was offending the TLC, which still adhered to its nonpartisan, Gomperist position. The divisions within the trade union movement, once again over craft- or industrial-based organization and the position of the CIO, as well as between national and international unions, made any leadership initiatives by the CCF extremely complex to calculate.[52] Nevertheless, the CCF leadership's constant awareness of the need to improve its links with the unions and its industrial support base brought an emphasis on strengthening ties with unions: unions as they were, with their underdeveloped sense of class-consciousness and without a radical critique of the capitalist system. This too contributed to the weakening of the socialist analysis within the CCF's platform.

Once the CIO was founded, the federal CCF began to take on some of the colouration of a labour party, but the process was not well engaged immediately prior to the 1940 election. This was a wartime election, and, having failed to develop a strong position previously among the Canadian working class, the divisions within the CCF over the war threatened to diminish its influence even more. Largely under the influence of its pacifist leader, J. S. Woodsworth, the CCF in 1936 declared itself neutral in any war. But, by 1939, amidst wartime propaganda and alarming press reports from Western Europe, the party membership began to question the propriety of this commitment. The war issue was passionately debated in 1939, and a compromise was finally struck, but at the cost of Woodsworth's resignation. The party would support the war effort, but only in so much as it meant sending goods and not men to Europe. To an electorate convinced of the necessity of a total war effort to halt the Nazi hordes, the CCF appeared less than patriotic.[53]

The 1940 election was in many ways a non-election. The country was preoccupied with the war, and there were few developments either within or outside the party system which could detract from this overarching concern. The TLC was not opposed to war, as it had been in 1914. Canadian labour for the most part was initially convinced of the necessity of collaboration with the government to ensure the war effort. Nor was there measurable opposition to the Liberal Party from the other federal parties.[54] The Conservatives had not yet recovered from their 1935 debacle. Although Bennett had resigned and a new leader, Dr. R. J. Manion had been recruited, the party survived on a day-to-day basis. Party faithfuls had hoped that Manion, a Roman Catholic, would bolster support in Quebec, but when war broke out hints of Conscription reopened old wounds. The Conservatives were unlikely, because of their historic positions, to benefit from that issue. In addition, Manion was thought too radical by some businessmen, and few funds were made available to the party in the 1940 campaign.[55]

Therefore, the Liberals faced little opposition from the other parties, either organizationally or ideologically, and the contingencies of war only served to strengthen this position. King resisted appearing overtly partisan, and partisanship was presented as inappropriate in a wartime election.[56] The war strengthened the federal state and, with it, the Liberal Party. In the final analysis, the 1940 election proved merely an exercise designed to legitimate the state's continuation of the war. If the war demanded a united country, this was held to apply to all spheres of social and political action, including partisan politics.

The circumstances surrounding the 1940 campaign were optimal for bourgeois politics. Class and even partisan considerations were deemed irrelevant in the face of the external fascist threat. In essence, the subordinate class organizations were encouraged to collaborate with the state and forego all personal demands for the cause. The Liberal Party gained a plurality of the votes in all provinces east of Manitoba and substantially improved its 1935 position in each of the western provinces. The Conservative Party also improved its vote in all but the Prairie provinces, but the gains were marginal at best. Conversely, all the third parties fell from their 1935 levels. Both the Social Credit and the CCF declined in popularity in all provinces, with the exception of the CCF in Saskatchewan. The electorate seemed to move back to the Liberals.

With few issues except the necessity of amassing a full-scale mobilization for the war effort surfacing in the 1940 campaign, the two major parties, by and large, did not appeal to specific groups in either the rural or urban milieux, as shown in Table 7:1.[57] While the Conservative party regained its urban character in the West, none of the federal parties had a uniquely urban identity in the East in 1940. The CCF, which had shown a strong measure of urban support in 1935 appeared to have lost its differentially urban support among eastern constituencies. Moreover, in the West the zero-order coefficient indicates no relationship between CCF vote and urban contexts. However, the urban support base for the CCF is masked by rural support for the party in Saskatchewan. When the effect of that province's strong CCF showing is eliminated, the CCF vote does appear to have a certain urban character, albeit at statistically insignificant levels.

Similar observations can be gleaned from Table 7:1 regarding the voting behaviour of rural constituencies in 1940. In the East none of the

Table 7:1
THE 1940 ELECTION: THE CORRELATION BETWEEN PARTY VOTE AND CONSTITUENCY TYPE, BY REGION
(Pearson's r)

	Urban	Rural
East		
Conservatives	.00	–.04
Liberals	.00	.09
CCF	.10	–.27*
Social Credit	–.06	–.01
West		
Conservatives	.21*	–.22*
Liberals	.12	–.17
CCF	.01	.21*
Social Credit	–.19*	.10

* p < .05
Source: See Appendix A.

parties appears to have developed a differentially rural support base, and the CCF does markedly poorly in regard to this relationship. Dissimilarly in the West, the rural constituencies continue to provide some evidence of class-based voting. However, this rural pattern was largely due to CCF support in Saskatchewan. When this province is excluded from the analysis of rural support for the CCF in the West, there is actually a negative relationship between the CCF vote and rural constituencies. (-.22*, p < .05). Overall, then, the vote was not structured along class lines in 1940. The rally to war meant that considerations of the "nation" were once again of overarching importance. As a result, the Liberals were given the strong mandate they had asked for, gaining no less than 52% of the popular vote and 74% of the seats in the House of Commons.[58]

The Development of Welfare Politics (1943-1945)

Despite the lack of class divisions in the 1940 results and despite the weakness of all its opponents, the Liberal Party, only three years later, faced an alliance between the most militant wing of the trade union movement and the CCF, whose star was very much on the ascendant. There was a prospect that this alliance would result in a major reorientation of federal partisan politics. The prospect was raised by the Canadian Congress of Labour's decision to endorse the CCF, which itself came from a more long-run evolution within the forces of social democracy. As a result, the CCF seemed to be the "opposition party." For a few years, it grew in strength and members, and polls showed that the party could potentially become the government or at least come close. The CCF appeared to have become a major party.[59]

The CCL developed a practice which differed from that of the TLC. In its 1943 endorsement of the CCF as the "political arm of labour" and in its recommendation that its members join the party, the CCL departed from its exclusively trade union actions and moved into the sphere of direct partisan activity.[60] Despite divisions within the CCL over the endorsement, by 1943 the leadership could not ignore the anti-labour attitudes and practices of the federal government. In addition, there was a change in the CCL's leadership, making endorsement feasible.[61] The CCF found, at last, in the CCL a possible organizational ally which would allow the party to emphasize the attractions of its form of social democracy for an industrial and urbanized labour force. There had always been militant CCF'ers in the CCL, and these people had worked in their trade union activity to pull the CCL closer to the CCF.[62] The CCF criticisms of the Canadian capitalist system seemed to find a sympathetic echo in the CCL's actions for collective bargaining rights and higher wages.

The total commitment to destroying the fascist threat which characterized the electorate in 1940 was slowly giving way to pervasive apprehension about the future. It was obvious to most that the war had pulled the Canadian capitalist system out of depression, but capital, labour and government all worried about the economic conditions that might prevail at the war's end. Memories of high unemployment and dislocation of hundreds and thousands of veterans from the First World War and more recent recollections of the tragedies of the Depression were rekindled. Canadians wanted assurances that such experiences would not come again, and a blueprint for the future. The CCF's political platforms of the wartime period progressively switched from emphasis on large-scale nationalization to a new kind of reformism which proposed to modify capitalism only as much as was necessary to achieve welfare goals for the population. The essential tool for the implementation of these reforms was the state. By 1942, the CCF leadership described the party platform as having:

> . . . three very basic and simple ideas. The first is that the primary duty of the state is to secure the welfare, both cultural and material, of the people who form the vast majority of the population. The second is that welfare must be provided now, in very tangible forms, such as health, education, good homes, etc. . . . The third is that this welfare will be attained only if the state develops the national resources of the country under a general economic plan, free from the dictates of private interests, so that the material foundations for a just society can be securely laid.[63]

Capitalism was to be controlled and regulated through the mechanisms of the state and not eradicated as was the original intent of the Regina Manifesto. This particular language of politics was more appealing, party leaders argued, to a voting public which had been educated to equate such terms as socialism and nationalization with Bolshevism. The CCF feared that too much emphasis on social ownership, on nationalization of the means of production, was alienating Canadian voters who had no experience with a language of politics, other than that of national unity and national development. Class analysis was not well understood, even among those voters who clearly knew that something radical had to be done to the capitalist system in order to prevent it from reproducing disaster. The CCF was not clear on how welfare programmes could be explained or justified, beyond the immediate effects of improving conditions. For the CCF, radicalism consisted of arguing that capitalism had to be replaced by social ownership. Since, for the CCF, nationalization constituted the only way to "eradicate" capitalism, less nationalization could only mean more capitalism, curbed but still present. During the war, the party proposed to nationalize only large or monopoly capital and leave private enterprise to organize smaller-scale activity.[64]

Gone was the emphasis on destroying capitalism and building the co-operative commonwealth. A more moderate language of politics was seen within the CCF as a means of winning elections.[65] The first, and most general reason for the change was that social democratic parties in advanced capitalist countries were preparing for what looked to be a much-increased opportunity for success in the coming postwar elections. They were concerned to have the programmatic tools to combat the unregulated capitalism which had led to the Depression and the development of those warped forms of capitalism, fascism in Nazi Germany and Italy. The programme of postwar reforms prepared by the CCF was no exception. It was based on an understanding that postwar politics would potentially be very different from what had gone before. Thus, the programmes developed in 1942 and 1944 were very close to those that appeared in Britain at the time.[66] What the CCF did not understand was that while the postwar politics would differ in programmes, these programmes would not remain the domain of social democratic parties. The bourgeois parties would also offer welfare packages to the electorate. A failure to anticipate this development left the CCF in a state of confusion for many years.

A second factor leading to this moderation and "patching" approach to welfarism, was the contradiction within the party between the parts that formed the federation. The farmers were, as we have described previously, less and less supportive of the idea of radical social transformation. Their petit bourgeois class position led them to demands for amelioration, not transformation, of Canadian capitalism. Although the CCF support in Saskatchewan was growing and would eventually lead to a provincial government in 1944, this movement was less important to the federal party and the national headquarters than what was happening in more industrialized areas like British Columbia and Ontario. The Saskatchewan party was, and had long been, very independent of the federal party and was not considered to represent that which was newest and most promising within the CCF.[67]

There was also the trade union movement. The CCF leadership and CCF militants within the unions (who were in many, but not all cases, the same people) continued to attempt to forge formal ties between the unions and the CCF. The goal was to bring the unions into a relationship similar to that in the United Kingdom, where unions were directly affiliated with the Labour Party and provided a goodly portion of its funding.[68] The Canadian trade unions, with their history of organizational divisions, internecine conflict and strong non-partisan roots, had not become carriers of radical social and political critiques. Organized labour, even within the CIO, was, on the whole, more conservative than the CCF, and the party was pressured into moderation and a great deal of emphasis on immediate benefits, in order to build the long-desired coalition. The unions and their members were interested in the amelioration of union conditions (collective bargaining) as well as a better distribution of the profits of expanded wartime production (higher wages) and the reduction of the possibility of a return to Depression conditions (unemployment insurance, pensions, housing). These were the demands they brought to the CCF, along with their offer of greater union support. They did not bring these demands wrapped in a fundamental expectation of socialist change.

For these reasons, the programmes that the CCF advocated were almost the same as those put forward by the two bourgeois parties. The Canadian bourgeoisie and its parties had come to the realization that they could not go on as before and survive. Thus, in a period of only a few years, the CCF found itself undercut in its programmatic distinctiveness by the other parties, the Liberals in particular. During the early years, however, the CCF was more radical, and, while the major parties fumbled for a new political practice, the electorate was changing quickly beneath them. As never before, the population was urban, industrial and organized. It was attuned to the aspirations of the CCF, and the war years brought it remarkable successes in provincial politics. In BC, for example, the CCF gained 33% of the popular vote in 1941, forcing the Liberals and Conservatives into a coalition to stop the socialists. Similarly, the Ontario provincial election of 1943 brought the CCF to the status of official opposition, with thirty-four members, nineteen of whom were trade unionists. In the following year the CCF took the Government of Saskatchewan, and in 1945 the Manitoba CCF forced the bourgeois parties into a coalition to retain office.[69]

The emergence of the CCF in Canadian politics had clearly broadened the range of political alternatives available to the population. Politics, for a time, was no longer merely a question of growth, or the National Policy or of being French or English. It now included the possibility of individual benefits to be gained from the state, social responsibility for subordinate classes and regulation of capital. In other words, the politics of the major parties, notably that of biculturalism and national consensus, was under increasing pressure from those who wanted to raise new issues. For a time there was a difference between the parties, a chance of incorporating a new analysis and a new language into political discourse. However, the hiatus was brief.

The two major parties recognized not only the partisan threat posed by the CCF, but also the need for a new style of bourgeois politics. A postwar settlement was needed. Gradually the political and partisan content of the "Keynesian revolution" was revealed in the bourgeois parties' programmes and the elections of the 1940s. The Conservative Party was the first to come to the realization that it would have to change if it were to survive as a federal party. What had been tentative with Bennett's "New Deal" became clearer. The reconstruction of the Conservative Party began in earnest in 1942. John Bracken, the longtime leader of the Manitoba Progressive Party and Premier of that province, was chosen leader, and the party's name was changed to Progressive Conservative. Bracken's image and programme were central to the new design, and advertising agencies, freshly equipped with the skills of wartime propaganda, were employed for the first time in a federal campaign in 1945 to engrave this image on the public's mind. Bracken was to be a composite attraction for all those voters the Conservatives wished to recover from the CCF. At times he was described as a hard worker and at others as a farmer, an administrator or an experienced politician who stood "four square for private enterprise and individual freedom against socialism and state control."[70]

The development of this image reveals the goal of the Progressive Conservative strategy of modifications in programme to support capitalism. The new platform, as well, underlined that the short-term interests of the bourgeoisie might have to be compromised if the party were to survive. The Port Hope Conference of 1942 outlined the parameters of the compromise which had begun, albeit with a rocky start, in the thirties. The party still emphasized free enterprise as the solution to the economic needs of the country, but it recognized the need for state intervention, particularly during periods of crisis. It adopted important programmes directed toward labour, farmers and the disadvantaged. These included national health programmes, large scale government-supported housing projects and encouragement of trade unions.[71] That the party hoped to recapture support leaning toward the CCF prior to the 1945 election was clear. As described in a journal of the time, "It will not, after Port Hope, be possible for the Conservative Party to attempt to insinuate itself to the Right of the Liberals. (Its only course) is to seek public approval as a party somewhat further Left than the Liberals but not so disturbingly Left as the CCF."[72]

Only the Liberal Party seemed to remain a protagonist of the old order. However, it soon became apparent that they too would have to change if they were to remain the government party. In many respects the response of the Liberal Party involved nothing less than the transformation of the activities of the state.[73] The federal state had the experience and lesson of wartime control and economic planning to draw on and the expertise of all those bureaucrats brought into the federal government for the management of the war. They had seen, and taught the Liberals, that massive capitalist expansion could occur simultaneously with much greater state intervention. The dependence of capitalists on an active state was, in wartime, very obvious. The transfer of these ideas to peacetime thinking was not a difficult or unlikely step, given the increasing popularity of Keynes' ideas among Canadian bureaucrats. The programme announcements were correlated with the electoral advances of the CCF, but they grew more from a thorough and modern analysis of advanced capitalism than from mere calculations of electoral success.

The new policy initiatives of the King government also involved major accommodations to organized labour. In 1943, Prime Minister King announced a new wage policy which included a cost-of-living bonus, and, early in 1944, compulsory bargaining rights were established by Order-in-Council.[74] This second accommodation brought a sharp reduction in strike activity, and it also served to draw the CCL and the TLC into a closer relationship with the federal government. Canada's collective bargaining act retained a clause, described above, which called for state conciliation and other forms of intervention. For a labour movement nurtured on the habits of economism, this potentially determinant role of the state in bargaining demanded the best possible relations with the agents of the state. Thus, only a year after the CCL had declared the CCF the political arm of labour, the CCL Congress repudiated that endorsement and began to compete with the TLC for the favours of the federal government.[75] Labour would not be a political force opposed to the practices of capitalism but rather an interest group organized to affect the decision-making process on labour matters.

If the electoral threat of industrial unionism seemed pushed aside, the CCF remained an important challenge to the Liberals in the impending federal election. The Liberals had lost two of the four by-elections in the West to the CCF in 1943, and public opinion polls of 1944 underlined that these were not isolated phenomena. The polls indicated that the CCF's popular support was strengthening each month, from a low of 10% of the electorate in January 1942, to 23% in February 1943, to a high of 29% in September of that same year, when it took one percentage point more than either of the two major parties.[76] The polls also indicated that there was a radical trend in the public's very conception of the proper activities of the state. Moreover, early in 1944 the polls showed that there was growing public support for trade unions and distrust of big business.[77]

Bourgeois politics and its partisan vehicles were embroiled in a crisis of authority, but party strategists were clearly aware of the type and direction of change that the conjuncture demanded. In essence, the Liberals' response, like that of the Progressive Conservatives and, for that matter, many of the other bourgeois parties in the western world at this time, was a moderate reform platform. In 1943, the Liberals outlined a new programme which contained, among other things, family allowances, a recommended floor on farm prices, improved health assistance and a massive housing programme.[78] In effect, the platform pushed the Liberals back into the centre of the political spectrum. It was still a bourgeois party, but it was ready to make certain sacrifices of the short-term interests of the bourgeoisie, in order to have a workable capitalism. The demands of the subordinate classes would have to be met by the state to some extent, even if the costs cut somewhat into capital accumulation. On the other hand, a second aspect of the programme was the creation of conditions for sustained capitalist expansion, via state intervention in the management of the economy. Thus, the Liberals and the Progressive Conservatives offered virtually the same programmes as the CCF but for different reasons. It suited the purposes of the bourgeois parties to have it seem that they were "pushed" into these programmes by the CCF, rather than because the development of a new role for the state was very much on the agenda for the reconstruction of postwar capitalism. Seeming to bend before electoral pressure was more ideologically accept- able than arguing that it was capitalism, itself, which needed the reforming.

If all parties now had a reformist platform, the problem became one of competition between them and the basis on which that could be organized. They had to begin to re-establish grounds for distinguishing themselves. The CCF leaders were concerned that they should not be pushed by their competitors into appearing as the "radicals," the central- izers or the totalitarian bureaucrats. They knew the costs that could be inflicted on them by the propaganda of their opponents. Nevertheless, their efforts to appear moderate and within the mainstream of Canadian society were hampered by propaganda campaigns of sometimes amazing proportions. A massive public relations campaign, financed by several banks and businesses, was launched against the CCF. Beginning shortly after the CCF successes in Ontario and Saskatchewan, pamphlets attack- ing the CCF were mailed to every household in the country, and some employers went so far as to put notes in their employees' pay envelopes urging them not to vote for the socialist party. Their message was a familiar one. They warned that the CCF in government would substitute a "foreign-born scheme of State Socialism for our democratic way of life" and "turn over to the CCF politicians complete control over our lives." Not satisfied with merely evoking the threat of centralization, of an "un- Canadian" variety, the campaign also played upon wartime sensibilities by reminding the voters that Nazi was an abbreviation of the proper name of the party, National Socialist.[79]

In the meantime, the Liberals and Progressive Conservatives fell back on the familiar politics of ethnicity, which would lead, after the emphasis on wartime nationalism was no longer available, to a whole series of issues of "Canadian" nationalism. In the wartime period, up to the 1945 election, the Conservatives were at a distinct disadvantage and struggled to find a position. Bracken attacked the Family Allowances Bill as a case of favouritism towards French Canada. He made ". . . an open denunciation of the Liberal government and its leader. The Family Allowances Bill, he declared, was 'legal bribery' for prolific French Canada."[80] But even this resort to the tried and true was not a success. With the opposition parties all in support of the bill and "family life," and with John Diefenbaker reminding the House that the Progressive

Conservatives also believed in social legislation, the bill passed its introductory vote without a single dissenting voice.[81]

The Liberal Party had a distinct and critical advantage over its partisan opponents. It was in office, and, hence, it could use its control over the state machinery to transform questions of redistribution into questions of administration before they became electoral cleavages. Thus in January 1944, the Speech from the Throne announced new government departments like Reconstruction, Health and Welfare and Veterans Affairs, and the government stated its intention of establishing family allowance and health insurance programmes. While the latter was to be postponed for over twenty years, the "baby bonus" appeared immediately. It gave the electorate with children under sixteen years of age a vested interest in rewarding the Liberal Party with re-election, to the tune of $8.00 a month per child. The Department of Veterans Affairs would administer programmes for veterans, which would help to avoid too much dislocation in the labour market by funding the business ventures of some with credit programmes and by, most importantly, keeping a large number of them out of the labour market altogether by sending them into the universities. In the meantime, women were enticed out of the labour market by inducements for starting families and by salaries high enough that only one per family would be sufficient. For the duration of the term of Parliament, act followed act, crowned with the White Paper on Unemployment and Income only a month before the election. Keynesian in design, it announced that the federal government was prepared to use fiscal policy to guarantee full employment, business growth, and hence, once again, prosperity for all.

In this way the Liberal Party stood prepared for the 1945 campaign. Over only one year it had managed to defuse the radicalism of the industrial unions, create a reformist current within the party's ranks and outline a plan for full employment designed to quell apprehension about the postwar society. Equally important, it had demonstrated that the new programme was possible without resort to the uncertainty of a socialist party. With the new image firmly in place, King put forward his campaign slogan: "Vote Liberal and Keep Building a New Social Order in Canada."[82]

The Progressive Conservatives were deflated by the Liberal Party's opportune manoeuvres prior to the 1945 campaign. Their new and "radical" image hardly appeared to be so after the Liberals had shifted the political centre of gravity so much that the Conservatives were forced out of the middle-of-the-road position they held so briefly.[83] The Conservative Party had been pushed back to its customary position on the right of the political spectrum while, in addition, yet another conscription crisis destroyed the party's potential for making inroads in Quebec. King's plebiscite called in 1942, to release the government from its firm promise not to introduce compulsory conscription, had profoundly reinforced the bicultural cleavage. Once again, the contingencies of war had pitted English against French Canadians, and, once again, Conservative politicians and newspapers in English Canada advocated immediate conscription and issued invidious statements about French Canada.[84] Thus, even though the plebiscite resulted in divisions among rank and file Liberals and resignations from the King cabinet because of the position taken by the Conservatives, the Liberals remained the party of Quebec.

The 1945 election promised to restore bourgeois politics, albeit a new and improved variety, to the federal sphere. The new and moderate image of the CCF deprived it of any distinctiveness and it was left to do battle with the bourgeois parties "on their own terms."[85] The inter-election strength of the CCF did reduce the percentage of the popular vote won by the Liberals and Conservatives, as compared to the last election. The CCF almost doubled its proportion of the vote from its 1940 level but the 16% it received was far below that which the Gallup Poll had promised in September 1944.[86] The CCF made gains in every province and particularly in Ontario, Manitoba and Saskatchewan where the provincial wings of the party had had some success. However, only in the West did it achieve a measure of support equal to or greater than that gained by the two older parties. Thus, even though the Liberals had pre-empted the CCF's challenge in the East, they could not regain their old dominance in the West.

The two major parties modified their programmes to include Keynesian planning and social welfare programmes, in an attempt to achieve a consensus in federal politics. If their strategies were successful, we would expect to find little evidence of a class-based division, in this case as indicated by predominance in urban or rural constituencies. In other words, if there were a consensus, both parties, but especially the Liberals, should draw support from a broad range of constituencies.

This effect can be observed in the correlation coefficients for the 1945 campaign, displayed in Table 7:2. Neither the Liberals nor the Conservatives developed a distinctly urban base in 1945. While the CCF did emerge as an eastern, urban party, the correlation is weaker than might have been expected given the party's showing in the Ontario provincial election of 1943 and in the Gallup Polls about federal politics. In the West, the zero-order coefficients show no relationship between CCF support and urban constituency context. However, as in 1940, rural support for the CCF in Saskatchewan masked a quite strong urban support base in the remaining western provinces ($.33$, $p < .05$).

The 1945 election also brought the end of a distinctly rural voting pattern in the West. Neither of the major parties nor the two minor parties appear to have been supported disproportionately by the agrarian constituency, which had since the early years of the century a rich tradition of class-based voting. In the East, on the other hand, the Liberals as

Table 7:2
THE 1945 ELECTION: THE CORRELATION OF PARTY VOTE AND
CONSTITUENCY TYPE, BY REGION
(Pearson's r)

	Urban	Rural
East		
Conservatives	.05	.02
Liberals	−.03	.20*
CCF	.18*	−.38*
Social Credit	−.08	.12*
West		
Conservatives	.11	−.16
Liberals	.01	.00
CCF	.04	.05
Social Credit	−.16	.07

* p < .05
Source: See Appendix A.

well as the Social Credit appealed disproportionately to a rural constituency.[87]

Conclusion

The 1945 election was a victory for the Liberal Party which had within a few short years altered its image from a party of the status quo to one of Keynesian reformism. In the same process it transformed the question of the welfare state, which had provided the main appeal of the CCF, into a question of administration. The CCF had attempted to develop an electoral cleavage by distinguishing itself from the bourgeois parties with the promise of an interventionist state and social welfare policies. However, when the two major parties fully embraced the same orientation and the Liberal Party, in particular, started to implement policies similar to those proposed by the CCF, the foundations for such an electoral cleavage eroded. The CCF felt itself outflanked by these manoeuvres and in the immediate postwar years looked for an explanation of the events of the last years of the war. It had to come to an understanding of how the Liberals had managed to, as it seemed, adopt many of its most precious positions. The CCF's explanation, both to the electorate and, most importantly, to itself, was that it had, through pressure, forced the Liberals to do what they did not want to do. Harking back to Mackenzie King's offer of a pension plan in exchange for the parliamentary support of Woodsworth's small band of labour representatives in 1926, the CCF announced that, during the war, it had done the same thing but on a much more massive scale. What they did not understand was that the world, and the capitalist system, of 1946 was extremely different from that of 1926. While it might have suited King to label the CCF as Liberals-in-a-hurry and explain to part of the electorate that the new programme was due to popular pressure, the purposes of the programme for the Liberal Party were clear, consistent, and what they wanted to do. The problems faced by the CCF in subsequent years because of this failure to understand the difference between the pensions of 1926 and the employment policies, baby bonuses, veterans in universities and the collective bargaining of 1945 allowed that party to go from decline to decline and defeat to defeat.

NOTES

[1] O. J. Firestone, "Industrial Development" in J. M. Careless and R. Brown, eds., *The Canadians* (Toronto: Macmillan, 1967), p. 462.

[2] S. M. Lipset, *Agrarian Socialism*, revised and expanded edition (Los Angeles: University of California, 1971), p. 46.

[3] Alvin Finkel, "Origins of the Welfare State in Canada," in Leo Panitch, ed., *The Canadian State* (Toronto: University of Toronto, 1977), pp. 348-349, 358.

[4] *Ibid.*, pp. 351-352.

[5] Canada, *Labour Legislation: A Study Prepared for The Royal Commission on Dominion-Provincial Relations* (Ottawa: Queen's Printer, 1939), pp. 5-6; emphasis added.

[6] Finkel, *op. cit.*, p. 345; David Wolfe, "The State and Economic Policy in Canada, 1968-75," in Panitch, *op. cit.*, p. 252.

[7] The GNP rose from $5,598 millions in 1939 to $11,897 millions in 1944. Colonel C. P. Stacey, "Through the War Years," in Careless and Brown, *op. cit.*, p. 284; Wallace Clement, *Continental Corporate Power* (Toronto: McClelland and Stewart, 1977), p. 82.

[8] The concept of "industrialization" is difficult to define. During the First World War, the national income derived from manufacturing exceeded that from agriculture. However, a greater proportion of the labour force was employed in agriculture than in manufacturing until World War Two. Thus Clement shares Firestone's characterization of this period as one in which the country "came of age industrially." See *ibid.*, p. 95; Wallace Clement, *The Canadian Corporate Elite* (Toronto: McClelland and Stewart, 1975), pp. 87-89; O. J. Firestone, *Canada's Economic Development* (London: Bowes and Bowes, 1958), p. 182.

[9] Firestone, "Industrial Development," *op. cit.*, p. 462.

[10] During the war, the Canadian state spent $700 million on industrial plant expansion, and 75% of this took the form of investment in wholly-owned Crown Corporations. *Ibid.*, p. 464.

[11] Clement, *The Canadian Corporate Elite, op. cit.*, p. 88.

[12] For a more fully developed discussion of this theme, see David A. Wolfe, "Canadian Economic Policy, 1945-1957," *Journal of Canadian Studies*, Vol. 13, No. 1, (Spring, 1978), pp. 3-20.

[13] Wolfe, "The State and Economic Policy in Canada," *op. cit.*, p. 258.

[14] In Britain, a Labour government was formed for the first time in 1945 while in France, the Socialists and Communists took part in a Liberation government

with non-collaborationist forces. The growth of the Italian Communist Party was substantial in the postwar period, as a result of its anti-fascist activities both before and during the war. In most western European countries, there was a substantial electoral shift to the Left.

[15]Wolfe, "The State and Economic Policy in Canada," *op. cit.,* pp. 252-254.

[16]See L. Panitch, "The Role and Nature of the Canadian State," p. 22 and D. Wolfe, "The State and Economic Policy," *op. cit.,* p. 256

[17]Panitch also notes that the predominance of the petite bourgeoisie prior to WWII retarded Canada's development in this respect. *Ibid.,* p. 20.

[18]For the basis of this argument see Ian Gough, "State Expenditure in Advanced Capitalism," *New Left Review,* Vol. 92, July-August 1975, especially pp. 56-65. Gough argues that the state expanded its programmes both in response to and in anticipation of class conflict. Thus, the specific content and form of the postwar settlement to labour in western democracies reflected the balance of class forces in each country and the type and intensity of class conflict of the period.

[19]See Wolfe, *op. cit.;* Finkel, *op. cit.;* For a general history of Canada's social welfare legislation see Kathleen Herman, "The Emerging Welfare State: Changing Perspectives in Canadian Welfare Policies and Programs, 1867-1960," in D. Davies and K. Herman, eds., *Social Space: Canadian Perspectives* (Toronto: New Press, 1971), pp. 131-141.

[20]Calculated from F. A. Angers and P. Allen, *Evolution de la structure des emplois au Canada,* (Montreal: Ecole des Hautes Etudes Commerciales, 1954), Table IV, p. 34.

[21]*Ibid.*

[22]Firestone, "Industrial Development," *op. cit.,* p. 464.

[23]Clement describes the movement of most employment into the service sector and concludes that "in Canada the economy changed from primary to tertiary without developing the area of secondary production." Clement, *Continental Corporate Power, op. cit.,* p. 96.

[24]For a general discussion of these trends, see D. Bell, *The Coming of Post-Industrial Society* (New York: Basic Books, 1973), *passim,* pp. 127-128.

[25]Irving M. Abella, *Nationalism, Communism, and Canadian Labour* (Toronto: University of Toronto, 1973), p. 3, Chapter 1, *passim.*

[26]This was almost the same process which occurred in the American unions, at the same time and for similar reasons. See, for example, I. Bernstein, *Turbulent Years: A History of the American Workers, 1933-1941* (Boston: Houghton, Mifflin, 1970).

[27]Abella claims that the CP organizers stepped into a gap left by the failure of the CCF to take on responsibility for union organization and leadership. The CCF was, at the time, still little organized and searching for an identity within the contradictions and internal competition due to its alliance of labour, farmers and socialists. See Abella, *op. cit.,* pp. 24-25.

[28]This strategy in no way implied that they could expect financial or organizational assistance from the CIO. Although they shared a common name, they were wholly national and self-supporting. Indeed, during the early period "the CIO was not even aware of what was being done in its name in Canada." *Ibid.,* p. 5.

[29]*Ibid.,* p. 6.

[30]For a detailed discussion of this incident, see *ibid.,* Chapter 1.

[31]That the Premier's motive was to protect the mine owners was made clear on several occasions during the strike. In one instance, the Premier declared, "Let me tell Lewis (J. L. Lewis of the CIO) here and now that he and his gang will never get their greedy paws on the mines of Northern Ontario, as long as I am Prime Minister." Shortly after, Jules Timmins of Hollander Mines reiterated confidently that, "under no circumstances will we recognize the CIO, and should the CIO interfere with our operations, we have the assurance of the government that ample protection will be given our men who are desirous of continuing work." In other words, Hepburn was pledged to help the mining magnate break the CIO. Abella, *op. cit.*, p. 19.

[32]This incidence of labour/state relations is remarkably evocative of Winnipeg in 1919. The coercive aspects are obviously the same, as are the efforts to play on an ideology of anti-Americanism. In discussing Hepburn's attack on the CIO, Brebner says "[Anti-Americanism] had been used in May, 1919, during and after an almost general strike in Winnipeg and has been a characteristic weapon against Canadian trade unionism, particularly in the metal-mining industry." J. B. Brebner, *North Atlantic Triangle: The Interplay of Canada, the United States and Great Britain* (Toronto: McClelland and Stewart, 1966), p. 306.

[33]Abella, *op. cit.*, p. 28.

[34]H. F. Quinn, *The Union Nationale: A Study of Quebec Nationalism* (Toronto: University of Toronto, 1967), p. 205.

[35]H. Blair Neatby, *The Politics of Chaos* (Toronto: Macmillan, 1972), p. 117.

[36]The process of manpower movements has been described in this way:

Au Québec, dans les régions périphériques, l'attrait de la main-d'oeuvre pour les grandes entreprises forestières et minières se fit par le biais du développement d'une agriculture non productive, aidée par les subventions gouvernementales et supportée par l'idéologie répandue principalement par l'église catholique, de la supériorité de la vie rurale et par le mouvement de retour à la terre.

A. Dubac, "Le fondement historique de la crise des sociétés canadiennes et québécoises," *Politique aujourd'hui*, no. 7-8 (1978), p. 44.

[37]As Mallory points out, provincial autonomy appeared secure but far more permeable when provincial legislation threatened the interests of the financial bourgeoisie. J. R. Mallory, *Social Credit and Federal Power in Canada* (Toronto: University of Toronto, 1954), p. 176.

[38]For a discussion, see Abella, *op. cit.*, Chapter 2; Gad Horowitz, *Canadian Labour in Politics* (Toronto: University of Toronto, 1968), p. 66.

[39]Throughout the thirties the state machinery had been used to hold back unionization by repression of the Communists and the CIO, as the experience of Ontario and Quebec show. Thus, in 1939 the rate of unionization was not much greater than it had been in 1930. See Finkel, *op. cit.*, p. 357.

[40]In 1939, 84% of Canadian wage earners received less than $10 per week, at a time when the minimum subsistence level was set at $21.50 by the government. Abella, *op. cit.*, p. 39.

[41]Horowitz, *op. cit.*, p. 70.

[42]Clement, *Continental Corporate Power, op. cit.*, p. 82.

[43]H. A. Logan, *Trade Unions in Canada: Their Development and Functioning* (Toronto: Macmillan, 1948), p. 530.

[44]Abella, *op. cit.*, p. 70.

[45]Bryce M. Stewart, "Wage and Manpower Controls in Canada," in W. D. Wood and P. Kumar, eds., Canadian Perspectives on Wage-Price Guidelines (Kingston: Industrial Relations Centre, 1976), pp. 156-167.

[46]Unlike the TLC, the CCL did not support the war unequivocally. Its leadership was extremely critical of both the extension of the IDIA and the government's wage control policies. Indeed, so adamant were they on the wage control issue that some organizers were arrested for "anti-war" activities. Abella, op. cit., p. 48.

[47]Initially, the federal government responded by a half-measure. In December, 1942, it ordered all Crown Corporations to bargain collectively with their employees. H. D. Woods, Labour Policy in Canada, 2nd ed. (Toronto: Macmillan, 1973), p. 73; S. Jamieson, Industrial Relations in Canada, 2nd ed. (Toronto: Macmillan, 1973), pp. 90-91. The pressures for collective bargaining rights during this period were so pronounced that even Premier Hepburn, faced with a provincial election in 1943, promised to introduce legislation similar to the Wagner Act for Ontario workers. Laurel MacDowell, "The Formation of Canadian Industrial Relations Systems During WW II," paper presented at the Annual Meeting of the Canadian Political Science Association, University of New Brunswick, Fredericton, NB, June 1977.

[48]The American Wagner Act was used as the model for legislation relating to union recognition, certification and collective bargaining. However, the principles of conciliation, compulsory arbitration, delay and state intervention were retained from the IDIA of 1907. The 1943 Order-in-Council was the basis for the postwar Industrial Relations and Disputes Act (1948). Jamieson, op. cit., pp. 91, 123.

[49]Norman Penner, The Canadian Left (Scarborough, Ontario: Prentice-Hall, 1978), p. 194; Walter Young, The Anatomy of a Party (Toronto: University of Toronto, 1971), p. 33.

[50]Young, op. cit., p. 48. This characterization of the CCF as having eastern leadership and western voters masks the effects of the electoral system, which played its part in magnifying the contradiction within the party. The CCF had more voters in the urban areas of Ontario and BC than it did among wheat farmers, but this support was not translated into seats. Indeed in 1935 the CCF gained 127,927 votes in Ontario but won no seats in that province while 69,376 votes in Saskatchewan yielded them two parliamentary seats. Seats were won in the farm areas and thus, the CCF appeared to be a party of farmers, first. See ibid., p. 13; Beck, op. cit., pp. 220-221.

[51]See J. W. Bennett and C. Krueger, "Agrarian Pragmatism and Radical Politics," in Lipset, op. cit.

[52]See Young, op. cit., Chapter 4 for a discussion of this process and, especially, for this period, pp. 77-80.

[53]Young, op. cit., pp. 103-104.

[54]The Reconstruction Party had withered away as quickly as it had emerged on the federal scene, while the Social Credit Party narrowed its focus to provincial politics in Alberta. Stripped of its reformist aspirations by political practice and federal disallowance, it steadily modelled itself as an alternative to the "Socialist threat." C. B. MacPherson, Democracy in Alberta: Social Credit and The Party System (Toronto: University of Toronto, 1962), p. 206.

[55]J. L. Granatstein, The Politics of Survival: The Conservative Party of Canada, 1939-1945 (Toronto: University of Toronto, 1970), Chapter 1, 2, passim.

[56]The press also nurtured the semblance of neutrality. Of the one hundred Canadian dailies, only twenty-five took the side of one party or another. At the

same time, the federal government issued larger and larger numbers of official statements which either directly or indirectly enhanced the profile of the King government. The partisan implications of this practice so outraged Mitch Hepburn that he banned the *March of Time* film "Canada at War," from Ontario theatres for the duration of the war. See J. M. Beck, *Pendulum of Power* (Scarborough, Ontario: Prentice-Hall, 1968), p. 230.

[57]Because we have neither demographic nor occupational data matching constituency boundaries for the 1940 and 1945 elections, we base our observations on the voting patterns of rural and urban constituencies. See Appendix A.

[58]Beck, *op. cit.*, pp. 238-239.

[59]See L. Zakuta, *A Protest Movement Becalmed* (Toronto: University of Toronto, 1964), Chapter 5.

[60]Of course, at the time, the CCF had hoped for more than an endorsement. It wanted affiliation, and all the preparations seemed made, until they were squashed by a combination of opposition from Communists within the CCL unions, the appeal of the American CIO's example of independent Political Action Committees, the fear of giving the TLC an advantage in its increasingly close relationship with the government and the failure of the CCF to push on to electoral success. Horowitz, *op. cit.*, pp. 78-82.

[61]In its formative years the CCL did not develop radical political philosophies or engage in direct political action. One reason which inhibited these developments was the existence of deep divisions between unionists about politics. The Communists, who had been initially against the war, were by 1943 (following the Nazi attack on the USSR) bitterly opposed to the CCL's critical position on the war. In addition, the CCL housed from the beginning, both CCF militants and Communists who were in conflict over political strategies. The Communists, for complicated reasons, supported the Liberals as the best opponents of fascism and refused to align with the CCF. Therefore, from the beginning, the leadership was forced to minimize any partisan activity which had the potential for dividing the new labour organization. By 1943 the Communists had been either discredited because of the frequency of ideological flip-flops or sufficiently displaced from positions of influence that the CCF endorsement could pass the CCL Conference.

[62]Zakuta, *op. cit.*, p. 67.

[63]This view was put forward by Frank Scott, LSR member and one of the co-authors of the Regina Manifesto, as quoted in Young, *op. cit.*, p. 109.

[64]The two important policy statements on these matters are "For Victory on Reconstruction" (1942) and "Security with Victory" (1944). See Zakuta, *op. cit.*, pp. 60-62.

[65]For a discussion of the controversy within the party around these changes, *ibid.*, pp. 60-62.

[66]Scott's statement quoted above was modelled on *The Beveridge Report*. It provides further evidence that the CCF was thinking always of itself as a social democratic party similar to the British Labour Party. See Young, *op. cit.*, p. 109.

[67]*Ibid.*, p. 109.

[68]It was very important for its evolution, that the CCF chose to model itself on the British Labour Party. It was one of the only major social democratic parties which had direct union affiliation. In Sweden and Norway, the party and unions were linked, but the affiliation was local, not national. Zakuta, *op. cit.*, p. 148.

[69]*Ibid.*, Chapter 5.

[70]Beck, *op. cit.*, p. 246.

[71]Ibid.

[72]Jane Jenson, "Party Strategy and Party Identification: Some Patterns of Partisan Allegiance," Canadian Journal of Political Science, IX:I, (March, 1976) p. 33, footnote 17.

[73]For a comprehensive development of this thesis see R. Whitaker, The Government Party (Toronto: University of Toronto, 1977).

[74]Logan, op. cit., pp. 540-542; H. A. Logan, "The State and Collective Bargaining," Canadian Journal of Political Science and Economics, 5 (November, 1944), p. 486.

[75]With the withdrawal of the CCL's endorsement of the CCF, the Political Action Committee (PAC) modelled on those of the CIO, became more important. It was a committee designed to "implement" CCL political policy decisions. It soon became the location of hard-fought disputes between partisans of different parties over the question of political action and, more specifically, the extent to which the CCF should be the only party supported. See Horowitz, op. cit., p. 99 ff.

[76]Beck, op. cit., p. 251.

[77]Whitaker, op. cit., p. 138.

[78]Ibid., p. 144.

[79]See Beck, op. cit., p. 252; Walter Young, Democracy and Discontent (Toronto: McGraw-Hill Ryerson, 1969), p. 74; D. Creighton, The Forked Road (Toronto: McClelland and Stewart, 1976), p. 102.

[80]As quoted in Creighton, op. cit., p. 89.

[81]Ibid., p. 90.

[82]Beck, op. cit., p. 248; Creighton, op. cit., p. 102.

[83]Creighton, op. cit., p. 104.

[84]See Beck, op. cit., pp. 244-245. In the country as a whole, 2,945,514 people voted to release the government from its "no conscription" pledge as against 1,643,006. In Quebec, the proportion was reversed: 376,188 voted for, and 993,663 voted against. See Colonel C. P. Stacey, op. cit., p. 294.

[85]Creighton, op. cit., p. 104; Young, The Anatomy of a Party, op. cit., p. 118.

[86]Beck, op. cit., pp. 256-257.

[87]While we cannot show the ethnic vote in 1945, it should be noted that the weight of the Social Credit support in the East fell in Quebec. In contrast to the 1940 election when Social Credit offered only two candidates in Quebec, no less than forty-three contested election in that province in 1945, as compared to only eight in Ontario. Ibid.

Chapter 8

1945-1965—Social Democracy for an Affluent Society

Introduction

Canada's economy and social structure settled into its modern form during these two decades. The industrialization stimulated by the demands of wartime production was consolidated in a prospering peacetime economy with the aid of American direct investment. Canada's economic activity was increasingly shaped to respond to the demands of the American market and its giant multinational corporations. These changes in Canada's postwar economy were reflected in the class structure and relations between its organizations. The bourgeoisie developed more tangible links with its American counterparts and increasingly pursued a continental development strategy. The subordinate classes changed in composition as the independent petite bourgeoisie and blue collar workers began to be overshadowed in number by new types of salaried workers—technicians, white collar workers and state employees. These new categories of workers, by and large, remained unorganized during these years, but in more familiar sectors of the labour force, trade union membership grew, and the major industrial and craft unions finally achieved organizational unity.

While these changes had important political potential for the future, they also came into play in the partisan politics of these decades. Years of their rivalry was stilled by the merger, in 1956, of the Trades and Labour Congress and the Canadian Congress of Labour into a single central organization, the Canadian Labour Congress (CLC). In turn, the new congress was a major participant in the founding of the New Democratic Party which, although sharing many characteristics of its predecessor, the CCF, was a social democratic party especially shaped for the new times. This period was also marked by the beginnings of a new nationalism. The Quiet Revolution in Quebec, most obvious after 1960, grew out of the urbanization, industrialization and secularization of the earlier postwar years. Similarly, a pan-Canadian nationalism which rejected American domination of the country's economic, political and cultural life also began to gather some force. The more radical manifestations of these movements would appear in the second half of the sixties and the seventies, but they began as the logical consequence of the development strategies and ideologies of the Canadian bourgeoisie after the Second World War.

As the war ended, and in preparation for the first postwar election, policy packages based on new understandings of the state and capitalism were put forward by all the parties. The boom conditions which followed seemed to justify this new role of the state. The predicted postwar recession had been "avoided," and, with only minor setbacks, Canadians enjoyed peak levels of employment and affluence. However, the particular form of the Canadian state's intervention encouraged even higher levels of foreign investment and in turn, a fundamental transformation of the bourgeoisie and its conception of the national interest. In contrast to earlier years, the postwar development strategy was founded on the "internationalization" of the Canadian economy and bourgeoisie. It provoked a reaction and raised the possibility of a new political alliance of the left, based on an analysis of Canadian capitalism which demanded the "re-nationalization" of the Canadian economy as a first step toward a new social order.

The labour movement also found itself in conditions of fundamental change, as the social formation rapidly accommodated more white collar and professional employment, increasing numbers of state employees and a massive entry of women into the labour force. The unions' ability to cope with these changes was only partial during these two postwar decades, but boom conditions eliminated many of the tensions between the industrial and craft centrals, and a merger was achieved. For the first time in decades, three-quarters of organized labour in Canada spoke with a single voice. Diversity had been "conquered." With this unity, after years of hard work on the part of the leadership of the CCF, came the first important proposal for a national labour party since the First World War. The New Democratic Party was founded with solid organizational links to the newly-formed Canadian Labour Congress (CLC). It was hoped that the CCF's transformation into the NDP, complete with organizational and financial links with organized labour and a new programme designed explicitly to appeal to the "middle classes" would bring Canadian social democracy out of the political wilderness to which it had been confined in the affluent postwar years. Unfortunately for the NDP, this self-transformation was not the most promising for the years that lay ahead. Not only did it not capture the support of the federal voters immediately, but it was not prepared for events to come, especially those after 1965. The NDP had moved with a current which was submerged by the long-term consequences of the Canadian postwar development strategy in the context of bicultural politics, and the new party had few ways to abandon the path that it had set for itself.

The Political Economy: 1945–1965

When the Economic Council of Canada (a body established to monitor and advise government on the state of the economy) issued its First

Annual Review in 1964, it found many reasons to pronounce itself satisfied with the postwar experience. There had been expansion, at times unprecedented expansion, in the economy under the guidance of the state, and, despite brief setbacks, it seemed economic growth would continue. The organizing principles for the period had been provided by the White Paper on Employment and Income of 1945, which noted that:

> ... the Government has stated unequivocally its adoption of a high and stable level of employment and income, and thereby higher standards of living, as a major aim of Government policy. It has been made clear that, if it is to be achieved, the endeavour to achieve it must pervade all government economic policy. It must be whole heartedly accepted by all economic groups and organizations as a great national objective, transcending in importance all sectional and group interests.[1]

The achievement of this optimistic state of affairs required fulfilling five policy objectives, some of which were in potential conflict with others. They were: (i) full employment, (ii) a high rate of economic growth, (iii) price stability, (iv) a viable balance of payments and (v) an equitable distribution of rising incomes.[2]

The federal Liberals, who, after all, had been responsible for the White Paper, had discovered a new formula to provide "prosperity for all," economic growth and, as a consequence, what seemed to be a new position for Canada in the world. Combined with some social programmes and the encouragement of foreign investment to assure sufficient development capital, the social unrest and unemployment which had characterized the post-1918 years had not been repeated. In fact, the unemployment rate was very low, settling around 2.8% in the period 1946-1953, and organized labour was placid as wages rose rapidly and consumer demand, pent up during the war years, was satisfied.[3]

In 1964, however, there were a few clouds on the horizon. Between 1958 and 1962, the unemployment rate pushed up to 6.7%; all indicators of economic growth had turned down since the mid-fifties, and labour costs were rising rapidly. In addition, on all of these dimensions, the Canadian record was worse than other developed countries.[4] Canada's economy remained export-oriented, and resources were the most rapidly growing export sector. This emphasis was in marked contrast to the trends of other industrialized countries. Despite considerable growth in the postwar period, manufacturing exports in Canada, as a proportion of all non-agricultural exports, were no higher in 1963 than they had been in the late 1920s. Although 16% of the GNP was due to exports (compared to 4% in the USA and 14% in the UK), most of these exports were unprocessed or only semi-processed primary products.[5] This meant that the Canadian economy remained inherently vulnerable, being neither highly technologically developed nor labour intensive. If world demand for, or Canada's supply of, resources fell off, economic troubles were a certainty. In addition, it was obvious that full employment would be increasingly difficult to achieve. More distressing for policy-makers, at least the thoughtful ones, was the realization that the whole economic structure was predicated on the continuation of high rates of growth. If this growth did not continue or could not be induced by the state, the edifice threatened to collapse or, at least, develop major cracks in its foundations. Such a tenuous economic balance had great political implications.

How did this situation arise, and what were its partisan effects? During the war, as the previous chapter described, there was a great deal of unease about what the end of the war might bring. The greatest fear was that the end of wartime manufacturing would cost thousands of Canadians their jobs and send unemployment rates to record levels. However, the state employed both Keynesian economic planning and more traditional policies, designed to induce investment, to achieve a smooth transition from a wartime to peacetime economy. Tariffs were again used to encourage import-substitution manufacturing. Similarly, many of the Crown Corporations set up for wartime production were sold, often at prices far below their market value (frequently at approximately one-third of that value) on the condition that the purchaser maintain employment in the plant for a minimum period of five years.[6] The effects of these policies were similar to those of the National Policy of 1878. The tariff and very attractive depreciation allowances encouraged even more American branch plants to establish in Canada.[7] Crown assets were sold to any purchaser largely because the desire to keep jobs in Canada outweighed any concern about the potential consequences of an over-reliance on foreign capital.[8]

These policies, in addition to international conditions, which were already encouraging a huge expansion of American multinational corporations, produced a net result that direct investment by Americans in Canada almost doubled in the 1945 to 1952 period alone. The shift in ownership of the Canadian manufacturing sector was extremely rapid, such that in a decade the percentage of foreign control grew from 35% in 1946 to 50% in 1953 to 56% in 1957 and, finally, to an unprecedented 60% in 1963. The increase of foreign control in mining and smelting and petroleum and natural gas was even more pronounced.[9] This movement of American capital into the resource sector in particular reflected a renewed interest in the creation of a continental economy. Integration of the two economies would allow Americans access to plentiful supplies of natural resources, especially those rapidly depleting in the United States. For Canadians, this integration represented a continuation of traditional staple export policies.[10] It seemed a natural strategy to pursue the American market, which had only discovered that it had potential supply problems. The Paley Report of 1952 warned the American government about the dangers involved in the rapid depletion of that country's own natural resources and pointed out that these materials were in abundant supply in Canada where they were not "needed" because of the relatively underdeveloped state of production.[11] This "Resources for Freedom" Report further suggested that American corporations assure themselves "safe" sources of supply, especially as the Cold War made such sources a primary strategic concern. Thus, both internal and external factors encouraged direct foreign investment, and the Canadian economy was progressively integrated with that of the United States.[12]

Whether the concern was the maintenance of employment or the exploitation of advantages in the resource sector, the source of capital invested in Canada did not alarm the Canadian government or for that matter the political parties and public opinion of the period.[13] The consequences and contradictions inherent in such dependency on American capitalism were to become apparent only in the late fifties and then only slowly. This recognition came about partially because of the changes in the social formation that occurred in these years, many of which were also a consequence of the new development strategy. The first important change was in the character and the orientations of the Canadian bourgeoisie. The second affected the composition of the labour force and labour organizations.

It will be recalled that from the pre-Confederation period, the commercial and financial elite were the most visible and politically important fraction of the Canadian bourgeoisie. With the industrialization and merger movement of the early twentieth century, this fraction expanded into corporate capitalism. Firms were bought and sold and production reduced or expanded, in order to maintain profitable conditions within the context of a domestic market stretching across the country. The capital to develop Canada's manufacturing sector was largely foreign in origin. This reliance on foreign capital, its regional manifestations and its political effects have been examined. A further consequence of this process, one which became extremely important in this period, was the restructuring and reorientation of the capitalist class in Canada.

In the postwar years, the Canadian bourgeoisie faced an economic order which demanded new strategies and fresh perspectives. The Depression and the Second World War taught the Canadian bourgeoisie and the state, just as they did in most of the developed capitalist world, several important lessons.[14] The first lesson was that the policy of national isolationism, so common during the early years of the Depression, had disastrous economic repercussions. Second, it was agreed that depression conditions could be avoided if the state took an active role in the organization of employment and investment and in the provision of social welfare. While the bourgeoisie might rely on the state to nurture a purely national market, isolation of that market from foreign competition was no longer a viable strategy. The state was needed not only to maintain conditions of stability within capitalism, but also to sustain a capitalism with international and multinational connections. The bourgeoisie recognized the new international order and its implications. Given the existing situation, within which they found themselves and which had been shaped by earlier development strategies, as well as the impulse from the war and postwar reconstruction, this could mean one thing:

> From 1940 to 1957, the ruling class of this country was radically reshaped. In 1939, the United Kingdom still seemed a powerful force, and the men who ruled Canada were a part of the old Atlantic triangle. They turned almost as much to Great Britain as to the United States, economically, culturally, and politically. After 1940, the ruling class found its centre of gravity in the United States.[15]

The Canadian bourgeoisie was integrated into an international network, but it was not eliminated or submerged in the process. It continued to be influential within Canada (and increasingly abroad), maintaining its position as a supplier of services to both national and multinational corporations. It continued to be active in transportation, commercial and financial activities while leaving the industrial transformation of the country to foreign capital.[16] As part of the process, the Canadian elite sat on boards of directors of firms which were partially- or even wholly-owned subsidiaries of foreign corporations.[17] In fact, Canadians often sat on boards of corporations which they had owned before those corporations were purchased by American capital.[18] The Canadian bourgeoisie, in turn, also provided capital for expansion from the national financial institutions which they controlled and marshalled the forces of the state to keep the process working.[19]

In essence, these changes reflected a fundamental transformation of the conception of the national interest. A new development strategy was adopted which was no longer based on a fear of integration with Americans. This is the difference between the 1850s and the 1950s. The dream of continentalism was once again realizable. Moreover, the Canadian bourgeoisie, in a multinational world, was not personally threatened by US expansion. They had found a place in the board rooms and banks of international capitalism.[20] As Lester B. Pearson, the Canadian Secretary of State for External Affairs in 1954 announced, Canada had become the "junior partner of a North American partnership."[21] This change in the national interest was recognized by Mitchell Sharp, who as one-time senior bureaucrat and Cabinet Minister in the Pearson government, both observed and aided the shift:

> At the time of Confederation and until the 1920s, there were strong countervailing forces promoting an East-West bias in Canada's economic development. . . . Over time, however, the exploitation of our mineral and forestry resources assumed more importance and these

found a large and expanding market in a rapidly industrializing United States. The economic axis was gradually turning in a North-South direction.[22]

National economic growth was, as always, founded on exports, but there were differences in this period. Agricultural exports dropped to 9% of the total market while natural resources such as pulp and paper rose to 34% and non-ferrous metal to 17% of Canada's export trade.[23] In addition, the United States increasingly became Canada's major trading partner. By 1950, two-thirds of Canadian exports went to the US which supplied Canada with the same proportion of its imports.[24] However, the latter was less "trade" than transfers between parent corporations and their branches in Canada.[25]

It could only be expected that the development strategy of the state would reflect these transformations in the economy and bourgeoisie. The fact was that the conceptions of the "national interest" and "national development" which had motivated federal state activity since 1867 began to take a radically different tone. Gone, for the moment, was the necessity of achieving independence for Canada from the vagaries of international trade. Gone too was the reliance on the wheat farmer. Now the motor of growth came from outside of Canada's borders, from the expansion of multinational American capitalism. Canada would grow, prosper and "develop" on the coattails of the American postwar economic boom and the growing international economic and political dominance of the United States.[26] The Canadian bourgeoisie understood this strategy of growth and involved the state in creating the necessary conditions for its unfolding and for dealing with political movements that might interfere with continental economic integration. Both the nationalists and socialists constituted such a danger.

The "Pipeline Scandal" of 1956 graphically illustrates the dimensions of this new development strategy, the role of the state in its accomplishment and some partisan consequences. Discoveries of vast reserves of oil and natural gas in Alberta confirmed Canada's advantages as a source of raw materials. The marketing of the natural gas was then on the agenda but how were these supplies in isolated (isolated from industrial activity, that is) Alberta to be brought to the markets of Ontario and the eastern US? The Alberta government in 1954 authorized the sale of 500 million cubic feet of natural gas per day to eastern Canada.[27] However, the massive infusion of Alberta energy into the industrial heartland demanded the construction of an elaborate and expensive pipeline—a project the federal government was all too willing to support. Indeed, Prime Minister St. Laurent considered the project to be equivalent in magnitude and importance to the building of the CPR.[28] The analogy was partially appropriate because, as in the case of the construction of the national railway, the federal government was to be a major financier of the Trans-

Canada Pipeline. However, there was a crucial difference between the two national projects. While the CPR was designed to integrate the national economy, the pipeline was "transnational" or continental in scope. It was not competing with but rather facilitating the activities of American capital. After the Alberta government offered 500 million cubic feet per day for sale, the federal government ruled that only 300 million was needed to meet Canadian needs, and the rest was open for sale to the United States. The Americans were quick to grasp the opportunity, and an export charter was issued to Trans-Canada Pipe Lines Ltd., a corporation controlled by American financial interests. Plans and agreements soon in hand, the federal government had every reason to believe that, in accordance with their desires, construction would be well under way before the next federal election. However, in the spring of 1956, Trans-Canada procrastinated, arguing that it needed an $80 million loan to build the line from Alberta to Winnipeg, the part of the pipeline which was essential for the export market.[29] The subsequent "Pipeline Scandal" actually involved the Liberal government's unorthodox application of closure to force a bill authorizing the loan through Parliament. Nevertheless, the question of American domination in the Canadian economy was raised by both the Progressive Conservatives and the CCF during the debate.[30] 1956, then, marks the beginnings of political reactions to the rapid modification of the Canadian social and economic structure. This was the year not only of the Pipeline debate but also of the establishment of the Royal Commission on Canada's Economic Prospects, chaired by Walter Gordon, which in years to come provided documentation for the critiques made by the new Canadian nationalists.

This shift in the focus of the national development had several unintended consequences which potentially threatened the existing organization of partisan relations. First, there was a strong propensity towards structural unemployment. In advanced capitalism there is generally an unemployment problem, as more and more machinery replaces labour in the production process. In Canada, however, "industrialization by branch plant" and "development by resource export" aggravated this tendency. Essentially, there were fewer employment opportunities in Canada's postwar development strategy. One of the expected benefits of economic growth is increased employment, but, in Canada, this effect was muted because resource industries are capital rather than labour intensive. Raw materials were exported for processing elsewhere or with only minimal processing. Manufacturing, once again heavily influenced, particularly in the most advanced sectors, by foreign ownership, was usually limited to production for the home market and not for export. American corporations no longer needed to use Canada as a base to export because they had either implanted branch plants in foreign markets or supplied them directly from the parent corporation.

Despite its level of economic development, Canada had only a small percentage of its population working in the manufacturing sector, and the numbers were not growing rapidly. In fact, in the period 1946-1963, employment in goods-producing industries increased by only 1% as primary industry employment decreased by 40% and employment in secondary production increased by only 44%. This can be compared to employment increases of well over one hundred per cent in public utilities, finance, insurance and real estate and in other service industries.[31] As government advisers and economists looked into the future, they could see signs of increasing unemployment.

That this unemployment was regionally concentrated was a second important factor threatening the political future. American branch plants were disproportionately located in the central provinces because of the availability of resources and their proximity to the parent companies. The regional differences in investment in manufacturing, unemployment rates and income can clearly be seen in Table 8:1. In the sixties, Atlantic Canada, for example, had the lowest investment level in manufacturing, the lowest per capita income and more than double Ontario's unemployment rate. Quebec was also distinguished from provinces to its west by high unemployment and low incomes. This pattern of regional underdevelopment held out the potential for regional discontent if it could find or be organized into an appropriate partisan vehicle.

In addition to structural unemployment and regional disparities, major changes in the occupational structure also held out the potential for a new alignment in the federal party system. As Table 8:2 shows, similar to the experience of other advanced capitalist countries, Canada witnessed a significant growth in the service or tertiary sector during this period. The number of white collar workers in Canada leaped in the period 1941-1961. Indeed, in the ten years between 1951 and 1961 alone, their numbers increased by 45%.[32] The increase was more rapid than previously, reflecting the nature and advances of modern industrialization. Once again, the increase in white collar work was due to a shift

Table 8:1
SOME INDICATORS OF ECONOMIC ACTIVITY, BY REGION (1960-1969)
(Canada = 100)

	Value Added in Manufacturing	Earned Income Per capita	Unemployment Rate
Atlantic Provinces	35.1	65.7	167.1
Quebec	101.1	89.0	134.0
Ontario	150.7	118.4	73.1
Prairies	39.9	94.4	62.7
BC	88.8	110.1	116.7

Source: Compiled from P. Phillips, *Regional Disparities* (Toronto: Lorimer, 1978) Chapter 2.

Table 8:2
CHANGES IN EMPLOYMENT BY INDUSTRY, 1946–1963

Industry	Employment 1946	Employment 1963	Total Change	Percentage Change
Goods Producing	2,809	2,883	74	+1
Primary	1,371	819	–552	–40
Secondary	1,433	2,064	626	+44
Service Producing	1,858	3,482	1,624	+87
Transportation, storage and communications	344	455	111	+32
Public utilities	33	75	52	+158
Trade	573	1,019	446	+78
Finance, insurance, real estate	124	254	130	+105
Other services	784	1,669	885	+113
All Industries	4,666	6,365	1,699	+36

Note: Newfoundland is not included in data for 1946. Other services include community services, public administration and defence (excluding armed forces) recreational services, business, private and personal services.

Source: The Economic Council of Canada, First Annual Review: Economic Goals for Canada to 1970, Table 46, p. 155.

within manufacturing industries which required fewer production and more office and administrative workers. The percentage of administrative and office workers within the manufacturing sector grew from 17% in 1947 to 29% in 1964.[33] By the mid-sixties, almost one-third of all employees in manufacturing were performing white collar work. At the same time, there was a huge expansion of state workers, many of whom were also white collar workers. The post-1945 welfare state and full employment policies induced the provision of greater and greater numbers of state jobs.[34] Staff was needed to administer the new programmes, and even more jobs were created by the state in times of unemployment to take up the slack in the labour market.[35] These two factors in addition to a more generally service-centred economy produced the changes described here.

It is equally important to note here, for later consideration of union and party actions, that the shifts which occurred in the labour force were of a particular kind. Among the white collar workers, clerical and financial-commercial categories increased relative to the rest.[36] Such workers have little training and are least independent in defining and determining their conditions of work. Second, there was a very rapid decline in self-employment during these years, partly but not completely due to the decline of agricultural work. Between 1911 and 1941, the per cent of wage-earners in the labour force increased from 60% to 67%. In the following decade, it rose another 10%, and, by 1961, 82% of the labour force were wage earners.[37] Third, in the postwar period, and accounting for some of this decline in self-employment, there was a huge increase in the numbers of salaried professionals. Between 1951 and 1961, the number of professionals in Canada increased by 65%, but, in contrast with earlier times, most were salaried wage-earners rather than self-employed.[38] They were a different type of professional:

> Almost all of the "new professionals," ranging from social workers to systems analysts, work for an employer. And salaried professionals tend to be concentrated in *large* work organizations that may not easily adapt to the culture of professionalism.[39]

In 1961, the percentage of wage-earning professionals ranged from as high as 100% among teachers and nurses to over 90% among engineers and 85% among accountants and auditors. Even such traditionally independent professions as law and medicine had, in 1961, a large contingent of salaried wage-earners.[40] The evolution from self-employed to wage-earner among professionals has been rapid, and it continues.[41]

A nother notable change in the occupational structure involved the appearance of more and more women in the work force, especially as a pool of cheap labour for unskilled jobs. In 1941, 23% of working-age women were in the labour force, but by 1961, this had grown to 29% and to 37% in 1967.[42] These women were largely concentrated in low-paying and non-production sectors and had little control over their conditions of work.

The long-term consequences of the postwar development strategy with its effects on employment and regional disparity were potentially disruptive to the traditional party system, and the compositional changes in the labour force provided a possible support base for a new political alignment. Who would take these issues and organize these workers, explain the workings of the system in partisan terms and propose a solution? As the following section will show, both the trade union movement and the CCF were slow to realize the potential for a new alliance of those who bore the costs of Canadian capitalism. Although conditions in this period offered a foundation for a coalition far surpassing, in numbers, the unrealized alliances of the twenties and thirties, there was no nationwide vehicle to mobilize the disaffected. The Progressive Conservative Party was successful, if only briefly, in forging a new coalition among its ranks. However, as we shall see, labour settled into a mood of complacency after the war, and the CCF floundered in the political wilderness. And, although late in this period, the CLC did participate in the creation of a new national labour party, the new party's design was not the most appropriate for the future.

The Unionism of Cold War Affluence

The postwar decades were, at one and the same time, a period of growth and expansion for the trade unions and a time of discouraging decline for the CCF. Trade unions had emerged from the war in a relatively strong position, although they were slow to organize the burgeoning new categories of state and white collar workers. With new collective bargaining and union rights, unions were confident that they had carved a legitimate place for themselves in the Canadian social fabric.[43] Reflecting this new legitimacy, membership began to grow, especially after the TLC accepted the fact that the traditional definition of craftwork was outmoded and began to organize greater numbers of semi- and unskilled workers.[44] The proportion of the labour force organized into trade unions rose, in consequence, from 15.7% in 1945 to 23.6% ten years later, where it remained for the next decade.[45]

However, in contrast with the war years, the postwar labour movement was conservative in outlook and moderate in its approach to industrial relations. Legal and social acceptance and organizational gains were achieved in such a way that the union movement was encouraged to remain economistic in outlook. Its new legal status, for example, involved, as before, the interventionary role of the federal state. Increasingly, the state would be involved in labour-management relations and in the resolution of industrial disputes.[46] Thus, union officials had real incentives to pursue good relations with the government rather than confront it. Labour's conservatism, especially in the late forties and early fifties, was also nurtured by the ideology of the Cold War which, in both the international and Canadian contexts, cast suspicion on radical politics and socialism in particular. The hysteria of the Cold War, reflected most spectacularly in the Gouzenko spy affair in Canada and McCarthyism in the United States, had a far more pervasive effect than these two events would suggest. It directed hostility against the left and Communists in particular, so much so that this competing organization was purged from the union movement.[47] In this atmosphere of hostility, it became virtually impossible to sustain any radical critique of capitalism. The Cold War conditions emphasized the "foreignness" of socialism and the advantages of the "new capitalism" of the welfare state, which, it was argued, made socialism unnecessary. The combination of the Cold War and the economic boom were disastrous for the remnants of socialist analysis within the labour movement and Canadian social democracy more generally. With the successful transition from a war to peacetime economy, the labour movement settled into a period of complacency.[48] Militancy declined and strikes were less frequent largely because employers almost voluntarily increased wages rather than face losses in production time. These conditions reinforced the economistic tendencies of the unions, and they became preoccupied with gaining a better deal for their membership to the exclusion of political action.

While the major trade unions were not concerned with developing a critical understanding of capitalism among their membership, neither were they much concerned with organizing the new categories of state and white collar workers.[49] Although growing in number, these workers either remained outside the ranks of organized labour, especially the internationals, or they were members of small, and poor, national trade unions. These new workers, despite their growing significance in the labour force and the balance of class forces, presented numerous organizational problems.[50] First, and perhaps most important, there were ideological barriers. For the most part, they did not consider themselves to be workers in the traditional "blue collar" sense of the term. Some harboured attitudes of professionalism while others simply failed to equate their working conditions, for instance, as file clerks or technicians, with those of factory workers. Moreover, the trade unions, rather than challenge this view with organizational drives and educational work, generally accepted it. North American unions had little experience organizing these types of workers, and the international unions in Canada got little guidance from their American headquarters. Few North American white collar workers and state employees were organized by the mid-sixties, a situation in marked contrast with the European situation. International unions still dominated the organized labour movement. In fact, from 1945 until 1960 traditional industrial and craft unions—the Autoworkers, Steelworkers and Carpenters, foremost among them—constituted the ten largest unions in Canada. Because the most rapidly expanding sectors of the labour force were not being organized by the internationals, the proportion of the trade unionists among the labour force remained low. Indeed, the percentage of the labour force organized in unions remained fixed at 23% from 1955 to 1965. As late as 1967, effective organizations were overwhelmingly concentrated in typically blue collar rather than white collar sectors. For example, as late as 1967, approximately one-half to three-fifths of the forestry, mining, construction and transportation workers were unionized compared to 8% of the trade and 12% of the service workers.[51]

By contrast, in Quebec, labour unions, with the very society itself, reeled with change. Wartime industrialization and urbanization set in motion a process of secularization which through the fifties and sixties undermined the cultural and ideological influence of the Roman Catholic Church. In the process, a strong, secular union movement grew up to challenge the non-conflictural class analysis of Church-directed unions. Indications that the Church was losing its influence in the Quebec labour movement were evident early in the 1940s. New industrial unions were rapidly eroding the CCCL's membership, and the percentage of unionized workers organized by CCCL affiliates dropped progressively from its high of 74% in 1935 to 28% in 1943.[52] That the internationals were successfully gaining ascendancy over the CCCL was especially disturbing to Church officials because the internationals were seen as both materialistic and centralizing. In the words of the Bishop of Rimouski, "Communism glides through their shadows like a serpent."[53]

In effect, the internationals posed a threat not only to the Church's direction of the Quebec labour movement, but also to the dominance of its world view. It was evident that something had to be done to bolster the CCCL's membership, and, beginning in 1943, the Church reluctantly made a few concessions in the direction of secularization. However, the process of secularizing the Quebec labour movement really gained momentum only after the war when a younger leadership took over the CCCL. Thereafter, the Church's influence in the CCCL steadily diminished until finally, in 1960, the CCCL was dissolved and the collection of Catholic unions gave way to the secular Confédération des Syndicats Nationaux (CNTU).[54] Over the course of several hard strikes, the CNTU increased its influence among Quebec labour, participating in the social and political changes which underlie the cultural tensions of the 1960s and 1970s.[55] The CNTU was also more successful than unions in English Canada in mobilizing and realizing the advantages of white collar unionism. From 1960 to 1965, the percentage of service and professional unions in the CNTU rose from 27% to 52%. At the same time, the CNTU membership increased from 102,000 to 150,000.[56] However, these new unions, at least initially, brought neither a socialist critique of the existing relations of production nor a departure from the linguistic and cultural isolation of the province's union movement.

Throughout the country the atmosphere of the fifties and early sixties was not conducive to radical union activity or radical politics. The repression of the organizations carrying and propounding fundamental societal critiques, the fear of socialism and the economism of the unions combined with the organizational habits of the union movement to produce a particular version of social democracy in Canada. From 1956 until 1961, the CCF was remaking itself with the help and guidance of the unions. These were, however, conservative unions with limited expectations or hopes for change. They were unions implanted in a small segment of the Canadian labour force, and they were the unions of the traditional working class. They were the unions of industrial and craft workers rather than unions of the rapidly expanding work force which would have to be included in any future successful left alliance. The potentiality of these workers, as union members and left voters, was not fully appreciated by the new party. Both the CCF and the NDP used a class map which placed these workers in the middle classes. The organization of the NDP went forward for the most part without them.

From the CCF to the NDP—Fifteen Years of Travail

Why did the CCF not rise on the wave of postwar social democracy, so important in other advanced capitalist societies? Why was its wartime advance halted? Part of the explanation can be found in the short history of the CCF, which was very much junior to the better established and more experienced European parties. However, this is not a completely satisfactory explanation. The specific strategy followed by the CCF in response to the new postwar politics must also be understood. What appeared in 1943 to be the CCF's long-awaited take-off in federal politics proved to be but a brief public flirtation with social democracy. As we have shown in the previous chapter, the major parties discovered the benefits for capitalism of regulation, planning and social welfare programmes. In these years, the CCF found itself pushed aside as the Liberals adopted "their" social programmes, one after the other. By 1948 and its Tenth Annual Conference, the CCF was reduced to self-congratulatory interpretations of its electoral failures. It pointed with some pride to how it had forced the Liberals to adopt some of its social welfare policies. However, this self-laudatory posture was not founded on a realistic assessment of modern conditions. The social policies of most advanced capitalist countries in the postwar years were more or less the same, and, in Canada, the actual level of social services and the redistribution of wealth was lower than most. Why, then, had the CCF not only not come to power, but also not pursued and elaborated upon the radical critique of the Regina Manifesto? Why, in short, had the CCF failed?

It is usually argued that the CCF was confronted with a choice between remaining faithful to its socialist principles or going "a-whoring after the Bitch Goddess"—electoral success.[57] However, this explanation is partially contradicted by the experience of some European socialist parties during the same period. Confronting similar economic and ideological changes, some of those parties did manage to retain, expand and even occasionally enact their principles by means of electoral victories, even if they did not bring about a complete transition to socialism. The fundamental weakness of the CCF strategy was not that it wanted to win elections. The party's difficulties arose from decisions to progressively moderate the party's platform based on a particular analysis of capitalism fundamental to the party's theory. The party had a theory and a strategy which would never enable the CCF to carve its place in the federal party system. In essence, the CCF strategy did not result in the partisan organization of the Canadian working class, the unending task of any workers' party. The CCF accepted the Canadian classes as it saw them and tried to work with them. However, the classes that it saw were, in fact, the "classes" of the liberal ideology of classlessness. Instead of challenging this ideology with its own class map, the CCF accepted it. It played by the rules of the bourgeois parties' game, and it could not win.

The CCF did not develop a language of politics which allowed it to construct a working-class alliance. It accepted the existing language of politics rather than developing its own. It accepted postwar liberalism's pronouncement of the "end of ideology." It accepted the view of society and its mapping and relations of classes which characterized North American liberalism. Doing these things, the CCF offered no alternative world view, no explanation of their conditions to the social groups and class fractions which advanced capitalism created. It could not explain to the new white collar workers, the state workers, the women, the workers in non-central regions, how their lives were created by the capitalism of postwar Canada. It could not explain the actions of the state, or of the Liberal Party, in a way which reflected an understanding of the welfare state. If it could not explain to these workers, and they formed a larger and larger proportion of the population, their life conditions, it could not lead their struggles. It could neither organize them in partisan politics nor provide a programme for resolution of the problems these workers and all workers faced. By failing to understand the Canadian "case" the CCF could not be other than a left wing of the Liberals—a more moral, a more democratic but essentially similar party.

The progressive reorientation of the CCF's socialism began early in the war years when the party issued cautious interpretations of the concept of nationalization in order to avoid alienating the western farmers and the conservative trade unionists. This strategy of moderation accelerated after the war and throughout the fifties until, in 1956, the party adopted a new statement of principles, the Winnipeg Declaration, which would provide the theoretical foundations for the New Democratic Party. The decision to draw the CCF and its successor, the NDP, closer to the ideological centre of the federal party system reflected disappointments stemming from the party's seeming inability to reverse its dismal electoral fortunes. Throughout the late forties and the fifties the CCF "had been slowly bleeding to death at the polls."[58] As early as 1950, the party's convention accepted that a restatement of the party's aims and purposes was necessary because it was felt that the Regina Manifesto was out of step with the times. The logic of this argument for moderation was based on the workers' need for allies. There were no longer sufficient numbers of farmers to form a winning alliance with the working class. The obvious allies were the "middle class" and organized labour. Therefore, the CCF had to appeal to these groups if it was to win elections and have access to the means to build socialism. However, these middle classes, and even organized labour, were neither socialist nor interested in socialist goals like nationalization and collective ownership. Therefore, if they were to be electoral allies, CCF programmes must be "moderated" so as not to frighten them away. The "moderate" Winnipeg Manifesto reflected this logic. The only remaining target of CCF wrath was large capital, whose power would have to be destroyed either by nationalization or by other measures to compel activity in the interest of the Canadian people. After its wartime statements, the CCF announced that it would nationalize only large-scale enterprises.[59]

The problem faced by the CCF was dramatic—the ideology of the Cold War, the return of economic prosperity, the institution of the welfare state, the gradual disappearance of the farmers as a radical force in federal politics, the growth of the "new" middle classes, the party's falling membership, finances and electoral fortunes—and all of these factors seemed to demand a change in the party's orientation to the electorate and, ultimately, the transformation of the CCF into the NDP in 1961. As defeat followed defeat, the CCF leadership became increasingly convinced that the solution to the party's ills lay in two related directions. It was argued that Canadian social democracy would not emerge from the political wilderness unless, and until, the party, first, followed the British Labour Party's example and forged strong organizational links with the trade union movement, and second, redesigned the party platform so that it would appeal to the Canadian "middle class" voter, who was seen as very conservative indeed. In 1956, T. C. Douglas expressed that party's dilemma which, in view of its postwar failures, was recognized and accepted by many party militants:

> We have to look very realistically over the period of the last ten or fifteen years and recognize that we have lost ground. . . . We also have to recognize that the capitalist groups have learned a great deal. . . . They have applied some of the Keynesian techniques and they have been admirably successful up to a point. . . . We . . . like socialist parties all over the Western world, are on the defensive . . . [The] indictment of capitalism [in the Regina Manifesto] is still basically true, but it is not as apparent as it was in 1933, and it is harder to sell.[60]

This redefinition and attempts to broaden the party's support base in the direction of organized labour and the middle class occurred throughout this period, culminating ultimately in the formation of the NDP. Paradoxically, it was precisely the CCF's efforts and tactics to make itself more palatable to the Canadian electorate which denied it, and later the NDP, a strong presence in the federal party system. There are three elements of the CCF's new approach which merit further attention because they circumscribed the electoral potential of social democracy. The first is their redefined class map and the position of the new middle classes within it. The second element concerns the CCF's understanding of the postwar state, and the third is the emphasis it placed on trade union affiliation. In the case of the first two elements, the CCF accepted the dominant definition of the class structure and the capitalist state. With regard to the trade union movement, it followed the unique, but not entirely appropriate, model of the British Labour Party.

Every party of the left, if it proposes a fundamental transformation of society, needs a road map. It needs a theory which describes the situation it faces, including a map of the class structure and strategies of how to proceed. The early CCF and its leadership did have a view of Canadian society in the thirties and a Canadian road map to socialism. Recognizing the importance of farmers, both in terms of numbers and political consciousness, and the relative weakness of labour, the CCF proposed to build Canadian socialism by means of an alliance between farmers and labour which would act in concert in Parliament to achieve change. The programmatic implications of this theory and strategy, defined in the Regina Manifesto and the CCF's early electoral platforms, did contain fundamental contradictions between the expectations of independent commodity producers and workers, but this strategy might have worked if the wartime escape from the Depression had not simultaneously and fundamentally altered the social formation of Canada.

As the previous chapter documents, the occupational structure of the country was changed radically by war-induced industrialization. As western farmers became less relevant both in numbers and economic importance, manufacturing and service-sector workers increased in number. The modern industrial economy was very different from what preceded it. It was an industrial, scientific and commercial economy which required large bureaucracies with specialized white collar employees to co-ordinate complex production and marketing processes. It was also a service-oriented economy designed to meet the demands of a more affluent society for a greater variety of consumer goods, personal services, education, leisure-time facilities and commercial activity.[61] It was the CCF's theoretical understanding of these changes which led to its strategy for the 1950s and its move into the NDP. This understanding was the same as that of the dominant ideology.

As already described, these years were marked by the growth of white collar work, state employees and professional and service workers. While the proportion of manual workers remained virtually constant during this period, white collar and service work increased dramatically. The CCF considered all these new workers to be part of the "middle class" because they were not blue collar workers—that is, by definition. They were middle class because of their lifestyles, and they were middle class because they were not unionized and, in many cases, not eligible for trade union membership. In other words, in the CCF's view two non-capitalist classes were the working class, those workers who had manual occupations and belonged to trade unions, and the middle class, those who did not meet these criteria.

In addition, these middle class people were considered to have interests and values which set them apart from blue collar workers. It is at this point that the class map of the CCF almost replicates that of the dominant ideology. The 1950s, with the Cold War and the postwar boom, produced an ideology which declared the "end of ideology."[62] In its simplified form, it was argued that affluence, Keynesianism and social welfare policies were rapidly but certainly eliminating the class divisions of capitalist society. According to the end-of-ideology thesis, everybody, including unionized workers (because their wages were high and would go higher), could acquire the symbols of the middle class such as a house, a car, well-educated children—in short, social mobility. Since the class structure had been broken down and everyone could aspire to and presumably attain a middle class life, socialism was no longer seen as necessary. Socialism may have been an ideology appropriate to earlier periods of capitalist development, but it had outlived its meaning and utility in post-industrial societies. Proponents of the end-of-ideology thesis only had to point to many of the policies which once were the stock-in-trade of prewar socialism (full employment, unemployment insurance, higher and more available levels of education, medical care and pensions) and now were either implemented or promised by the bourgeois parties. With both pervasive affluence and the welfare state, end-of-ideology ideologies asked, why would anyone vote socialist? Moreover, the argument was often buttressed with critiques of existing socialism, which, as the Stalinist experience of the USSR and Eastern Europe seemed to demonstrate, led to excessive centralization, regulation and a disregard for basic liberties. Both the end-of-ideology thesis and the Cold War image of Stalin's communism eroded the support base of socialist parties during this period.

Nevertheless, the view that a middle class utopia had arrived failed to take into account the conditions of these workers and the basis for their momentary affluence. It confused the consumer durables of affluence—the products of technology—with the relations of hierarchy, power and exploitation which produced those goods. There was an assumption (and not only among liberal thinkers but some socialists as well) that white collar work gave people access to the world of the petite bourgeoisie—the world of independence in work, of individual initiative and rewards and of working conditions better than the lot of the manual workers; in essence, a world where capitalist relations of production were less imposing and less binding. However, an examination of the conditions of white collar work in the 1950s does not conform to this simple view of an ever-expanding petite bourgeoisie. Certainly white collar workers did have higher levels of education, in general, than did other workers, and, with education, there did come certain expectations about mobility and lifestyles.[63] But, the greatest expansion of white collar workers was among the least skilled, the lowest paid and the least independent at work. Clerical work was in great demand, which meant that more people (and increasingly these were women) were needed for the routine and mechanical tasks of administration. Second, professional workers were increasing in number, especially in the state sector, but they were not the traditional professionals—the doctors and lawyers of the independent petite bourgeoisie—but salaried professionals employed in large institutions. Technological change brought whole new categories of work, requiring highly trained technicians and scientific workers, for example, which were essential components of modern automated industry, but this work was performed in company labs or in factories on tasks defined for them by the production process and their corporate employers.

Classifying all these workers as middle class and thus setting them off from the "real workers" could not explain to them why they experienced such a gap between expectation and reality or why, despite their white collar, education and personal affluence, they found themselves with little personal freedom and less and less initiative in larger and larger impersonal work units. Moreover, it did not explain why, not infrequently, they received lower wages than seemed "appropriate" for their responsibilities and status. Gradually these workers would, themselves, recognize that they were not "middle class" and that they were, in fact, not all that different from the blue collar workers. With this recognition would come increased militancy in collective action, especially in the late 1960s and the 1970s. But, this movement was not inspired by any theory of capitalist society emanating from the CCF/NDP, and these workers did not necessarily turn to that party for an understanding of their life conditions nor for a leader of their struggles.

The reaction of the CCF and, later, the NDP to these new social groupings did little to rally them behind the party in the elections of the 1950s and 1960s. The CCF leadership recognized that the new middle classes would be valuable allies along with the organized workers in their struggle for political power. However, they were also keenly aware that these social groupings were not at that moment socialist nor open to socialist goals such as nationalization and collective ownership. In view of this fact the leadership thought it necessary to dilute the party's programmes and platforms so that these potential supporters would not be frightened away. Throughout the fifties, then, the CCF's critique of capitalism was steadily reduced to a criticism of the worst abuses of large-scale capitalism. Monopolies, the party argued, would have to be destroyed either by nationalization or by other measures to force them to act in the interests of the Canadian people. The radical critique of the thirties gave way to statements that CCF socialism meant the nationalization of less and less. Indeed as early as the party's 1948 convention, the self-assigned task of the CCF government was defined as "helping business fulfill its legitimate function."[64] However, the party's approach to the electorate was most fundamentally altered with the adoption of the Winnipeg Declaration of Principles, the statement of purpose which would guide the formation of the NDP. In order to appeal to the perceived conservatism of the "middle classes" and to make themselves more acceptable to the trade unions who were also seen as conservative, the party's leadership purged the party of references to nationalization and socialism. Instead of the Regina Manifesto's aim to "replace the present capitalistic system," CCFers would now seek a social order in which everyone could "enjoy equality and freedom, a sense of human dignity and an opportunity to live a rich and meaningful life."[65] In its desire to capture the support of what it saw as a conservative electorate, the party had effectively transformed itself to more closely resemble the bourgeois parties. It was more liberal than socialist. As one party historian of the period observed:

> If the CCF of today is compared with the party before the war, the missing qualities are the most striking. Along with so many socialist parties, the CCF has lost much of its indignation and, with it, most of its hope for a socialist utopia. The "capitalist boss" has almost vanished as a symbolic, rallying enemy, and with his disappearance the sectarian spirit fled.[66]

Thus, lacking a coherent critique of capitalist relations and a class map for the future, the CCF largely failed to draw these new categories of workers into the party. It had moderated its programme so that these new workers were left to the two bourgeois parties to organize, in the elections of the fifties and sixties, along cleavages other than class.

The second important gap in the CCF's theory was its understanding of the advanced capitalist state. While the CCF did recognize that monopolies were gaining more and more influence in Canada and that capitalism in the fifties seemed as strong as ever before, there was little understanding of the role of the state in these developments. The CCF had accepted an analysis of corporate capitalism which took the separation between the ownership and management of capital to imply a fundamental change in the nature of corporations. The CCF posited that if, somehow, these corporations could be purged of their capitalist owners, they would lose their exploitative qualities and function for the common good.[67] Underlying this version of corporate capitalism was a liberal view of the state. The state became the tool for this transformation because it was seen as more or less a neutral actor between capital and other interests in society which could restrain one in the interest of the others. This led the CCF to emphasize that change in the policy direction of the state, and ultimately corporate decision-making, could be achieved simply by replacing personnel. While it was clearly understood that the Liberal government was not "neutral" in its dealings with Canadian capital, the CCF thought that the state's biases could be eliminated with the installation of a new party and a new elite in power. The CCF saw itself as comprising that new elite, but it offered the electorate policies and options which were little other than more of the same. It proposed a better welfare programme and more humanistic leadership, but the party had no theory of how these programmes reinforced capitalism and no theory of how to break the capitalist state free of those tasks it performed for the reproduction of capital. In other words, there was little understanding that some programmes of social reform could benefit capitalism as well as provide tangible improvements in the population's living conditions. The benefits also accruing to capital from, for example, improved education, unemployment insurance monies injected into a low demand economy, the nationalization of certain infrastructural necessities and the absorption of excess labour by state employment were not seen as contradictory in the party's philosophy. The state was not understood to be more than merely captured by the interests of monopoly capital and itself, in a complicated way, implicated in the reproduction of that system.

In many ways, the CCF's theory of the state is illustrated by its appreciation of what the Liberals had done in the postwar period. In the CCF's view, the Liberals had "stolen" their programme to circumvent the CCF's electoral threat. In 1950, the reflections of Frank Underhill, one of the authors of the Regina Manifesto and an original member of the LSR, outlined how many CCFers saw the party's relationship with the bourgeois parties.

> The CCF was launched at a moment when both capitalist economic institutions and North American political parties appeared to be finally bankrupt. It was very easy then to conceive of the socialist heaven as shortly about to be inaugurated by a new political party. . . . But eighteen years of experience since 1932 should have made us mature enough to realize that other political parties will continue to keep alive by helping themselves to all of our planks that turn out to be good vote-getters, that some kind of mixed economy is all there is any likelihood of seeing in our time.[68]

In helping themselves to the CCF planks, the old parties were thought to have acted solely out of expediency rather than from conviction or necessity.[69] The CCF believed that they had forced the Liberals to initiate programmes which they otherwise would not have done. As the Winnipeg Declaration assured, "Many of the improvements [the Regina Manifesto] recommended have been wrung out of unwilling governments by the growing strength of our movement and the growing political maturity of the Canadian people."[70] What the CCF did not see, despite being told so by the Liberals and their supporters, was that the state thought it needed full employment and social insurance programmes if another depression were to be avoided. The CCF seemed not to have heard the Montreal Board of Trade tell the Royal Commission on Dominion-Provincial Relations that:

> . . . taxation for the purpose of social services transfers purchasing power from the richer to the poorer classes, raises the standard of living of the poor, increases their demand for commodities and thereby tends toward industrial stability and prosperity.[71]

The federal Liberals, the Progressive Conservatives and influential business leaders made similar arguments on several occasions.[72]

The CCF's failure to understand or explain the role of the state in times of capitalist expansion, meant that the party did not constitute a clear alternative to the electorate. With its liberal view of a neutral state, the CCF had one argument to rally support behind it—vote CCF for more honest government. However, the party's inability to recognize the contradictions inherent in the Keynesian state was more debilitating in times of economic downturn. It had few alternatives once full employment and price stability policies came into conflict with each other. When the continued economic growth upon which these policies were premised grew more and more difficult to achieve, the CCF was as confounded as the two bourgeois parties.

The CCF was not the only party which confronted theoretical problems concerning the "new middle classes" and the modern capitalist state. Most socialist parties were forced to make some adjustments in their theories and political strategies. Among these was the British Labour Party whose postwar line was embraced in large part by both the CCF and its successor the NDP. Increasingly across this period, the Labour Party's electoral strategy reflected the "embourgeoisement" theory of postwar capitalism. Most simply, the proponents of this view argued that the affluence of the postwar period had mended the class divisions of capitalism. Everyone, but particularly the working class, was becoming middle class, more bourgeois. Guided by this perspective, the Labour Party modified its image and programmes, placing less emphasis on the working class character of its programmes and appealing more to the new categories of the middle class voters. This programmatic switch, principally associated with the leadership of Hugh Gaitskell, however, had many unexpected and unwelcomed consequences for the electoral fortunes of the party. Throughout the sixties, there was a significant drop in the voter turnout in British elections, and the BLP lost some of its trade union and working class support. In effect, the Labour Party, while searching for the middle class vote, had begun to demobilize the British working class. It had ceased to create and sustain its traditional class constituency.[73]

However, even though the strategy supported by the leadership of the Labour Party changed, there remained within the British labour movement and also, very importantly, among leftist intellectuals, a fundamental opposition to the theory and strategy. They criticized the party's position throughout the sixties and when the electoral results began to confirm their analysis, the Labour Party attempted to recoup what it had lost and modified its line.[74] The CCF in contrast largely lacked these responses among its rank and file. Similar to the Labour Party, it had moderated its programme to appeal to the growing but illusive middle classes, but it had done so before implanting itself among the Canadian working class. It failed to create a working class constituency and continued to accept prevailing notions that the new categories of workers of the fifties and sixties formed an affluent middle class, living within a new capitalism and new relations of production.

The CCF's inability to understand changes in the state in addition to the changed occupational structure restricted the party's electoral strategies in the fifties. Across the postwar period, the party's platform was progressively moderated until in 1956, it redefined the party's goals in the Winnipeg Declaration. As we have argued, the programmatic moderation was considered a political necessity in order to appeal to the growing middle class, their values and their lifestyle. But at the same time and because of the CCF's theoretical weaknesses, it never did develop an appropriate approach to this electorate. It took the CCF many years to realize that the postwar depression was not going to materialize and that affluence was real.[75] It continued to stress the existence of poverty and the recurrence of depression at the same time that it steadily moderated its proposed solutions to the deficiencies of capitalism. The CCF failed to explain to the electorate why their very real affluence was in many instances predicated on continued relations of hierarchy and the private accumulation of profit as well as the expectation of an ever-expanding economy without which structural unemployment and even more glaring regional disparities would emerge. Instead the party recalled to the electorate a distant past and predicted depressions which did not materialize.

The CCF found itself in an untenable position in the elections of this period. For example, during the 1945 election it conjured up the Depression with campaign pictures of haggard men hunched over soup bowls under the caption, "What Capitalism does to Canadians." At the same time, it promised to provide the electorate with electric refrigerators, radios, houses and cars as the fruits of its policies.[76] However, the Liberals promised the same and soon presided over their arrival. In the contests for short-term prosperity the Liberals won all the prizes. The CCF refused to concede this fact, continually portraying the Liberals in the elections of the fifties as the purveyors of poverty for many. Their campaign literature depicted in comic book form, "John and Jane Public who lived in a shack with twins but no washer or other conveniences—such as chairs."[77] It is not surprising that this stress on poverty and immiseration found little echo with an electorate which was increasingly well off. Canadians were indisputably more affluent in the 1950s. (Although, of course, poverty and suffering did exist, it never approached that of the thirties). What was needed was not a party to tell them they were not well off but a party that could account for their lives which, despite the houses, cars, washers and social mobility, were lived within and in the face of large bureaucracies, with less real freedom of choice. Moreover, there was little discussion of the fact that Canada was increasingly influenced by cultural and economic conditions outside its borders and beyond the influence of even its government.

In the CCF's new statement of purpose, the 1956 Winnipeg Declaration, capitalist society was condemned as "society motivated by the drive for private gain and special privilege" and as "basically immoral" requiring social planning to build the desired society.[78] However, this Declaration did not speak of the state nor of the exploitive nature of capitalism. Unlike the Regina Manifesto, it was not an apocalyptic document. It did not give a radical critique of the fifties nor did it provide a viable prediction for succeeding decades.[79]

There is little doubt that the CCF looked to the example of the British Labour Party when it modified its programme throughout the fifties.[80] For most of its history, the CCF had modelled itself on the British party. Before the CCF was transformed into the NDP, this emulation had meant the importation of much of the thought of the BLP. However, it had also meant the continuing pursuit of tighter links with the trade union movement, so that the CCF's structure could match that of the Labour Party. Much energy was expended from the earliest years of the CCF in trying to induce unions to affiliate with or endorse the CCF. However, while it was evident to most of the CCF's militants that the party would have to establish closer links with labour to survive in the postwar years, it was precisely the emulation of the Labour Party's structure which constitutes the third factor inhibiting the growth of social democratic forces in Canada during this period. The analogy to the British Labour Party was not entirely appropriate. It paid very little heed to the historical contingencies which forged such an alliance in Great Britain early in the twentieth century or to the existing conservatism of the Canadian trade union movement in the fifties which brought additional support for the forces of moderation within the CCF.[81] Even after the CCF formally rewrote its principles and then restructured itself as the NDP, its electoral fortunes would not improve as had been anticipated.

A Canadian party resembling the British Labour Party had been a long-term goal of the CCF leadership, particularly of its full-time organizer David Lewis. First and foremost, realization of this model involved the creation of formal links between the CCF and the trade union movement. The history of the CCF's efforts to bring the trade unions into direct relationship with the party is a long one well recounted elsewhere.[82] However, as the previous chapter describes, the process began in earnest during the war when CCF leaders worked within the CCL to have that body endorse the CCF as the "political arm of labour." After the war, these efforts were extended to the TLC, which was traditionally reluctant to engage in partisan activity. Attempts to involve the trade union movement only intensified in the face of the CCF's electoral defeats of the fifties. There were few reasons to resist changing the party's policy and programme if not its very structure. The party was weak at the polls; its membership was falling, and its coffers were empty.

By 1953 an extremely delicate campaign was begun to bring the TLC and CCL into an alliance with the CCF. There were several reasons why direct union affiliation was so keenly pursued by the CCF leadership. Most obviously it would provide a firm financial foundation for the party, as a portion of union dues would be directed to the party. In addition, it was thought that union leadership would be able to mobilize trade union-ists behind what was to be "their party." It was hoped that the electoral successes of the British Labour Party would be replicated in Canada.

Efforts to forge such an alliance were facilitated and hastened when, in 1955, the AFL and CIO amalgamated to form the AFL/CIO. Following the lead of their parent bodies, the TLC and CCL merged together in the Canadian Labour Congress (CLC). One of the questions which was thought to be of vital concern as well as potentially divisive and even an obstacle to merger was that of the endorsement of a political party of labour. The pre-merger 1955 Statement of Principles, in fact, made no reference to the matter, leaving it to the CLC to decide the question.[83] This was a great victory for the CCF militants because the shrewd manoeuvring on their part eventually led to a potentially more rewarding result than the endorsement of the obviously foundering CCF as the "political arm of labour."[84] The merger made possible and set in motion the movement for a new labour party, the New Democratic Party.

The 1958 CLC convention endorsed a call for "a fundamental rea-lignment of political forces in Canada" which would involve all those "interested in basic social reform," and resolved to set up a joint com-mittee with the CCF to investigate the possibilities of establishing a new party which would allow for a "massive union wing" similar to that housed by the BLP.[85] These were the beginnings of what was to culminate in 1961 in the dissolution of the CCF and the inauguration of the NDP. The NDP would accept the CCF's moderate restatement of principles, the 1956 Winnipeg Declaration, as its guiding principle and would have mechanisms for union affiliation similar to the British Labour Party. In fact, the main difference between the ageing CCF and the NDP was structural. The NDP could affiliate trade unions and extend delegate rights to them on the party's convention floor.[86]

As discussed, the CCF leadership had hoped that a party structure resembling the BLP would lead rank and file trade unionists into the party's electoral coalition. The hope for electoral success seemed to be based on the logic that if unions supported a party, as did the British, then the union membership would too, as did the British. However, the analogy with the BLP and the weakness of this electoral logic were not fully explored as the links between the CCF and CLC grew more entwined. Unions would provide the NDP with some money and person-nel for election work, but the most important link between labour and the NDP were the CCF militants themselves who had struggled most of their political lifetimes to realize their dream of a labour party in Canada.[87] First and foremost, the CLC campaign for a new party was a campaign orchestrated from above, a campaign of the leadership and not of the rank and file. Moreover, it was a campaign among a very particular segment of the trade union leadership. While the trade union movement as a whole had not been directly involved in partisan politics for some fifty years, its leadership was not politically neutral. Indeed, many had strong ties with the bourgeois parties, specifically the Liberals. Bourgeois party partisans permeated almost every layer of the trade union movement.[88]

The fact that the NDP was created from the top had very predictable and particular influences on the evolution of the NDP and its electoral fortunes. The first problems the NDP encountered concerned the nature of union affiliation to the party. Rather than create channels for the affiliation *en masse* of all the unions affiliated with the CLC, the NDP only made provisions for the affiliation of individual trade union locals. The decision to affiliate was left to individual locals, and many simply did not take the initiative to join. There were several reasons why the potential for union affiliation remained greater than what was actually achieved. The Canadian labour movement had little history of formal affiliation with a political party, and, in addition, the NDP was a new party. Moreover, the leadership of some important unions were Liberal partisans and did not favour formal affiliation with the new labour party. In fact, few union locals took the initiative to affiliate without the blessings of the union leadership. In particular unions, where the national or international headquarters were not aligned with the CCF, few locals defied their own headquarters by joining.[89] Overall, the union links with the NDP remained more formal and financial rather than being designed for mobilization of the union membership in support of the NDP.

Second, the NDP was largely a marriage of notables, and most of the organized work force showed little interest in the new labour party. Canadian trade unionists were unfamiliar with, if not hostile to, social democracy, and neither the CCF/NDP nor the union movement had done much to educate them otherwise. That portion of the labour force which was organized in unions in Canada was not yet interested in social transformation. It was not about to risk its high wages and affluence for the promise of a new society. It was not ready because it had not been made ready. The Canadian working class had little faith in socialism because no party had prepared the way or supported radicalism within the trade union movement. Instead, in a mistaken analogy to the British Labour Party, the NDP, armed with the CCF's very moderate Winnipeg Declaration of Principles, conformed to the labour movement's conservatism rather than shaping its perspectives concerning socialism. While the formal organizational structure may have been similar, the NDP was not the British Labour Party.

The British Labour Party was created and gained office under very different conditions of capitalism and with a very different union movement. It also had fifty years of experience and history behind it. Only inattention to the importance of history and the partisan mobilization of the working class could produce imitation in such a different situation. The Labour Party was founded, contested elections, and took power before Keynesianism. In fact, it was the Labour Party that implemented the postwar settlement in Britain. These historical differences meant that its electorate, its working class, was created on the basis of a critique of capitalism, and there were remnants of this critique in the unions and the party even when the party line and strategy changed in the fifties. In Canada, the union movement had been relieved, sometimes with the assistance of the state, of its most critical elements (for example, with the expulsion of the Communists). Moreover, the NDP was created with the help of unions implanted in only a small segment of the work force. They were the unions of the traditional working class, often the internationals. They were the unions of the industrial and craft workers rather than the unions of the rapidly expanding work force which would have to be included in the alliance of any future successful left-wing party. The potentiality of these workers as union members and left voters was not fully appreciated by the new party which tended to assign them to the middle class. Thus, the NDP's obsession with affiliation meant that the union movement had to be accepted as it was—without class consciousness, without a history of struggle for socialism, without a sense of responsibility for the creation of the welfare state or, for that matter, without political experience. This meant that the CCF/NDP was required to moderate its programme in the interests of gaining the existing and, most often, international union leaders who, in turn, recognized the conservatism of their rank and file membership or were politically conservative themselves.

What consequences did this moderation hold for the NDP? In Keynesian Canada with a Liberal Party actively implementing a social programme, "moderation" meant more of the same. However, the Liberals were a major party while the NDP had little chance of forming the federal government. Therefore, there was little reason to expect union members to support the CCF/NDP when they could have almost the same thing with the Liberals. There was no historic alliance of workers with a party which they themselves had built, as in Britain. There was not a conscious working class in Canada, as the CCF/NDP ceased to address its anticipated electorate in a language of politics cast in class terms. The workers had not been organized into a class, and they would not act as one in federal elections.

The NDP was thus founded within the "end-of-ideology" ideology. This thinking was reflected in its programmatic statements, policies and leadership. Unfortunately for the NDP, within five years ideological conflict would resume as crisis began to threaten western capitalism. The Canadian social democrats were ill-prepared to meet the turnabout in the economy or to offer alternatives to the electorate.

However, in the NDP's first years, Canadian unionists had little reason to feel the need for a fundamental change. With no residue of radical politics or radicalism which would allow them to see the current conditions of capitalism as anything other than permanent growth, the CLC, as the TLC and CCL of earlier years, pulled the CCF/NDP toward a politics of economism and a perspective which made it difficult for the NDP to compete with the bourgeois parties, which were already instituting many reforms. Under these conditions, the electoral fortunes of the CCF/NDP were disastrous. With little to distinguish the party, the Liberals and Conservatives could resort to their emphasis on national unity and biculturalism. Thus, in the immediate postwar years the language of politics remained largely unchanged. With prosperity and national development came the usual politics of competition between the two major parties.

The Elections of Postwar Affluence

In the postwar years there appeared to be a consensus among all three federal parties about the interventionist role of the state in postwar capitalism. However, the Liberal Party, as the government, had a distinct advantage over its competitors in successive partisan contests. In the years immediately following the war, the Liberals remained comfortably in power, administering the new social programmes which eased the threat of postwar depression and discontent. Affluence and the unveiling of Keynesian-type policies guaranteed that the Liberals would hold their pre-eminent position in the partisan arena, but this also posed an identity crisis for the cadres of the Conservative and CCF parties. The glaring class disparities of the Depression which had given rise to the CCF were blurred by high employment levels, better wages and higher standards of living. In the face of these advantageous economic conditions, the CCF, as we have seen, at first moderated its programmes to appeal to what it saw as an ever-expanding middle class while forging an as yet untested alliance with organized labour. Industrial development, a changing occupational structure and, most fundamentally, an inappropriate appreciation of the policies which the governing party had set in motion eroded the meagre space in the electorate that the CCF had carved out during the thirties and the war years. The old coalition of farmers, labour and socialists gave way to a formal union with the labour movement, but the benefits of this alliance remained more potential than real throughout these years. Both the new labour party and the labour movement neglected to educate and mobilize Canadian workers. Reorganization of the social democratic hierarchy could come about, but a strong class cleavage in the electorate would not automatically materialize in response.

The Progressive Conservatives also confronted grave problems in the face of a Keynesian Liberal Party, for with the Liberals' admirable provisions for Canadian capitalism, there seemed room for only a single bourgeois party. Although the Conservatives had attempted to reorient themselves with their Port Hope statement during the war years, they were effectively pushed aside by the Liberals by the war's end. It was, after all, the Liberals who brought peace and managed the prosperity of the immediate postwar period. The Conservatives would flounder, as the CCF had, in an attempt to find an appropriate identity. The party experimented with new leaders and resurrected old symbols, and, for a short while, under the leadership of John Diefenbaker, it would make a populist appeal against the Liberals. However, Diefenbaker's Conservatives did not gain unprecedented electoral victory by developing and mobilizing a class cleavage, although they did mobilize the Prairie farmer (that group which, since 1921, had been most open to class-based appeals). Diefenbaker's definition of politics addressed pan-Canadian nationalism and unveiled a new national policy designed to exploit the northern frontier "for the benefit of all." It was yet another variant of federal politics in the "national interest."

For much of this period, then, partisan politics revolved around the tried and tested electoral rhetoric of national unity, resource development and the politics of culture. This was especially reflected in the elections of the late forties and early fifties. For example, even though the Depression and the war had substantially weakened and altered the attraction and power of the British Empire, there were sufficient remnants of allegiance within the Progressive Conservative Party and the electorate to prevent a complete purge of Imperial symbolism in Canada. These symbols were resurrected again and again to block the growing penetration of American influence in Canada's cultural and economic life. In fundamental agreement about the need for Keynesian-type state activities, the Conservatives skirmished with the Liberals over the "nefarious" influence of French Canada on the governing party, a Canadian flag, the mailboxes and patriation of the British North America Act and its amendment procedures. In the absence of other cleavages, federal politics was an orgy of symbolism. For example, the two major parties debated about the proper place for the word "Dominion" in federal legislation and on public documents, a Citizenship Bill and a new flag, the design of which was eventually abandoned in the face of threats by Francophone ministers to resign if it were accepted. By 1951, it was parliamentary debate over the revisions of the "*Dominion* Land Surveys Act," the "*Dominion* Election Act" and whether the mailboxes should be designated "Royal Mail" or not. Prime Minister St. Laurent was worried by the political consequences of this issue because,

> ... Pickersgill had persuaded him that the row about "royal" was politically "far more dangerous than the fuss about Dominion"; and, early in 1952, he took advantage of a special press conference to make a careful explanation of the rules governing the use of the word "royal."[90]

Such matters were not much to fight elections about. Rather, the Liberals rested comfortably with their Quebec majority and successfully cultivated their image as sound administrators, even if ones not terribly respectful of traditions.

The politics of the late forties and early fifties left little space for the Tories and the CCF and little basis for partisan distinctiveness. Both parties suffered electorally in consequence. Indeed, the 1949 and 1953 campaigns were similar in many respects, with the same leaders, issues and results.[91] Mackenzie King retired in 1948, making way for Louis St. Laurent. Two months later the Progressive Conservatives, in their continuing search for a workable formula and a winning strategy, swung back from their wartime radical chic and chose George Drew as their leader. He was a former Premier of Ontario and a good representative of the traditional Toronto. With little to divide the parties, 1949 and 1953 seemed to be contests between these two men and their "teams." St. Laurent campaigned on the Liberals' record in office while Drew battered away at the government party for being as tired and arrogant as its ministers. In addition, the Conservatives deplored the federal government's apparent incursions into fields of provincial jurisdiction, its "statism" and the increasing presence of American interests in the Canadian economy. They offered, however, no clear alternative definition of how to conduct the business of the modern state.

The CCF was similarly demoralized, as the Liberals implemented at least parts of their social democratic programmes which had appeared so radical at the time of the CCF's birth, and there was no sign of the severe unemployment and economic dislocations that the CCF had warned would occur in the immediate postwar period. Prosperity, combined with growing distrust of anything left-wing or "socialistic," made it difficult for the CCF to convince the electorate of either the defects of capitalism or the merits of socialism.[92]

The CCF leadership felt their only recourse was to moderate their critique of capitalism, and this they did leaving less and less reason for workers to rally behind the party's cause while at the same time failing to retain the traditional agrarian base of the party. The return to prosperity multiplied the migration of the Prairie farmers, an already diminishing breed, from the party, and the evacuation was nearly completed with the CCF's transformation into the NDP. While the CCF attempted to reassure this segment of the electorate that the party's proposals for public ownership did not extend to agriculture, when Depression-like conditions disappeared, most of the farmers were lost to the party. The CCF's very foundations were in shambles, and its popular vote dropped persistently in its final years. In contrast, the Liberals, riding on their record, scored comfortable victories in both 1949 and 1953.

The Liberals' record, however, would not sustain them in office throughout these two decades. Late in the fifties, some of the weaknesses in their postwar development strategy began to appear. Unemployment rose dramatically and rapidly; Prairie farmers grew restless as carloads of wheat overflowed western grain elevators without visible markets, and many other groups in Canada—the disabled, pensioners, small business-men especially in the hinterland regions—grew disenchanted as prosper-ity seemed to pass them by. These factors created a space for opposition parties to challenge the Liberals' commanding position in the federal party system. However, only the Conservative Party would grasp the opportunity and mobilize the discontented behind their new leader, John Diefenbaker. Once again the CCF was caught off-guard and ill-prepared. It was too deeply engrossed in its own remodelling to see that conditions had finally turned in its favour. They were theoretically at a loss to explain to the electorate the downturn of the welfare-state economy.

The remaining elections of this period witnessed first the outburst and then the gradual erosion of the Progressive Conservatives' populist experiment. The chorus of discontent, the space in the electorate, found a leader in John Diefenbaker. Nevertheless, his meteoric rise to power in the late fifties would not alter the content of federal partisan politics or the dominant language of culture. He merely voiced discontent about the "inequalities" and malfunctioning of the Canadian economic system and not the capitalist system itself. In fact, with the possible exception of the attention paid to Prairie farmers, Diefenbaker's appeals did much to rein-force the politics of culture. While he was able to mobilize those segments of the electorate which suffered from the short recession of the fifties, he also addressed this assembly in the traditional Tory symbols of renewed Imperial ties, less emphasis on a distinct French Canadian heritage within Canada and a nationalistic anti-Americanism. He offered the electorate a new national dream cast in terms of the "national interest," one which ignored class inequalities and exploitation. Indeed, Diefenbaker was fond of drawing parallels between his national dream and that of his chosen historical model, Sir John A. Macdonald. As he explained in 1958:

> Sir John A. Macdonald opened the west. He saw Canada from East to West. I see a new Canada—*A Canada of the North!*[93]

The Liberals did little to counter this new vision. Nor did they take many steps to lessen the grievances of the discontented. In both the 1957 and 1958 campaigns, they attempted to arrest the Conservative challenge by maintaining a solid Liberal Quebec and reminding the rest of Canada that only the Liberal Party could elect members in that province. St. Laurent mimicked his predecessors:

> No one wants a one-party state but . . . there is only one party which has sufficient strength in every province to assure the country a stable government, and that party is the Liberal Party.[94]

Be that as it may, the Conservatives were willing to forfeit Quebec, gambling successfully in 1957 that they could win at least a minority government if they swept the remaining provinces. Essential to the Tories' experiment was an energetic courting of the Prairie petite bourgeoisie which historically demanded that its class interests be addressed by the federal party system. The Conservatives had promised action where the Liberals had not acted, and the Diefenbaker government, although a minority in 1957, was quick to consolidate this image among Prairie farmers and farmers generally. The Prairie Grain Advance Payments Act which extended advance payments to the wheat farmers was assented to less than a month after the Twenty-third Parliament reopened. In January, 1958, John Bracken, a former Liberal-Progressive premier of Manitoba and Progressive Conservative national leader, was appointed a one-man Royal Commission to investigate the problems of grain transportation. In addition, Conservatives proved to be able middlemen for the wheat farmer, negotiating massive grain sales to the People's Republic of China. The farming community, especially in underdeveloped regions, was also bolstered by the Agricultural and Rural Development Act (ARDA, 1961), which funnelled much needed capital into the rejuvenation of Canadian agriculture.[95] All told, there was good reason for the farmer to support Diefenbaker's Conservatives. However, none of these appeals to the agricultural community were necessarily cast in class terms nor were other reforms such as increased old-age pensions, income tax reductions and improved subsidies for the Maritimes. In essence, Diefenbaker minimized the class basis of politics when he could and offered specific appeals to a limited number of groups. In fact, in 1958, so successful was his coalition that he won the confidence of virtually every major social category in the country.[96]

The official launching of the NDP in 1961 renewed efforts to forge a worker-owner cleavage in the electorate. However, for reasons already discussed, the new labour party did not take off in the 1962, 1963 or 1965 elections. In these contests, the NDP revealed itself to be an even more moderate party than the ageing CCF. After more than three years of planning and discussion, labour's party advocated a continuation of Keynesian-style economic management and rejected thoroughgoing socialism and nationalization. It anticipated a flood of class-based voting in its favour but did little to mobilize the workers, appearing to be little more than a left-wing variant of the two major parties. Like the Liberals and Conservatives it too pronounced its dedication to full employment policies, and, criticizing its partisan competitors, it promised to be a better guardian of the economy. Albeit, the party did advocate a national investment board, public and co-operative ownership of utilities and national resources and the curtailment of foreign ownership, but the class biases in the prevailing economic system and the necessity of their policies were never fully articulated to the electorate. The party's ability to do so was limited somewhat by available financial resources but few efforts were made even to politicize the trade union movement. The NDP had achieved affiliation with the peak organization of the Canadian labour movement, but its contact with the mass of workers was still very tenuous. Indeed, a public opinion poll conducted after the 1962 federal election indicated that a greater percentage of union households had voted for the Liberal Party than for the NDP.[97] A vehicle for the expression of a class cleavage in the federal party system had been forged in this period, but much of its anticipated constituency had not been developed politically. As before, most continued to be organized in partisan politics around the familiar cultural cleavage.

Given these partisan practices, we would predict several trends in the voting patterns of Canadians in these years. First, the bicultural cleavage should persist, given the emphasis placed on the politics of language and national identity by both major parties. Second, we would expect little development of an occupational polarization. Finally, the politics of western farmers should be in flux as their party of the 1930s abandons them for a concerted attack on the vote of organized labour. The correlation coefficients shown in Tables 8:3 and 8:4 largely confirm the persistence of the bicultural cleavage, especially in the East, in the elections studied here. As Table 8:3 demonstrates, even after the effects

Table 8:3
CORRELATION OF PARTY VOTE AND FRENCH ETHNICITY
CONTROLLING FOR LABOUR FORCE** BY REGION
(3rd order partial)

	East			West		
	Lib.	Con.	CCF/NDP	Lib.	Con.	CCF/NDP
1949	.42*	−.53*	−47*	.32*	−25*	−.03
1953	.52*	−.53*	−49*	.33*	.11*	−.06
1957	.68*	−.65*	−47*	.22*	.01	−.08
1958	.64*	−.47*	−.41*	.43*	.02	−.12
1962	−.17*	−.58*	−.56*	.34*	.03	−.12
1963	−.08	−.72*	−.40*	.34*	.09	−.20*
1965	.13*	−.61*	−.34*	.39*	.17	−13

* p < .05
** controlling for worker, farmer, white collar
Source: See Appendix A.

of the occupational composition of the constituency's labour force on the vote is accounted for statistically, there is a strong relationship between voting Liberal and the number of Francophones in the constituencies in the period 1949–1957. However, the flowering of the Créditiste party in Quebec (just as the Nationalist Party of over fifty years before) dramatically reduced this trend in the elections of the sixties. In contrast, a tendency to vote Progressive Conservative or CCF/NDP continued to decline as the proportion of French-speaking Canadians in the constituency increased.

Table 8:4 outlines the other side of the bicultural cleavage. When the effects of the occupational composition of the labour force are held constant statistically, both the Conservatives and CCF/NDP, and particularly the former, remained the party of English-speaking constituencies in all seven elections. However, a comparison of the strength of the correlation coefficients in both Tables 8:3 and 8:4 emphasizes that the bicultural cleavage was more pronounced in the East than in the West. While the constituencies with more Francophone voters in the West showed a greater propensity to support the Liberal Party, English constituencies do not appear more likely to support the CCF/NDP as in the East. Similarly, the tendency for the Progressive Conservative vote to increase with the proportion of English-speaking Canadians in the constituency in the West falls off dramatically after 1957—that is, after the Diefenbaker government offered programmes designed for the western farmer.

The correlations in Table 8:5 support the above observation and demonstrate the instability of the western agrarian vote in this period.[98] The table shows that while, in the East, the percentage of the labour force involved in agriculture is positively related to the constituency's Con-

Table 8:4
CORRELATION OF PARTY VOTE AND ENGLISH ETHNICITY
CONTROLLING FOR LABOUR FORCE, **BY REGION**
(3rd order partial)

	East			West		
	Lib.	*Con.*	*CCF/NDP*	*Lib.*	*Con.*	*CCF/NDP*
1949	−.38*	.57*	.33*	−.30*	.63*	−.18
1953	−.51*	.60*	.38*	−.35*	.25*	−.09
1957	−.67*	.69*	.33*	−.36*	.38*	−.16
1958	−.63*	.55*	.30*	−.15	.13	−.01
1962	.09	.64*	.46*	−.01	−.09	−.03
1963	.00	.77*	.29*	.00	−.25*	.04
1965	−.21*	.68*	.24*	−01	−.24*	−.02

* p < .05
** controlling for worker, farmer, white collar
Source: See Appendix A.

Table 8:5

CORRELATION OF PARTY VOTE AND AGRICULTURAL LABOUR FORCE CONTROLLING FOR ETHNICITY** BY REGION

(3rd order partial)

	East			West		
	Lib.	*Con.*	*CCF/NDP*	*Lib.*	*Con.*	*CCF/NDP*
1949	−.09	−.00	−.40*	−.10	.00	.00
1953	−.09	.22*	−.35*	.22*	.02	−.10
1957	−.11	.29*	−.30*	.21*	−.06	−.13
1958	−.09	.37*	−.34*	.15	.13	−.19
1962	−.16*	.29*	−.38*	−.13	.55*	−.46*
1963	−.19*	.44*	−.43*	−.42*	.67*	−.48*
1965	−.14*	.36*	−.37*	−.33*	.61*	−.43*

* $p < .05$
** controlling for English, French, German
Source: See Appendix A.

servative vote, in the West, the correlation swings between the two major parties. An agricultural labour force in the constituency is positively related to the Liberal vote in both 1953 and 1957, but the correlation shifts to the Conservative Party in the early sixties.

The voting patterns of the constituencies with a high concentration of mining, manufacturing and construction workers exhibit a similar instability in the West during this period. Table 8:6 indicates that, in the East, neither the Liberal nor Conservative Parties were disproportionately supported in constituencies with such a labour force composition. In fact, the opposite is the tendency. Constituencies with a large blue collar component did tend to support the CCF/NDP as urban constituen-

Table 8:6

CORRELATION OF PARTY VOTE AND BLUE-COLLAR LABOUR FORCE CONTROLLING FOR ETHNICITY** BY REGION

(3rd order partial)

	East			West		
	Lib.	*Con.*	*CCF/NDP*	*Lib.*	*Con.*	*CCF/NDP*
1949	−.04	.25*	.09	−.13	−.09	−.11
1953	.03	−.22*	.37*	−.29*	−.12	.15
1957	−.11	−.25*	.39*	−.28*	−.14	.23*
1958	−.16*	−.22*	.40*	−.16	−.35*	.31*
1962	−.12*	−.22*	.40*	.05	−.64*	.53*
1963	−.20*	−.20*	.42*	.29*	−.74*	.56*
1965	−.23*	−.23*	.37*	.20	−.69*	.50*

* $p < .05$
** controlling for English, French, German
Source: See Appendix A.

cies had in the past. What is striking is that this cleavage was only marginally, if at all, improved after the CCF officially transformed into the NDP. In the West, the relationship between the CCF/NDP vote and the working class composition of the constituency remained weak until after the new labour party was launched. Nonetheless, it is important to point out that this tendency did not enhance the party's popular vote except in Ontario and then only in 1965. Across this period, constituencies with a large blue collar component did tend to more clearly align with the NDP, but the party's popular vote edged upward only marginally from 13.5% of the total electorate in 1962 to 17.9% in 1965.

Beginning in 1965, it is possible to examine some of the patterns with data about individuals drawn from post-election surveys of the Canadian population. The 1965 aggregate data displaying the voting patterns of federal constituencies are supported by a national election study conducted shortly after the campaign. The results of this survey indicate that 50% of the farmers surveyed supported the Conservatives compared to 35% and 9% for the Liberal and NDP parties respectively. Only 20% of skilled labour and 11% of the unskilled labour workers surveyed supported the NDP. Approximately one-half of both these groups supported the Liberals in 1965. Moreover, the data about individuals confirm that the NDP was principally composed of workers even if the majority of Canadian workers supported the bourgeois parties. In 1965 45% of the NDP votes came from labour, especially unionized labour, compared to 39% and 29% of the Liberal and Conservative voters respectively.[99] The NDP's electoral core was labour but most workers chose one of the other parties.

Earlier in this chapter, we devoted considerable discussion to the unprecedented growth, during the postwar years, of what is commonly described as the "new middle class." It was argued that the state workers, technicians, clerks and salaried professionals constituted an important potential support base for the CCF/NDP. However, rather than speak to the conditions and organize these workers, both the social democratic party and the labour movement described these new categories of workers as the dominant ideology did—as affluent and conservative voters whose interests were incompatible with those of the labour movement.

Under such conditions, there is little reason to expect that these categories of voters would not be organized by the two major parties, along other possible cleavages. Unfortunately, it is difficult to isolate and analyse the voting behaviour of the new categories of voters either in the aggregate or survey data available for this period. Most categorizations combine the 'old' and 'new' middle class and do not specify, for example, whether professionals are salaried or not. However, CIPO surveys, conducted between 1953 and 1963, and a 1965 national election study suggest that this group tended to move between the Liberal and Conservative Parties during this period. In addition, in the elections between 1953 and 1965 the CCF/NDP did not even achieve its national mean of support among professionals, white collar, clerical and sales workers and the university-educated. What these surveys of Canadian voters do show is the instability of support patterns among these groups. In 1953, for example, professionals, white collar workers and the university-educated were most likely to support the Liberal Party. In contrast, in the Diefenbaker sweep of 1958 the majority of professionals, clerical and sales workers and the university-educated supported the Conservatives. However, in the next election, 1962, the largest proportion of these voters once again were found within the Liberal Party where they remained for the next two elections.[100] These types of workers were unstable partisans, an available support base migrating among the parties, although this migration did not particularly benefit the CCF/NDP.

Conclusion

The "Diefenbaker interlude" marks the first appearance, in a major way, of the two issues which have since dominated recent Canadian federal elections—Canadian and Québécois nationalism. It was also a time when the Tories experimented with a slightly different electoral strategy. They harnessed much of the discontent that existed at the time about the day-to-day workings of postwar capitalism among the many groups in Canada who had begun to feel disenchantment with the status quo. This chorus of discontent found a leader in John Diefenbaker, but what he led was merely discontent with the "inequalities" and malfunctioning of the Canadian system. It was neither a fundamental critique nor a demand for transformation. Diefenbaker appealed to those segments of the population who, in the short recession at the end of the fifties, saw their position rapidly deteriorate. The deterioration would soon be chronic, but in 1957, 1958 and 1962 it was only expressed as "time for a change." Diefenbaker collected together those voters who had not received the full benefit of the postwar boom and whose life conditions were precarious. Nevertheless, while he did assemble the discontented, he also dressed this assembly in the traditional Tory symbols of renewed Imperial ties, anti-Americanism and less emphasis on the distinctiveness of French Canada.

There was, in the Diefenbaker campaigns, the first real evidence that American influence in Canada would be, along with the status of Quebec, the issue of the sixties. His stress was heavy on emotional anti-Americanism, although the facts and figures of the shocking truth had begun to appear. The Royal Commission on Canada's Economic Prospects (with Walter Gordon as chairman) had been sent out by the Liberal government to investigate the result of the strategy they had been following. This was neither a popular idea in the government nor one whose long-term importance was clearly understood in 1956. Indeed, the stirrings of Canadian nationalism in whatever form had formidable opposition.

These were very dangerous thoughts in the Canada of the 1950's. To criticize the American economic domination of North America, or to question the American leadership of the "Free World," were heresies virtually as appalling as the profession of Protestant opinions would have been in sixteenth-century Spain. How could Canadians possibly conceive of an independent foreign policy when the menace of international Communism demanded the defence of a united West under American command? How could Canadians be so infatuated as to profess a separate economic interest when American capital was promoting the rapid development of their national resources and establishing what seemed to be a permanent prosperity throughout the entire North American continent?[101]

Nevertheless, the Gordon Commission did exist, and its Report excited some partisan comment and electoral discussion.

Meanwhile, modernization seemed, at last, to have come to Quebec. Although always willing to accommodate capital's needs in the 1930s and 1940s, by the 1950s the alliance of Duplessis' Union Nationale and the Church was more of a hindrance than a help for modern capitalism interested in Quebec. A more skilled, educated, urban and mobile work force was needed, and traditional pre-capitalist ideological campaigns, described in previous chapters, could not provide it. Quebec society was breaking decades of fetters, and, by 1960, the "quietly revolutionary" government of Premier Jean Lesage grasped all the symbols of the new and pushed forward the modernization process. Quebec society was changing rapidly, and, by 1965 and after, the federal Liberals would be hard pressed to manage and master the bicultural cleavage which was the source of their electoral strength. Only nine years after the Gordon Report, the Royal Commission on Bilingualism and Biculturalism would uncover the facts about the effects of a century of bicultural politics and federally-directed economic development on Canada's ethnic groups. This too would mark a change in Canadian politics.

However, in the late fifties and early sixties these issues were developing but not fully grown. Stances were experimentally adopted and either abandoned or developed further. The Tory experience with Diefenbaker's populism is one of the most striking of these experiments. For the CCF, and later the NDP, this sudden shift within the Progressive Conservative Party proved disastrous. The Tory campaigns based on the effects of the "interests" of the "common people" and especially the westerners, cut deeply into what little remained of the traditional, prewar agrarian discontent housed within the NDP. Diefenbaker appealed to, among others, western farmers and populists, and these groups transferred their support to the Progressive Conservatives. In this way the new party seemed to lose the farmers without gaining the workers.

NOTES

[1] Quoted in Economic Council of Canada, *First Annual Review: Economic Goals for Canada to 1970* (Ottawa: Queen's Printer, 1964), p. 8.

[2] *Ibid.*, p. 7.

[3] *Ibid.*, p. 9.

[4] *Ibid.*, pp. 9-10, 12-17, 19-21.

[5] *Ibid.*, pp. 88-89.

[6] For details see David Wolfe "Economic Growth and Foreign Investment: A Perspective on Canadian Economic Policy, 1945-1957," *Journal of Canadian Studies*, vol. 13, no. 1 (Spring, 1978), p. 5.

[7] Indeed, when the Department of Trade and Commerce found that Canadian corporations were unwilling or unable to produce an item blocked by the tariff, it actively sought an American corporation, willing to extend its operations to Canada, to produce the product, *Ibid.*, p. 7.

[8] The representatives of the Canadian government were fond of informing potential investors that they were unconcerned about the 'nationality' of capital in Canada. For example, in 1954, C. D. Howe told potential American investors that, "Canada has welcomed the participation of American and other foreign capital in its industrial expansion. In Canada, foreign investors are treated the same as domestic investors." Quoted in Wallace Clement, *Continental Corporate Power* (Toronto: McClelland and Stewart, 1977), p. 85.

[9] *Ibid.*, p. 80; K. Levitt, *Silent Surrender* (Toronto: Macmillan, 1971), p. 61.

[10] This attitude is shown by the position taken by Canadian negotiators not only *vis à vis* the Americans but also in the negotiations for the General Agreement on Tariffs and Trade (GATT) after the war. There, Canadians were most concerned to maintain the traditional position of comparative advantage in the export of certain natural resources. See Wolfe, *op. cit.*, pp. 8-9.

[11] Of the twenty-nine key commodities identified in the Report, Canada was a potential supplier of twelve. In addition, Canada was considered a desirable source for these products because it was secure politically and militarily. See Clement, *op. cit.*, p. 84; A. Dubac, "Le fondement historique de la crise des sociétés canadiennes et québécoises," *Politique aujourd'hui*, no. 7-8 (1978), pp. 38-39.

[12] Levitt claims that Canada was at this time somewhat unique with respect to foreign investment. The usual pattern in developed countries was the penetration of markets by multinationals producing within the host country. In less developed countries, in contrast, the emphasis was on the exploration and export of natural resources. Canada's uniqueness lies in having both forms. See Levitt, *op. cit.*, pp. 61-62.

[13] Gallup polls of these years indicate that the majority of those sampled were not concerned about the growth of foreign ownership in Canada. In fact, in 1950, 60% of the sample wanted a greater American capital inflow. In 1956, 63% of the sampled group felt the US influence on Canada was not excessive. Philip Resnick, *The Land of Cain: Class and Nationalism in English Canada, 1945-1975* (Vancouver: New Star Books, 1977), p. 73.

[14] For a succinct discussion of this process, see Jean K. Laux, "Global Interdependence and State Intervention," in B. Tomlin, *Canada's Foreign Policy: Analysis and Trends* (Toronto: Methuen, 1978).

[15] George Grant, *Lament for a Nation: The Defeat of Canadian Nationalism* (Toronto: McClelland and Stewart, 1965), pp. 9-10.

[16]Clement characterizes the bourgeoisie's relationship as one of partnership and not "dependence." However, the maintenance of this position implies a continuing commitment to a continental economic system. Wallace Clement, *The Canadian Corporate Elite* (Toronto: McClelland and Stewart, 1975), pp. 354-357, 120-121, 205.

[17]There was an increase, over time, in the number of elite positions which were controlled by foreign corporations. In 1951, 27% of all positions in the Canadian corporate elite were under foreign control. By 1972, the statistic was 40%. See *ibid.*, footnote 7, p. 123.

[18]A United Nations study shows the following comparative pattern of acquisition of existing companies by US multinationals.

	pre-1946	1946-1957	1958-1967
Canada	29%	45%	58%
Other Countries	24%	28%	41%

Cited in Clement, *Continental Corporate Power, op. cit.*, p. 88. This means that Canadians often sat on boards of companies that had previously been theirs and controlled stock which was part of the conditions of transfer of the corporations.

[19]This marshalling process was at least partially based on the wartime integration of business and government within the state apparatus itself. The personnel of big business ascended to steering roles within the government to conduct the war effort according to the logic of business management. Magnates such as H. R. MacMillan of MacMillan-Bloedel and E. P. Taylor of Argus Corporation were recruited to the federal bureaucracy as "dollar-a-year men" for the duration of the war. In effect, total mobilization of the country's productive capacities for a maximum war effort achieved an integration of the state and the bourgeoisie which came to resemble the situation in the first years of Confederation.

> "To the end of his career, Mackenzie King had kept insisting that, in Canada, the Liberals were the friends of the "little man" and the Conservative Party was the party of "big business." This worn out fiction was moribund even before the war; but by 1951, it survived only as a kind of Greek myth, with all the irrelevance of a Greek myth and none of its charm. Howe had not merely linked big business and the Liberal Party, he had virtually identified them."

See D. Creighton, *The Forked Road* (Toronto: McClelland and Stewart, 1976), p. 223.

[20]By the mid-1950s, there was a high level of participation of Canadians in foreign-controlled subsidiaries. A study for the Royal Commission on Canada's Economic Prospects found that, of the corporate subsidiaries which had majority foreign ownership, 60% (284/447) of the directors were Canadian. For wholly-owned subsidiaries, there were 46% (199/429) Canadian directors. See John Porter, *The Vertical Mosaic* (Toronto: University of Toronto, 1965), pp. 271-272.

[21]Resnick, *op. cit.*, p. 74.

[22]Quoted in Clement, *Continental Corporate Power, op. cit.*, p. 87.

[23]Clement, *The Canadian Corporate Elite, op. cit.*, p. 89.

[24]*Ibid.*, p. 102.

[25]*Ibid.*, p. 108.

[26]One example of this increased American dominance is seen in the decline of the

British position in the postwar world. For a discussion of the US compulsion of the U.K. to accept a new status, which was based on making postwar reconstruction aid conditional on an acceptance of the American goal of a "... single world-wide economic community, based on the principles of multilateral trade, non-discrimination, and free convertibility of currencies," and Canada's role in the process, see Creighton, *op. cit.*, p. 123ff.

27Peter C. Newman, *Renegade in Power: The Diefenbaker Years* (Toronto: McClelland and Stewart, 1963), p. 38.

28Clement, *The Canadian Corporate Elite, op. cit.*, p. 101.

29Newman, *op. cit.*, p. 38.

30Progressive Conservative Party leader, George Drew, for example, argued that "Canadians should declare their economic independence of the United States," and called for "an all-Canadian pipeline under Canadian control." Cited in Resnick, *op. cit.*, p. 104. However, the Tory leader soon moderated this tone as Bay Street interests, closely aligned with the party, opposed his stand on the pipeline. Newman, *op. cit.*, p. 43.

31See the Economic Council of Canada, *First Annual Review: Economic Goals for Canada to 1970, op. cit.*, Table 46, p. 155.

In the US in 1947, 30% of the population was engaged in the production of manufactured goods or construction. Three years further into the postwar boom, in Canada in 1951, the equivalent statistic was 25%. For Canadian figures see F. A. Angers and P. Allen, *Evolution de la structure des emplois au Canada* (Montreal: Ecole des Hautes Etudes Commerciales, 1954), *passim* and especially, pp. 23, 43-45. American figures are from D. Bell, *The Coming of Post-Industrial Society* (New York: Basic Books, 1973), p. 131.

32S. B. Goldenberg, *Professional Workers and Collective Bargaining* (Ottawa: Task Force on Labour Relations, Study no. 2 PCO, 1970), p. 14.

33S. G. Peitchinis, *Canadian Labour Economics* (Toronto: McGraw-Hill, 1970), Table 5.2.

34For a full discussion, see H. Armstrong, "The Labour Force and State Workers in Canada," in L. Panitch, ed., *The Canadian State* (Toronto: University of Toronto, 1977), p. 290 especially; G. W. Adams, "Collective Bargaining by Salaried Professionals," *Relations industriales—Industrial Relations*, vol. 32, no. 2 (1977), p. 190.

35Between 1946 and 1964, the per cent of state workers went from 8.9% to 21.2% of the labour force, a rate of increase of 365%; one-third of all new jobs in the period were created by the state. Armstrong, *op. cit.*, pp. 296-301.

36Leo Johnson, "The Development of Class in Canada in the Twentieth Century," in Gary Teeple, ed. *Capitalism and the National Question in Canada* (Toronto: University of Toronto, 1972), p. 165.

37*Canadian Industrial Relations*, The Report of the Task Force on Labour Relations (Ottawa: PCO, 1968), Table 1, p. 23.

38Goldenberg, *op. cit.*, p. 15.

39Adams, *op. cit.*, p. 188. On the ideology of professionals, see also Goldenberg, *op. cit.*, p. 20ff.

40Goldenberg, *op. cit.*, p. 15.

41By 1971, for example, 43% of lawyers and doctors were not in private practice. Adams, *op. cit.*, p. 188.

42G. A. C. Cook, *Opportunity for Choice* (Ottawa: Statistics Canada, 1976), Table 4.1, p. 106. The 1967 figure is from "Women in the Labour Force: Facts and Figures—1977," Labour Canada, 1977, Part One, Table 1b, p. 9.

[43]Collective bargaining in areas of federal jurisdiction was established by the Industrial Relations and Disputes Act of 1948, and most provinces were quick to pattern their own legislation on the federal act. See *Canadian Industrial Relations, op. cit.*, p. 16ff, especially p. 19; and H. A. Logan, *State Intervention and State Assistance in Collective Bargaining: The Canadian Experience* (Toronto: University of Toronto, 1956).

[44]Porter, *op. cit.*, p. 321.

[45]Colin Campbell, *Canadian Political Facts* (Toronto: Methuen, 1977), Table 9, p. 136.

[46]David Wolfe, "The State and Economic Policy in Canada," in Leo Panitch, ed., *The Canadian State* (Toronto: University of Toronto, 1977), p. 255.

[47]We will not go into the complicated details of how the campaign against the Communists was mounted and carried out. The anti-Communism of the CCF leadership within the unions was probably unparalleled but it was an anti-Communism founded primarily on the recognition of a competitor in the partisan field, as well as a distrust of the Communists because of their frequent changes of official line in the period 1934-1941 and their subsequent collaboration with the Liberals at the end of the war. For a detailed discussion of the story see, M. Lazarus, *Years of Hard Labour* (Don Mills, Ontario: Ontario Federation of Labour, 1974), pp. 49-51; I. M. Abella, *Nationalism, Communism and Canadian Labour* (Toronto: University of Toronto, 1973), especially Chapters 5-8; N. Penner, *The Canadian Left* (Scarborough, Ontario: Prentice-Hall, 1977), Chapter 5; G. Horowitz, *Canadian Labour in Politics* (Toronto: University of Toronto, 1968), Chapter 3, especially pp. 117-131.

[48]S. Jamieson, *Industrial Relations in Canada*, 2nd ed., (Toronto: Macmillan, 1973), pp. 92-93.

[49]In 1963, the CLC commissioned a study on the unionization of white collar workers. For details see Resnick, *op. cit.*, p. 63.

[50]Although the percentage of state workers among all workers, for example, grew from 8.9 in 1946, to 12.6 in 1956, to 19.1 in 1966, these workers did not all have the right to unionize throughout the period. *Ibid.*, Table 2.19, p. 59.

[51]Campbell, *op. cit.*, pp. 136-137. In 1960, CUPE with a membership of 44,873 became the fourth largest union, and by 1965, it was the second largest union. For the sectoral percentages, see *Canadian Industrial Relations, op. cit.*, Table 4, p. 26.

[52]Herbert Quinn, *The Union Nationale: A Study in Quebec Nationalism* (Toronto: University of Toronto, 1963), Table VII, p. 205.

[53]Porter, *op. cit.*, pp. 333, 331-334.

[54]For a general discussion of unions in Quebec, see *Annuaire du Québec* (Quebec: Province of Quebec, 1972), pp. 384-386.

[55]For a brief discussion of two very important strikes in Quebec during this period, notably the Asbestos and Murdochville strikes, see Lazarus, *op. cit.*, pp. 57-59, 62-63; for a more detailed analysis of the Asbestos strike and the new union philosophy in the early 1950s see P. E. Trudeau *et al.*, *The Asbestos Strike* (Toronto: Lorimer, 1974).

[56]D. Ethier, J. M. Piotte, et J. Reynolds, *Les travailleurs contre l'état bourgeois* (Montreal: L'Aurore, 1975).

[57]For the best known interpretations of this dilemma, see W. Young, *The Anatomy of a Party* (Toronto: University of Toronto, 1969); L. Zakuta, *A Protest Movement Becalmed* (Toronto: University of Toronto, 1964). For a new formulation of the old question, see R. A. Hackett, "The Waffle Conflict in the NDP,"

in H. Thorburn, *Party Politics in Canada*, 4th ed., (Scarborough, Ontario: Prentice-Hall, 1979).

[58]Young, *op. cit.*, p. 128.

[59]This logic, as well as emerging from the quotation of Douglas given in the text, is described in most secondary literature on the CCF of this period. See, for example, Young, *op. cit.*, pp. 114-115, 123-26, 135; Horowitz, *op. cit.*, pp. 172-73.

[60]Cited in Horowitz, *op. cit.*, p. 172.

[61]For a more general discussion, see Bell, *op. cit., passim.*

[62]The "end-of-ideology" argument was pervasive and much written about. For a summary argument, see D. Bell, *The End of Ideology: On The Exhaustion of Political Ideas in the Fifties* (N.Y.: The Free Press of Glencoe, 1961).

[63]For the educational levels of different categories of workers, see Economic Council of Canada, *First Annual Review: Economic Goals for Canada to 1970, op. cit.,* Table 47, p. 162.

[64]Young, *op. cit.*, pp. 114-115.

[65]*Ibid.*, p. 129.

[66]Leo Zakuta, "Membership in a Becalmed Protest Movement," *Canadian Journal of Economics and Political Science*, vol. 24, no. 2 (May, 1958), pp. 192-193.

[67]As with the "end-of-ideology" debate, this question had deep roots in the political conditions of the 1950s and was influential in more places than the CCF. The impact of the "managerial revolution" is summarily described in R. Miliband, *The State in Capitalist Society* (London: Weidenfeld and Nicolson, 1969), p. 28ff.

[68]Frank Underhill, *In Search of Canadian Liberalism* (Toronto: Macmillan, 1960), p. 139.

[69]Zakuta, *A Protest Movement Becalmed, op. cit.*, pp. 89-90.

[70]Young, *op. cit.*, p. 313.

[71]Quoted in A. Finkel, "Origins of the Welfare State in Canada," in Panitch, *op. cit.*, p. 357.

[72]*Ibid.*, p. 316.

[73]For a discussion of this process of party decision-making and its effects, see L. Minkin "The British Labour Party and the Trade Unions: Crisis and Compact," *Industrial and Labour Relations Review*, vol. 28, (October 1974). This issue is a symposium on European labour and politics and is a useful source of comparative information about how parties of the left faced the crises of the fifties—the increasing affluence, new middle classes and Cold War.

[74]See *ibid.*, p. 72. See also J. H. Goldthorpe, D. Lockwood, F. Bechofer and J. Platt, *The Affluent Worker in the Class Structure* (London: Cambridge University, 1969). The latter is a very important academic study which challenged the "embourgeoisement" thesis and provided contrary evidence to be used by the Labour leadership to justify its strategy.

[75]Zakuta, *A Protest Movement Becalmed, op. cit.*, pp. 86-87.

[76]Young, *op. cit.*, p. 118.

[77]*Ibid.*, pp. 136-137.

[78]*Ibid.*, p. 315.

[79]For a discussion of the internal party debate at the time of writing the Winnipeg Declaration, see Zakuta, *A Protest Movement Becalmed, op. cit.*, Chapter 7.

[80]Young, *op. cit.*, p. 126.

[81]*Ibid.*, pp. 120-122.

[82]See Young, *op. cit.*; Horowitz, *op. cit.*

[83]Horowitz, *op. cit.*, pp. 167-171; Porter, *op. cit.*, p. 321ff.

[84]The manoeuvring to prevent the CCF from being endorsed, so as not to frighten the more conservative forces within the TLC, was a familiar one for the CCF leadership. For example, in 1942 at the CCL convention, David Lewis managed to keep all resolutions in favour of nation-wide affiliation with the CCF off the floor and at the CBRE convention was busy blocking resolutions "too favourable" to the CCF. All this was in the interest of not alienating the TLC, so that at its Convention in 1942, also, the CCFers spoke against motions for affiliation. Their strategy was silence in the face of possible opposition. The leadership realized that the passing of an endorsement of the CCF by the union centrals would require much work and many years. Their reward came in 1958. See Horowitz, *op. cit.*, pp. 76-77.

[85]Horowitz, *op. cit.*, p. 191.

[86]Penner, *op. cit.*, p. 237.

[87]The fact of declining membership and a pressing need for funds cannot be ignored in the discussion of reasons behind a desire for union support. See Zakuta, *A Protest Movement Becalmed, op. cit.*, pp. 105-06.

[88]D. Morton, *NDP: Social Democracy in Canada*, 2nd ed. (Toronto: Hakkert, 1977), p. 30.

[89]*Ibid.*, pp. 202-203.

[90]Creighton, *op. cit.*, p. 229. See also p. 128ff. and 226ff. for a full discussion.

[91]J. Murray Beck, *The Pendulum of Power* (Scarborough, Ontario: Prentice-Hall, 1968), p. 276.

[92]*Ibid.*, p. 263.

[93]Laurier LaPierre, "The 1960s," in J. M. Careless and R. Brown, eds., *The Canadians: 1867-1967* (Toronto: Macmillan, 1967), p. 346.

[94]Beck, *op. cit.*, p. 294.

[95]David E. Smith, "Grits and Tories on the Prairies," in Thorburn, *op. cit.*, pp. 279-285.

[96]Peter Regenstreif, *The Diefenbaker Interlude* (Don Mills, Ontario: Longmans, 1965), p. 33.

[97]Morton, *op. cit.*, p. 38.

[98]The demographic and occupational measures for the 1949 elections are estimated from the 1951 census data and should be interpreted with caution. In addition, the 1949 measure of "farmer" differs from other years because in 1949 this category included all primary workers. The category for the elections 1953 through 1965 measures only agricultural work force. See Appendix A for further details.

[99]See H. Clarke, J. Jenson, L. LeDuc and J. Pammett, *Political Choice in Canada* (Toronto: McGraw-Hill Ryerson, 1979), Figure 4.3, p. 109.

[100]Regenstreif, *op. cit.*, Chapter 1, Tables 3, 6, and 7; Clarke *et al.*, *op. cit.*, Figure 4.3.

[101]Creighton, *op. cit.*, p. 257.

Chapter 9

The Lull Before the Storm: 1965-1974

Introduction

The Liberal Party gained a distinct partisan advantage because of its quick wartime recognition that Keynesian demand-management techniques and specific social programmes would increase consumption and stabilize capital accumulation, thereby avoiding a recurrence of the 1930s Depression. From the end of the war until the early 1970s the new economics seemed to work. The economy grew while unemployment and inflation rates remained low. There were, however, a few disturbing signs on the horizon which would soon become chronic problems. Relative productivity rates were slowing; exports formed a larger proportion of the Gross National Product than elsewhere; and unemployment rates were rising slowly but perceptibly. These negative economic indicators were the symptom of a contradiction at the heart of postwar economic strategies. Keynesian politics had been based on the assumption of expansion. With an expanding economic pie, both capital and labour could have more in absolute terms. Capital accumulation could go forward at the same time as workers' wages rose and state-organized social programmes grew. Without expansion, the edifice might tumble.

In these years of prosperity founded on expansion, the balance of power among labour, capital and the state shifted in most advanced capitalist countries. In North America, as in Western Europe, the concessions of the so-called "postwar settlement" strengthened the position of the labour movement. While it was only in some countries that unions gained access to the state and capitalist decision-making bodies, everywhere they expanded their legal rights and organization improved, while wage bargaining produced real gains for their constituency. At the same time the structure of capital became more concentrated. Nevertheless, capital still relied on national states to meet its needs for collective services, for infrastructure, for an educated and healthy workforce and for minimal levels of industrial peace. States became more interventionist and increasingly caught between the demands of labour and capital. This does not mean that the state was an impartial arbiter of the interests of capital and labour. Rather, it was a "balance wheel" which regulated the whole economy, assuring simultaneously the accumulation of capital and the continuity of class relations. This role enabled the state to make important concessions to labour's demands. Having an essential role to play in industrial capitalism, the state could not withdraw, even when it found itself caught, once the expansionary economy went into decline, between trying to satisfy the competing demands of capital for accumulation and labour for collective benefits and higher wages.

Canada did not diverge substantially from these general patterns of development. As the previous chapter shows, the growth of social services and state activity and the evolution of labour and capital paralleled the experience of other advanced capitalist countries, albeit somewhat more slowly. But the problems confronting the Canadian state were also particular. One fundamental consequence of years of continental integration was less room for the state to manoeuvre. Foreign ownership meant less national control of the economy; crucial economic decisions often were made elsewhere and responded to the needs of multinationals with interests much larger than those of their Canadian operations. These problems of loss of control were magnified by the fact that more than two-thirds of Canadian trade was with a single country, the United States. By the middle of the 1970s, it had become evident that ongoing reliance on economic integration with the United States had trapped Canadian decision-makers, leaving them fewer instruments to respond to the economic ruptures which rocked the international economy in the mid-seventies and beyond.

As in the past, however, the organization of partisan relations and the language of politics did not reflect these developments. None of the federal parties provided a theory and a strategy adequate for the new conditions. It is not surprising that the bourgeois parties did not meet these needs because they were, of course, never likely to provide a sustained critical analysis of the postwar development strategy, including continentalism. The Liberals, in particular, were kept busy with the politics of biculturalism, which threatened to slip the bonds of mere symbolism, having spawned a major nationalist movement which demanded independence for, and thus isolation of, a large portion of the industrial heartland and domestic market. The political difficulties accumulating during this period were acute. On the one hand, the politics of culture was available to the major parties to distinguish themselves and, for the Liberals, to construct a winning partisan coalition. On the other hand, its continued use had left space for the mobilization of new nationalist movements in Quebec, the growth of which required real adjustments in the relations between the two cultural groups. Quebec was rapidly organizing for independent linguistic and economic action. The major preoccupation of the Liberals, the governing party during this period, was to quell the rising nationalist fervour for a reallocation of power within federalism, if not outright political independence.

What was less understandable, on the surface, was the failure of the social democratic party, the NDP, to grasp the political potential of the period. The NDP had been born when socialist and left-wing forces were on the run because of their seeming irrelevancy during the Cold War decade of economic boom. By the late sixties, such retrenchment was no longer typical of the left around the world, which was resurgent politically and ideologically. In Western Europe new analyses of postwar capitalism appeared and were inserted into the everyday language of partisan politics. Yet the NDP, with its "end of ideology" ideology and links with the most traditional of industrial unions, was ill-prepared for new circumstances. In the early 1970s the forces of the old order within the party beat back an important challenge to the assumptions which had structured the NDP's activities since its founding. They confronted the NDP with an analysis of capitalism which prescribed the construction of a new alliance of progressive forces around the task of breaking Canada's dependence on American capitalism. Their proposed road to Canadian socialism emphasized escape from the American Empire as a condition of independent socialist action and, thus, laid the basis for a preliminary alliance across several social categories. This position, however, was rejected by the party as a whole. The process of internal conflict and the party's inability to find a compromise position endowed the NDP with a costly legacy of internal wounds and fear of strategic debate. It was incapable of coherent initiative when the economic crisis of the mid-1970s arrived in full force.

The Uneasy Boom

As Canadians prepared to celebrate the one-hundredth anniversary of Confederation confidence about the country's future abounded. With a few exceptions, the economic strategies pursued by the federal state had worked, ushering in a period of substantial growth since the war. Between 1950 and 1966 alone, GNP more than doubled, while the value of Canadian exports nearly trebled.[1] While there had been a few periods of high unemployment or inflation, particularly in the recession of 1957-61, Canada's growth record remained strong in the period between 1960 and 1973, when growth in real GDP and employment consistently exceeded the OECD average.[2] When the economy faltered momentarily, the state, equipped with Keynesian tools, generally tried to pick up the slack by stimulating demand or by creating employment in the state sector. Few observers in 1965 could have forecast the turbulent situation which would arrive in the mid-seventies.

At the same time, however, there *were* warning signs of impending economic difficulties. Labour costs were rising relative to slowing productivity growth; corporate concentration increased; job creation in the manufacturing sector stalled while the service, and especially the state sector, mushroomed in size; and the trade deficit was intractable. Canada was not alone with these problems by the mid-1960s; indeed its economic situation closely followed that of the USA. But neither was North America alone, since Western Europe and Japan also had similar experiences. Declining productivity, rising state spending, and labour militancy characterized most of the advanced capitalist countries. Canada's experience, however, was somewhat unique because of the continentalist component of its postwar development strategy.

The previous chapter described the federal government's move towards some demand-management, a partial commitment to full-employment and limited social welfare policies.[3] The strategy, however, contained contradictions which could, under certain conditions, stagnate the growth upon which the policies depended. New collective bargaining arrangements had brought a social and industrial truce in the postwar years and the reconstruction of capitalism did proceed. But it did so with policies which strengthened organized labour. The combination of rapid capital accumulation, leading to economic growth, and expanding government spending for Keynesian-inspired social programmes (which led to more state-sector jobs), produced a tighter labour market throughout the 1960s. As workers became more militant, both in their demands for higher wages and in their opposition to the speed-ups, over-time and other manifestations of deteriorating working conditions, the tighter labour market often made such workplace militancy effective.[4] There was a shift in the balance of power among organized labour, management and the government. Moreover, since the state had publicly committed itself to be the guarantor of economic well-being in its postwar development strategy, conflict over the distribution of the surplus of the production process increasingly appeared as a political question. The government was embroiled in attempts to influence the share of national output going to labour and the share going to capital.[5]

Several initiatives appeared at this time. The burden of taxation was slowly but perceptibly shifted from corporations to individual wage-earners.[6] Mechanisms were set in place to slow inflation, even at the cost of greater unemployment.[7] And, finally, since both the government and business assigned the economy's problems to rising wages, there were concerted efforts to tie wage increases to growth in productivity. The Liberals turned to a standard postwar economic response, more familiar in Western Europe than Canada. There incomes policies, which often involved granting other rights and benefits to workers in lieu of wage increases, had been used as part of tripartite arrangements since 1945.[8] In 1968 the Canadian Minister of Finance proposed an incomes policy, involving voluntary wage restraint guidelines tied to increases in productivity. Unionists, however, saw this call for wage restraint as one which could only worsen their situation, without bringing significant benefits of any sort.[9] Organized labour was in a strong position to resist, because of the conditions of the labour market. Union memberships dissatisfied with existing distribution of income—especially as taxes increased and inflation mounted—continued to be militant in their demands not only for higher wages but also for improvements in working conditions and more benefits.

The state as employer also began to face serious problems of its own. Between 1946 and 1971 the percentage of the labour force on government payrolls expanded from 9% to 22%, largely because of more provincial and municipal government hiring.[10] Moreover, by 1967, 14% of Canadians under major collective agreements worked in the public sector; by the mid-seventies, the proportion approached one-half.[11] Both the federal and provincial governments, then, found themselves the target of wage demands from their own employees for parity with private-sector workers. Public-sector unions won large catch-up wage settlements, which further squeezed state revenues and encouraged private-sector unions also to bargain to restore traditional differentials.

Canada's postwar development strategy had revolved around four central elements: freer trade, organized by international institutions inspired by the Bretton Woods agreements; encouragement of resource exports; promotion of additional manufacturing in Canada; and Keynesian-inspired stabilization policies. These elements, in combination, were expected to bring about diversification of the Canadian economy, making it less dependent on resource extraction and providing new jobs. Nevertheless, beginning in the late 1960s, many Canadians recognized that the economic effects were not quite what was expected. Manufacturing jobs did not increase relative to the other sectors, as corporations turned to new, less labour-intensive technologies and service sector jobs rose in number.[12] Moreover, current account uncertainties plagued the economy, and foreign investment did not flow into the country in the same volume as it had earlier.

Several factors contributed to this situation, not the least of which were advanced capitalist economies' vulnerability to movement of capital. Gradually in these years Canada became a less attractive milieu for foreign investment. It had a small population and corporations were less willing to absorb higher costs to serve only the Canadian domestic market. With tariffs moderating as the result of international agreements, there was little incentive to keep branch plants in full production in host countries. Multinational corporations began shifting their direct investment in manufacturing from Canada to Europe or the Third World while, at the same time, they pumped investment into the resource sector.[13] Canada, like other countries, began to discover that multinationals could profitably manufacture parts and components where labour was cheap and simply assemble the final product where it was to be sold.[14] In doing so, corporations could avoid "cumbersome" government regulations about working conditions and the rights of workers as well as high wages where relative productivity growth was slackening. Throughout this period, Canada had one of the lowest rates of productivity increase among OECD countries.[15]

The flaws in the continentalist component of the postwar development strategy became starkly evident in August, 1971 when President Nixon announced a co-ordinated series of measures fabricated to repatriate the economic activity of American multinationals and to alleviate the balance of payments problem. This programme was the American response to general shifts in the international economy, and it caught Canada, its largest trading partner, in a very vulnerable position. The programme extended generous tax credits to corporations making capital investments in the US while allowing American corporations exporting goods to write off 50% of their taxes on foreign sales. In addition, a 10% surcharge was placed on all American imports.[16] In effect, the Americans had put up a wall against imports, including those from Canada.

The "Nixonomics" of the early seventies shook the whole international economic system but held especially chilling prospects for Canadian decision-makers. The federal government immediately expressed its shock that the United States had "broken trust" with Canada and pleaded, unsuccessfully, for special exemptions. Mitchell Sharp, then Minister of External Affairs, expressed the official disbelief in the apparent rupture in Canada's special relationship with the United States in the following manner:

> I hate to think that the United States is now turning its back on a partnership in the development of North America that has served both our societies well for centuries.[17]

But turn it had and there were few protective mechanisms available to a federal government which was already losing its grip on the development of the economy. Tax breaks and other incentives were extended to encourage investment, but the momentum of capital mobility was already well established and the pull of American incentives too great. Increasingly, multinational corporations assigned their Canadian branch plants the task of assembling parts produced elsewhere. Even Canadian multinationals were drawn by the promise of higher profit margins in the American South.[18]

A number of government reports, prominent politicians and economists predicted the economic liabilities inherent in dependence on foreign capital for industrial development, especially at a time of declining productivity and international economic restructuring. Walter Gordon, for example, as early as 1957, and continuing through the 1960s, warned his colleagues in the Liberal Party of the need to "repatriate" Canadian industry. Similarly, the Gray report of 1971 argued that:

> Canada's openness to direct investment has meant that Canadian industrial development and priorities have in large part been determined by foreign

corporate interests and the industrial policies of other governments. This has led to a greater emphasis on the resource sector in comparison with manufacturing. Furthermore, other governments will put increasing emphasis on obtaining secure supplies for their resource needs and will likely continue to find Canada relatively attractive. . . . Over-development of the resource sector many not accord with Canadian objectives or priorities including long-run employment objectives for a growing population.[19]

It was only slowly, however, that the federal government tentatively began to address the problem. In the early seventies, the Trudeau government undertook a number of initiatives to lessen foreign ownership and reduce the economy's dependence on the United States. None of these were particularly bold changes in direction but they nevertheless irritated sections of capital in both Canada and the United States. First, in 1971, the Liberal government launched the Canadian Development Corporation (CDC) with a mandate to stimulate and underwrite indigeneous entrepreneurship.[20] Second, the Department of External Affairs attempted to forge a "Third Option" for Canada, composed of diversified trade links with the European Economic Community and Pacific Rim countries. At the same time, and in keeping with the recommendations of the Gray Report, the government established the Foreign Investment Review Agency (FIRA) in 1973 to review and, if necessary, refuse foreign investment which did not promise to be of "significant benefit to Canada."[21] Also in that year, the federal government became an actor in the oil industry with the creation of Petro-Canada. Both these latter measures were undertaken under considerable pressure from the NDP, which held the balance of power in Parliament after the 1972 federal election. Thereafter, the Science Council, as well as other governmental advisory bodies, urged a greater role for the state in research and development which, they argued, would encourage the growth of Canadian-controlled technology, modernization and job creation.[22] A coherent and encompassing state-directed industrial strategy, however, failed to materialize during this period.

The Labour Movement: Winds of Change

Although the Canadian trade-union movement would undergo important transformations in the next decade, in 1965 it was much the same type of organization it had been in the 1950s. Approximately the same proportion (23%) of the civilian labour force was organized as in 1955.[23] Moreover, as in the mid-fifties, unions affiliated with the AFL-CIO international unions dominated the Canadian Labour Congress in both membership and leadership. Organized labour did not deviate from its long-established tradition of avoiding the thicket of partisan politics. Even though the CLC had formally endorsed the New Democratic Party as the political arm of labour and some affiliated locals contributed dues to the party's election chest, strong electoral ties between rank-and-file unionists and the new party had not been forged and the CLC did little to tighten the party-union link.

Nevertheless, by the early 1970s there were important changes occurring in the labour movement. It was growing in size at the same time as it was becoming less dominated by international industrial and craft unions and increasingly militant and willing to strike.[24] One of the major reorientations of the labour movement during these years involved a shift in the balance of power within the CLC from private-sector workers and international unions to public-sector workers and national unions. The postwar years had brought rapid changes in the occupational structure. Growing numbers of wage earners were not on factory floors or construction sites but in offices, schools, hospitals and federal and provincial bureaucracies. In the mid-sixties many of these workers organized into large national unions affiliated with the CLC. So rapid was the growth of public-sector workers that the Canadian Union of Public Employees (CUPE) went from being the fourth largest union in Canada (with approximately one-half the membership of the largest union, the Steelworkers) in 1960 to the largest in 1975. In the same year, the Public Service Alliance passed the Autoworkers for third place. Thus, the union movement as a whole grew in numbers during these years, with the increased membership coming largely from the public sector. The rapid growth of the state-sector and its rising rate of unionization were the major factors behind the increase in unionists affiliated with national unions. As a result, the proportion of international unionists among organized labour decreased from approximately three-quarters to one-half.[25]

State workers, however, were not the only unionists without ties to the internationals. In both Quebec and the rest of Canada, private-sector workers began to set up national unions in industries previously under the jurisdiction of the international unions. This growth in national unions, without ties to the USA, reoriented the Canadian labour movement, which had been dominated by international unionism for the entire twentieth century.

Two issues, in particular, tended to encourage tensions between national and international unions within the CLC. One, which will be discussed shortly, involved confrontation with the state. The other concerned the question of Canadian nationalism and autonomy from "international" unionism and the American-based AFL-CIO. On several occasions CUPE led an attack on the leadership of the CLC, which was disproportionately drawn from the internationals, over American influence. Such actions constituted a challenge to the power structure within the CLC. During the early 1970s, the number of resolutions at CLC National Conventions dealing with "Canadian autonomy" was larger than ever before in the CLC's history, rising from seven in 1970, to fourteen in 1972 to thirty in 1974.[26] These calls, issuing from both the leadership of national unions such as CUPE and rank-and-file nationalists within international unions, were defused by international union officials who perceived CUPE, in particular, as a threat to the once unchallenged dominance of international unionism within the CLC.[27]

Ironically, the reorientation of the Canadian labour movement during the seventies toward increasing autonomy grew as much from the actions of the Nixon administration and the AFL-CIO—which seemed to betray its Canadian affiliates—as from the organization of critiques by national unions alone. Nixonomics brought threats of unemployment to the membership of international unions in Canada. Particularly distressing for Canadian international unionists was the fact that the AFL-CIO was a major lobbying force behind the protectionist measures designed to bring jobs back to the United States. The AFL-CIO's principal concern at the time was the flow of industrial jobs from the United States to low-wage Third World countries. Despite promises to the contrary the American international leaderships were willing to sacrifice their Canadian membership, which comprised only about 8% of the whole, to bolster employment opportunities in the United States.[28]

Members of both national and international unions reacted with disbelief and condemnation of the Nixon Administration and the AFL-CIO. Dennis McDermott, then head of the Canadian region of the United Auto Workers, for example, while defending the internationals, conceded that "one day very soon there has to be a wholesale review by labour itself of the US based unions in Canada."[29] In the meantime, CUPE organized a "reform group" to force the question of international domination at the 1974 CLC Convention. The leadership of the CLC, however, held firm, perceiving attacks against the internationals largely as challenges to their organizational position.[30] This convention magnified ongoing tensions within the CLC between public and private-sector workers and between the national and international unions. Throughout the early seventies this conflict within the unions intersected with the debate and conflict within the NDP over Canadian nationalism.

The autonomy debate, while simmering throughout this period, was necessarily quelled by the actions of some provinces and the federal government which threatened the rights and viability of national and international unions alike. As the economic malaise grew more severe and workers demanded higher wages, governments found themselves hard-pressed to hold public-sector costs down. Moreover, wage settlements in the public sector were starting to set precedents for settlements in the private sector. At the same time, uncontrolled inflation and rising taxes consumed workers' incomes. In a system of labour-management relations where unions were accustomed to thinking only in terms of their collective bargaining situation, the most likely reaction to threats to workers' income was to demand higher wages and/or cost-of-living allowances (COLA).

The push for higher wages to "catch up" with mounting prices and taxes initially came from public-sector workers. State workers were among the first to feel the squeeze of the economic crisis. The state was much more likely than private employers to hold back benefits from its employees.[31] In the early seventies, public-sector workers reacted to these conditions with strike actions. The new militancy among state workers was perhaps most visible in Quebec. In that province, the three major union centrals, the Confederation of National Trade Unions (CNTU), the Quebec Federation of Labour (QFL), and the Corporation des Enseignants du Quebec (CEQ) joined forces in a "Common Front" to negotiate with the provincial government. As negotiations bogged down in the spring of 1972, state workers engaged in general strikes to support their contract demands, even after provincial legislation was passed to force workers back to work. Refusal to accept the back-to-work legislation resulted in forty union leaders being sentenced, including the leaders of the three centrals, each of whom was jailed for one year.[32]

Public-sector militancy broke out in other provinces, especially Ontario, in following years.[33] By 1974, it was evident that public-sector unions were taking the lead in reorienting the Canadian labour movement towards more strikes. Militancy increased as the Consumer Price Index edged upwards, the latter increasing by 21% between 1973 and 1974 alone. Inflation brought a precipitous decline in the standard of living of all workers. While private-sector workers' demands for higher wages resembled those of the public sector, their employers, by and large, were unwilling to allow what they termed "excessive" settlements. Negotiations frequently broke down, leading to a record-breaking 9.4 million work-days lost in strikes and lockouts across the country in 1974 and over 10 million the following year, a near record among OECD countries.[34]

Escalating wage demands and industrial unrest were sources of concern for both business and the federal government. One solution to the problem, at least for some, was the imposition of compulsory wage controls which would curtail collective bargaining rights, keep wage increases to a minimum, and force labour to accept a reduced share of national income. The first federal party to grab for this seemingly obvious solution was the Progressive Conservatives and they offered it to the electorate in 1974. During the campaign both the Liberals and the NDP criticized the scheme as being unfair to workers and ineffective in dampening the inflationary spiral. The Conservatives lost the election but, as we shall see in the next chapter, the victorious Liberals implemented wage controls even though the policy was a blatant contradiction of their 1974 electoral platform. The Liberal Party's dishonesty and wage controls proved to be instrumental in drawing the Canadian labour movement behind the NDP in the politics of the late seventies and eighties.

Problems on the Left

When the NDP was founded in 1961 one of its expressed intents was to focus more of its electoral efforts in central Canada, especially Ontario.[35] This focus was clearly different from that of the CCF which had been predominantly a western party. Given the goals of the new party and the distribution of the federal electorate, this Ontario-centred strategy was fundamental to the new party's electoral future. The NDP was in principle to be a party with close links to trade unions, and most of organized labour was in the central regions of the country.[36]

In its first statement of principles the NDP proposed to establish an improved welfare state in Canada and to control, largely through planning, the worst abuses of the capitalist economy. While the NDP did, in its 1961 Founding Resolution, identify the major issues which would inform the content of Canadian politics for the next two decades—the increasing influence of large corporations, poverty in the midst of plenty, employment and unemployment, and Quebec's position in Confederation—its proposals were for amelioration of the status quo rather than fundamental change. Socialism was not mentioned as the NDP's goal, nor did the word itself appear in the document. Gone too was that symbol of the CCF's socialism—nationalization. Instead, the NDP proposed to establish an Investment Board to plan and regulate investment, "including that derived from company reserves," and to "promote steady economic growth and full employment without inflation."[37] To cope with increasingly visible Americanization, a Canadian Development Fund was proposed, to "mobilize and channel the funds of insurance, trust, and similar companies" so as "to give Canadians a greater opportunity to invest in the future of their country." Another proposal was for minimum percentages of Canadians on company boards of directors.

The new party did not, as the previous chapter demonstrated, make a great deal of headway in the frequent elections of the early sixties, although it managed to gain twenty-three parliamentary seats in 1965. The years following, however, brought a challenge to the NDP's strategy. After more than two decades of seeming oblivion, the left was on the rise in many liberal democracies. And, it was a "new left" with goals and strategies different from the left of either the pre-World War II period or the Cold War era. In Canada, as elsewhere, the movement took off from what it saw as the failure of the traditional left—both parties and unions—to mobilize the forces of change within society. As we have described, parties of the left were badly hurt by the experience of the fifties—growing economic affluence, Cold War anti-Communism—which led some left parties to moderate their programmes and move closer to the bourgeois parties. The reluctance to use a class-based language of politics, in turn, contributed to class disorganization and demobilization.

Events were rapidly changing this environment, however. The Vietnam War challenged the Cold War assumptions about global relations and power. The contradiction between full employment and price stability policies was becoming more evident, as both unemployment and inflation began their upward spiral. Opposition among workers to both their wages and the labour process resulted in many wildcat strikes and other outbreaks of militancy. State workers struck for "catch up" wage increases. University students, a category which had expanded dramatically during the postwar boom, became restive under educational rules designed for much more elitist and undemocratic institutions. There was, in other words, a collection of different conflicts which, while independent of each other, broke out together in an uncoordinated fashion. The events of 1968 in many countries were a decisive turning-point from the politics of postwar affluence. Events in such scattered quarters as Paris and Chicago demonstrated that the old ways would not go on forever and that change might be possible. The Cold War was over and the left could come out of the bunkers without risking destruction.

In Canada the "rebirth of the left" pressured the NDP for a redefinition of its strategy and tactics. Taking encouragement from what was happening in other countries as well as in Canada, critics of the NDP's middle-of-the-road electoral strategy began to organize and soon acquired the name Waffle.[38] They organized to put pressure on the party to turn further left which in 1968 meant emphasizing more democracy within the party and society, more participation by people in their community and in workplace decisions and more social ownership. The Waffle wanted to move further away from the statism and parliamentarism which the NDP embraced. The movement shared the belief that people themselves could build their own socialism, with less need for either a directing party leadership or for strong state technocrats to design controls within capitalism.

The Waffle began with the publication of a Manifesto, "For an Independent Socialist Canada," which reintroduced into NDP politics a language which had been absent for years. The Manifesto began: "Our aim as democratic socialists is to build an independent socialist Canada. Our aim as supporters of the New Democratic Party is to make it a truly socialist party."[39] The new group also proposed an alliance between nationalists and socialists. While acknowledging that the Depression had been the catalyst for the founding of the CCF, by 1969, "the major threat to Canadian survival today is American control of the Canadian economy. The major issue of our times is not national unity but national survival, and the fundamental threat is external not internal." Wafflers identified the continentalist component of the state's postwar development strategy as discriminatory along national lines so that all Canadians who bore its costs could be assembled into a democratic movement for political and economic change. The NDP convention of 1969, with resolutions partially inspired by the Waffle, identified "millions of Canadians [who] share our faith in Canada and our determination to strengthen and enrich Canada's independence and place in the world" because "continental integration has become so pervasive that Canadians who value an independent Canada and New Democrats who reject the values of corporate capitalism now share a common agenda."[40] The logic of this alliance strategy was that continental integration distributed its high costs inequitably and that a socialist transformation was itself impossible without first gaining national control of the institutions which directed economic development. An additional component of the Waffle Manifesto was that economic, social and political decisions should not be centralized. To the traditional NDP goals for the redistribution of wealth and welfare were added an insistence on workers' participation in industrial decision-making and a move towards economic and social democracy. This was clearly a move away from NDP parliamentarism towards identifying the sources of change *in society*.[41] To the NDP's scenario for top-down reforms, implemented after gaining elected office, the Waffle counterposed a vision of change involving societal mobilization, and thus centring party activity less exclusively on elections.

Neither the Waffle's vision of Canadian society nor its strategy of transformation were shared by the mainstream of the NDP which firmly believed that Canadian workers and the middle classes would tolerate no more than a better-organized Keynesian state. According to the NDP itself, socialism was not on the agenda for the party's electorate. Nevertheless, the NDP *was* concerned about the source of capital invested in Canada, although it did not see American capital as a fundamental impediment to planning the economy and establishing welfare state programmes. Therefore, rather than attacking American influence directly, the party proposed various planning mechanisms, with the pride of place going to a Canadian Development Fund, which would deploy Canadian capital (in particular, insurance, trust funds and other collections of savings) in a coherent fashion so as to counteract the effects of unregulated foreign investment. Thus, according to the 1967 Federal Convention's "Resolution on Economic Independence," Canada could "preserve economic and political independence by bold public initiatives" alongside private capital, whether domestic or foreign.

In the late sixties, then, the NDP was not completely complacent and the process of self-examination had begun even before the Waffle appeared in the pages of *Canadian Dimension* in the fall of 1969. In fact, critics of NDP practice, actively pressing for more radical positions within the party—whether relating to Quebec or American ownership—had some of their analyses "appropriated" by NDP leaders.[42] The necessity for a re-evaluation of the party's positions, however, became even more apparent after the 1968 election when the Liberals' new leader, Pierre Trudeau, captured the loyalty of young middle-class Canada, which the NDP considered its special preserve. This was the very constituency that the NDP had so assiduously cultivated since the late fifties. Suddenly the new-image Liberals had "stolen" their voters, their Canadian Development Fund (now the Canadian Development Corporation) and their medicare.

Contemplating this disaster, which made starkly evident the difficulties of federal politics since 1961, the problem was defined as one of "distinguishing" the NDP from the Liberals. Charles Taylor, a prominent party member, reacted to these events by arguing that the NDP had failed to be sufficiently distinctive.

> We have pulled our punches in the past, largely because we have been hovering between two strategies. The first is that of the revisionists, who play down the opposition between socialist goals and the corporate system *per se* and focus the attack on the existing political elites. The left then offers itself as a "swinging" technologically literate alternative. (But the Liberals can do as well). . . . Now the disadvantages of the revisionist strategy are evident. One doesn't frighten the sacred cows, but at the same time one creates a certain credibility gap which centres around the question: how are you going to get the money?[43]

The other strategy, which Taylor would have preferred, was one which might initially have frightened off voters but which ". . . would open the way to forming a public which is attuned to the basic opposition between corporate power and social priorities." It would do this by making the "mechanisms of our society transparent." The alliance proposed was between "affluent workers (including white collar and a substantial number of professionals, of course) and those groups most disadvantaged by our society."[44] It is worth noting here that Taylor's work at that time was the first major theoretical working document within the NDP for several years.[45] Even before the Waffle appeared, then, the NDP had begun to re-evaluate postwar strategies.

It was partly because of this self-questioning that Waffle members could make headway within the NDP. By the 1969 Federal Convention, a well-organized Waffle faction participated in policy debates and saw many of its positions passed. The Waffle challenged traditional NDP theory and strategy in two fundamental ways. First, the Waffle emphasized the need for the NDP to undertake the creation and organization of the working class. Second, it defined a new alliance strategy for the passage to socialism. On the first point, the Waffle assigned responsibility of a party of the left to create its own constituency, by challenging the language of politics, before gaining power and *in order to* gain power. This principle was clearly advanced in the second paragraph of the Waffle Manifesto:

> The achievement of socialism awaits the building of a mass base of socialists, in factories and offices, on farms and campuses. The development of a socialist consciousness, on which can be built a socialist base, must be the first priority of the New Democratic Party.

Within the NDP, this position was at times presented as a distinction between electoral activity and other forms of grassroots democracy, and, therefore, it appealed to those longtime New Democrats who had always been suspicious of their party's almost exclusive attention to electioneering. The Waffle's focus on "extra-parliamentary activity" implied the need to prepare, through grass-roots actions in unions, tenant associations and other social movements, support for radical social change which would provide the necessary foundations to allow a democratically elected NDP government to transform Canadian society.[46] Wafflers claimed that if anything more than reformism and the social democratic management of capitalism were to result from electoral victory, such preparation was not only desirable but essential.

Of course, these notions of how to bring about fundamental social change were alien to years of CCF/NDP practice. To some people it appeared that the Waffle had put the "horse behind the buggy." For decades the CCF had claimed that the party had to capture the reins of parliamentary power before it could begin to build socialism. This analysis, informing years of CCF/NDP political practice, had been a justification for the strategic focus on electoral politics and technocratic statism reflected in the 1956 Winnipeg Resolution and the Founding Resolution of the party. It also provided the rationale for confining the activities of the left-wing of the party, so as to assure party unity for electoral activity.

This strategy was epitomized in one of the few NDP successes of the lean years—the mass canvassing technique. Developed by Stephen Lewis in 1963 in Riverdale, canvasses of all households by NDP party workers resulted in the election of an underdog NDP candidate, and within two months worked again in another by-election. For a victory-starved party, the campaign technique appeared to provide a way out of the political wilderness. Subsequently, the technique was popularized, forming the basis of NDP electoral campaigns and, to some extent, was even imitated by the two major parties. The technique embodied two crucial assumptions, one about the voters and the other about NDP activists. The voters were, under no conditions, to be "alienated" by the canvass, which meant that they were not to be engaged in a debate to discuss the merits or demerits of the NDP, its programme or its philosophy. According to the NDP, "the whole purpose of canvassing is to find these potential New Democratic voters, persuade them to support the party and ensure that they get out to vote." The persuasion was to be done by official campaign literature, as clearly outlined in the NDP pamphlet describing the canvassing technique—"The voter should talk, the *leaflet should argue*, the canvasser listens." There were three proposed leaflets. The first introduced the candidate with photo and biography. The second identified the candidate with the issues, using a centrally produced party leaflet and adding the local candidate's special concerns, if any. The third emphasized the importance of voting.[47] In sum, the campaign was centrally directed and decided, and the interaction between NDP activists and voters was kept to a minimum.

NDP activists became free labour for a party lacking funds to use more sophisticated and costly communications media. They did not have to be politically sophisticated, since they personally did not have to convince voters to vote NDP. The canvassing technique was a time-consuming activity which provided little opportunity or encouragement for the development of a class-conscious party cadre. This type of mobilization of activists and voters was anathema to socialists who saw as necessary the creation of a mass and class-conscious political movement in order to bring the party to power.

The Waffle's second disagreement with the traditional NDP strategy attracted most attention. Its alliance strategy identified economic nationalism as the first step on the road to socialism and was founded both on a nationalist desire for an independent Canada and on a criticism of American imperialism which grew out of opposition to the Vietnam War.

> The American Empire is held together through world-wide military alliances and by giant monopoly corporations. Canada's membership in the American alliance system and the ownership of the Canadian economy by American corporations precludes Canada playing an independent role in the world. These bonds must be cut if corporate capitalism and the social priorities it creates is to be effectively challenged.

Moreover, American imperialism, Canadian independence from it, and socialist transformation were inherently linked. The nationalist movement was to be a way of mobilizing for a full socialist transformation. According to this argument,

> Canadian nationalism is a relevant force on which to build to the extent that it is anti-imperialist. On the road to socialism, such aspirations for independence must be taken into account. For to pursue independence seriously is to make visible the necessity of socialism in Canada.[48]

This was not the route the NDP had in mind, however, for solving the problems of Canada. The Waffle argued for a very different strategy which raised difficult questions for those people involved in the continental economic system, the workers in multinational corporations and members of international unions.

The mobilization of the Waffle within the NDP called for a response by the party leadership and the supporters of the traditional strategies. At the 1969 Federal Convention of the NDP, there were attempts at accommodation by moderating Waffle resolutions sufficiently to enable their passage by the full Convention. After two more years of organization within the NDP and a good deal of public attention, however, the battle grew more divisive, especially during the 1971 Federal Convention which selected a new leader. The representative of the "old order" (and the person probably more responsible than anyone else for the evolution of the CCF into the NDP, with a parliamentarist strategy), David Lewis, had his candidacy threatened by a challenge from Waffle-supported Jim Laxer. The convention debate and vote were dramatic; Laxer gained about one-third of the vote.

In subsequent months, the conflict among Wafflers and non-Wafflers grew more divisive, especially in the Ontario and Saskatchewan provincial sections of the party.[49] The party hierarchy decided that it could no longer accommodate the radical faction and found constitutional grounds to end the existence of the Waffle within the party (which occurred in 1972 in Ontario). The argument was that the Waffle constituted a "party within the party," a situation which was in direct violation of the NDP's constitution. It quite explicitly stated that NDP members could belong to one and only one party.[50] Waffle members were given an ultimatum either to drop their separate structure or to leave the NDP.

While there were constitutional grounds for this action, the causes of the expulsion must be sought behind these proximate reasons. In essence, the Waffle represented not only a personal challenge to the party leadership but also a political challenge to years of strategic development. In particular, the Waffle came to represent a direct confrontation with trade-union influence within the NDP. The possibility of corporate and American state reprisals, as well as the threat of lower rates of economic growth, if Waffle positions were ever implemented, haunted the international union leaders who sat on the governing councils of the NDP, especially in the Ontario wing. Moreover, the Waffle reintroduced the language of "socialism" which had been missing from the NDP, partly because of the anticipatory "conservatism" of some of the affiliated trade unions.

The Waffle presented the internationals with an organizational challenge, as well as a material and ideological one, when the group supported the establishment of Canadian national unions in direct challenge to the jurisdiction of the internationals. It also began to mobilize a militant rank-and-file challenge to the established leadership of the unions. Waffle activity in Windsor, the home of the Autoworkers, around Auto Pact questions appeared menacing to the international unions, simply as unions.[51]

Finally, the Waffle's commitment to extra-parliamentary action challenged the legitimacy of the existing labour leadership both within the NDP and in the union movement at large. The Waffle argued that rank-and-file unionists should pursue workers' control in the workplace as well as displace the existing leadership structure and take more direct control over union affairs themselves. It implied or directly indicted the labour establishment for being bureaucratic, conservative and "staff professionals of internationals," who were remote from, if not unrepresentative of the membership.[52] The labour leadership responded with equal rancour. The Waffle was described as a "haven for social misfits," practicing "snobbery for assuming that workers are stupid enough to permit the union leadership to manipulate them."[53]

Underlying all of this animosity was one bottom-line issue for the unionists: The party had no business interfering with the trade-union movement. The intervention of elements of the party into the internal affairs of its labour affiliates was an innovation in the politics of the NDP. In its eagerness to draw labour into a partisan coalition, the NDP had always accepted the labour movement as it was and tried to build a new party around it. The Waffle's call for national unions and greater extra-parliamentary action drew the party perilously close to sacred ground which, if crossed, could destroy the fabric and logic of the party. Ultimately, then, the Waffle threatened the party's hierarchy, whose entire postwar electoral strategy hung in the balance.[54]

The continued existence of the Waffle was, therefore, a threat on several fronts and posed a difficult choice for the NDP. Should it embrace a radical faction and risk losing labour (along with its considerable financial and organizational resources), thereby giving up any hope of the NDP's long anticipated electoral "take-off" among Canadian workers? Or, should it force the Waffle to dismantle and toe the party line at risk of losing it and the new elements it appeared to be attracting to the party? Under the leadership of David Lewis, the NDP eventually chose the latter course of action, reaffirming its ties to the union movement and its hope for electoral support among workers. The solution implemented by the Ontario provincial section was to force the end of the "separate organization" within the party. Stephen Lewis, the Ontario NDP leader, denounced the Waffle, blaming it for its "sneering, contemptuous attitude towards official trade unionism and the labour leadership."[55]

This kind of internal, factional fight within a political party always has great costs, and this case was no exception. Not only did the party lose some of its membership, but the legacy of conflict endured. The party membership remained divided and disenchanted and the revival of the old bogey of "union power" reminded many NDPers of the days of decline, the 1950s. The resolution of the Waffle conflict represented a reaffirmation of statist social democracy—stressing parliamentarism and technocratic solutions to the effects of the capitalist system—coupled with electoralist populism. It marked the marginalization of the "societal transformation perspective," which the Waffle had offered.[56]

One immediate consequence of the reinforcement of these positions within the NDP appeared in the 1972 election campaign, the first led by David Lewis. This campaign was conducted around the notion that the Canadian tax system had produced a large number of "corporate welfare bums." Lewis identified specific large corporations which were "ripping off" Canadian taxpayers as well as the Canadian government because they were permitted tax breaks and other concessions. Day after day during the campaign Lewis identified such giants as the International Nickel Company of Canada, Celanese Canada Limited, Electrohome, Shell Oil, Canadian Westinghouse and many others as "freeloaders" in Canada. The NDP proposed that corporations should be more fairly taxed, while a tax-cut to individuals would create the necessary demand to generate new jobs in a lagging economy.[57] Once again, then, the NDP offered the Canadian people a fairer, more just, and more equitable capitalism. It was a populist attack against the "robber barons," a strategy of identifying "bad capitalists" rather than one of exposing the class inequalities of capitalism of which "bad capitalists" were only a part. But the populism appeared to reap electoral dividends and it was repeated in the 1974 campaign.

The theme of corporate welfare bums rewarded the NDP with thirty-one seats in the House of Commons in 1972, its best results ever, and gave it the balance of power in the minority Parliament. The party's success, however, also created a predicament; the NDP had to decide whether to prolong or terminate the life of the new Parliament by choosing to align with either the Liberals or the Conservatives on parliamentary divisions. Immediately after the election, David Lewis announced the party's conditions for support of either of the two major parties. These included legislative measures to combat unemployment and the increasing cost of living, more effective legislation to curb foreign ownership, and reform of the tax system.[58] While the Liberals appeared to take these conditions into account in the Speech from the Throne, in the end, few concessions, with the exception of the establishment of FIRA and Petro-Canada, were actually made.[59]

With the NDP's support for the Liberal Party bringing few immediate results, the party's credibility declined both in the electorate and among party rank and file. For some people the NDP, which had always seemed to stand apart from the two major parties, had reversed its line and pressure mounted within the party to defeat the government if only to save the NDP from further loss of credibility. But there were also opposing forces which feared public condemnation if the NDP precipitated a premature election. Moreover, several MPs felt that their own seats were threatened by the Progressive Conservatives' rise in the public opinion polls. Therefore, in the face of disagreement among party activists, the parliamentary caucus held on until spring 1974 when the Liberal government fell over its budget. For many party members, however, the defeat came too late and at too great a cost. In the words of one veteran NDP MP, "after the defeat of the last government . . . Canadians perceived the NDP as one of the old-line parties."[60]

The NDP suffered from internal confusion, disenchantment and division in 1974. The party attempted to revive the spirit of 1972 with concerns about "who controls the Canadian economy" and frequently tried, without success, to make its bland, if not ambiguous campaign slogan, "People Matter More," fire the public's imagination. But conditions had changed and organized labour, in particular, found this orientation unconvincing in the face of certain wage controls if the Progressive Conservatives were elected.[61] The campaign offered the electorate a clear alternative between the two major parties with established positions—controls or not—while the NDP stood in the wings, armed only with the same arguments against controls that the Liberals were already making to greater effect. The 1974 election did not return the NDP to its former standing in the House of Commons, and it cost David Lewis his parliamentary seat and the party leadership.

In sum, then, the NDP did not make great headway either in the electoral arena or in the creation of a solid working-class constituency during this decade. The 1972 electoral high appeared as an aberration between the two low points of 1968 and 1974. Therefore, for party strategists, the problem was serious indeed. Moreover, while the NDP had survived a bitter internal conflict, it had done so at the cost of purging the party of many of its youngest, most energetic members who had represented an effort to adjust to new times. The resolution of the bitter conflict involved reassertion of the positions of statist social democracy and electoralism which had been developed for the previous decades. As economic conditions worsened and as capitalism restructured in dramatic ways, pressure mounted on the NDP to "catch up" with the new times both in its theory and its alliance strategies. The post-1975 years would bring even greater debates about strategic directions, even if the depth of conflict never reached that of the Waffle years.

The Elections of 1968-1974: The Politics of Culture Rejuvenated

These years mark the revival of intense conflicts revolving around the politics of culture. In 1968, Canada had just turned into its second century, and Canadians, not yet fully aware of the economic challenges which awaited them in the seventies, were confident about the future. The two major parties offered the electorate new leaders, one of whom seemed to embody the aspirations of Canadian "nationhood" in the face of growing disenchantment in Quebec with existing federalism. The artificial calm, however, proved short-lived.

In many ways, these years were dominated by one man, Pierre Trudeau. The 1968 campaign revolved around Trudeau, with few issues capturing the electorate's attention other than his leadership and ability to defend federalism in the face of growing demands for greater autonomy in Quebec.[62] The new Conservative leader, Robert Stanfield, and NDP veteran Tommy Douglas unsuccessfully attempted to draw economic issues and the Liberal government's record into partisan debate. The pivotal issue remained leadership, especially in cultural politics, and both Stanfield and Douglas suffered in comparison. Trudeau refused to be held accountable for his party's record and offered the electorate little more than a vague promise of a "Just Society" for the future. The NDP leader protested that the 1968 campaign was "nothing but a theatrical performance . . . contemptuous of the democratic process," but the voters seemed to disagree.[63]

The only issue to gain much attention during the campaign, one virtually inseparable from Trudeau's leadership, was the question of national identity and the relationship between Anglophones and Francophones. In the years leading up to the 1968 campaign, the Progressive Conservatives, in particular, had attempted to meet the challenge of Quebec with new orientations. Their solution was to recognize that Canada was composed of two founding peoples. Unfortunately for the Tories their solution had consequences which they never intended. "Two peoples," translated into French, became *"deux nations"* which, when translated back into English is "two nations."[64] The Liberal Party under Trudeau's leadership took advantage of this merry-go-round of language arguing that the concept was divisive, encouraging only greater isolation of the two linguistic groups. Throughout the campaign, the Liberals held out the *deux nations* concept as evidence of the Conservatives' inability to understand Quebec or Canadian nationhood. The Liberals argued that Canada was "one nation" which for English Canada meant no special status for Quebec and for French Canada implied greater representation for Francophones in Ottawa.

The 1968 campaign reinforced the language of culture in Canadian politics. The Liberal Party offered the electorate the vision of a "Just Society" and its guardianship of the Canadian nation. Class-based definitions of politics remained unarticulated and Canadians continued to divide among themselves in federal elections on the basis of cultural criteria. Given the NDP's continued reluctance to contradict this partisan discourse with a new definition of politics, it remained a weak third option. The Liberals marched to power without being challenged about the class inequalities in their "one Canada."

Events in Quebec soon reinforced the bicultural cleavage in federal politics. In 1970 a small group of nationalist extremists precipitated the October Crisis by kidnapping a British trade commissioner, James Cross, and then a provincial cabinet minister, Pierre Laporte. The federal government's subsequent imposition of the War Measures Act along with the assassination of Laporte guaranteed that bicultural politics would persist as an important issue in the 1972 federal election campaign. Even though unemployment was climbing, the Liberals entered the campaign with the complacent theme "The Land is Strong" and their familiar appeals to national unity. By 1972, however, the public mood had changed, being much less confident about the country's possibilities than in 1968. In particular, there was a considerable backlash against the government's attempts to establish the "French fact" in Ottawa. In the civil-service ridings surrounding Ottawa, the Official Languages Act, which designated numerous key posts in the public sector as bilingual, brought strident criticisms of the government's language policies. Elsewhere, concern mounted over recent legislation of the Quebec Liberal government which declared French the only official language in that province. In the meantime, forces for independence were gathering momentum in the province. Trudeau did not appear to be managing the Quebec issue as the Liberal Party promised that only he could.

While both opposition parties capitalized on the apparent inconsistency between the Liberals' vague appeals to national unity and the existing state of affairs, this cultural definition was not all-encompassing. The NDP, as discussed earlier, centred its campaign on inequalities in the federal taxation system. The Conservatives also stressed economic issues, promising tax cuts and legislation to reduce unemployment, a strategy which reaped handsome dividends for the party everywhere except Quebec.[65] The land was apparently not all that strong, and the electorate responded to the proposals of the opposition parties. The 1972 election returned a chastened Liberal minority government. While both the Conservatives and NDP had made gains by contesting the Liberals' assertion that national unity was the only relevant political issue in the campaign, the results of the election revealed a "division of the country into two camps, one francophone and one anglophone."[66] The politics of national unity once again had been made manifest as entrenched national division.

By the 1974 election, in the face of an economic downturn and disturbing manifestations of the new international economic order, it was becoming more difficult to maintain the politics of culture as the dominant language of politics. This election was fought on the issue of wage and price controls. While the immediate "cause" of the election was the defeat of the Liberal government following the NDP desertion of the coalition which had kept the government in power since 1972, the Progressive Conservatives quickly took the lead in organizing the election around the issue of wage controls when Robert Stanfield promised to implement controls as a way of curbing inflation. This promise provided the Liberals with their campaign issue and forced the NDP into the impossible position of trying to promise "more protection" from wage controls than the Liberals were already offering. With the Conservatives committing themselves early in the campaign to the position, it was easy for the Liberals to claim that the Tories' proposals would hurt the wage earners of Canada more than they would help inflation, which the Liberals asserted was a "worldwide phenomenon" outside the control of a single state.[67]

To the country's obvious concern with inflation and its consequences, the Liberals offered few concrete proposals beyond the assurance that, by refusing to accept controls, they would do nothing to hurt wage earners' ability to keep up with the rising costs. In such a campaign, the NDP was out-manoeuvred because its criticisms of the impact of wage controls sounded suspiciously similar to those of the Liberals, the same party that it had kept in power for the previous two years. In this context, the old loyalties held and the Liberals were returned with a majority.

Given the nature of the issues and the debates which characterized these three elections, several trends in federal party support might be predicted. First, since much of the partisan debate during this period continued to focus on national unity and identity, especially in 1968 and 1972, the bicultural cleavage in the East should remain intact. Second, except perhaps in 1974, little occupational polarization within the electorate should be expected. Finally, a decline in the distinctiveness of the NDP as a workers' party might be predicted because of the party's continuing moderation throughout this period, the union movement's continued avoidance of federal partisan politics, and the Liberals' ability to capitalize on the wage and price controls issue in 1974.

The third-order partial correlation coefficients displayed in tables 9:1 through 9:4 support these expectations. As Table 9:1 demonstrates, the

Table 9:1
CORRELATION OF PARTY VOTE AND FRENCH MOTHER TONGUE CONTROLLING FOR LABOUR FORCE** BY REGION
(3rd order partial)

	East			West		
	Lib.	Con.	NDP	Lib.	Con.	NDP
1968	.27*	−.50*	−.40*	.29*	.06	−.14
1972	.38*	−.73*	−.49*	.30*	.00	−.14
1974	.39*	−.57*	−.45	.20*	−.02	−.10

*p < .05
** controlling for worker, farmer, white collar
Source: See Appendix A.

bicultural cleavage remained strong across the three elections, even after the effects of the occupational composition of the constituency are controlled statistically. In fact, the relationship between the Liberal vote and the proportion of Francophones in the constituency actually strengthened in these elections. The intensification of support for the Liberal Party in Quebec can also be traced in the popular vote. The Liberals' proportion of the Quebec popular vote increased from 46% in 1965 to 54% in 1974.

Table 9:2 illustrates the other side of the politics of culture. The NDP and the Progressive Conservatives remained the parties of English-speaking constituencies, after the effects of labour force composition on the vote are held constant. The relationship between the proportion of English-speaking constituencies and the Conservative vote is especially apparent in 1972, when the federal campaign was marked by an English backlash against the government's language policies.

Table 9:2
CORRELATION OF PARTY VOTE AND ENGLISH MOTHER TONGUE CONTROLLING FOR LABOUR FORCE** BY REGION
(3rd order partial)

	East			West		
	Lib.	*Con.*	*NDP*	*Lib.*	*Con.*	*NDP*
1968	−.34*	.62*	.22*	−.10	.21*	−.16
1972	−.39*	.77*	.34*	−.09	.14	−.13
1974	−.43*	.62*	.35*	−.02	.19	−.22*

*p < .05
** controlling for worker, farmer, white collar
Source: See Appendix A.

The third-order partials shown in Table 9:3 support the expectation of a decline in the level of blue-collar constituency support for the NDP in both the East and the West. Even though the 1968 election revolved around leadership and culture rather than class issues, the relationship between the NDP vote and the proportion of blue-collar workers in the constituency was strong, at least in the East. In 1974, however, the relationship decreased, especially in the East. Nevertheless, while the NDP did lose some of its distinctiveness in blue-collar constituencies, its popular vote did not decrease substantially in Ontario, the most industrialized province. The party's popular vote declined by only 1% in the period between 1968 and 1974. Thus, while the NDP's popular vote fluctuated only slightly, it was less clearly defined as a party of blue-collar workers. This trend should not be surprising, given the NDP's omnibus tendencies throughout this period.

Table 9:3 also demonstrates that the Liberal Party, which always attempted to minimize class dialogue and appear to be the party of "all

Table 9:3
CORRELATION OF PARTY VOTE AND BLUE COLLAR LABOUR
FORCE CONTROLLING FOR MOTHER TONGUE** BY REGION
(3rd order partial)

	East			West		
	Lib.	*Con.*	*NDP*	*Lib.*	*Con.*	*NDP*
1968	.00	−.22*	.37*	.29*	−.64*	.42*
1972	−.04	−.21*	.30*	.08	−.46*	.45*
1974	.09	−.20*	.23*	.12	−.33	.34*

*p < .05
** controlling for English, French, German
Source: See Appendix A.

the people," does not have a distinct identity among blue-collar constituencies. Support for the Conservative Party, in contrast, decreases as the proportion of blue-collar workers increases across all three elections. As in the past, the Liberals were more successful than the Conservatives in appealing to a broad coalition of voters.

While the agricultural labour force was less important in determining the outcomes of federal elections in the seventies than in the twenties, Table 9:4 indicates that the patterns of party support in agricultural constituencies have remained fairly stable since the Diefenbaker era. When the effects of ethnicity are controlled, the Conservative vote remains positively related to the proportion of the labour force involved in agriculture in the East and the West. The table, however, also exhibits greater instability of electoral cleavages in the West than in the East. The Conservative Party's identity in agricultural constituencies, in fact, declined precipitously in the seventies. This does not imply, however, that the party's popular support has declined in the region. Rather, the Conservative Party appeared to be gaining a greater diversity of support

Table 9:4
CORRELATION OF PARTY VOTE AND AGRICULTURAL LABOUR
FORCE CONTROLLING FOR MOTHER TONGUE** BY REGION
(3rd order partial)

	East			West		
	Lib.	*Con.*	*NDP*	*Lib.*	*Con.*	*NDP*
1968	−.30*	.35*	−.28*	−.58*	.58*	−.22*
1972	−.32*	.36*	−.32*	−.33*	.41*	−.41*
1974	−.33*	.34*	−.26*	−.21*	.22	−.21*

*p < .05
** controlling for English, French, German
Source: See Appendix A.

in the West during this period, losing its distinct identity as the party of western agriculture, a mantle it inherited in the Diefenbaker years.

While suitable aggregate data for an examination of the support patterns of white-collar workers are not available, as in the last chapter, some observations about the voting behaviour of these occupational groups can be gleaned from post-election voting surveys. The parties made few appeals to white-collar workers as workers during this period so that it might be expected that they would distribute themselves among the parties on the basis of matters other than class. Voting survey results, in fact, suggest that this is the case. In 1974, for example, the Liberals were supported by 53% of the professional, business and managerial categories and 55% of the clerical and sales workers surveyed. Among skilled workers, however, 53% also supported the Liberals. In contrast, voting studies show that NDP support between 1965 and 1974 among skilled workers decreased from 20% to 14% while increasing only marginally among unskilled workers from 11% to 14%.[68]

These data on the voting behaviour of individuals lend support to the aggregate relationships discussed above. Between 1968 and 1974, NDP support among its traditional constituency eroded, without substantial increases in support from the "middle classes" which it attempted to cultivate with its path of moderation. In essence, the NDP demobilized some of its blue-collar constituency in the period examined here. In fact, survey results show that the proportion of labourers in the party's support group decreased by 5% during these years.

Conclusion

This chapter documents the immediate economic and political background to the federal partisan politics of the 1980s—an ambiguous politics in which many of the seemingly immutable features of the political landscape began to blur. Although the period began in relative economic prosperity and political tranquility, three themes which would dominate federal politics after 1974 soon disturbed it. These were a declining economy and an increasingly difficult trading relationship with the United States; the regionalization of the federal party system with the emergence of the Progressive Conservative Party as the party of the "New West," and the necessity of adjusting federal arrangements to accommodate rising aspirations for autonomy in Quebec.

This period witnessed the beginning of the decline of the postwar development strategy as a path to economic growth and prosperity. The movement of international capital and American protectionism (reflecting shifts in the international economy) aggravated Canada's problems of manufacturing trade deficits and compounded its persistent difficulties with high unemployment and low productivity. Moreover, these patterns had the effect of dividing the bourgeoisie into two fractions, which were, for the most part, regionally-based. One fraction sought an intensification of the use of resources (especially energy) as a foundation for future economic development. This development would be founded on a continental strategy and promised to shift the locus of economic activity from the Centre to the peripheries, especially the West. In contrast, another fraction of Canadian capital advocated the preservation of existing Canadian manufacturing sectors and new state-directed development of the industrial and service sector. These positions began to take shape during this period and, in the years to follow, opposing forces representing different visions of Canada's future would compete to control the political agenda of the 1980s.

These forces also would become manifest in the federal party system and in the policies and support bases of the major parties. This chapter has shown how the Conservative Party began to be identified as the party of the West while the Liberals, under the leadership of Pierre Trudeau, maintained their traditional hold over the Centre, especially Quebec and urban Ontario. The development of these deep regional divisions would prove to be an important basis for change in the federal party system. No longer would "regionalism" be expressed by the "protest" of third parties. Instead, the two major parties would propose alternative responses to an increasingly unstable economic order. These real changes in federal partisan politics would dominate the politics of the 1980s but their origins can be located in the National Policy and the postwar development strategy.

The regionalization of federal partisan alignments occurred despite the NDP's continued efforts to remodel itself as a left-wing alternative in the federal party system. Created in the Cold War and the economic boom, the new party has had to face fundamental choices since its conception. Its responses to the changing occupational and economic structure did not reap the electoral rewards the NDP anticipated. Rather than pursuing an unambiguous class analysis which incorporated the expanding categories of new workers such as public-sector workers or developing a clear alternative to the economic strategy of the Liberals, the NDP pursued its statist social democracy and maintained its links with the traditionally more conservative international trade unions. Although economic disarray became increasingly evident during this period, the party failed to come to grips with the changing economic and social order of the postwar world and to provide an alternative to the major parties' definition of politics. Thus, working-class support, which the NDP always assumed would accrue to the party after formal links with organized labour were established, did not materialize. The NDP experienced some demobilization of its working-class constituency without gaining the support of the middle classes its populist positions were designed to attract.

The third theme emerging during this period was the necessity of accommodating Quebec's growing economic and cultural nationalism. The predictable consequence of one hundred years of cultural politics was the growth of a strong movement within Quebec for greater autonomy. In these years, the Liberal Party attempted to respond to the "Quiet Revolution" in Quebec by electing a new leader who appeared to embody the French fact in Canada and by adjusting federal laws and bureaucratic recruitment practices to facilitate the greater participation of Francophones in national politics. Yet here two widely divergent views of Canada's future emerged. One envisioned a bilingual and bicultural Canada and the other sought to create a Francophone homeland within Quebec. In the years to follow, the politics of culture would reach proportions sufficient to threaten the continuation of Confederation and bring profound changes both to federal arrangements in Canada and to federal partisan politics.

NOTES

[1] C. Campbell, *Canadian Political Facts, 1945-1975* (Toronto: Methuen, 1977), pp. 124, 127.

[2] Royal Commission on the Economic Union and Development Prospects for Canada, *Report*, vol. 2 (Ottawa: Supply and Services, 1985), pp. 48-49.

[3] For a comparison of the Canadian experience with several other countries see N. Apple, "The Rise and Fall of Full Employment Capitalism," *Studies in Political Economy*, no. 4, 1980.

[4] The experience of the auto industry is quite typical here. Autoworkers in the mid-1960s participated in a set of wildcat strikes and other labour actions which the UAW itself did not initially support. See Charlotte Yates, "From Plant to Politics: The Canadian UAW, 1936-1984," Ph.D. Thesis, Carleton University, 1988, Chapter 6; W. Roberts and J. Bullen, "A Heritage of Hope and Struggle: Workers, Unions, and Politics in Canada, 1930-82," in M. Cross and G. Kealey, *Modern Canada, 1930s-1980s* (Toronto: McClelland and Stewart, 1984), pp. 128-131.

[5] D. Wolfe, "The State and Economic Policy in Canada, 1968-1975," in L.V. Panitch, ed., *The Canadian State: Political Economy and Political Power* (Toronto: University of Toronto Press, 1977), p. 255.

[6] For Canada see *ibid.*, pp. 276-77. The Canadian government was not alone in this move. For information on other OECD countries, see I. Gough, "State Expenditure in Advanced Capitalism," *New Left Review*, no. 92, 1975, p. 87.

[7] Wolfe, *op. cit.*, pp. 266-68.

[8] For details see L.V. Panitch, "The Tripartite Experience," in K. Banting, *The State and Economic Interests* (Toronto: University of Toronto, 1986), p. 47.

[9] Wolfe, *op. cit.*, pp. 264-65.

[10] P. Resnick, *The Land of Cain* (Vancouver: New Star, 1977), p. 59.

[11] R. Starks, *Industry in Decline* (Toronto: Lorimer, 1978), p. 44.

[12] Because the Canadian economy was less industrialized in the postwar years, it always had a lower proportion of manufacturing jobs. Therefore, as other advanced industrial countries experienced important percentage shifts from

manufacturing to service work, Canada kept a relatively stable albeit low proportion of its labour force in the secondary sector.

[13]Canada's share of all US direct foreign investment was 34% in 1959 and 27% in 1972. Europe's share during the same period increased from 18% to 33%. Resnick, *op. cit.*, p. 35. See also J. Laxer and R. Laxer, *The Liberal Idea of Canada* (Toronto: Lorimer, 1977), p. 41.

[14]*Ibid.*, p. 42.

[15]The increase in real GNE per person employed declined from 3.5% in 1947-56 to 2.3% in 1967-73. Royal Commission, *op. cit.*, pp. 8, 48.

[16]Wolfe, *op. cit.*, p. 269; Laxer and Laxer, *op. cit.*, p. 43.

[17]Resnick, *op. cit.*, p. 150.

[18]Starks, *op. cit.*, pp. 52-56.

[19]Canadian Forum, *A Citizen's Guide to the Gray Report* (Toronto: New Press, 1971), p. 19.

[20]Apparently the CDC was not initially a strong government priority. Early in 1970 Trudeau told a student audience that the CDC was seventy-fourth on a list of seventy-four government bills in terms of priorities. Resnick, *op. cit.*, p. 265, footnote 8.

[21]*Ibid.*, p. 147.

[22]Science Council Committee on Industrial Policies, *Uncertain Prospects: Canadian Manufacturing Industry, 1971-1977* (Ottawa: Minister of Supply and Services, 1977), p. 14.

[23]Campbell, *op. cit.*, p. 136.

[24]R. Byrm, *The Structure of the Canadian Capitalist Class* (Toronto: Garamond Press, 1985); L.V. Panitch and D. Swartz, *From Consent to Coercion: The Assault on Trade Union Freedoms* (Toronto: Garamond, 1985), p. 24.

[25]There was a differential rate of organization among national and international unions, as national unions paid more attention to the "coverage" of all eligible workers. See J. Lang, "The Million-Dollar Question: The CLC and the Canadian Unions," in D. Drache, ed., *Debates and Controversies From This Magazine* (Toronto: McClelland and Stewart, 1979), p. 197.

[26]R. Laxer, *Canada's Unions* (Toronto: Lorimer, 1976), p. 136.

[27]T. White, "Canadian Labour and International Unions in the Seventies," in S. Clark, J. Grayson, and L. Grayson, eds., *Prophecy and Protest: Social Movements in Twentieth-Century Canada* (Toronto: Gage, 1975), p. 293.

[28]Laxer, *op. cit.*, p. 118.

[29]*Ibid.*, p. 118.

[30]For an account of the 1974 CLC Convention and the major resolutions, see *ibid.*, Chapter 15; Lang, *op. cit.*, p. 194.

[31]Laxer, *op. cit.*, p. xii.

[32]*Ibid.*, p. 183.

[33]Laxer and Laxer, *op. cit.*, p. 121.

[34]Royal Commission, *op. cit.*, p. 693.

[35]D. Morton, *NDP: Social Democracy in Canada* (Toronto: Hakkert, 1977), p. vii. The CCF-NDP failed to develop a viable electoral organization in Quebec at either the provincial or federal level.

[36]In 1961, 38% of all members of unions and employees' associations lived in Ontario while a further 24% lived in Quebec.

[37]NDP, *New Democratic Policies 1961-1976* (Ottawa: NDP, 1976), p. iv for the Founding Resolution and *passim* for the resolutions of the 1961 Federal Convention.

[38]The origin of the group's name is not agreed upon. For two possibilities, see Robert Hackett, "The Waffle Conflict in the NDP," in H. Thorburn, ed., *Party Politics in Canada*, 4th ed. (Toronto: Prentice-Hall, 1979).

[39]All quotes from the Waffle Manifesto are from "For an Independent Socialist Canada," in *Canadian Dimension*, vol. 6, no. 3-4.

[40]*New Democratic Policies, op. cit.*, p. 9.

[41]For a more detailed discussion of this aspect of the Waffle/mainstream conflict, particularly with reference to intellectuals, see N. Bradford "Ideas, Intellectuals and Social Democracy in Canada," in A. Gagnon and B. Tanguay, *Canadian Parties in Transition: Discourse, Organization and Representation* (Toronto: Nelson, 1988), pp. 149-50.

[42]Bradford states that Kari Levitt's analysis, which eventually appeared in *Silent Surrender*, was reflected in the 1967 Convention resolutions. Another example is Charles Taylor's modification of Gad Horowitz's writings on "two nations" which moved the NDP beyond its usual positions on federalism. See *ibid.*, p. 148.

[43]See C. Taylor, "A Socialist Perspective on the '70s," in *Canadian Dimension*, vol. 5, no. 8, p. 36. This position document was prepared for a policy meeting of the federal NDP caucus.

[44]*Ibid.*

[45]See J. Laxer, "The Socialist Tradition in Canada," in *Canadian Dimension*, vol. 6, no. 6.

[46]See *Canadian Dimension*, vol. 6, no. 6, p. 44, for the Waffle resolution on "Extra-Parliamentary Activity" to the 1969 Convention.

[47]See NDP, *With Your Help: An Election Manual* (Ottawa: NDP, 1965), *passim*. The same text was used for new pamphlets until the 1978 canvassing programme was developed.

[48]Both quotes from *Waffle Manifesto*.

[49]The federal structure of the party made the provincial organization the primary unit of the party.

[50]Indicators of separate organization were that the Waffle kept its own membership and mailing lists, ran Waffle-identified candidates in the 1971 Ontario election (under the NDP banner, to be sure) and issued its own public statements, which were sometimes in fundamental contradiction with what the party leadership was saying. For a detailed account see D. Morton, *The New Democrats 1961-1986: The Politics of Change* (Toronto: Copp Clark Pitman, 1986), pp. 130ff.

[51]See Hackett, *op. cit.*, p. 197.

[52]R. Hackett, "Pie in the Sky: A History of the Ontario Waffle," *Canadian Dimension* (November 1980), p. 41.

[53]Dennis McDermott, then leader of the UAW, as quoted in *ibid.*, pp. 33-34.

[54]See J. Brodie, "From Waffles to Grits: A Decade in the Life of the New Democratic Party," in H. Thorburn, ed., *Party Politics in Canada*, 5th ed. (Toronto: Prentice-Hall, 1985), p. 209.

[55]Morton, *NDP*, p. 132.

[56]Bradford, *op. cit.*, p. 149.

[57]For a discussion of the corporate welfare bum tactic and the chance discovery of the major campaign issue of 1972 see Walter Stewart, *Divide and Con: Canadian Politics at Work* (Toronto: New Press, 1973), Chapter 4 and David Lewis, *The Good Fight* (Toronto: Macmillan, 1981).

[58]The NDP's increased emphasis on nationalist issues reflects not only the legacy of the Waffle but the increase in popular support for action against foreign influence. See Resnick, *op. cit.*, p. 148; Hackett, "The Waffle Conflict," pp. 195, 200.

[59]See W. Irvine, "An Overview of the 1974 Federal Election in Canada," in H. Penniman, ed., *Canada at the Polls: The General Election of 1974* (Washington: American Enterprise Institute for Public Policy, 1975), p. 34 and Morton, *The New Democrats*, pp. 146-47.

[60]J. Surich, "Purists and Pragmatists: Canadian Democratic Socialism at the Crossroads," in Penniman, *op. cit.*, p. 134.

[61]Morton, *NDP*, p. 166.

[62]J. M. Beck, *The Pendulum of Power* (Toronto: Prentice-Hall, 1968), p. 400.

[63]*Ibid.*, p. 405.

[64]*Ibid.*, p. 408.

[65]For a discussion of the 1972 campaign see Stewart, *op. cit.*, *passim*.

[66]*Ibid.*, p. 227.

[67]H. Clarke, J. Jenson, L. LeDuc and J. Pammett, *Political Choice in Canada* (Toronto: McGraw-Hill Ryerson, 1979). Chapter 8 discusses the development of the inflation issue.

[68]*Ibid.*, p. 109.

Chapter 10

Into the 1980s: The Politics of Uncertainty

Introduction

In the three decades following the Second World War, the Liberal govern-ment tried to stabilize the economy with Keynesian demand-management techniques and social welfare policies, while at the same time, tightly linking Canada's economic development to that of the United States. It dominated both the electoral terrain and the political agenda with ongo-ing appeals to national unity and a national identity. By the early 1970s, however, this strategy began to unravel. While worrisome economic trends occupied economic policy-makers from the late 1960s, "Nix-onomics" gave a clear and distressing signal to Canada that it could no longer take the old order for granted. Events after that only served to erode further the postwar orthodoxies. The Canadian economy staggered and then tumbled in the face of extraordinary economic shocks and structural crises. The Organization of Petroleum Exporting Countries (OPEC) raised oil prices in 1973 and again in 1979. But this was only one nail in the coffin of postwar economics. Productivity in the industries which had driven the postwar boom had already begun to falter. In the meantime labour, both organized and unorganized, stepped up its de-mands for improved working conditions as well as higher wages. Capital continued its movement around the globe seeking locales with low wages and fewer restrictions on labour practices. As a result, the industrialized world faced uncontrolled inflation, declining growth and rising unem-ployment which, in the early 1980s, culminated in a recession of propor-tions unseen since the 1930s.

The past two decades have witnessed dramatic changes in the inter-national economy, which have displaced the United States as the un-rivalled leader of global capitalism. By the mid-1980s, the United States joined the ranks of the net debtor nations of the world while Japan assumed the influential role of the world's most important banker.[1] These years also saw the rise of Newly Industrializing Countries (NICs) as major exporters in both the primary and secondary sectors. In sum, the old order crumbled and with it most of the assumptions which structured economic thinking since the Second World War.

In Canada the legacy of the postwar development strategy was not sustained economic growth but an economy increasingly immune to the counter-cyclical interventions of the federal government. As the tried and true instruments of the postwar years faltered, national politics by the late

1970s turned to debates about alternative ways of coping with the economic crisis. This debate—inside state institutions as well as political parties—involved two decidedly different visions of the role of the state and the future course of economic development. One would have installed a nationalist-inspired industrial strategy, requiring an expanded role for the state in the direction and stimulation of the economy, while the other began from the premise that the state was, in large part, the cause of the economic malaise and that the economy should be governed by market forces. For a time immediately after the 1980 election and Quebec Referendum, these opposing views organized divisions within the federal party system. During these years, the Liberal Party introduced, but could not implement, a resource-based, nationalist-inspired developmental strategy while the Progressive Conservative Party, advocating free trade as its development strategy, recast itself as the party of the "national interest." In the meantime, the NDP struggled to find a progressive response to an increasingly volatile economic and political environment.

The Economics of Crisis

Most advanced capitalist economies have experienced similar trends in economic performance in the postwar years. They prospered after 1945 largely because of the growth generated by postwar reconstruction and a new regime for international trade. Mass production industries experienced steady increases in productivity while mass consumption lifestyles—made possible by rising wages (both individual and social)—sustained demand. The social stability, which came from a trade-off in which workers gave up control over production decisions in exchange for rising wages, was an important element of the whole package.[2] In Canada, this trade-off was installed in collective bargaining arrangements by a series of important strikes and settlements in the late 1940s and 1950s. And, this system worked well to produce economic growth. Between 1948 and 1973, world trade expanded by approximately 7% annually while world output grew at a yearly rate of approximately 5%. But, by the mid-seventies, productivity growth slowed, labour militancy increased and stagflation—an economic condition unthinkable to orthodox Keynesians—took root.

By the mid-1970s falling productivity rates, mounting inflation and unemployment plagued the Canadian economy. Growth was particularly slow: between 1974 and 1979 growth in the Canadian real GDP dropped by over 2% from the preceding five-year average. The economy continued on this uncertain course, falling again in 1976-77, slipping once again in the mild recession of 1979-80 and collapsing into a full-blown recession in 1981-82. In 1982, growth in real GDP was a negative 4.4% while the official unemployment rate climbed to 11% (the unofficial rate was estimated to be double the official figure). The mid-eighties brought a fragile and uneven recovery but unemployment rates remained persistently high.[3]

The instability of the international economy during this period can be attributed, in part, to an astronomical climb in energy prices. The dual oil shocks of 1973 and 1979 represented a massive transfer of capital from industrialized to oil-producing countries. Wealth was similarly transferred within oil-rich countries such as Canada and power and influence shifted to resource producers. In response to the inflationary spiral in the mid-1970s, governments made monetarism rather than more traditional Keynesian responses the core of economic policy. This, in turn, pushed up interest rates and slowed investment and job creation.[4] By 1981, OECD countries experienced virtually no job creation and, in the following year, with the onset of the recession, existing jobs began to disappear at an alarming rate. In 1982 employment growth in Canada was negative (-3.3%).[5]

One important characteristic of the ongoing economic crisis is that there has been a serious problem with productivity. The classic postwar forms of the labour process (mass production industries organized according to Taylorist principles) reached their limits in the late 1960s.[6] Workers began to object to their working conditions while firms began to seek technological innovation which would allow them to maintain productivity. These two responses interacted. As strikes, lockouts and militant demands for new working conditions increasingly characterized labour relations, companies either dropped their militant workforces by moving their operations or tried to reorganize the labour force by introducing more "flexible" labour processes. Flexibility became a euphemism for hiring part-time or temporary workers who were not unionized and were less likely to dispute with management and for new forms of labour-management relations such as "quality circles." In Canada, as elsewhere, both kinds of labour force restructuring occurred. As labour militancy climbed and productivity fell (because less could be forced out of the old machines), new technologies restructured labour processes, collective bargaining rights were reduced.[7]

There also were important international forces at play in restructuring economic relations. Most significant was that the United States was rapidly losing its commanding position in the international economic system. Its share of world exports dropped from 22% in 1950 to 10% in 1980. The American industrial machine, unchallenged in technological superiority and efficiency at the end of the war, rapidly lost ground to competitors around the globe. It faced stiff competition from the European Economic Community (EEC) which by 1980 constituted the world's largest trading bloc with an external trade matching the combined shares of the United States and Japan. In the meantime, labour-intensive industries grew in the newly industrializing countries of the Pacific Rim and South America. They attracted multinationals to take advantage of low wages and their exports ate up increasingly large proportions of world markets.[8]

The declining status of the United States in the international economy posed especially vexing problems for Canadian investors and policy-makers already facing similar problems of falling productivity, labour militancy and industrial restructuring. The postwar development strategy had been constructed on four fundamental pillars—mass production for the domestic market; freer trade, especially with the Americans, Keynesian-inspired demand management, and development of resource exports. Policy-makers assumed that both domestic manufacturing and resource development would depend upon expanded foreign investment. True to design, the United States became Canada's largest trading partner: three-quarters of Canada's trade, amounting to 156 billion dollars in exports and imports in 1984, went south of the border.[9]

As discussed in the previous chapter, the economics of the early 1970s began to reveal the less positive side of the postwar development strategy. Branch-plant industrialization left in its wake an inefficient, uncompetitive and technologically dependent manufacturing sector. Therefore, when productivity began to decline and technological innovation was on the agenda, there was little space in the Canadian system for autonomous innovation or re-structuring. Decisions over the future of Canada's industries—whether they would wind down or be restructured—depended on actors outside the country's borders. The conditions described in the last chapter deteriorated further during the late seventies and early eighties. Canada's overall productivity growth declined from an average annual rate of 2.3% in the 1967-73 period to virtually zero between 1974 and 1981. The manufacturing sector continued to shrink, accounting for only 20% of the total labour force in 1981, a drop of almost 10% in the postwar period. As the international economy restructured, Canada's share of total direct foreign investment fell from 16% in the early 1960s to a negative figure in the early 1980s.[10]

The crisis in the manufacturing sector reached unimagined proportions during the 1981-1982 recession, which was due, in part, to the American Federal Reserve Board's decision to slow inflation by restricting the U.S. money supply.[11] This monetarist approach successfully reduced inflation but it undermined growth. Interest rates soared to over 20% and industry began to contract, being no longer able to finance either existing inventories or capital expansion. This was a global recession but its impact was extremely pronounced in Canada, partially because it coincided with long-delayed increases in oil prices. In 1981-1982 alone, capital investment in Canada dropped in real terms by 26% (compared to 16% in the U.S.).[12] Business bankruptcies reached record-breaking peaks and unemployment ballooned. In one year alone, 321,000 jobs were lost in the nation's goods-producing industries, 194,000 of these in the manufacturing sector.[13]

Canada's worsening economic prospects during this period were not confined to its truncated manufacturing sector; the resource sector also reeled in response to changes in the international economy. Resources have always held the key to Canadian economic prosperity, providing the activity necessary to underwrite the persistent trade imbalance in finished goods. Throughout this period, however, resources (excluding oil) played an ever-diminishing role in the nation's output. By the early 1980s, the primary sector's share of the GDP had fallen to less than half of its 1947 level.[14] Put differently, the resource sector's share of the nation's total output had fallen to 14% by 1982.[15] Hidden within these statistics were pronounced changes in the relative importance of various resources. There was a boom in mining in the twenty-five years after 1945, placing Canada among the world's top producers in all fourteen major minerals except coal. In recent years, however, the production of all minerals (except potash and sulphur) declined. Third World countries such as Chile, Zaire and Zambia have challenged Canada's leadership in the production of minerals while technological change has made redundant once important Canadian minerals. Glass fibres, for example, have replaced copper wiring.

In sum, since 1973 there was a deterioration in most aspects of Canada's economic performance; this situation only worsened during the early eighties.[16] While all advanced industrialized countries faced problems of this type, there was a fear that Canada might have "painted itself into a corner." Because so much manufacturing was done by branch plants of American corporations, there was little opportunity for an autonomous response by these firms to the pressures for restructuring. Branch plants did not control their own technology. Nor did they do much research and development. Many corporations which were manufacturing in Canada depended upon responses to restructuring made elsewhere. And, often such decisions involved plant closures and the relocation of production sites rather than the modernization or expansion of the Canadian plant.

The continentalist element of the postwar development strategy of continental integration also meant that the Canadian economy was extremely vulnerable to American economic policy. Throughout this period, it became increasingly clear that the United States was no longer prepared to grant Canada any special concessions in formulating its economic policy. "A new doctrine of protectionism" swept through the American Congress, identifying Canadian goods, particularly primary products such as lumber, as unfair competitors and thus subject to American countervailing duties.[17] Even more troubling was the Americans' increasing reliance upon non-tariff barriers, government procurement and similar policies, which were designed to keep production in the United States and to lock foreign goods out of the American market. The combined effect of countervailing duties and non-tariff barriers prompted an increasing number of Canadian firms to relocate branches or move their entire operation to the United States, thereby intensifying the crisis in the Canadian manufacturing sector.[18] In short, a major effect of Canada's postwar economic strategy was to tie domestic development to the demands of the American economy. Paradoxically, the very success of this strategy left Canadian policy-makers few options and, as we will see, an increasingly bleak vision of the future.[19]

The growth of provincial power also limited the capacity of the federal government to respond to volatile international conditions. Implicit in the continental economic design was the gradual replacement of traditional East-West trading linkages within Canada, which were forged by the National Policy, with North-South ones. Throughout the seventies, Ottawa lost its power to manage the national economy as the provinces began to implement their own development—or "province-building"—strategies to achieve the economic diversification that had been denied them by over a century of federal economic policy-making.[20]

The challenge to federal power was most pronounced in the resource-producing provinces which historically existed in the unenviable role of economic hinterland for Central Canada. Rising oil prices and, to a lesser extent, international demand for potash, sulphur and other selected resources, affected a dramatic, if fragile, shift in the balance of power between the federal and provincial governments and between provinces within Canada. The coffers of the oil-producing provinces ballooned, providing them with the fiscal means to promote development within their respective jurisdictions. Meanwhile, the population shifted to participate in the economic boom in the western provinces.[21] These changes brought the federal government and resource-producing provinces into increasing conflict with respect to both the control and distribution of resource rents and more fundamental issues about the role of the federal state in the economy. Decidedly different conceptions of the future course of Canadian economic development emerged. Throughout the seventies, the premiers of the resource-producing provinces, especially in the West, introduced and popularized an alternative vision of Canadian development, one which emphasized decentralization of the federal government's economic prerogatives, market-driven economic development, and accelerated continental economic integration. This alternative vision was embraced by the Progressive Conservatives in the late seventies and provided the ideological underpinnings for a fundamental shift in federal politics in the mid-eighties.[22]

In the meantime, the situations of Ontario and Quebec, long dominant in the national economy, altered. The difficulties of the manufacturing sector and the western resource boom effectively weakened Ontario's once unchallenged position in the Canadian political economy. Between 1970 and 1977, it had the lowest growth rate in the country, as its share of GDP dropped from 42% to 39%. The massive transfer of wealth from oil-consuming to oil-producing provinces meant that, for the first time Ontario qualified for federal equalization grants (forcing the federal government to introduce special legislation to disqualify it from collecting). The balkanization of the national market as a result of provincially-based development strategies compounded Ontario's sagging fortunes. By the mid-1980s, five provincial governments had legislation which favoured provincial suppliers for government contracts.[23] Ontario's supremacy as the purveyor of industrial goods to the Canadian market was no longer assured.

Before 1945 Quebec and Ontario formed the industrial centre of Canada and together their populations determined the outcome of federal elections. Then two important developments dislocated Quebec from the centre and made it susceptible to different political alignments. First, Quebec did not share in equal measure with Ontario the industrial "spin-offs" of the postwar development strategy. The construction of the St. Lawrence Seaway drew commerce away from Montreal to Toronto and the manufacturing stimulated by the Auto Pact located disproportionately in Ontario. Meanwhile, traditionally Quebec-based industries such as textiles, clothing and leather goods went into decline as trade liberalization brought cheaper foreign goods into the Canadian market.[24] The net effect of all of these factors was that between 1960 and 1980 Quebec's share of the nation's manufacturing production slipped from a third to a quarter.[25] Since 1960, then, successive "province-building" governments in Quebec have linked the province's future to resources, especially hydro-electric sales to the United States. In the process, Quebec has shifted its political alliances within federalism to the side of the resource-producing provinces, often leaving Ontario isolated in the current debate about economic futures.

In summary, these years were marked by dramatic shifts in centres of economic power both between and within nations, wavering policy responses by the federal government in the face of economic crisis, and uncertainties about the future. These uncertainties were multiplied in the early 1980s by a deep recession and an unstable trading relationship with the United States. But beneath all of these manifestations of instability and trouble was the ongoing process of economic restructuring for an uncertain future. Postwar capitalism appeared to have reached the limits of expansion under the old system. Thus Canadian capital and the state responded to this crisis with new forms of production, new labour processes, new products and new social relations. In short, the rules of the game were rapidly changing and the labour movement and other progressive forces had to struggle to catch up.

Labour in the Crisis

In the first half of the 1970s, Canadian labour responded to the growing economic malaise with militancy. Demands for wage increases to keep up with inflation came from both public- and private-sector unions and neither the government nor business could successfully resist. Between 1973 and 1975 two economic indicators, the Consumer Price Index and labour compensation per unit of output, more than doubled.[26] Mounting inflation resulted in large part from the rapid increases in the price of resources, particularly oil. This price rise brought higher costs to domestic consumers but it also meant a mini-boom for the Canadian economy, which saw increases in both incomes and the international value of the Canadian dollar. Strength in resources, however, did not bolster other sectors of the economy. The manufacturing sector continued to face productivity problems; plants closed, activity declined, unemployment rose and modernization proceeded unevenly. Moreover, the repatriation of profits by foreign-owned companies and restrictions on oil exports aggravated Canada's balance of payments problem.[27]

Confronted with a multitude of negative economic indicators, but still not convinced that the conditions which had sustained the long postwar boom had disappeared, the federal government turned to a policy instrument that had long been in the repertory of postwar governments, although not used in Canada since 1945.[28] In October 1975, it imposed wage and price controls and established the Anti-Inflation Board. According to the federal government's analysis, the economic crisis found its root in an imbalance between workers' incomes and capital investment. Accordingly, if the relationship could be rebalanced, economic growth would necessarily follow. Prime Minister Trudeau justified the dramatic reversal of his opposition to wage controls, expressed in the 1974 election campaign, as a temporary measure which would "teach" Canadians to adjust to the new conditions. Wage controls were touted as the way to halt union demands for higher wage settlements, thereby dampening internally-generated inflation and restoring business confidence in the Canadian economy. Assigning the cause of inflation to "too many people and too many groups" attempting to "increase their money incomes at rates faster than the increase in the national wealth," Trudeau explained that controls involved "nothing less than a wrenching adjustment of our expectations—an adjustment of our national lifestyle to our means."[29]

Throughout the controls period, wage increases were held at rates well below inflation (which was only minimally reduced from 10.8% in 1975 to 8.9% in 1978). Workers' real wages fell under the controls regime and continued to fall well into the 1980s. In fact, estimates show that the average employed worker had a thousand dollars less purchasing power in 1984 than five years earlier.[30] At the same time, business received generous allowances to improve its profit margins; corporate profits before taxes dropped only slightly from 15.1% to 14.3% during the controls regime.[31]

Wage controls were an extraordinary if temporary governmental response to the growing economic crisis, but it was not the only policy instrument embraced by state economic decision-makers during these years. In a move away from the postwar economic othodoxy, the Bank of Canada decided to institute a tight money policy.[32] The "new monetarism" was announced by Gerald Bouey, Governor of the Bank of Canada, one month before the federal government imposed its anti-inflation programme. In contrast to the analysis which informed the move towards wage controls, Bouey claimed that the inflationary spiral of the mid-seventies found its cause in a dramatic increase in the supply of money made available by central bankers in the early seventies in their combined efforts to stimulate the slowing economies of the industrialized world. His solution was to reduce the growth rate of the money supply in order to break inflationary expectations, even at the cost of slow growth and unemployment in the short term. The Bank of Canada doggedly pursued this policy until the early 1980s but the anticipated drop in inflation rates failed to materialize.[33] Inflation continued to edge upward, reaching 12.5% in 1981, a level not surpassed since 1948.[34]

The union movement considered all of these actions as an attack on its hard-won postwar victories. Resistance to the government's actions was the first response. Labour leaders saw wage controls as an effort to curtail collective bargaining rights. And they were, since they brought no influence over government policy-making or decision-making in the workplace as a substitute for the sacrifice of wage increases. Canadian unions' long-standing focus on the workplace and privatized labour-management relations left them with no strategy of demanding greater political power or non-wage benefits, as European unions often did when confronted with incomes policies.[35] They saw the imposition of wage controls simply as an attack on union rights and fought it as such. In industries where unions were strong enough to resist, they did so; in the other cases, they had to accept the law.[36] Unions also rejected controls as an unfair sharing of the burden of inflation—only the waged were forced to restrain themselves.

In the 1974 election campaign, both the Liberals and the NDP condemned controls. They criticized the Tories' advocacy of wage controls as being both an ineffective way to dampen inflation and unfair to workers. But if labour had equated a vote for the Liberals as a vote against controls, they were soon disappointed. Shortly after the election, the Minister of Finance, John Turner, approached the CLC leadership with a proposal for voluntary controls. The union leaders, seeing an offer which would only worsen the situation of their members, rejected the proposal out of hand. The search for consensus ended and, on Thanksgiving evening 1975, Trudeau announced compulsory controls.

Labour leaders and rank-and-file unionists alike were outraged and calls for resistance emanated from all quarters. But the possibilities for an effective fight against controls were limited. Government leaders used "tough talk" to discourage labour's opposition, threatening to jail any union leaders who did not accept the jurisdiction of the Anti-Inflation Board (AIB). Some unions—CUPE in particular—called for a general strike and the postal workers and Toronto secondary school teachers did strike. The most visible union response, however, was the 1976 "Day of Protest" which pulled over one million unionists off the job and sent hundreds of thousands to Parliament Hill. While seen as a major success for the CLC, the Day of Protest did not end controls. Moreover, the CLC lost its challenge to the constitutionality of the legislation when the Supreme Court found that the AIB legislation fell under the federal government's prerogative to act for the "Peace, Order and Good Government" of Canada.

The union movement's failure to end controls underscored its lack of effective political resources to fight the increasingly harsh assault on collective bargaining rights. By the end of the 1970s, business and government were on the offensive to weaken what they both described as the excessive power of organized labour. Many corporations had concluded that the labour process and labour-management relations needed restructuring if companies were ever to climb out of their economic difficulties. Both the requirements of new technologies and the workers' opposition to the organization of assembly-line work encouraged managers to experiment with new forms of industrial organization. One experiment involved the introduction of "quality of working life" reforms in which workers assumed more responsibility for production decision-making.[37] Semi-autonomous work groups and flexibility in job assignment provided managers with ways of maximizing the new production technology, especially robots and complicated computer-assisted designs. Often, but not always, managers presented such changes in working conditions as advantages to workers which could off-set the fact that collective bargaining was not producing higher wages. In more dramatic circumstances, firms demanded concessions from their workers to cut back previously won wages and benefits. Sometimes new working conditions were offered in exchange but, as often, employers simply threatened to close down if the concessions were not forthcoming. Other companies reorganized their production processes so that they could lower labour costs. These procedures often involved by-passing the unionized and militant work force altogether, subcontracting or hiring among categories of the labour force—women, in the first instance—that traditionally has eschewed militancy and had a history of temporary or irregular participation in the workforce. As a result, the numbers of part-time workers in Canada climbed.[38] Some companies simply tried to dispose of the problem by displacing workers altogether, substituting new technology for the skills of workers.[39] Finally, in assessing the total restructuring process, many firms concluded that new technology and labour processes only could achieve their full objectives if their operations were fully continentalized.[40] Therefore, they began to pressure the federal government for free trade arrangements which would allow for the continental rationalization of productive capacity.

All of these responses by business to the new economic conditions threatened the unions' position in the postwar economy. New work rules, more flexible job assignment, consultation between labour and management on production design, re-classification of existing job hierarchies and free trade, all imperilled the position that unions had constructed in the workplace after 1945. Unions' strength depended on their ability to represent their members in wage negotiations; concession-bargaining would only undermine that role. One way that unions exercised their power was by threatening to strike, but another way was by refusing to co-operate in the production process. Work roles and systems of job assignment which by-passed the unions and made relations between managers and workers more direct, would also undermine that basis of power. Similarly, free trade was likely to mean rationalization of production in fewer plants within Canada and probably plants without unionized work forces. At a more basic level, part-time work and homework—much favoured in high-technology production—made union organization difficult because the workers did not even share a single workplace. For all these reasons, then, the labour movement confronted a dilemma. It had to find a strategic response to the restructuring demands of capital. But, no matter the response, it was always constrained by the general atmosphere of labour-management relations which had become hostile to organized labour.

In the late 1970s and into the 1980s, governments as employers led the assault against union power. In light of the contradictions and tensions in economic policy—reflected in the simultaneous pursuit of wage controls and monetarism—the federal government sought greater coherence. In 1978 Prime Minister Trudeau, along with other Western leaders attending the Bonn Economic Summit, tacked cuts in government spending and employment in the public sector onto monetarism. The federal government tied its rate of expenditures to increases in the GNP. As a result, government's share of the GNP has remained virtually static since 1975. In this way, the government attempted to shift the composition of its spending away from social programmes which raised the social wage to a formula that would more directly bolster capital accumulation. It reduced unemployment insurance benefits, cut its contribution to post-secondary education and health care through a new funding formula and partially de-indexed social security payments. The net effect was that the share of total government expenditures for social programmes dropped from 46% in 1976 to 40% in 1982.[41]

But the most important political element of the whole package was the initiative to control the government payroll by controlling public-sector wages. In 1982 the federal government instituted the "6 and 5" programme which removed the right to strike from public-sector workers, extended the life of existing contracts, and set wage increases without negotiation at 6% the first year and 5% the second.[42] When the Tories replaced the Liberals in 1984, the Mulroney government's neo-liberalism brought the combined responses of privatization and deregulation which effectively curtailed collective bargaining among many public-sector workers if it stood in the way of restructuring the public service. This whole package also inspired provincial governments to introduce similar restraints. In the process, public-sector workers were given the clear message that they could no longer count on having the right to strike while private-sector employers were encouraged not to bow to the "excessive" demands of their employees.

In this hostile environment, the union movement needed new and bold strategies. One response—tripartism—drew upon the arsenal which unions in other countries had deployed in the postwar years. The CLC developed the concept of "social corporatism" as a means of gaining greater influence within government by securing an unchallenged position to "speak for labour." At its 1976 Convention, CLC leaders declared themselves ready to pursue social corporatism with government and business, by which they meant a scheme to extend participation to labour and business in planning the government's post-control policies. Convention delegates, representing a number of different unions, however, opposed the proposal from the floor and gave a stronger than usual endorsement of the NDP. Public-sector union leaders opposed the CLC initiative because they recognized the potential for conflict if the union central engaged in tripartism with their employer. For others, like Dennis McDermott of the Autoworkers, tripartism was only desirable when a strong social democratic party existed. Provincial federations of labour also opposed the visibility that such a scheme would necessarily give to the CLC. In general, however, the proposal lost its lustre as the Anti-Inflation Board handed down decisions which controlled only wages and not prices. But tripartism continued to have a lingering appeal for unionists and government officials. State-organized task forces to investigate industrial sectors appeared in 1978 and the Major Projects Task Force, which was co-chaired by representatives of business and labour, reported in 1981.[43] The Mulroney government continued this practice with the 1985

National Economic Conference, which brought together representatives from labour, business, government, and other sectors to discuss the future direction of the Canadian economy. These consultative efforts, however, remained episodic and intangible in their effects.

Throughout these years the union movement continued its search for an effective response to the changed economic and political environment. The CLC recognized that the new economic conditions called for more than collective bargaining and the occasional foray into lobbying. Beginning in the late 1970s, then, the CLC began to formulate a strategy for industrial restructuring, one which rejected continental free trade, favouring instead more natural resources processing in Canada, enhanced regulation of foreign investment, more research and development within Canada, and the restoration and improvement of social programmes.[44]

While decidedly labour-focused, the CLC's plan dove-tailed with those of other actors in Canadian politics in these years. Moving to take advantage of this convergence, the CLC instituted two political initiatives to press for its industrial restructuring programme. The first was a concerted effort to strengthen the NDP by more activism in federal partisan politics. This initiative by organized labour was, in many ways, a legacy of wage controls, when the Liberal Party flagrantly reneged on its campaign promise to protect labour. The CLC set out to convince the rank and file that the old-line parties had proven themselves, once again, to be only the friends of big business and that unionists had no alternative but to support "their party," the NDP. As the 1979 federal election approached, the CLC executive decided to increase its funding of the NDP and to press union locals to mobilize their members into a voting block. The CLC's president, Dennis McDermott, always more open to active partisanship than many other labour leaders, announced that:

> The Canadian trade union movement is mounting a massive information campaign to tell Canadians in general and workers in particular that the time has finally come for people to make their frustration known the best way this can be done: at the ballot box.[45]

In a campaign termed "Canadian Labour Calling," the CLC set up telephone centres in target ridings where volunteers and union votes were plentiful. The telephone campaign stressed the realities of shrinking pay cheques, unemployment, the erosion of trade-union rights under the Liberal government, and the need for a new and comprehensive industrial strategy. Labour continued its partisan activity in support of the NDP in both the 1980 and 1984 federal campaigns, but their effects on electoral outcomes were limited.

The labour movement did not put all of its eggs in the electoral basket, however. By the mid-1980s it had become a major force in what the authors of *The Other Macdonald Report* have termed "the popular sector," presenting an alternative vision to the free trade, market-based development strategy promoted by many bourgeois politicians.[46] Building on the notion of a more independent industrial strategy, a rebuilding of the Canadian economy around a continued commitment to social programmes and economic redistribution, many unions and the CLC leadership have emerged as leaders of one of the lines of opposition to the "new consensus" the Mulroney government is promoting. In particular, it contributed to the broad-based coalition of groups opposed to the free trade agreement in 1987-88.

For example, the Ontario Federation of Labour (OFL), whose membership is most immediately threatened by the bilateral trade pact has co-ordinated a multi-faceted campaign, including research, phone banks, direct mail, television appeals and coalition-building among a broad spectrum of political actors. Electoral support for the NDP also remains crucial to its strategy, as an OFL briefing note clearly details:

> Let there be no question that this campaign is also about removing Brian Mulroney and his big-business-backed Conservatives from power. Workers know only too well the history of the Liberal Party and its leader's ties to the business world to ever trust them again. But there is a political party that is always prepared to stand up for ordinary people. That party is the NDP. Ed Broadbent has been leading the Parliamentary battle against the free trade deal from the start. By sticking together and continuing to work closely with Bob Rae and Ed Broadbent, we'll not only stop Mulroney's sellout, but also we'll elect an honest and caring NDP government for Canada.[47]

As the rest of this chapter shows, the "popular sector" proposals faced formidable opposition. Not only are the forces for free trade and market-based restructuring strong because they have their representatives in power in Ottawa and in several provincial capitals but also because the opposition is divided.

Overtaken By Events: The NDP in the Debate about Alternative Futures

The events of the first half of the 1970s created deep and bleeding wounds within the NDP. The Waffle conflict had divided the party, led to the departure of much of a generation of young activists, and pushed the party back onto the traditional positions of parliamentarism. As one long-time NDP supporter wrote: "What the Waffle left behind in the NDP was a serious generation gap in the party's intellectual wing and a nervous awareness of the dangers of policy discussion."[48] Support for the minority government from 1972 to 1974 also had demoralized many NDPers, while blurring the boundaries between the NDP and the Liberals. This haziness continued in the first few years of the new decade, as the Liberals swung sharply in a more nationalist direction, implementing programmes similar to those long advocated by the NDP.

Yet, as conflict over alternative futures emerged in Canadian politics—within the state, the labour movement, and the popular sector, and between the Liberals and Progressive Conservatives—the NDP remained mired in difficulties. Debate did occur within the party, but it often failed to materialize in its public actions. By the late 1970s, many NDPers were articulating their concerns that the party had failed to provide coherent proposals to face the ongoing economic crisis, thereby enabling the other parties and business opinion leaders to blame "big unions" and "big government" for the economic downturn.[49] A lively debate inside the NDP did lead to a detailed new perspective, but it also was one which deepened parliamentarism, being founded on an electoralist strategy of accumulating voters from a broad spectrum of Canadian society. The NDP did not lead wide-spread public debate about alternative futures.

From its conception, the NDP had advocated an expanded role for the state in the Canadian economy, but by the mid-1970s, the party's central tenets of centralized federalism, planning and Keynesianism sat less well with party theoreticians, strategists and activists. Thus, in these years the NDP set out to discover its own post-Keynesian future.[50] It was obvious to NDP strategists that the postwar world had altered and new policies were necessary. A first response, in the late 1970s, brought an industrial strategy based on "supply-side" state intervention. Manipulation of fiscal policy would support and consolidate Canadian firms in key sectors which promised to become internationally competitive. A proposed Canadian Investment Fund would encourage corporations to invest profits in projects meeting state criteria and tax savings would encourage firms to invest in research and development.[51] The NDP offered state-directed initiatives to foster and co-ordinate the economic restructuring which the economic crisis made necessary. These were efforts to counter the emerging neo-liberal criticisms that it was postwar policies of state intervention and spending that created the economic difficulties in the first place.

In the face of the neo-liberal version of postwar history, with its market-led solutions, the NDP offered another view. It attributed Canada's economic uncertainties to the distinctiveness of Canadian industrial development, in particular the legacy of foreign investment. To compensate for this inheritance, the NDP advocated a broader mandate for the state than simply providing more comprehensive and equitable social programmes. The model for social democracy shifted in these years from British Fabianism, with its statism and dominance by organized labour, to Sweden where investment funds and careful restructuring involving the state, labour and capital seemed able to keep the economy afloat over the shoals of economic crisis.[52]

This post-Keynesianism did not come easily to the NDP. In the early 1980s, debate again rocked the party over whether or not its policies were adequate for the changed economic environment. Prominent leftists, such as ex-Wafflers James Laxer and Mel Watkins, claimed that the Liberals, especially with the National Energy Programme, had a better vision of the post-Keynesian future.[53] Laxer, in particular, was profoundly critical of the NDP's emphasis on "distribution" rather than on "production." The Laxer Report, published just before the 1984 election, chastised the NDP for holding to its postwar course which, by the mid-eighties, appeared to be "short-sighted, old-fashioned and contradictory."[54] The embrace of much of the language and analysis of neo-liberalism in the Report implied a concomitant shift in interest from workers to Canadian companies and middle-class technocrats. Such a shift would obviously elicit objections not only from the union movement but also from socialists who sought to update party strategy without giving away a commitment to traditional democratic socialist values.

But it was not only neo-liberalism in the guise of updating social democracy which threatened the NDP at the time. As troublesome was the growing "western revolt" within the party which challenged the NDP's steadfast advocacy of a strong centralized federal state. On each of the major issues which pitted the Centre against the West during the early eighties—questions of oil pricing, the National Energy Programme and the new constitutional division of powers—the NDP sided with the Liberals and, thus in many minds, against western interests. The resulting malaise, evident among the party's rank and file, parliamentary wing and provincial leadership, erupted at the party's national convention in 1983. The Regina Convention was intended both to celebrate the 50th anniversary of the Regina Manifesto and to confirm an updated Manifesto.[55] When Allan Blakeney and Grant Notley, along with their supporters, arrived in Regina with an alternative Manifesto, calling for greater space for provincial diversity and questioning the NDP's industrial strategy worked out with the CLC in the late 1970s, the celebration turned sour. It became dominated by a series of divisive backroom negotiations aimed at cooling the apparent "western revolt" in the party. Eventually dissension was contained within the new Manifesto by recognizing a need for "stronger provincial and local governments capable of realizing important tasks of economic and social development," and "the demand by Canadians to decentralize, where feasible."[56] Provinces were to be able to become laboratories for social change.

In many ways, the NDP had been caught by its failure to recognize the political consequences of the western shift in economic activity. The party's roots and much of its electoral support came from the western provinces. Indeed, twenty-six of the party's thirty-one MPs elected in 1980 represented western constituencies—constituencies which were increasingly antagonistic toward both the power of the federal government and Ontario's historically dominant position in the Canadian economy and politics. The party's strategy for an electoral "take-off" continued to be tied to developing a support-base in Ontario. Thus, on most of the major political issues of the eighties, the party was paralyzed by the choice of appealing to the Centre and alienating its traditional support-base in the West or the reverse.

But the objections raised by western NDP leaders were not only to federalism. They too incorporated a critique of Keynesianism and what they saw as excessive attention to organized labour's desire for protection of jobs, any jobs.[57] Their basic economic proposal was for an incomes policy, based on a new "social contract." This idea would require a good deal of explaining to the union movement which had been living through the Liberals' 6 and 5 wage control programme and saw, in both Laxer's and the westerners' view of labour as "just another interest group," a clear threat to its social power.

Explanations and discussion, however, never occurred in any concerted manner. The divisions at Regina were papered over; electoralism could be used to support a demand for party unity. Indeed, the very intensity of internal debate and the range of disagreement contributed to the fact that much of this economic discussion did not appear in the NDP's electioneering. Moreover, the tactic of electoralist catch-all populism also discouraged clear position taking. Therefore, while the NDP did have an industrial strategy as part of its official platform, and was debating alternative futures for democratic socialism in crisis, these issues received little play in elections.

In 1979, all three parties stumbled about for position, with the Tories in particular unwilling to repeat the 1974 disaster wrought by taking a clear position on an issue. In this context, the NDP discovered a new asset—Ed Broadbent. He topped the leaders in popularity polls, running far ahead of the NDP itself. While the CLC's telephone campaign went on (despite making some NDPers nervous that it would conjure up the old bogey of "too much" labour influence over the NDP), the major thrust of the whole campaign turned on the slogan, "Vote Ed—Instead."[58] The 1980 election followed only nine months later, and "for the NDP, as for its rivals, campaigning had to be a matter of recycling the speeches, candidates, and strategies of the 1979 campaign."[59] The CLC's support was accepted, but both campaigns were careful to point out that labour was only one component of the NDP's constituency. Therefore, in the NDP's effort to broaden its populist appeal to "working people," the new initiatives of organized labour were obfuscated and in the end Canadian trade unionists did not vote as a block for the NDP.

In 1984, "except for references to a made-in-Canada interest rate, the imposition of a levy to finance worker training and some tax reforms, the economic policy presented by the NDP involved little more than fiscal stimulation to create jobs and preserve the welfare state."[60] In essence, the party appeared to be advocating more of the same even though traditional

Keynesianism had been much discredited by the events of the preceding decade. Moreover, the NDP plumped completely for a populist strategy. Refusing its pollster's advice to stress its economic ideas, the NDP put together a campaign in which it offered Broadbent "Standing Up for Ordinary Canadians."[61] Its electoral slogan for the late eighties—"For People Like You"—carries a similar message.

Pulled by the ever elusive promise of electoral success "if only" the right appeal could be found, the NDP presented no coherent response to economic restructuring and the changing circumstances of the Canadian economy. The NDP too was caught in many of the changes which had remade Canadian society and politics. Its provincial leaders—who after all had brought the only electoral successes the party had—were reluctant to line up behind an industrial policy which stressed rebuilding Canadian manufacturing at the Centre. Moreover, after 1984, for the first time in its history, public opinion polls showed the NDP gaining strength in Quebec, where centralized federalism does not sell well. The federal wing itself was divided over the ways to modernize its thinking, as the controversies over the Laxer Report and incomes policy clearly demonstrated. Finally, when the CLC finally began to give greater support to the NDP, the party itself was already far along a populist road which refused to grant any privileged position to the labour movement in its doctrine or constituency. The unions, therefore, turned towards more independent mobilization, both around collective bargaining and in broad coalitions with sympathetic political actors. The CLC found more solid allies for its industrial strategy in the Science Council of Canada, the Canadian Centre for Policy Alternatives, the Coalition Against Free Trade and the Canadian Conference of Catholic Bishops than in NDP election rhetoric. The relative public silence of the NDP meant that it left the stage to the other parties to formulate a response to economic restructuring and thereby define the boundaries of partisan debate about alternative futures.

Alternative Futures: From the Politics of Culture to Free Trade

The debate about alternative futures, we should always remember, occurred in the context of a declining economy which had not responded either to the medicine of traditional postwar economics—wage controls— or to the monetarism of the Bank of Canada. Therefore, attention turned to decidedly different possibilities. One of these was a new development strategy of state-encouraged, and even state-led, industrial restructuring. The other opted for neo-liberal retrenchment of state spending and a greater reliance on market forces, which, by the mid-1980s, included accelerated continentalism through free trade.

The call for a coherent state-centred industrial strategy arose as the costs of branch-plant industrialization became a growing source of concern for government officials, economists and some voters. The Gordon,

Watkins and Gray reports all demanded that the federal government take steps to "repatriate" Canadian industry from foreign interests if the manufacturing sector was to survive, let alone grow, in the new international conditions. In response, the federal government established the Canadian Development Corporation (CDC) in 1971, announced an ill-fated and vaguely formulated industrial strategy and created the Ministry of State for Science and Technology in 1972, introduced the Foreign Investment Review Agency (FIRA) in 1973 and launched Petro-Canada in 1975. The underlying concern of each of the policy instruments was foreign (American) investment, a fact which provoked a negative response from the continentalist fraction of the Canadian bourgeoisie and the American government.

By the mid-seventies, however, proponents of an industrial strategy were concerned about both the *fact* of foreign investment and the *form* that future investment in the industrial sector might take. Of course, as the history of the Canadian economy well demonstrates, the source of investment is not easily separated from the form of industrial activity. Nevertheless, the distinction is an important one because it suggested that the government should not be concerned simply with "buying back" industry but, instead, should be actively launching and supporting the specific industries likely to prosper in the new international economy. Proponents of this position began to argue that the most appropriate industrial strategy for Canada would involve the state "picking winners," specifically industries with a high value-added component and research and development potential.

The NDP's industrial strategy of the late 1970s was indebted to this type of argument. While a number of agencies promoted this approach, its most consistent advocate was the Science Council of Canada which claimed that "technological sovereignty" would provide salvation from certain economic decline.[62] State-directed technological development promised to end Canada's dependence on imports of finished goods, open new markets and recapture the manufacturing sector from foreign ownership, which it identified as "the single most important obstacle to developing such technology." To achieve this goal, the Science Council advised government to develop a procurement policy to open a market for Canadian-made goods, play an entrepreneurial role in developing new technologies, become joint partners with private industry, and finally, establish technology centres to promote research and development.[63] In other words, the Science Council prescribed more—not less—government support for capital accumulation via actions which were specifically oriented toward sectors of the economy which had attenuated under the postwar developmental strategy.

As a result, the Liberal government found itself pressed to develop an "industrial strategy" which would make Canada a producer of specialized products rather than a full range of manufactured goods. But, not everyone shared this enthusiasm for new state action. The Liberal party, in fact, continued to harbour strong supporters of greater continentalism and less government intervention. More threatening than its internal party divisions, however, was the fact that the Liberals found themselves losing the support of powerful elements of the business community. The Canadian Manufacturers' Association, for example, spoke out continuously against attempts to regulate foreign ownership while other supporters of continentalism warned that the federal government's actions were reducing investor confidence and interfering "with the natural process of continental integration."[64] Therefore, Prime Minister Trudeau hastened to assure the Economic Club of New York in 1978 ". . . that foreign investment is welcome in Canada, that we need it, that we want it, and that we hope it will come." At the same time, the Canadian government accepted the line of the Bonn Economic Summit that government spending lay at the root of the economic difficulties all countries were experiencing.

While the Liberal Party tentatively embraced fiscal conservatism in the late seventies, this interpretation of the economic future was being fully elaborated in other quarters. The neo-liberal Margaret Thatcher won elections in Britain in 1979 and Ronald Reagan became President of the United States in 1980. In Canada, a powerful coalition of conservative think-tanks, provincial and federal politicians and business leaders adopted this viewpoint, tacking onto it support for continental free trade. According to the neo-liberal orthodoxy, the crisis of advanced capitalism derived from over three decades of Keynesianism which had pushed capitalist economies to the brink of collapse. Governments, through social welfare programmes and extensive growth in the public service, had become too large, fiscally irresponsible and oppressive to the "creative elements of society" (read capitalist) with increasingly onerous taxation. Given these truisms, the solution was simple: reduce the size of government and let the private sector resume its supposedly historic role as the creative, efficient and productive engine of capitalist growth.[65] This coalition urged Canadian policy-makers to minimize the role of the state, cut back social welfare policies, reduce regulation and allow trade liberalization to proceed.

These views on the future course of Canadian development became increasingly popular among governmental and business circles in the late seventies and early eighties. Influential bodies such as the Economic Council of Canada (ECC), the Ontario Economic Council (OEC), the Fraser Institute, the C.D. Howe Institute and a relatively new player, the Business Council on National Issues (B.C.N.I.) all proclaimed the new orthodoxy.[66] Each espoused the neo-liberal virtues of free enterprise and free trade, opposed the concept of a state-centred industrial strategy, and advocated decreased government spending, deregulation and reduced corporate taxes. They became fixated, however, on the size of the federal deficit.[67]

During the late seventies, this vision was increasingly interwoven into the positions of the Progressive Conservative Party. The party's transformation began during the leadership of Joe Clark, who brought together an unstable coalition of western capital and its supporters, province-building politicians and some progressive elements in the party (the so-called Red Tories) in 1976. This coalition self-destructed during the short-lived Clark government of 1979, but was recast—largely without the progressive faction—behind Brian Mulroney in 1983. It was the rise of Clark to the leadership of the Conservative Party, however, which revealed to Tory strategists an apparently winning formula in the federal arena.

For most of the postwar period, the Conservatives had been relegated to the status of the party of the peripheries, the party of those dispossessed by the postwar development strategy. Indeed, it was precisely this persona which had prompted Diefenbaker's meteoric rise and fall in federal politics. The seventies had changed this electoral arithmetic, however. The western provinces were now powerful actors in the Canadian economy and increasingly frustrated with the continuing centrist orientation of the federal Liberal Party. The growing western malaise, however, was not, as it had been in the past, tied to progressivism. Rather, it was increasingly informed by neo-liberalism. The western premiers utilized the combined themes of regionalism and neo-liberalism—with their call for decentralization and a return to free enterprise—throughout the seventies to protect their jurisdiction over natural resources against federal incursions. They used the notion of less state intervention as a shorthand for no *federal* intrusion in provincially-oriented and state-directed provincial developmental policies. This rhetoric was consistent with the growing right wing of the federal Progressive Conservative Party and increasingly vocal business elites, who regardless of their partisanship, wanted to wind down state enterprises, drastically cut social welfare expenditures and deregulate the economy.[68]

In these years there was an uncharacteristic, if incomplete, polarization in federal party politics. The Liberals and Conservatives, for the first time in many years, disagreed over three fundamental orientations which had formed the basis of consensus for much of the postwar period. The first was decentralization of economic policy-making. The postwar inter-party consensus favoured federal power. By 1979, however, the federal Conservatives began to articulate a different conception of Canada, with the ambiguous phrase "community of communities." They campaigned with the promise that key federal powers over resources, culture and communications would be turned over to the provinces. Meanwhile, the Liberals held fast to the notion that Canada was more than a sum of its parts and that the federal power should not be surrendered to the provinces.

The proper role for government in the economy was the second point of contention between the two major parties. The Liberals, while cutting back state activities during the late seventies, maintained a positive orientation toward an activist state, a posture which became very clear for a short time after their re-election in 1980. The National Energy Policy (NEP) and a resource-driven restructuring of the industrial sector were presented as new tools to replace the Keynesianism of the postwar years. The Progressive Conservatives, however, increasingly adopted the "buzz-words" of the New Right. For example, addressing his new constituency, Clark said:

> Big government is not the answer. It is a more dangerous giant than Big Business or Big Labour, because government has the power to write the rules. I advocate greater use of the free market, and less concentration of economic power. A decentralized economy will reflect Canada's diversity, foster a sense of community, and provide opportunities for personal risk-taking and creativity.[69]

The third major area of interparty disagreement was economic nationalism. For most of the postwar years the Liberals had been continent-alist, an orientation that was consistently opposed by the NDP and by the Conservatives under Diefenbaker. Throughout the seventies, however, they had taken a few tentative steps in the direction of economic national-ism. The Conservatives argued that regulatory instruments such as FIRA were unnecessary restrictions on the private sector and that discouraging foreign investment was a luxury the economy could ill-afford.

The Petro-Canada issue, in particular, embodied the fundamental differences in the strategies of the two major parties. Petro-Can had been established by a minority Liberal government, under pressure from the NDP, as a public corporation in the petroleum industry to counterbalance the power of multinational oil companies. At first resisting the idea, the Liberals increasingly relied on the Crown corporation as a means of opening new energy projects to Canadian capital. For the Conservatives, however, Petro-Can embodied all that was wrong with the postwar development strategy—federal dominance over provincial concerns and an unnecessary intrusion by the state into the private sector. Thus, even though public opinion polls favoured retention of the Crown corporation, the Tories promised to "privatize" it if they were elected in 1979.

By the 1979 federal election, then, the rhetoric of neo-liberalism found its way onto the platforms of the federal parties. But, the transition was incomplete. While Joe Clark led the Conservatives to victory in 1979, he failed to achieve the majority his government needed to implement this new vision of Canada's future. Yet, the new government claimed that it could act *as if* it had a majority, and introduced a hard-hitting "austerity" budget which included an eighteen-cent-a-gallon tax on gasoline. Much to the Conservatives' surprise, the government fell on the NDP's vote of non-confidence in the budget and the subsequent "eighteen cent" election rewarded the Liberal Party, under the revived leadership of Pierre Trudeau, with a majority government.[70] The Liberals appeared to have recaptured the mantle of the party of the national interest.

Neither the elections of 1980 or 1984 gave Canadian voters advanced warning of the subsequent political agendas of the bourgeois parties.[71] Trudeau entered the 1980 campaign mocking the obvious ineptitude of the short-lived Clark government, accusing it of being the dupe of the western premiers and the multinational oil companies, promising a made-in-Canada energy policy which would be less onerous for consumers, and pledging his ongoing commitment to renewing federalism. The electoral campaign was clearly a divisive one, pitting yet again the central provinces against the peripheries, especially the West. On election night, the CBC proclaimed a Liberal majority before the polls had even closed on the Prairies.

After the 1980 election defeat of the Tories and the success of the *Non* position in the Quebec referendum, a confident Liberal government put together a policy package of unanticipated policy initiatives. What Donald Smiley terms the "Third National Policy" was designed to halt the regionalizing forces in Canadian politics and to provide a new vision of a single community.[72] Central to it was patriation of the British North America Act and entrenchment of the Charter of Rights and Freedoms, implementation of the National Energy Programme, unveiling of a resource-driven industrial strategy and introduction of the Western Development Fund. These initiatives were both nationalist and centrist. The Charter of Rights and Freedoms, for example, stressed individual rights over those of provinces or collective rights while the National Energy Programme and the Western Development Fund strengthened federal goals for economic development. Both the provinces and the Conservative Party were obviously suspicious of, if not down right opposed to, these actions.

The Liberal government's initial response in 1980 to economic crisis and the process of industrial restructuring was a peculiar hybrid which adapted some of the key planks of the "technological sovereignty school." Key to this new approach was the National Energy Programme and a White Paper entitled "Economic Development for Canada in the 1980s" which the government introduced with its budget in November 1981. The two were complementary components of an economic masterplan which would tie industrial growth to federally-directed resource exploitation in the peripheries.

The NEP was unveiled in Parliament in October 1980 only three weeks after the Constitutional resolution had been placed before the

House. Trudeau had promised a made-in-Canada energy policy during the election, but the boldness of the policy initiative both delighted the nationalist left and outraged the oil-producing provinces, the US-based multinational oil companies and, ultimately, the American government.[73] The programme had three stated objectives: security of supply organized by creating independence from the international market; Canadianization of the industry; and fairness in prices and the distribution of revenues. Few could argue with these almost platitudinous goals, but the chosen means to accomplish them aroused hostility in numerous quarters. First, the government announced that it would unilaterally set the price of oil and natural gas below world levels; it thereby antagonized the oil companies and the western provincial governments. Second, it introduced measures to increase the federal government's share of oil rents, thus creating a direct cost to the treasuries of the producing provinces. In addition, it extended incentives to firms that would increase their activity in land under federal rather than provincial jurisdiction. Finally, the federal government retroactively reserved for the Crown (Petro-Canada) a 25% interest in the development rights of the Canada Lands, a provision which incensed the American multinationals already exploring Canada's off-shore and Arctic oil reserves.[74]

NEP had a number of hidden objectives, not the least of which was to return some control to Ottawa over the direction of the national economy and to bolster the federal government's sagging revenues by exacting a cut of the provincial resource rents. It also was meant to appeal to Canadian capital which had been effectively closed out of the most lucrative game in town—energy. The Liberals knew that Canadian corporations (such as Power and Argus) wanted to get into the energy business and they expected that independent Canadian oil companies (such as Dome) would align with the federal government if federal incentives were arranged in their favour.[75] To sweeten the pot, FIRA was directed to block foreign oil companies from takeovers of Canadian enterprises while the NEP announced that the oil and gas industry would have majority Canadian ownership by 1990. What followed in the next months, then, was a "spate of takeovers of foreign firms so extensive that the value of the Canadian dollar was threatened."[76]

While the NEP was presented to the Canadian public as an initiative undertaken by the federal government in the "national interest," it certainly was not perceived as such in the oil-producing provinces. The reaction of the western provinces, especially Alberta, was quick and dramatic. Premier Lougheed likened NEP to "having strangers take over the living room" and announced cuts in oil production.[77] The western provinces viewed the NEP as yet another example of a federal government elected by and acting on behalf of central Canada. When the federal government argued that Canadian industry would gain a competitive advantage by holding the domestic price at 75% of world levels, producing provinces interpreted this as a subsidy to Ontario. The Liberals had hit rock-bottom electorally in the western provinces in 1980 and the NEP only further reinforced the regionalization of the federal party system. Not even the promise of a Western Development Fund could heal these wounds.

Federal officials had anticipated resistance from both the producing provinces and the multinational oil companies but they did not expect that most independent Canadian producers would join ranks with the provinces, the multinationals and the American government in opposition to the new energy policy. By all accounts, these Canadian companies reacted against the policy as "capitalists, not Canadians," viewing both the nationalist and interventionist dimensions of the NEP as antagonistic to their long-term interests.[78] This united opposition forced a few changes in the original legislation, but the federal government held fast to the programme's overarching design and goals.

The Liberals could not back down on their energy programme because it was a central thread in the new industrial strategy which envisioned the revival of the industrial core by means of mega-project development. The Major Projects (Blair-Carr) Task Force, reporting in 1981, estimated that, by the year 2000, investors would spend over 400 billion dollars on large projects and recommended that the federal government institute procurement and other policies to ensure that Canadian industry reaped the spin-offs.[79] The Liberal government accepted the thrust of the Task Force report in its White Paper, "Economic Development for Canada in the 1980s."[80]

Declaring that the "Government of Canada must assume a leadership role in the field of economic development," the federal government asserted it would be a partner in mega-project development, using the "back-in" provisions of the NEP and other mechanisms, to direct and stimulate Canadian manufacturing and research and development. While the White Paper stressed that this new industrial strategy did not exclude foreign capital and that "NEPing" other sectors of the Canadian economy was not appropriate, the American government took umbrage. Within the course of two years, the federal government had strengthened FIRA, legislated a reduction in foreign control of what the Americans perceived as "continental energy reserves," and finally, introduced a White Paper which, although veiled in co-operative terms, could not conceal its nationalist aspirations. Washington was not prepared to accept protectionism in Canada or, for that matter, "any deviations from its historic role as a resource hinterland and a captive market."[81] Thus, the US government took steps to challenge FIRA and other Canadian legislation in the international courts.

The "Third National Policy," collapsed, however, not because of

American protest but because of flaws in its own design. Like its predecessors, it was a resource-driven strategy, which meant that its success was tied to the vagaries of the international commodities market. The whole plan depended on rising energy prices but predictions of such rises proved unfounded. Only months after the federal government announced its vision of Canada's prosperous future, oil prices began their downward spiral, reducing federal (and provincial) revenues and making many proposed mega-projects much less feasible. Work on existing mega-projects, such as the Tar Sands plants in Alberta, ground to a halt and interest in proposed "mega-projects" such as Hybernia and Arctic development abated.[82]

The Liberals' Third National Policy thus resembled a "shooting star," visible at one moment but gone the next, as the global economy entered the recession of 1981. Not only had the Liberals failed to imprint an overarching national design on the balkanized provincial economies of the country, but they had alienated significant segments of the electorate and the capitalist class in the process. The government had run out of ideas and options to cope with the growing economic crisis. Thus, in the fall of 1982, it appointed Donald Macdonald to head the *Royal Commission on the Economic Union and Development Prospects for Canada* and charged it to recommend "appropriate national goals and policies for economic development."[83] Before the Royal Commission could report, however, Brian Mulroney displaced Joe Clark as Leader of the Opposition, Trudeau retired and the new Prime Minister, John Turner, led his party to a resounding defeat at the polls. A new era in federal partisan politics had opened.

While the Liberal government beat its retreat from interventionism in the last years of its tenure, the Tories promulgated a Canadian variant of neo-liberalism. After several years of back-stabbing, the right wing of the Conservative party successfully forced a leadership convention in 1983 and replaced Joe Clark with Brian Mulroney. In him, they found a leader that was not only sympathetic to multinational capital but drawn from its ranks; charismatic in a way that Joe Clark, after years of media ridicule, could never be; and a fluently bilingual Quebec native son. Mulroney also had developed the art of walking the fine line of politics in the 1980s, one time expounding the virtues of the free enterprise system and next time referring to social programmes as "the dimension of tenderness" and pledging to "demonstrate compassion for the needy and assistance for the disadvantaged."[84]

In the 1984 federal election both major parties hugged "the centre of the political spectrum," avoiding controversial policy debates.[85] It was much more a fight between two new leaders, who were depicted by the NDP as the "Corporate Clones" and "Bobbsey Twins of Bay Street." In fact Mulroney and Turner *were* very similar candidates in terms of economic philosophy, background and support networks. Both promised better management of the economy, trade liberalization, more jobs, and more co-operative federalism. The difference was that Turner was saddled with a legacy of Liberal policy failures, a weak organization, and a party with a dubious reputation for patronage appointments.[86] As the campaign progressed, it was clear that the Conservatives would win the election; the only question was by how much.

One of the novelties of the 1984 campaign was the attention devoted to women voters by all three parties, in response both to the mobilization of women when the Constitution and Charter were passed and a gender gap which emerged in the federal party system. In 1979 more women than men voted for the Liberal party. This gap in favour of the Liberals widened to 6% in 1980 and to 10% in 1983 opinion polls, where it remained until a few weeks before the 1984 election. All parties reacted by including specific planks for women in their campaign platforms, discussing programmes more, and participating in a special debate on women's issues. Yet, all of this attention only seemed to underline how unfamiliar and uncomfortable the leaders, of the two major parties in particular, were with the policy concerns of the women's movement. Both Turner and Mulroney took virtually the same position on a broad range of issues, ranging from jobs to daycare to poverty.

Yet, while Mulroney and Turner made gestures to women as a political constituency, it was equally clear that the policy demands of the women's movement were fundamentally incompatible with the neo-liberalism of both major parties. How could they promise to reduce government regulation of the private sector and, at the same time, impose affirmative action programmes to move women out of their traditional job ghettoes? How could the major parties promise to reduce the deficit and, at the same time, deliver on their promise of universal and affordable daycare or income security for elderly women? They could not and they would not and, in the end, the gender gap closed. Women and men supported the Tories at approximately the same rate. Thus the Liberals' lost their slight advantage while the NDP, clearly the most progressive choice for women in 1984, made marginal gains. For the first time since national election studies have recorded gender differences in party preferences, the NDP's support base in 1984 was no longer disproportionately male. A week before the election the NDP claimed 19% of decided men and 18% of decided women.[87]

The 1984 election culminated with the largest landslide ever recorded in a federal election. The Tories swept the West, shattered the Liberals' historical dominance of Quebec and won Ontario and the Maritimes. They took 211 seats to the Liberals' 40 and the NDP's 30. Yet, in the early months of the Mulroney administration, it was not clear what kind of government the Canadian public had so whole-heartedly endorsed. The

1984 campaign, like the 1980 one before it, had not telegraphed the agenda and policies of the government. The Tories' new approach, however, soon became clear with its May 1985 budget, which coincided with the release of the long-awaited Macdonald Commission Report.

The Mulroney government made it clear that its major concern was economic recovery and that it would employ the policy instruments of neo-liberalism to achieve this goal. It unveiled a four fold approach to recovery: re-orienting public policies to encourage entrepreneurship, investment and risk-taking; rationalizing the management of government resources and programmes; balancing the budget; and reducing both the size and role of government.[88] To this end, the new government replaced FIRA with Investment Canada, which would seek out rather than review foreign investment, announced its intention to privatize federal Crown corporations such as the Canadian Development Corporation, and altered the tax system to favour corporations and the wealthy.[89] The Tories made no apologies for the obvious inequities in the new taxation regime; theirs' was a market-driven approach to economic recovery which rewarded "risk-takers."

The Conservatives unexpectedly found support for their agenda in the *Report of the Royal Commission on the Economic Union and Development Prospects for Canada*, which had been appointed by the Liberals three years earlier. After months of public consultation, the compilation of briefs and the commission of hundreds of studies by the most established academics in Canada, the Royal Commission concluded that a market-driven approach, including free trade with the United States, was the only viable option available to Canadian policy-makers. Indeed, on each of the issues which seemed to distinguish the Liberals and Conservatives in the early 1980s, the Commission appeared to side with the latter's position. On the question of a state-directed industrial strategy, for example, it concluded that:

> Relative to current practice, Commissioners favour a more market-oriented industrial policy. More particularly, we favour letting the market work and placing less emphasis on government intervention to protect declining industries. We have reviewed the possibility of a more specifically targeted approach—the strategy of picking winners—but we believe it is unlikely that such a highly interventionist approach would meet with greater success overall than would a more neutral policy.[90]

A market-driven approach absolved the Royal Commission of making a clear pronouncement about the second point of division between the two major parties—the centralization or decentralization of economic policy-making. The Commission's response to this heated federal-provincial debate was a simple one: neither level of government should take precedence over the market. Nevertheless, the Mulroney government already had made significant movements toward decentralization, especially in the energy field. The Atlantic Accord with Newfoundland and the Western Accord with three western provinces were signed early in 1985. These agreements gave the oil-producing provinces much more control over resource development and returned to the provinces resource taxes which had been claimed by the Liberals under NEP. The Accords also diluted the elements of NEP aimed at increasing Canadian ownership. In short, "the Conservatives had carried out their threat to dismantle the centrepiece of the Liberals' new nationalism."[91]

The most controversial recommendation of the Macdonald Commission, however, was its outright rejection of economic nationalism and an endorsement of free trade. Of course, the shadow of free trade has always lurked in the wings when the Canadian economy falls into disarray and the Macdonald Commission was not the first to propose this panacea. The concept had already been heartily endorsed by the Economic Council of Canada, the Senate's Committee on Foreign Relations, the four western premiers, the Canadian Chamber of Commerce and most influential business lobbies.[92] But, the federal parties had traditionally resisted the idea of a formal pact with the United States, especially since trade liberalization was rapidly progressing as a result of successive rounds of GATT. Certainly, the notion was incompatible with the thrust of the Liberals' "Third National Policy" and, as late as 1983, it was rejected by all but one (John Crosbie) of the candidates for the leadership of the Conservative Party. Joe Clark labelled it "very dangerous" because of its potentially destructive impact on Ontario's economy; Michael Wilson felt it was "simplistic and naive" because Canadian industry was not strong enough to compete in a free trade environment; and Mulroney likened free trade to "sleeping with an elephant." He said, "it's terrific until the elephant twitches and if it rolls over, you're a dead man."[93] He continued:

> That is why free trade was decided in an election in 1911. It affects Canadian sovereignty and we will have none of it, not during leadership campaigns or at any time.[94]

So what had changed? Why were the same Conservative politicians prepared to embrace free trade in 1985 when they had so roundly rejected it only two years earlier? One reason, as the Macdonald Commission's analysis so clearly indicated, was that, after years of pursuing a strategy of continental integration, Canadian policy-makers had painted themselves into a corner. Canada could not penetrate world markets while the Americans too confronted large and sometimes exclusive trading blocs. Thus, rationalization and industrial restructuring within the context of the 1980s suggested rationalization of the North American market. American companies could use their unused capacity to supply the Canadian market while Canadian resources would be exempt from non-tariff barriers and countervailing duties on the American market. In absence of a strong coalition of Canadian capitalists supporting a state-centred and nationalist-inspired industrial restructuring, free trade emerged as the popular option in the face of an increasingly protectionist trading partner.

Free trade with the United States, as the Commissioners readily admitted, ultimately required a "leap of faith" by Canadians, but it was justified by neo-liberal principles. They argued that secure access to the American market would, in the long run, strengthen the Canadian economy by forcing firms to be more competitive. The *Report* forecast that free trade would cause dislocations (read unemployment) and recommended that the Canadian government institute "transitional assistance" for the workforce. While the Commission predicted growth in the Canadian manufacturing sector in the long run, a close reading of its analysis clearly indicates that it recognized that a free trade deal would rationalize the North American market and lock the Canadian economy into its historic role as resource hinterland for American manufacturing. As the *Report* explains:

> Whether our association with our neighbours is easy or not, we "need" the United States. It buys about a fifth of what we produce, and it sells us many of the products which make our lives rich and varied. We watch American television, drive American cars, eat American vegetables, drink American orange juice, and wear American clothes. The United States, however, also needs us. It needs our iron ore to make cars, our paper to print newspapers, our subway cars to travel to work, and our lumber to build homes. We are not only their best customer, but also their principal supplier.[95]

Yet, the story does not end here. There also was an even larger political agenda underlying the free trade deal which appealed to the Tories and business alike. Free trade's promise to create a so-called "level playing field" could pose a fundamental threat to Canada's social welfare and regional assistance programmes, which historically have been much more generous than those of the United States. Under a free trade regime, many programmes such as medicare and regional and sectoral assistance could be deemed a government subsidy and thus, an example of "unfair advantage," subject to downward revision. While the Conservatives continued to assure the Canadian public that social services would not be adjusted downward to match American standards, even the Macdonald Commission predicted that there would be pressures both from the United States and from within Canada to "level the playing field." Americans, for example, could regard state intervention in the fields of cultural policy and regional development as "violating the spirit, if not the letter, of a free-trade arrangement."[96] At the same time,

> . . . a bilateral free-trade agreement might lead to significant change in the configuration of political forces confronting Canadian decision-makers . . . they could be expected to arise primarily in relation to government policies that had the effect of "artificially" increasing the production costs of

Canadian enterprises over those of comparable and competing firms in the United States . . . for instance, labour codes, safety requirements, environmental regulations [and] any number of different forms of taxation.[97]

The Macdonald Commission and the Mulroney government have presented free trade as if it is governed by the neutral mechanisms of the market but, it is anything but neutral. It harmonizes perfectly with the neo-conservative political agenda and strategy for industrial restructuring which entails a market-driven approach to economic growth, continental rationalization, government cut-backs in social services, reduced rights for workers, and a lesser role for the state in the economy.[98]

The Tories' rapid embrace of the Macdonald Report and their frenzied efforts to seal a free trade deal with the United States before another federal election have enabled them to dictate the federal political agenda since the mid-1980s. It is also a political agenda which caught the Liberals and NDP, organized labour, interest groups and the Canadian public unprepared. The NDP has consistently opposed free trade, opting instead for its own industrial strategy. But the popularity of the deal, revealed in early public opinion polls, made that party wary of too strong an attack, especially when free trade continued to be popular in the West. Once again, the free trade issue forced the NDP to balance its position to keep its traditional constituency and, at the same time, attract Ontario. The Liberal Party at first accepted free trade, but the Liberals then recognized the partisan advantage that might be gained by opposing the "specific deal" cut by the Conservatives. It remains unclear what a new Liberal administration might do with the issue of free trade; the party has not developed an alternative economic strategy. As a result, the labour movement and the "popular sector's" mobilization against free trade has been the only systematic voice against it. Yet, despite all this the Tories spent most of their time in office after 1984 running third in the public opinion polls.

Conclusion

The federal politics of the late 1980s continued to be marked by change and uncertainty. These years have drawn the NDP to the verge of its long-awaited electoral take-off in the federal arena. It arrived at this point not by constructing a class-based political coalition but, instead, by presenting itself as the only "honest broker" in a brokerage party system which in the past decade was shaken by deceit, ambiguity and dissent. Whether the NDP continues to ride the crest of the opinion polls is a question that only history can answer. Playing the brokerage game exacts its costs, however, as the experience of the party over the last decade well attests. The electoral support of "ordinary Canadians" is volatile, easily swayed by the appeals of leadership at one moment and divided by regional or national loyalties the next. At the same time, brokerage politics strains and weakens the party's ties with labour and other progressive forces.

As the parties gear up for probably the final federal election of the 1980s, it is not immediately obvious how the party system and voting alignments will take shape. Each chapter of this book has documented processes and events which could not have been predicted by any deterministic analysis. The strategies of parties, developments within the labour movement, a changing economic and international order—all these factors make the constant tension among alternative definitions of politics a story without an end. Nevertheless, the party system has a past which weighs heavily on the possibilities of all parties, especially those of the left.

Chapter One discussed the conditions most commonly associated with the development of class-based electoral politics. The first condition for class voting is the existence of a political party which can contribute to the creation of a constituency of class-conscious voters. Without this prior condition, the evidence of a class cleavage in electoral politics should not be expected. In order to organize such a cleavage into electoral politics, in order to "create" the working class in elections, a party of the left must challenge the definition of politics put forward by the other parties. It must attempt to forge its own definition of politics in a way that *class* will be seen as the relevant political criteria for electoral choice and party loyalty. In the absence of a clear redefinition, workers and their potential allies will likely be organized by the bourgeois parties along cleavages other than class. It is this alternate organization which characterizes Canadian federal elections.

As the preceding chapters describe, class-based political discourse from 1867 until the present has had only brief and isolated expression in the federal party system. The politics of class in Canada has existed and does exist to be sure; the electoral organization of classes, however, does not. This book demonstrates that class-based left parties have never been absent from the federal partisan terrain, but, as we have seen, they have had few successes and many failures. While it is clear from this history that it is not inevitable that a class cleavage will come to dominate electoral politics in Canada, it is also obvious that the potential for the emergence of such a cleavage is always present. Its appearance is a matter of history, of social forces and of new discourses about classes and parties.

NOTES

[1]See J. Laxer, *Decline of the Super-Powers* (Toronto: Lorimer, 1987), p. xiii.

[2]G. Ross and J. Jenson, "Post-War Class Struggle and the Crisis of Left Politics," in R. Miliband *et al.*, eds., *The Socialist Register, 1985-86* (London: Merlin, 1986), pp. 23-28.

[3]See Royal Commission on the Economic Union and Developmental Prospects for Canada, *Report*, Vol. 1 (Ottawa: Minister of Supply and Services, 1985),

pp. 128-131; D. Wolfe, "The Rise and Demise of the Keynesian Era," in M. Cross and G. Kealey, eds., *Modern Canada: 1930-1980s* (Toronto: McClelland and Stewart, 1984), Table 1.

[4]Royal Commission, *op. cit.*, p. 128.

[5]*Ibid.*, p. 131.

[6]A. Lipietz, *Mirages and Miracles: The Crisis of Global Fordism* (London: Verso, 1987), pp. 41 ff.

[7]This is a generalized description of the patterns. National variations were very great, depending upon the ways in which political actors, especially trade unions, reacted to the new conditions. For an extension of this argument see R. Mahon, "From Fordism to ?: New Technology, Labour Markets and Unions," *Economic and Industrial Democracy*, vol. 8, 1987, pp. 5-60. For a discussion of the impact on women's participation rates see E. Hagen and J. Jenson, "Paradoxes and Promises: An Introduction," in J. Jenson, *et al.*, eds., *The Feminization of the Labor Force: Paradoxes and Promises* (London/NY: Polity/Oxford, 1988).

[8]Royal Commission, *op. cit.*, p. 225.

[9]*Ibid.*, p. 247.

[10]*Ibid.*, vol. 2, pp. 9, 27, 233. The fall off in direct foreign investment in the 1980s is attributable, in large part, to the provision of the National Energy Program which required that foreign-owned companies be acquired by Canadian interests.

[11]A similar strategy had been adopted by the Bank of Canada since the mid-seventies.

[12]Royal Commission, *op. cit.*, vol. 1, p. 136.

[13]Laxer, *op. cit.*, p. 124.

[14]Royal Commission, *op. cit.*, vol. 2, p. 27.

[15]*Ibid.*, p. 404.

[16]See *Ibid.*, vol. 2, p. 9.

[17]See S. Clarkson, *Canada and the Reagan Challenge*, updated ed., (Toronto: Lorimer, 1985), p. 8.

[18]The Macdonald Commission estimated that the percentage of American manufactured goods protected by non-tariff barriers rose from one-fifth to over one-third in the 1980 to 1983 period alone. *Op. cit.*, vol. 1, p. 161.

[19]Even "success stories" were contradictory. The 1965 Auto Pact rationalizing North American automobile production appeared to shore up the Canadian manufacturing sector and American demand for cars helped the Canadian economy pull out of the deep recession of 1981-1982. In 1984, the auto industry accounted for exports worth 30 billion dollars, nearly 27% of Canada's foreign sales of goods, compared to an insignificant 2.3% in 1964. But, continental rationalization also exacted costs which were paid primarily by Canadian auto parts manufacturers. Cars built in Canada increasingly used parts supplied from south of the border. By 1980 the Canadian parts industry supplied less than one-half of the dollar value of parts bought by Canadians—a drop from 90% in 1972. Canadian imports of auto products reached a value of nearly 26 billion by 1984, contributing significantly to Canada's balance of payments problems. See Laxer, *op. cit.*, p. 125 and Royal Commission, *op. cit.*, p. 227.

[20]See Clarkson, *op. cit.*, p. 11; G. Stevenson, *Unfulfilled Union* (Toronto: Macmillan, 1979); and D.V. Smiley, *The Federal Condition in Canada* (Toronto: McGraw-Hill, 1987), Chapter 7.

[21]The shift was so pronounced that in the late 1970s new federal constituencies were created and the electoral map revised such that for the first time in Canadian history the West would be as important in the federal electoral arithmetic as Quebec had been for the previous century.

[22]See, for example, J. Brodie, "Tensions from Within: Regionalism and Party Policy in Canada," in H. Thorburn, ed., *Party Politics in Canada*, 5th ed. (Toronto: Prentice-Hall, 1985).

[23]*The Sunday Star*, January 31, 1988, p. B5.

[24]See M. Ethier, "Regional Grievances: The Quebec Case," in K. Norrie, ed., *Disparities and Interregional Adjustment* (Toronto: University of Toronto, 1986).

[25]J. Laxer, *Canada's Economic Strategy* (Toronto: McClelland and Stewart, 1981), p. 121.

[26]Wolfe, *op. cit.*, Table 1.

[27]J. Jenson, "Economic Factors in Canadian Political Integration," in J.H. Pammett and B.W. Tomlin, eds., *The Integration Question in Canada* (Toronto: Addison-Wesley, 1984), p. 64. The decision to protect domestic supply by restricting oil exports means that the economy lost the factor which had enabled the country to maintain a surplus on the current account, which dropped from a surplus of $108 million in 1973 to a deficit of $4757 million in 1975. Of course, also contributing to this switch was the increased import of manufactured goods, which followed on the heels of the boom. See Wolfe, *op. cit.*, Table 2.

[28]In the late 1960s several ministers of finance conducted a round of discussions with business and labour leaders in an effort to construct a voluntary agreement for wage and price controls. Neither set of leaders was enthusiastic.

[29]W. Wood and P. Kumar, eds., *Canadian Perspectives on Wage-Price Guidelines: A Book of Readings* (Kingston: Industrial Relations Centre, 1976), p. 320.

[30]C. Gonick, *The Great Economic Debate* (Toronto: Lorimer, 1987), p. 116.

[31]Wolfe, *op. cit.*, Table 3, pp. 67-68.

[32]Jenson, *op. cit.*, p. 65.

[33]Gonick, *op. cit.*, p. 115.

[34]Wolfe, *op. cit.*, Table 1.

[35]Governments would try to obtain "voluntary" agreement of union leaders to limit their members' wage increases to an agreed-upon level in exchange for a union role in state economic decision-making, for greater union security in the workplace and some extension of the welfare state. See L.V. Panitch and D. Swartz, *From Consent to Coercion: The Assault on Trade Union Freedoms* (Toronto: Garamond, 1985), p. 31.

[36]C. Yates, "From Plant to Politics: The Canadian UAW 1936-1984," PhD Thesis, Political Science, Carleton University, 1988, Chapter 6.

[37]D. Swartz, "New Forms of Worker Participation: A Critique of Quality of Working Life," *Studies in Political Economy*, no. 5, 1981.

[38]I. Bakker, "Women's Employment in Comparative Perspective," in J. Jenson, *et al.*, *op. cit.*, Table 2-1, p. 21.

[39]R. Mahon, "Canadian Labour in the Battle of the Eighties," *Studies in Political Economy*, no. 11, 1983, pp. 151-52.

[40]*Ibid.*, 160.

[41]*Ibid.*, p. 117.

[42]Panitch and Swartz, *op. cit.*, pp. 39ff.

[43]Mahon, *op. cit.*, p. 168-69.

[44]*Ibid.*, p. 166.

[45]Statement by Dennis McDermott, President of the CLC, March 28, 1979.

[46]D. Drache and D. Cameron, eds., *The Other Macdonald Report: The Consensus on Canada's Future that the Macdonald Commission Left Out* (Toronto: Lorimer, 1985).

[47]Ontario Federation of Labour, *Let Canadians Decide: OFL Free Trade Briefing Notes* (Toronto: OFL, 1988), p. 9.

[48]D. Morton, *The New Democrats 1961-1986: The Politics of Change* (Toronto: Copp Clark Pitman, 1986), p. 155.

[49]*Ibid.*, p. 184.

[50]*Ibid.*, p. 192.

[51]For a discussion of the intellectual currents which encouraged the development of this new approach see N. Bradford, "Ideas, Intellectuals and Social Democracy in Canada," in A. Gagnon and B. Tanguay, *Canadian Parties in Transition: Discourse, Organization, and Representation* (Toronto: Nelson, 1988), pp. 153-57.

[52]This post-Keynesianism required a three-stage programme to enhance the key sectors of housing, transportation and food, strengthen the industries providing these basic needs, and finally support industries which exhibited investment potential. Morton, *The New Democrats*, p. 192.

[53]Laxer, *Canada's Economic Strategy*, pp. 195-202. For a discussion of the background to this position see Bradford, *op. cit.*

[54]Morton, *op. cit.*, p. 216. The Report was published as J. Laxer, *Rethinking the Economy: The Laxer Report on Canadian Economic Problems and Prospects* (Toronto: NC Press, 1983).

[55]*Ibid.*, p. 213.

[56]A. Whitehorn, "The CCF-NDP: Fifty Years After," in Thorburn, *op. cit.*, p. 201.

[57]For a detailed exploration of the "Western" position, as well as critiques of it, see J. Richards and D. Kerr, eds., *Canada: What's Left?* (Edmonton: NeWest, 1986).

[58]Whitehorn, *op. cit.*, p. 194.

[59]*Ibid.*, p. 198.

[60]*Ibid.*, pp. 162-163.

[61]The 1984 campaign strategy was controversial. Terry Grier and Gerry Caplan organized it, over the objections of other leaders and activists. The electoralist thrust was always front and centre. "As a theme, "ordinary Canadians," as Grier ruefully admitted, might be a lot more populist than socialist, but it plucked a deep chord in the party and among those who had never supported the NDP," Morton, *op. cit.*, pp. 217-19.

[62]For a summary of these positions see, Drache and Cameron, *op. cit.*

[63]Gonick, *op. cit.*, p. 198.

[64]J. Laxer and R. Laxer, *The Liberal Idea of Canada* (Toronto: Lorimer, 1977), p. 107.

[65]Laxer, *Canada's Economic Strategy*, p. 29.

[66]The latter, formed in 1977, represented a coalition, constituted by invitation only, of the "three most powerful segments of the Canadian Business Community—the resource companies, the branch plant manufacturers and the banks." *Ibid.*, p. 37. For a detailed analysis see D. Langille, "The Business Council on National Issues and the Canadian State," *SPE*, no. 24, 1987.

[67]According to the BCNI, C.D. Howe Institute and the ECC the federal deficit was both forcing up interest rates and crowding out private investment. A. Maslove, "The Public Pursuit of Private Interests," in A. Maslove, ed., *How Ottawa Spends, 1985: Sharing the Pie* (Toronto: Methuen, 1985), pp. 16-19.

[68]For further discussion of these points see J. Brodie and J. Jenson, "The Party System," in M.S. Whittington and G. Williams, eds., *Canadian Politics in the 1980s,* 2nd ed. (Toronto: Methuen, 1984).

[69]As quoted in Laxer, *Canada's Economic Strategy,* p. 148.

[70]See Morton, *op. cit.,* pp. 194-196.

[71]Smiley, *op. cit.,* p. 182.

[72]*Ibid.,* p. 179.

[73]Clarkson, *op. cit.,* Chapter 1.

[74]Royal Commission, *op. cit.,* vol. 2, pp. 485-486.

[75]D. Milne, *Tug of War: Ottawa and the Provinces Under Trudeau and Mulroney* (Toronto: Lorimer, 1986), p. 80.

[76]*Ibid.,* p. 82.

[77]*Ibid.,* p. 84.

[78]*Ibid.,* pp. 92-93.

[79]Clarkson, *op. cit.,* p. 109.

[80]Canada, *Economic Development for Canada in the 1980s* (Ottawa: Supply and Services, November, 1981), pp. 2-3.

[81]Clarkson, *op. cit.,* p. 276.

[82]Milne, *op. cit.,* p. 95.

[83]Royal Commission, *op. cit.,* p. xvii.

[84]As quoted in M. Prince, "Whatever Happened to Compassion? Liberal Social Policy, 1980-1984," in A. Maslove, ed., *How Ottawa Spends, 1984: The New Agenda* (Toronto: Methuen, 1984), p. 112.

[85]M. Prince, "The Mulroney Agenda: A Right Turn for Ottawa," in M. Prince, ed., *How Ottawa Spends, 1986-1987: Tracking the Tories* (Toronto: Methuen, 1986), p. 7.

[86]Morton, *op. cit.,* p. 219.

[87]See J. Brodie, "Reflections on the 1984 Campaign," *The Facts* (May 1985) and *Women and Politics in Canada* (Toronto: McGraw-Hill Ryerson, 1985), Chapter 8.

[88]Prince, "The Mulroney Agenda," p. 10.

[89]The new taxation regime shifted taxation from the corporate sector to wage earners and, among wage earners, from the rich to the poor. By 1986, the corporate share of total taxation revenue had fallen to 14% while personal taxes had risen to 45% (compared to 1951 figures of 28% and 24% respectively). Moreover, as a result of the 1985 budget, the average poor family ($15,000 a year) lost $135, the average middle class family ($35,000 a year) lost $208, while the rich family ($80,000 a year) enjoyed a tax saving of $631. Gonick, *op. cit.,* p. 125.

[90]Royal Commission, *op. cit.,* vol. 3, p. 425.

[91]Milne, *op. cit.,* pp. 109-111.

[92]*The Sunday Star,* June 9, 1985.

[93]*The Toronto Star,* June 8, 1985, p. A1.

[94]*Ibid.,* p. A6.

[95]Royal Commission, *op. cit.*, vol. 1, p. 300.

[96]*Ibid.*, vol. 1, 357-358.

[97]*Ibid.*, p. 359.

[98]See Drache and Cameron, *op. cit.*, Introduction.

Appendix A

Methodological Appendix

The Data

The data used in this analysis are derived from a number of sources. For the period 1908-1965, the data were collected by Donald Blake for his doctoral dissertation "Regionalism in Canadian Voting Behaviour 1908-1968" (Yale University). See also Donald Blake, "The Measurement of Regionalism in Canadian Voting Patterns," *Canadian Journal of Political Science*, 5 (March, 1972). The ethnic composition of each constituency was measured in percentages and was taken from the *Census of Canada* for the years 1911, 1921, 1951 and 1961. Census characteristics by electoral district of the election of 1949 were estimated from the 1951 *Census of Canada* (see below). Blake derived the election results from the *Canadian Parliamentary Guide* for 1908 to 1917; from Harold Scarrow, *Canada Votes: A Handbook of Federal and Provincial Election Data* (New Orleans: The Hauser Press, 1962) for the period 1921-1958; and from the *Report of the Chief Electoral Officer* for the period 1962-1965. Blake corrected some inaccuracies which he discovered in the Scarrow data. The data for the period 1968-1974 were obtained by merging federal election data compiled by Bruce D. Macnaughton and James Twiss of Carleton University and census data constructed to overlap with electoral boundaries by data archivists at the Institute for Behavioural Research, York University, Toronto. These data were made available by the Social Science Archive, Carleton University, Ottawa. Neither the original investigators nor the archive are responsible for their use here.

We wish to stress that the correlation coefficients presented in this text provide only an approximate overview of electoral trends among selected populations. Moreover, special caution should be taken in interpreting the 1949 election results. In this case, the constituencies' ethnic distributions were constructed from census subdivision information, and, in some cases, where constituency boundaries cut subdivisions, groups were allocated between constituencies in proportion to the constituency population unaccounted for by the summing of whole subdivisions. Because occupational distributions for subdivisions were not available, these were estimated using census information provided for incorporated cities, towns and villages exceeding one thousand. Rural constituencies were assumed to have the same occupational distributions as the rural part of the census division in which they fell.

Operational Definitions

Constituency type—urban/rural

Because the percentage distributions of occupational groups in each constituency were not available for the pre-1949 period, observations concerning farmers' and workers' politics are based upon the voting correlates of urban and rural constituency types.

The rural and urban variables employed in the period 1908-1945 were constructed by the authors from the *Reports of the Chief Electoral Officer*. Each constituency was coded as urban, rural or mixed according to the *Report's* designation of the nature of the district's polling stations. For example, if all the polls were designated rural, the constituency was coded rural. Similarly, if all the polls were designated urban, the constituency was coded urban. For the early period, however, these criteria were relaxed for western urban constituencies. In this case, those urban ridings with few deviant polling stations were coded according to the modal category as urban. All other constituencies being neither rural nor urban were coded as mixed.

Since the urban and rural variables were not used in the same statistical procedure at any point in our analysis, these variables were constructed as follows:

Urban/rural + mixed
Rural/urban + mixed

In other words, all other ridings were used as the comparison groups for urban and rural ridings respectively. The frequencies for each of these categories are displayed below by election year and region.

CONSTITUENCY TYPES
(Horizontal Totals)

	East* (Ont., Que., Maritimes)				West (Prairies, BC)			
	Urban	Rural	Mixed	Total	Urban	Rural	Mixed	Total
1908- 1911	21	83	79	(183)	5	16	13	(34)
1917- 1921	30	72	71	(173)	7	27	22	(56)
1925- 1930	36	74	62	(172)	10	38	20	(68)
1935- 1945	40	81	50	(171)	13	44	14	(71)

* Nfld. not included in this study.

Demographic Variables

The demographic and occupational variables are not equivalent measures across all election years because the census categories were altered over the period 1908-1974. Nevertheless, we have attempted to achieve as much consistency across election years as possible. The operational definitions for each period are as follows:

Variable	Operational Definitions
	1908–1911
	1911 Census
	% ethnic origin in riding
English	% British
French	% French
German	% German, Austro–Hungarian, Bulgarian (groups likely to be disenfranchised in 1917)
Eastern Europe	% Polish, Russian
	1917–1921
	1921 Census
	% ethnic origin in riding
English	% British
French	% French
German	% Austrian, German
Eastern Europe	% Polish, Russian, Ukranian
	1949
	1951 Census
	(Estimation Procedure see above)
	% ethnic origin in riding
English	% British origin
French	% French origin
European	% German, Jewish, Polish, Russian, Ukranian
	% male labour force by industry and occupational group
Primary	% primary (includes farmers, miners, labourers)
White Collar	% clerical, commercial, financial
Worker	% manufacturing, mechanical, construction

Variable	*Operational Definitions*
	1953-1965
	1961 Census
	% ethnic origin in riding
English	% British
French	% French
European	% German, other European (includes Jewish, Polish, Russian and other)[a]
	% total labour force by industry in riding
Farmer	% agriculture
White Collar	% managerial, professional, technical, clerical and sales
Worker	% mining, manufacturing, construction
	1968-1974*
	1971 Census
	*% mother tongue**
English	% English
French	% French
European	% German, Polish, Ukranian
	% male labour force by industry
Farmer	% agriculture
White Collar	% finance, insurance, community, business, service occupations
Worker	% manufacturing, construction, industry unspecified

* The census data available for the 1968-1974 period were categorized as Mother Tongue of family heads.

[a] This category does not include Italian, Dutch or Scandinavian.

The Analysis

Throughout our analysis we have measured the strength of the relationship between constituency characteristics and party support with the zero-order Pearson's correlation coefficient and the partial correlation coefficient. Pearson's r measures the degree of relationship between two metric variables and is relatively simple to interpret. The statistic ranges from -1 which indicates a perfect negative relationship through 0 which suggests that there is no relationship between the variables to +1, which indicates a perfect positive relationship.

The partial correlation coefficient is interpreted in the same way. However, this statistic accounts for the relationship between the dependent variable and 1 or more control variables. It employs a mathematical strategy which cancels out any variation in the dependent variable that could be explained (i.e. held in common) by the joint relationship between the independent variable and a control variable and second, between the control variable and the dependent variable.[1] Thus, the partial correlation coefficient enables the researcher to determine whether the zero-order relationship between the dependent and independent variable is independent, intervening or spurious; that is, the variation discerned between the dependent and independent variable is owing to the way both vary with a third variable.

The partial correlation technique, then, enables the researcher to reassess the original association between the independent and dependent variables so that it reflects a direct association, unmarred by the variables' association to a third extraneous factor.[2] The partial correlation technique may also be employed to control for the effects of more than one variable in the original relationship.

Second and third order partials were employed in our examination of the post-1945 period. These statistics control for the effects of two or more extraneous factors on the original relationship and are similar to the first order partial correlation coefficient. Interpretation of higher order partial correlation coefficients, however, can be confusing if not guided by a theoretical expectation concerning the necessity of statistical control of two or more factors.[3]

In this study, third order partials have been employed to control for the effects of certain historically relevant ethnic categories on the relationship between the constituency's party vote and the work force and certain theoretically relevant indicators of the class structure on the relationship between the constituency's party vote and ethnic composition. The zero-order correlations (the relationship between the dependent and independent variables prior to control procedures) are contained in Appendix B. The probability level throughout the book was fixed at $p < .05$ indicating that there are less than five in one hundred chances that the correlation coefficients presented are due to random variation or "chance" alone.

NOTES

[1] See T. Jones, *Conducting Political Research* (New York: Harper and Row, 1971), pp. 123-132.

[2] David Nachmias and Chava Nachmias, *Research Methods in The Social Sciences* (New York: St. Martin's Press, 1976).

[3] Robert H. Gordon, "Issues in Multiple Regression," *American Journal of Sociology*, 73 (1968), 592-616.

Appendix B

Zero-order Correlations of Party Vote 1949–1974 by Region

1949 LABOUR FORCE AND ETHNIC ZERO-ORDER CORRELATIONS OF VOTE BY REGION

	Primary**	Worker	White Collar	English	French	European
East						
Conservative	.17*	−.11	.09	.54*	−.49*	.01
Liberal	.04	.01	.01	−.38*	.42*	−.17*
CCF	−.39*	.04	.05	.19*	−.38*	.24*
Social Credit	.25*	−.26*	−.27*	−.20	.16	−.05
West						
Conservative	−.34*	.21*	.23*	.67*	−.28*	−.61*
Liberal	.06	−.27*	−.21*	−.32*	.37*	.16
CCF	−.01	−.03	−.04	−.16	−.02	.20*
Social Credit	.09	−.103	−.20	.03	−.05	−.06

* p < .05
** primary includes farmers, loggers, fishermen, miners

1953–1958 LABOUR FORCE AND ETHNIC ZERO-ORDER CORRELATIONS OF LIBERAL VOTE BY REGION

	Farmer	Worker	White Collar	English	French	European
East						
1953	−.00	.01	−.06	−.51*	.52*	−.22*
1957	−.02	−.07	−.05	−.65*	.68*	−.34*
1958	−.02	−.12*	−.16	−.62	.65*	−.35
West						
1953	.43*	−.40*	−.27*	−.46*	.38*	.34*
1957	.43*	−.40*	−.25*	−.47*	.28*	.40*
1958	.23*	−.23*	−.07*	−.22*	.44*	.07

* p < .05

335

1953-1958 LABOUR FORCE AND ETHNIC ZERO-ORDER CORRELATIONS OF CONSERVATIVE VOTE BY REGION

	Farmer	Worker	White Collar	English	French	European
East						
1953	.23*	−.28*	−.01	.60*	−.49*	.02
1957	.25*	−.28*	.05	.68*	−.60*	.14*
1958	.38*	−.31*	.03	.54*	−.42*	.00
West						
1953	−.23*	−.01	.38*	.42*	.02	−.35*
1957	−.40*	.08	.52*	.60*	−.11	−.55*
1958	−.06	−.24	.30*	.29*	−.02	−.24

*p < .05

1953-1958 LABOUR FORCE AND ETHNIC ZERO-ORDER CORRELATIONS OF CCF VOTE BY REGION

	Farmer	Worker	White Collar	English	French	European
East						
1953	−.43*	.43*	.25*	.29*	−.46*	.49*
1957	−.42*	.47*	.17*	.22*	−.42*	.52*
1958	−.43*	.47*	.18*	.20*	−.38*	.46*
West						
1953	.00	.06	−.08	−.10	.05	.18
1957	.05	.09	−.19*	−.23*	−.04	.31*
1958	−.12	.26*	−.10	−.04	−.11	.10

*p < .05

1962-1974 LABOUR FORCE AND ETHNIC ZERO-ORDER CORRELATIONS OF LIBERAL VOTE BY REGION

	Farmer	Worker	White Collar	English	French	European
East						
1962	−.23*	−.03	.20*	.11	−.20*	.21*
1963	−.26*	−.08	.32*	.04	−.14*	.21*
1965	−.21*	−.12*	.24	−.15*	.07	.08
1968	−.31*	.11	.43	−.14*	.24*	.06
1972	−.32*	−.08	.15*	−.35*	.37*	−.13*
1974	−.33	−.03	.18*	−.33*	.38*	−.07
West						
1962	−.21*	.01	.35*	.21*	.23*	−.22*
1963	−.51*	.31*	.59*	.37*	.12	−.37
1965	−.42*	.22*	.56*	.32*	.18	−.35
1968	−.69*	.52*	.73*	.44*	.13	.16
1972	−.45*	.33*	.60*	.32*	.19*	−.03
1974	−.38*	.35*	.48*	.34*	.14	−.18

*p < .05

1962–1974 LABOUR FORCE AND ETHNIC ZERO-ORDER CORRELATIONS OF CONSERVATIVE VOTE BY REGION

	Farmer	Worker	White Collar	English	French	European
East						
1962	.29*	−.29*	−.06	.64*	−.52*	.05
1963	.35*	−.25*	−.15*	.73*	−.63*	.13*
1965	.34*	−.31*	−.22*	.64*	−.51*	.02
1968	.33*	−.25*	−.27*	.38*	−.45*	−.16*
1972	.28*	−.03	−.02	.65*	−.71*	−.14*
1974	.32*	−.06	.01	.51*	−.54*	.07
West						
1962	.61*	−.69*	−.30*	−.30*	.15	.33*
1963	.76*	−.79*	−.46*	−.46*	.21*	.48*
1965	.70*	−.75*	−.40*	−.43*	.25*	.44*
1968	.61*	−.57*	−.29*	−.27*	.04	.14
1972	.45*	−.42*	−.21*	−.20*	−.00	.11
1974	.21*	−.24*	−.05	−.04	−.03	−.00

* p < .05

1962–1974 LABOUR FORCE AND ETHNIC ZERO-ORDER CORRELATIONS OF NDP VOTE BY REGION

	Farmer	Worker	White Collar	English	French	European
East						
1962	−.45*	.44*	.29*	.37*	−.53*	.53*
1963	−.50*	.49*	.35*	.20*	−.38*	.48*
1965	−.45*	.45*	.35*	.18*	−.35*	.47*
1968	−.24*	.49*	.18*	.32*	−.33*	.56*
1972	−.25*	.40*	.18*	.39*	−.43*	.52*
West						
1962	−.45*	.56*	.13	.13	−.17	−.14
1963	−.51*	.61*	.16	.22*	−.24	−.22*
1965	−.42*	.51*	.11	.13	−.18	−.10
1968	−.16	.23*	−.13	.00	−.10	−.03
1972	−.22*	.25*	−.12	.00	−.10	−.06
1974	−.04	.03	−.25*	−.20*	−.07	.11

* p < .05

Index

Aberhart, William, 175
Agricultural and Rural Development Act (ARDA), 249
Alien Labour Law, 63
All Canadian Congress of Labour (ACCL), 138, 165-166, 173
Amalgamated Clothing Workers, 193
American Federation of Labour (AFL), 32-37, 66, 69, 93, 97; (AFL-CIO), 193, 195, 242, 268-270
Anti-Inflation Board (AIB), 300-301
Auto Pact, 278, 299

Bennett, R.B., 148, 159, 162-163, 176-178, 188, 199, 204
Blakeney, Allan, 308
Bonn Conference, 303
Borden, Robert, 94-97, 102
Bouey, Gerald, 301
Bourassa, Henri, 46, 75-77, 94, 97
Bracken, John, 204-205, 207, 249
Bretton Woods, 267
Britain, 22-23, 54, 72, 122, 156, 203, 222
British Columbia Federation of Labour, 68
British Labour Party, 168, 233, 239, 241-244
Broadbent, Ed, 306, 309-310
Brown, George, 40
Business Council on National Issues, 312
Byng, Lord, 145

C. D. Howe Institute, 312
Canadian Catholic Confederation of Labour (CCCL), 136, 165-166, 173, 194, 229-230
Canadian Centre for Policy Alternatives, 310
Canadian Chamber of Commerce, 321
Canadian Charter of Rights and Freedoms, 315
Canadian Conference of Catholic Bishops, 310
Canadian Congress of Labour (CCL), 187, 195-196, 199-203, 206, 217, 241-242, 245

Canadian Council of Agriculture (CCA), 107, 142
Canadian Development Corporation (CDC), 268, 274-275, 311, 320
Canadian Dimension, 274
Canadian Labour Congress (CLC), 217-218, 227, 241-243, 268-270, 301, 304-306, 309-310
Canadian Labour Party (CLP), 93, 97, 106, 137-138
Canadian Labour Union (CLU), 30
Canadian Manufacturers Association (CMA), 70, 312
Canadian Pacific Railway, 46, 59-60, 223
Canadian Union of Public Employees (CUPE), 269-70, 301
Canadian Unionist, 173
Clark, Joe, 314-315, 318, 321
Coalition Against Free Trade, 310
Cold War, 228, 233-235, 264, 272-273, 280
Committee for Industrial Organization (CIO), 193-195, 242
Common Front, 271
Communists, 137-138, 163, 165-167, 193, 228, 244
Confederation des Syndicats Nationales (CNTU), 230, 271
Co-operative Commonwealth Federation (CCF) (founding), 157, 166-182
Corporate Welfare Bums, 280
Corporation des Ēnseignants du Quebec (CEQ), 271
Crerar, T.A., 107
Cross, James, 283
Crow's Nest Pass Agreement, 60

Diefenbaker, John, 207, 246, 248-249, 251, 254-255, 286, 313-314
Dominion Labour Party (DLP), 137
Dominion Securities Corporation, 181
Douglas, T.C., 233, 282
Drew, George, 247
Duplessis, Maurice, 194, 255

Economic Council of Canada, 218, 226, 312, 321
European Economic Community (EEC), 268, 295

Family Allowance Bill, 207
Farmers' Platforms, 75, 78-80
Farmers' Union, 146
Federated Labour Party of British
  Columbia, 106
Fielding, W.S., 107
Foreign Investment Review
  Agency (FIRA), 268, 280, 311,
  314, 316-317, 320
Fraser Institute, 312

Ginger Group, 112, 142, 148
Gompers, Samuel, 33, 93, 100-101
Gordon, Donald, 190
Gordon, Walter, 224, 254-255, 267
Gouzenko Affair, 228
Grain Growers' Association
  (GGA), 146
Grain Growers' Guide, 107
Grand Trunk Railway, 128
Gray Report, 267-268

Hepburn, Mitchell, 194
Howe, C.D., 189
Hudson's Bay Company, 22-23

Independent Labour Parties (ILP),
  106, 140, 147, 173
Industrial Disputes Investigation
  Act (IDIA), 64
Industrial Relations Dispute Act
  (IRDA), 196
International Workers of the World
  (IWW), 66-67, 91-92, 102
Investment Canada, 320

Just Society, 282
Keynesian Economics, 187, 190,
  204-205, 208, 210, 220, 233-234,
  239, 244-246, 249, 264-266, 274,
  293-295, 307, 309, 311, 314
King, Mackenzie, 109, 139, 141-145,
  148, 178, 195, 199, 205-206,
  208-211, 247
Knights of Labour, 30, 32-36

Laporte, Pierre, 283
Laurier, Wilfred, 72, 75-77, 94-96,
  98, 128
Laxer, Jim, 278, 308
League for Social Reconstruction
  (LSR), 165, 169-170, 198, 238
Le Devoir, 76

Lesage, Jean, 255
Lewis, David, 241, 278, 281
Lewis, John L., 193
Lewis, Stephen, 276, 279
Limitations of Work Act, 177
Lougheed, Peter, 316

Macdonald, Donald, 318
Macdonald, John A., 24, 40, 42-44,
  77, 248
Major Projects Task Force, 304
Manion, R.J., 178, 199
Manning, Ernest, 175
Maritime Rights Movement, 131,
  142-144
McCarthyism, 228
McDermott, Dennis, 304-305
Meighen, Arthur, 108-109, 144
Mercier, Honore, 46
Minimum Wages Act, 177
Montreal Board of Trade, 238
Mulroney, Brian, 304, 306, 313,
  318-320, 323

National Energy Policy, 308,
  314-318, 321
National Policy, 21-27, 40-41, 46,
  53-61, 65, 74-75, 77, 81, 108, 112,
  124-130, 138, 141, 158, 190, 204
Natural Products Marketing Act,
  177
New Democratic Party (NDP)
  (founding), 218, 230-245
Newly Industrializing Countries
  (NICs), 293
Nixon, Richard M., 267, 270
Nixonomics, 267, 295
Norquay, John, 45
Notley, Grant, 308

October Crisis, 283
One Big Union (OBU), 104-106, 138
On-to-Ottawa-Trek, 163, 166
Ontario Economic Council, 312
Ontario Federation of Labour, 306
Orange Lodge, 39-40, 71

Padlock Law, 194
Paley Report, 220-221
Pearson, Lester B., 222
Petro-Canada, 268, 280, 311, 314,
  316
Pipeline Scandal (1956), 223

Port Hope Conference, 205, 246
Prairie Grain Advance Payments
  Act, 249
Progressive Party, 107-112, 120-121,
  138-142, 149-150, 156-157, 168,
  197
Prophetic Bible Institute, 175
Public Service Alliance (PSA), 269

Quebec Federation of Labour,
  (QFL), 271

Reconstruction Party, 172, 176,
  179-181
Regina Manifesto, 168, 197-198,
  202, 231, 233-234, 236, 238, 241
Regina Riot, 164
Rerum Novarum, 36
Riel Rebellion, 44-45
Robertson, Gideon, 101, 163
Robson Report, 104-105
Royal Commission on Bilingualism
  and Biculturalism, 255
Royal Commission on Canada's
  Economic Prospects, 224, 254
Royal Commission on Dominion
  Provincial Relations, 189, 238
Royal Commission on Economic
  Union and Development Pros-
  pects for Canada, 318, 320-323
Russian Revolution, 81, 95, 104

Science Council of Canada, 268,
  310-311
Sharp, Mitchell, 222, 267
Smiley, Don, 315
Social Credit Party, 167, 175,
  179-181
Social Democratic Party (SDP), 106
Socialist Party of British Columbia,
  31
Socialist Party of North America,
  106
Stalinism, 235
Stanfield, Robert, 282, 284
Steel Workers Organizing Com-
  mittee (SWOC), 193
Stevens, Harry, 196
St. Laurent, Louis, 223, 247-249

Taylor, Charles, 275
The Globe, 40
Third Option, 268

Toronto Trades Assembly, 30
Trades and Labour Congress of
  Canada (TLC), 30-37, 64-68, 79,
  91-93, 97-101, 103, 105-106, 120,
  134-138, 140, 165-166, 173,
  195-196, 198-199, 201, 206, 217,
  228, 241, 245
Trades Union Act, 40
Trans-Canada Pipeline, 223-224
Trudeau, Pierre E., 268, 275,
  282-283, 288, 300-301, 303, 312,
  315-316, 318
Turner, John, 301, 318-319

Underhill, Frank, 238
Unemployment and Social Insurance Act, 177
Unemployment Insurance Act
  (1940), 191, 196
Union Government, 88, 95, 97,
  100-101, 105, 108, 111
United Auto Workers (UAW),
  269-270, 278, 304
United Farmers, 108, 140, 146-147,
  172, 175, 198
United Mine Workers (UMW), 105,
  193
United States, 22-24, 58, 76,
  122-125, 128-130, 156-158, 162,
  187, 189, 217, 219-224, 254-255,
  267-270, 293-295, 298-299,
  320-322

Vietnam War, 273, 277

Waffle, 273-280
Wagner Act, 193
War Measures Act, 102, 196, 283
War Time Elections Act, 88, 95-96
Wartime Industries Control Board,
  189
Wartime Prices and Trade Board,
  189
Watkins, Mel, 308
Weekly Rest and Industrial Under-
  takings Act, 177
Western Federation of Miners, 66
Western Labour Conference, 100,
  103, 147-148, 168
Wheat Board, 121-146
White Paper on Employment and
  Income, 191, 219
Wilson, Michael, 321

Winnipeg Declaration of Principles, 232, 236, 238, 240, 242-243,
276
Winnipeg General Strike, 70,
104-105, 134, 140
Woodsworth, J.S., 168, 199
Worker's Party, 137

Workers Unity League, 165-166,
193
World War I, 53-57, 87-89, 119, 122,
164, 189-190, 196
World War II, 55, 156, 177, 188-189,
217, 221